NUFFIELD EUROPEAN STUDIES

FEDERALIZING EUROPE?

FEDERALIZING EUROPE?

*The Costs, Benefits, and Preconditions
of Federal Political Systems*

Edited by
JOACHIM JENS HESSE
and
VINCENT WRIGHT

OXFORD UNIVERSITY PRESS
1996

Oxford University Press, Walton Street, Oxford OX2 6DP
Oxford New York
Athens Auckland Bangkok Bombay
Calcutta Cape Town Dar es Salaam Delhi
Florence Hong Kong Istanbul Karachi
Kuala Lumpur Madras Madrid Melbourne
Mexico City Nairobi Paris Singapore
Taipei Tokyo Toronto
and associated companies in
Berlin Ibadan

Oxford is a trade mark of Oxford University Press

Published in the United States
by Oxford University Press Inc., New York

British Library Cataloguing in Publication Data
Data available

Library of Congress Cataloging-in-Publication Data
Federalizing Europe?: the costs, benefits and preconditions of federal political
systems/edited by Joachim Jens Hesse and Vincent Wright.
— (Nuffield European studies)
1. Federal government—Europe. 2. European federation. 3. Federal government.
I. Hesse, Joachim Jens. II. Wright, Vincent. III. Series.
JN15.F396 1996 321.02'094—dc20 95-11267
ISBN 0-19-827992-2

1 3 5 7 9 10 8 6 4 2

Typeset by Best-set Typesetter Ltd., Hong Kong
Printed in Great Britain
on acid-free paper by
Bookcraft (Bath) Ltd
Midsomer Norton, Avon

Preface

Not since the great controversies of the 1950s has the constitutional and institutional development of the European Community and its constituent states been so widely and so intensely debated as at present, and nowhere has the political conflict over European federalism been more divisive or more misunderstood than in Britain. Fuelled by heated arguments about the very nature of federal political arrangements, their democratic contents, functional capacities, and stabilizing or destabilizing roles in the break-up of the Yugoslavian state, in the 'velvet divorce' of the Czech and Slovak Republics, or in the formation of the Commonwealth of Independent States, processes of federalization have come to the forefront of public debate. In some cases, they have become entangled in the rather confusing discussion of the elusive concept of subsidiarity. The fundamental disagreements which have emerged can be explained only partially by inadequate information about the actual workings of federal systems. Prejudices, rather than solid empirical analysis, appear to be playing a considerable role in assessing the performance of federations.

Against this background, we at the Centre for European Studies at Nuffield College, Oxford, thought that it would make sense to attempt a critical reappraisal of the political, economic, and socio-cultural potential of current federal political–institutional arrangements. The reappraisal, we decided, needed to include both an analysis of their necessary preconditions as well as an evaluation of their distinct advantages and disadvantages compared with other forms of state organization. A conference, entitled 'Federalizing Europe? The Costs, Benefits and Preconditions of Federal Political Systems', was devoted to these objectives. This book is the result of that conference.

The Centre would like to take this opportunity to thank all participants in the conference who responded so positively to our invitation. Our particular thanks go to those who prepared the papers and who also amended them in the light of the discussions and later comments. We should also like to acknowledge the financial support provided by the Anglo-German Foundation for the Study of Industrial Society and by the Nuffield Foundation, which made it possible to invite academics from both sides of the Atlantic and the Channel as well as from Australia. Finally, we should like to express our gratitude to the Warden and Fellows of Nuffield College who hosted the meeting and to Klaus Goetz and Stephanie Wright whose administrative efforts ensured the smooth functioning of the conference.

J.J.H.
V.W.

Contents

List of Figures   ix

1. INTRODUCTION
   Joachim Jens Hesse and Vincent Wright   1

Part I. The Context

2. EUROPEAN FEDERALISM: THE LESSONS OF PAST
   EXPERIENCE
   William H. Riker   9

3. THE POLITICAL THEORY OF FEDERALISM: THE
   RELEVANCE OF CLASSICAL APPROACHES
   Murray Forsyth   25

4. THE CONSTITUTIONAL ARRANGEMENTS OF
   FEDERAL SYSTEMS: A SCEPTICAL VIEW
   FROM THE OUTSIDE
   Cheryl Saunders   46

Part II. Federal Arrangements: Costs, Benefits, and Preconditions

5. THE POLITICAL DIMENSION, GERMAN
   PRACTICE, AND THE EUROPEAN
   PERSPECTIVE
   Uwe Leonardy   73

6. AN ECONOMIC PERSPECTIVE
   Dieter Biehl   101

7. THE CULTURAL DIMENSION
   Peter M. Leslie   121

Part III. The European Experience

8. GERMAN FEDERALISM AND THE CHALLENGE OF
   UNIFICATION
   Gerhard Lehmbruch   169

9. AUSTRIA: HAS THE FEDERATION BECOME
   OBSOLETE?
   Reinhard Rack   204

10. SWITZERLAND: THE MODEL IN NEED OF
    ADAPTATION?
    Daniel Thürer   219

11. SPAIN: A FEDERATION IN THE MAKING?
    Juan José Solozábal   240

12. THE REFORM OF THE BELGIAN STATE
    Robert Senelle   266

13. FROM THE USSR TO THE COMMONWEALTH OF
    INDEPENDENT STATES: CONFEDERATION OR
    CIVILIZED DIVORCE?
    Stephan Kux   325

Part IV. Conclusion: Federalizing Europe

14. CAN THERE BE A STABLE FEDERAL BALANCE IN
    EUROPE?
    Fritz W. Scharpf   361

15. FEDERALIZING EUROPE: THE PATH TO
    ADJUSTMENT
    Joachim Jens Hesse and Vincent Wright   374

Index   401

List of Figures

2.1 Types of government in terms of their degrees of
   centralization   11
6.1 The extended-cost concept   103
6.2 Distribution of 50 per cent of EU own resources per
   capita in 1987 according to hypothetical progressive
   financing, with the aid of an EU surcharge on
   national income taxes   118
7.1 Federalization: probable balance of cultural costs
   and benefits   130
12.1 The Communities of Belgium   320
12.2 The Regions of Belgium: their populations and gross
   national product   321
12.3 The Provinces of Belgium   322
12.4 The political structure of the Brussels-Capital Region   323
12.5 The political structure of Belgian government   324

1

Introduction

JOACHIM JENS HESSE AND VINCENT WRIGHT

This book, as its title indicates, deals with the subject of 'federalizing Europe'. And it does so at three levels: at the level of the European Community, at the level of its Member States, and at the level of the states of Central and Eastern Europe. This approach, it will be argued, is essential, because of the increasing interdependence and interplay of these three levels: nation-states in all parts of Europe influence one another, influence the Community, and are influenced by it. This is true in a variety of ways and to varying degrees. This book looks at one of those ways: the federalizing of previous unitary state systems or the reordering of existing federal arrangements. Clearly, not all European nation-states are involved. There are at least two notable exceptions in Western Europe: the United Kingdom, with its unprecedented drive to centralization (a phenomenon it misleadingly and critically attributes to the Community), and France, with a programme of decentralization which is essentially focused on the bigger communes and on the *départements*. Moreover, in Central and Eastern Europe events in countries such as (the former) Yugoslavia and Czechoslovakia have demonstrated, sometimes tragically, the vulnerability of federal or quasi-federal arrangements when attempting to deal with highly intense, non-negotiable, and politically salient cleavages. Ideally, this book would have examined some of these cases. Answering questions such as 'Why is federalization not on the political agenda in the United Kingdom and France?' and, 'Under what conditions are federal arrangements inappropriate or inapplicable?' would have extended the book's theoretical and empirical scope—but also its length. Furthermore, even the more modest approach of this book raises multiple and complex theoretical issues, and its more restricted empirical base has the advantage of providing greater analytical coherence.

The systematic comparative analysis of federations, and the body of political, economic, social, and cultural ideas and principles which underpin them has been in decline for nearly two decades. The 1950s and 1960s saw the publication of a string of influential studies on the theory and practice of federal government in a comparative perspective. Since then, the zeal for explicitly comparative work, which seeks to combine empirical description with analytical concerns, or even theoretical ambitions, has waned. True, there have been some recent, sporadic attempts at comparing the legal–constitutional frameworks of modern federal systems, with a view to developing more general theories of federal government. However, although they have been able to take account of important changes and new trends in some of the older federations, they have added relatively little to our understanding of the distinguishing features of federal governance.

This is not to say that research on federalism is, as such, underdeveloped. Britain alone has at least three specialized institutions designed to foster the academic study of federalism. In all the Western European federations, with the surprising exception of Germany, there exist one or more research institutes focusing on questions of federal governance; and whilst a comparable concentration of research effort is lacking in the German case (at least until very recently), problems of federalism have traditionally occupied a very prominent position in that country in the study of constitutional and public law. Since the early 1970s, German, Belgian, and Spanish political science has also become increasingly involved in federal studies, and has contributed to a widening of what tended to be a predominantly legal–institutional perspective, to include processes of policy-making and implementation. Turning to the United States—the first modern federation—one finds a number of social science research institutes whose research centres on federal–state relations. And in Canada, the study of intergovernmental relations has been a growth industry in recent years, reflecting the persistent and acute problems of keeping together the Canadian state. Furthermore, if one takes into account the work done in long-established federations such as Australia, it is clear that federal studies as a whole are flourishing.

However, at least as far as writing and research on the European experience of federalism are concerned, single-country studies still predominate, and references to other federal systems are generally perfunctory. One of the reasons for the relative paucity of comparative research is certainly the very diversity and fluctuating nature of existing federal and pre-federal (or quasi-federal) systems. This renders difficult meaningful comparisons that go beyond merely aggregate legal–institutional analyses. The difference is not solely one between long-established (or mature) federal systems and newly (and unstable) emerging ones. From a functional point of view, federal systems may be viewed as an institutional response to a wide range of political, economic, social, and cultural problems; structural arrangements reflect these different contextual conditions. Thus, federalization may, for example, be primarily the result of a conscious and deliberate rejection of oppressive central control under a previous authoritarian regime; it may be seen as an attempt at the institutional accommodation of salient cultural cleavages; or it may be undertaken in reaction to increasingly obvious performance deficits at the central state level in traditionally unitary systems.

The impression of diversity in European federalism is further enhanced if the analysis is not restricted to Western Europe, but seeks to take account of current developments in Central and Eastern Europe. Here decades of 'democratic centralism' have thoroughly discredited state authority, especially at the central level. As a result, there is a strong tendency within the emergent democracies to transfer powers to local and regional authorities. In fact, there is some evidence to suggest that the rapid functional and territorial fragmentation of policy-making may threaten the effective central co-ordination of reform processes in the political, economic, and social spheres.

It is scarcely surprising that in trying to reshape the legal–institutional framework of governance, Central and Eastern European countries should turn for guidance and inspiration to their Western neighbours and that the Western federations should have attracted particular attention. However, it has quickly become apparent that the contextual determinants of federal-type solutions are too case-specific to allow for any straightforward transplant of federal constitutional models. There remains an urgent need to find practicable constitutional solutions to the pressing problems of political, economic, and social instability in Central and Eastern Europe. Nevertheless, despite the limits to the applicability of Western experiences of federalism to the reform processes in Central and Eastern

Europe, it makes sense to re-examine Western processes of federalization, regionalization, and decentralization, with a view to drawing lessons that might be useful in the Central and Eastern European context.

In doing so, particular emphasis needs to be placed on the necessary preconditions for successful federalization and the political, economic, and socio-cultural costs and benefits of federal governance. What is required is a sober, historically informed assessment of the possibilities of, and limits to, federalization. This is not only necessary in relation to Central and Eastern Europe, where many of the essential prerequisites of federalization appear to be lacking. In view of the widespread calls for further federalization and regionalization in many Western European states, a more systematic inquiry into the political, economic, and social bases of apparently successful polities as well as a critical performance analysis may help to paint a more realistic picture of the problem-solving capacity of decentralized and fragmented political systems. Lastly, a comparative attempt along these lines may also throw light on the viability of a European Federation (or a 'United States of Europe'). With the opponents of a federal Europe not only questioning the desirability but also the viability of a federal European Community, the topicality of this issue is readily apparent.

On the basis of these considerations, this book is intended to contribute to a more balanced assessment of the political, economic, and socio-cultural potential of federal political-institutional arrangements, by exploring the costs, benefits, and preconditions of federalization. The basic question to be addressed is the following: What can reasonably be expected from federal systems, at what price, and under which conditions? In view of the substantial variations in the legal–institutional configurations of existing federations, it is reasonable to assume that the costs and benefits of federalizing unitary systems differ considerably between countries. They can also be expected to be different from those which occur if federal structures are rooted in previously autonomous polities. Some benefits of federalization can be realized only in specific institutional settings, just as certain costs are tied to particular institutional arrangements. The importance of national contexts is also apparent when one looks at the complex preconditions of federalization. Here, it may be argued that many of the rewards customarily associated with federal government are, in fact, preconditions for the successful creation and long-term survival of federative structures. Given the analytical and empirical questions which this book seeks to address, it was thought essential to complement the conceptual-theoretical discussion of costs, benefits, and preconditions with analyses of individual federations.

Part I of the book, which is devoted to a consideration of traditional approaches to federalism (with three chapters by the late William Riker, Murray Forsyth, and Cheryl Saunders) is followed by a section (with chapters by Uwe Leonardy, Dieter Biehl, and Peter Leslie) on the political, economic, and socio-cultural costs and benefits of federalization. This leads, in Part III, to chapters which analyse the experiences of five West European countries, and which examine the tensions and adjustment processes of three traditionally stable federal systems (Germany—Gerhard Lehmbruch, Austria—Reinhard Rack, and Switzerland—Daniel Thürer), and two traditionally stable centralized polities which are undergoing relatively radical federal or quasi-federal restructuring (Spain—Juan Solozábal and Belgium—Robert Senelle). Some of these chapters highlight the impact of membership (effective or imminent) of the European Community on domestic institutional arrangements at territorial level. A final chapter in Part III explores the particularly troubled case of the Commonwealth of Independent States (Stephan Kux), which has seen the refashioning of territorial structures and relationships.

The final part of the book (Part IV) then deals more specifically with the Community and the comparative dimension of federalization. Informed by a general sensitivity to national experiences, Fritz Scharpf raises the issue of whether there can be 'a stable federal balance in Europe'. The book concludes with an overall assessment, by the two editors, of the federalizing processes at work in Europe, both at the Community and the nation-state level. In doing so, they point to the problems, paradoxes, and likely outcomes of those processes, and they raise questions about some of the premisses of traditional theoretical approaches.

But perhaps the major lesson they draw from the studies presented in this book is that there are no easy lessons to be drawn. There are clearly difficulties in attempting to transplant foreign models, and not only because preconditions are unpropitious. Rather it is because many of those models (even the apparently most stable) are themselves under strain, being squeezed by both domestic and external factors. Institutional arrangements are rarely fossilized, and this is peculiarly so with territorial arrangements, because they are entangled with wider functional and often highly politicized issues, all of which are susceptible to change. They may not be entirely fluid and unpredictable, but they are far from static. Moreover, it is no less clear that partial experiments with federalization may create a dynamic with ripple effects that are difficult to control. Reform must, therefore, be embedded in a knowledge of the political, economic, social, and cultural context of the country, a wariness when confronted with foreign models, and a sensitivity to the wider issues which are inevitably raised when federalization processes are put in train. If this book contributes in a modest way to that knowledge, wariness, and sensitivity, it will, we hope, have served its purpose.

PART I
The Context

2

European Federalism
The Lessons of Past Experience

WILLIAM H. RIKER

1. INTRODUCTION

As we begin this consideration of European federations, it is worth while recalling that only in the nineteenth and twentieth centuries have federations been a widely used constitutional form. They were rare before the nineteenth century and it may be that they will become less attractive in the twenty-first century. But for now they are generally approved of. And this is surprising because this era has also been an era of nationalism when the nation-state, the sovereign political organization of the people, is also approved of. These two forms are in some ways inconsistent: nation-states derive from, justify, and separate out a single ethnic group, while federations may—and often do—bring together political units with different ethnic bases. So a difficult problem for interpreting federalism is to explain the twentieth-century support for this pragmatic, instrumental constitution in an era that embraces simultaneously the emotional and often irrational loyalties of nationalism.

In order to estimate whether or not federalism can transcend this internal contradiction, we must first determine just what federalism is or the notion of government by federation. One elementary feature is a two-tier government. A set of constituent governments acknowledge that a federal government has authority over all their territory and people for those functions covering the whole territory, while they retain for themselves those functions related just to their own territories. But, of course, all governments—except those with tiny populations—are decentralized, with at least two tiers. So the number of tiers cannot be the distinguishing feature of federalism.

If we take the word seriously, it must depend on an agreement. Its Latin root *foedus* is an agreement or covenant, but it is a very special kind of agreement because *foedus* is also *fides* or trust. So by its root a federation is a bargain about government, a bargain based, however, not on an enforcement procedure, but on simple trust itself. Ordinary bargains or contracts depend on a judiciary to punish reneging. But the agreement to create a judiciary can hardly depend on what is yet to be created, namely, the government within which the judiciary is located. So the special covenant of a federation is necessarily something which continues to be advantageous to all parties. When all are known to benefit, then each can reasonably rely on the others to keep the agreement. This is a self-enforcing agreement because the enforcement is rational mutual confidence.

The content of this agreement is the division of functions among tiers. As I have already pointed out, all governments larger than villages are organized in tiers, but federation embodies the arrangement of tiers in a permanent agreement. It ensures that governments at the constituent and central tiers always exist and retain their assigned duties. Governments that are not federations can reorganize the local units at will, destroying old regional units and creating new ones. But in federations the constituent units have agreed with one another that each will retain its identity and its unique functions.

Thus, federalism is a constitutionally determined tier-structure. If its constitutional feature is ignored, then it is merely some particular arrangement for decentralization. Unfortunately, in recent years this is how students of policy (and especially economists) have treated it. They have thereby overlooked the whole point of federalism, namely that the tiered structure cannot arbitrarily be revised, or even revised to adjust for changed conditions.

To visualize this concept of federalism, consider a set of geographically contiguous governments, each with its own territory. At one extreme they can be totally independent of one another. If they undertake concerted action, however, they at least need institutions to execute it. The simplest such institution is an alliance, where all the decision-making power continues to reside in the independent governments, but where there is also some executive authority (such as a military commander) to carry out the (usually unanimously decided) action. Alliances are, however, often fragile and ineffective. So if the independent governments want permanence and efficiency, they may federate and thereby create a central government with independent decision-making authority for some functions. Finally, at the extreme of integration, the independent governments may simply vanish into the imperial centre.

So we can illustrate the scale of centralization as in Fig. 2.1, which fairly sharply demarcates federation from other forms of government. For a federation to exist, the central government must have authority to decide on action for at least one function entirely on its own and without reference to the preferences of the constituent governments. (If the central government cannot do this much, then the organization is at best an alliance.) On the other hand, the constituent governments must also have authority to decide on action for at least one function entirely independently of the centre and each other. (If they cannot do this much, then the organization is completely unitary.) Federations thus cover a wide range of divisions of functions. Those close to the alliance end of the scale are said to be peripheralized and those close to the unitary end are said to be centralized.

The complexity of this description and the lack of clarity in the assignment of functions suggest an obvious question: why would framers of constitutions adopt so difficult a political form? The answer is, of course, that it enables the rulers of a set of independent states to accomplish some objective that is not feasible independently or in alliance. Of course, the rulers of one state might incorporate other states into their state in order to aggregate resources. Indeed, throughout recorded history this is what has usually happened. Imperial expansion is a far more frequent method of aggregation than is federalism. But imperial expansion is costly, if,

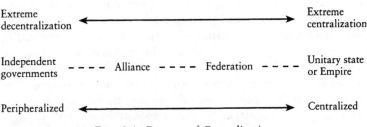

FIG. 2.1. Degrees of Centralization

that is, the potential victims resist. So occasionally, ambitious expansionists federate rather than conquer.

2. THE MILITARY MOTIVE

What goals are sufficiently desired to lead to federation? The goal most frequently observed is military, although, of course, that goal is always instrumental. Wars are not usually fought for their own sake, for the joy of fighting and dying, but rather they are undertaken aggressively for the sake of trade, territory, plunder, and tribute, or defensively, for the sake of resistance and independence. Success in war depends on resources. So the aggregation of resources for war is the primary, though instrumental, motive for federation. Indeed, the rulers of all successful federations, that is, federations that have lasted more than a few years, have initially displayed some kind of military purpose.

One frequent purpose has been rebellion or civil war. Subordinate units of an empire rebel simultaneously and then federate for better resistance. Thus the Dutch Republic facilitated the rebellion of the provinces in the Netherlands against Spanish dominion; the United States facilitated the rebellion of some American colonies against Great Britain; and the several Spanish American federations (Argentina, Mexico, Venezuela, Gran Columbia, and the Central American Federation, the latter two of which were short-lived) facilitated the rebellion against Spain. Another frequent purpose has been to defend against the imperial ambition of neighbours; for example, the Swiss confederation (against Habsburg ambition); the Soviet Union (against a potential Western threat which Lenin preferred to meet by seducing the non-Russian provinces rather than by conquering them, which he probably could not have done anyway); the Canadian confederation (against a threat of invasion from the United States, which had occurred three times previously and seemed likely again at the end of its Civil War); and the Australian commonwealth (against the new—in 1900—Pacific imperialism of Japan and Germany). A third military purpose has been to absorb neighbours in order to prepare for aggressive expansion. Thus Yugoslavia became a federation to further Tito's plans for a Central European empire (although Stalin beat him to the draw). And a fourth military purpose is to absorb neighbours, with less cost than conquest, mollifying them with the appearance of continuing sovereignty. The Delian League of the Athenian empire is an ancient example. Dual monarchies also have this character: the Austro-Hungarian empire in the nineteenth century and perhaps even Britain in the seventeenth. Surely the first German empire, which absorbed Bavaria and Württemberg after 1870, is a clear-cut example. The contemporary Indian federation has also proved an excellent way of absorbing the princely states of pre-Independence India. The Malay federation, which later became Malaysia, absorbed Singapore and Brunei; and the Nigerian federation enabled the north to subdue the east. Of course, many cases fall into two categories. India seems best placed in the fourth category, but it could just as easily fit in the second (in the sense of defence against Pakistan) and Malaysia was also defending against an aggressive Indonesia.

This outline of categories of military rationales for federation, within which I have included most well-known federations, makes it clear that, at their initiation, they all had some military purpose. This observation is strengthened by considering the instances of federations that did not work and were abandoned within a few years, returning to independent states or becoming fully unitary. These failures reflected the lack of any military purpose, defective structures (for example, one large and dominant unit, as in the USSR or in the short-lived Egyptian–Syrian federation, or very few units as in New Zealand), or both.

Many of these failed federations were initially established by the British government, which of course also set up some successful ones. After observing the success of the United States, the first federation formed from former British colonies, and after successfully acquiescing in Canada and Australia, the British government repeatedly urged its newly independent or about-to-be independent colonies to federate. Many did so. Canada, Australia, and India remain federations. But New Zealand (formed only on the inappropriate model of the United States), South Africa, Pakistan, the West Indies, and Rhodesia–Nyasaland all abandoned the federal form. Nigeria is an equivocal case: it has been a federation for two brief periods, and at other times a centralized dictatorship. Two of these states (Pakistan and Nigeria) had very defective structures (i.e. very few units and one dominant unit) and found they needed a unitary form for civil war. With geographically separated parts, Pakistan broke up into two non-federated independent states. Nigeria, with only three states, had a highly defective structure, which was revealed when one unit rebelled and civil war ensued. When once again a federation, Nigeria restructured into twenty-one states, although this did not prevent the second re-establishment of dictatorship. The future of a Nigerian federation is now quite unclear.

The other failed ex-British federations abandoned federalism because there was simply no military reason for them to be federal. There were no enemies on the scene and hence they did not need to worry about maintaining internal order. Non-British federations that were stillborn displayed the same range of reasons for failure: the French-sponsored Mali federation in West Africa had no military rationale and hence collapsed into unitary governments; the Javanese immediately rejected the Dutch-sponsored Indonesian federation, thinking it a Dutch trick and preferring to integrate by conquest; and several Spanish American federations collapsed as militarily unnecessary. In general, the history of failed federations implies the same conclusion as the history of successful ones: initially, there must be a compelling reason to aggregate resources, and this compulsion has until now invariably been military, though sometimes framers prefer imperial to federal institutions to solve the military problems at, perhaps, less cost.

The preference for an imperial, as against a federal, solution to the military problem of expansion is dramatically illustrated by the prompt Indonesian rejection of the federation devised by the Dutch colonial office when the Dutch empire collapsed. As the Javanese sensed, this federation had no obvious military purpose: it served mainly to separate other islands from Java, an outcome perhaps desired by Dutch and even non-Javanese politicians, but certainly not desired by the Javanese. Furthermore, Java had sufficient military resources to bring unwilling former Dutch colonies into a unitary Indonesia. Hence, it simply did not need a federation for expansion, which it could easily accomplish imperially, either by persuasion or force. Thus, a federal contract failed, not primarily because it was externally imposed, but mainly because it had no initial rationale.

Just as the existence of a compelling military purpose informs all successful new federations and just as the absence of a military purpose characterizes all new federations that fail to get going, so at the present time the end of the Cold War and the prospect of an end to major wars in general has induced the collapse of a number of marginally viable federations.

Perhaps the best recent examples are the Soviet Union and Yugoslavia, which have both collapsed. The Soviet Union was, as its name implies, initially conceived as a federation, a device to re-aggregate, both for defensive military purposes and for internal security, the separated units of the defunct Russian empire. It was a genuine federation for a few months, until Lenin was able to dominate the re-attached provinces. Thereafter, until about 1989, the nominal federation was, in practice, a unitary state. But the federal form reappeared when the Baltic provinces, and then Russia itself, began to operate independently of the Union. It was still quite centralized, but was, nevertheless, a federation. But this federation had no apparent military purpose: hardly anyone believed the Western alliance intended to invade the Union, the Union itself had already decided it could no longer afford a satellite empire, and the failed coup in the summer of 1991 revealed that the military could not act as an internal police-force to hold the Union together. Within five months this federation collapsed, to be replaced by a new, highly peripheralized federation, so peripheralized, in fact, that one wonders if it is a federation at all. The moral is that, with neither an external nor an internal military *raison d'être*, the unpopular and unwanted federation collapsed.

Something similar has happened to the former Yugoslavia, though the collapse began much earlier, probably with the realization that Yugoslavia had nothing to fear from the Soviet Union or its satellites, especially after the death of Tito. It kept together reasonably well with much economic decentralization. But when the Soviet satellites successfully deserted the empire, units of Yugoslavia began to rebel. The first to go was Slovenia, which was far enough away from the Serbian centre to avoid invasion by the Serbian-controlled Yugoslav army. Then Croatia fought itself free. Today, Bosnia is at war with Serbia and Macedonia is seeking recognition. Clearly, the military purpose of federation has disappeared. The original purpose—to attract a central European federation under Tito—disappeared soon after the federation was formed because Stalin beat Tito to the draw. Its continuing military purpose, externally to resist the Soviet empire and internally to police the outlying provinces, both disappeared, as the Soviet Union collapsed and the army proved unable to control Slovenia and Croatia. As the military purpose disappeared, so did the federation.

In other existing federations that have lost their military rationale, the federation has weakened, perhaps to the point of peripheralizing and then disappearing. Pakistan had already lost its federal agreement to oppose India when Bangladesh separated. Now the two parts of Czechoslovakia have separated. This federation, which was formed at the end of the First World War as a device to create a viable national government out of the debris of the Austrian empire, lost its military purpose, as it was absorbed, first, into the Third Reich and then into the Soviet empire. Once freed from Soviet shackles, the federation seemed to have no military justification and hence has broken up.

An interesting case of possibly incipient disintegration is Canada. The original military purpose was to defend against potential invasion by the United States. Fear of invasion was reasonable because the United States or its predecessor colonies had invaded Canadian lands three times in a century and some American politicians threatened to do so again at the end of the Civil War. Federation was thus a prudent military response to such threats. But over the next century the United States apparently lost interest in military conquest. Canadian cynics would say that economic conquest was easier, but most United States citizens would simply say that they hardly ever think about Canada. Hence, the initially centralized Canadian federation has tended to peripheralize generally and has specifically attempted to placate Quebec by recognizing its francophone identity. In recent years the Liberal party has sought to justify the federation as a protection against American economic competition. But this justification has seemed hollow, because its disadvantage is the exclusion of Canadian goods from the American market. So the Canadian federation is teetering on the edge of Quebec's nationalism. If Quebec goes, the future of other parts of the federation is unclear.

All these examples of federal disintegration and incipient disintegration in the wake of the outbreak of peace emphasize the fact that federations have almost invariably begun as military enterprises. If they remain basically that, then military considerations are a large part of the glue that holds them together. But of course a few federations have generated a kind of nationalistic or ethnic loyalty to the federations themselves, loyalties that supersede the loyalties to the provincial units. This has certainly happened in the most stable of current federations: Argentina, Australia, Brazil, Germany, Mexico, Switzerland, and the United States. In these states, the military purpose is less central than it was initially. Consequently, it is sometimes difficult for citizens of these successful federations to observe and recall the initial military purpose. Nevertheless, in the discussion of new federations it is important to remember the way that the now stable federations were formed.

Federations have appeared ever since ancient times: in ancient Greece (and some say in ancient Israel), in medieval Europe (the Swiss, Swabian, and north Italian leagues), and in early modern Europe (the Dutch Republic). But federalism began to flourish in the nineteenth century with imperial Germany as well as with the consequences of the Spanish, Portuguese, and British empires. The pace accelerated in the twentieth century with the break-up of empires, bringing new African, Asian, and European federations. What accounts for this burst of federalism? One step is the invention of centralized federalism in the United States in the late eighteenth century. The other is the collapse of empires.

The invention provided a viable organization that turned out to be useful in partially reassembling the debris of empire. Imperial administrators organize political units appropriate for their purposes and these units are typically too small to be militarily effective by themselves. Thus it made sense for eighteenth-century British administrators to govern through units as small as Massachusetts or South Carolina. And even in the twentieth century, units as geographically compact as Punjab and Baroda made good administrative sense. However, it is likely that none of these units was viable as an independent state in a hostile eighteenth- or twentieth-century world. So when they became independent, their politicians chose to combine them with adjacent units. Combinations by force would have been difficult in both cases, but combination by agreement into a centralized federation was acceptable in both cases. And in many others. Once centralized federalism was invented, framers of constitutions for ex-imperial units used it frequently.

Of course, not all the contemporary federations derive from collapsed empires. But even those that do not emanate from that source have adopted the centralized form. Switzerland reorganized in 1848 and Germany and Austria did so after World Wars I and II on the centralized model. The former Soviet Union and Yugoslavia—if their claims to be federations were justifiable—would probably never have adopted a federal structure if the centralized form of government had been available. Recent federalizing movements would probably make no headway without the centralized model. In Belgium, for example, the movement for federation is an effort to preserve a nation-state against the divisiveness of ethnic hostilities. If the peripheralized form of federation were available, federalism would achieve very little, and complete separation might do just as well. But centralized federation preserves the existing aggregation of national force, while simultaneously attenuating the ethnic divisiveness. So the invention of centralized federalism is crucial to the contemporary use and approval of federalism and, therefore, deserves explanation.

When the thirteen colonies that formed the United States rebelled against Britain, they initially formed a loose, peripheralized federation. Though the main organ (that is, the Continental Congress) of what became this federation did declare independence (in 1776), and sent ambassadors, organized an army, and borrowed money, it was kept on a tight rein by the new state governments which, as it turned out, really controlled taxes and military resources. A peripheralized constitution, the Articles of Confederation, adopted in 1781, embodied the principles of provincial control so that decisions on national policy were really made in the state capitals. Nationalist leaders, who controlled the federal government from 1781 onwards, were deeply discontented with this state of affairs. They tried several times to bring forward modest amendments to these Articles, but failed because of the unanimity requirement characteristic of peripheralized federations. Then, in a bold move, they attempted a complete revision of the constitution, based on a proposal by James Madison for a wholly national government, entirely uninfluenced by the states and fully in control of them. This would have been a government as unitary as any in the world. The delegates at the Philadelphia Convention of 1787 revised Madison's proposal to give the states unique functions, an independent juridical identity, and also a role in supplying national officials. Thus, by way of a compromise between nationalists and provincials, these nationalists created a new kind of centralized federation, one with almost as much governing strength as a unitary government, but also with unique functions and perpetual guarantees for the constituent units. It was this combination of features that rendered centralized federalism so popular in subsequent centuries.

3. THE MOTIVE OF TRADE RESTRICTION

The foregoing discussion suggests that people have welcomed federalism for purely instrumental reasons. In fact, however, many political philosophers have justified the federal form on moral grounds: that it promotes liberty by allowing freedom of action for small groups or units, or, more generally, that it limits big government and thus promotes individual freedom.

There is no question that federalism restricts the ability of the central government to prescribe public policy. The constitution prohibits central government action in functions reserved for the constituent units. Indeed, when the central government ignores these prohibitions, as, for example, in the Soviet Union from a few months after its establishment to its dissolution in 1991, then federalism is itself destroyed. A dictatorship cannot really be a federation. When the central government denies omnipotence and guarantees constituent governments unique functions, then groups that lose nationally have a chance to win locally. With such compensation for national losers, the society as a whole is not zero-sum. In that sense, federalism really does promote individual freedom.

It is possible, however, to exaggerate the freedom-generating effects of federalism. While the foregoing argument is valid in general, nevertheless local freedom of action may not in fact generate true liberty. The United States offers a perverse example. In 1787 one of the constitutional compromises provided that states govern the institution of slavery. After a generation, however, the northern, slave-free, more populous region deeply regretted that concession. In the southern, slave-holding, less populous region, federalism came to mean protection of slaveholders' property rights and the absence of freedom for the black-skinned slaves. Though a majority, the northern region lacked the two-thirds and three-quarters majorities necessary for constitutional amendments. Therefore, the only feasible method of eliminating slavery was the Civil War from 1861 to 1865. While that war did end slavery, it still left matters such as voting rights in the local jurisdictions.

Within a generation of the end of the Civil War, southern states had once again repressed the former slaves. Again, federalism, the supposed protector of minorities, turned out to be a device for condoning repression. Only in 1954–65 did the north become sufficiently populous and sympathetic to eliminate that second repression. Thus, for well over half of its history, federalism in the United States actually meant freedom for some southern whites to oppress blacks, hardly the conventional picture of federalism as guaranteeing freedom. Fortunately, in recent generations federal repression of blacks has ceased, so now federalism in the United States serves as an addition to the separation of powers and thus does, on the whole, serve the cause of liberty. Considering all the federations there have been in the world, I believe that federalism has been a significant force for limited government and hence for personal freedom.

Because of the success of federalism both as an instrument to aggregate resources and as a protection of liberty, many political idealists today hope to adapt it to new circumstances, such as a federal world or a federal Europe. If the description in this chapter of the origin of federations is even remotely correct, a federal world is a chimera. There must be a reason to aggregate resources, some external (or internal) enemy or object of aggression. Otherwise, no government would be willing to give up independence for aggregation. But a federal world precludes an enemy or an opportunity for attack and hence also precludes a reason for aggregation.

A federal Europe is a more complicated case. One frequently mentioned alternative incentive is the economic interaction with Asia and America. Federation is a pretty good device for trade warfare in two ways: on the one hand, if the federation has internal free trade—and most do—then federation immediately expands the free-trade area compared with its size before federation. On the other hand, a strong federation over a large territory can fairly effectively raise trade barriers in favour of some minorities of citizens of the federation. The combination may actually increase the incomes of a majority of citizens of the federation over what they were prior to federating. This may not be the optimal way to increase income, but it may be a feasible way. If so, there may be economic incentives for federation.

In the long run, it is probably true that this incentive is illusory. The main beneficiaries of a wider free-trade area are precisely those manufacturing and extractive industries that benefit the most from existing trade barriers. The oligopolists thus protected of course increase prices throughout the free-trade area, probably thereby absorbing most of the gains of the non-protected producers whose sole advantage is a larger market area. Consequently, for most participants the gains from federation may be very short-lived.

In the abstract, of course, trade between traders who are not forced by governmental regulation to deal with each other is necessarily advantageous to both parties. If it is not, then trade does not occur. Assuming that such free conditions exist, all traders benefit from trade and all increases in trade are advantageous. Consequently, deviations from this ideal world of completely free trade are harmful. This is the consensus of most professional economists and the evidence of great increases in income during the relatively free-trade eras (e.g. the latter decades of the nineteenth century and after World War II) is a powerful indication that the professional economists are correct.

But abstract long-term advantages in free trade may not mean much in the political world in which some groups can visualize immediate gains from trade restrictions. Consumers seldom observe such gains. No matter how much all citizens in their roles as consumers benefit from free trade, the benefit shows up only as lower prices than otherwise anticipated for imported goods or those domestic goods competing with imported goods. Since the higher anticipated price is never observed, the consumption benefit may not—indeed, usually, does not—appear to be a significant part of personal income, even though from an accounting viewpoint lower costs of living constitute higher incomes as much as increased earnings do. Hence the consumption benefit from free trade is relatively invisible to most citizens.

The producers' gain from trade restriction is, however, easily imaginable. Not all producers can benefit from trade restriction. Imagine an entirely autarkic economy. Each producer is able to increase prices in the absence of external competition. But what each gains from production income is cancelled out by increased costs of living. So no one gains. Relaxing the conditions to an economy with some, but not universal, trade restrictions, the producers whose products are protected—enabling them to increase domestic prices for all citizens—are able to gain from trade restrictions. Those whose products are not protected must sell at competitive prices and are unable to gain. Thus the main political question about trade restriction is: what proportion of producers can gain from managed trade?

In a small country, most of the production is for export and relatively little for domestic consumption. Consequently, in a small country very few producers can imagine a significant increase in income from charging protected higher prices in the domestic market, especially if other nations retaliate and thus reduce producers' foreign sales. But in a large country, where many producers sell mostly in the domestic market, those producers can anticipate significant gains of income from higher (i.e. protected) prices to their compatriots.

Other things being equal, increasing the size of a domestic market increases the proportion of citizens whose income derives primarily from sales in the domestic market. It follows, therefore, that any device, empire, or federation, that increases the size of the domestic market increases the proportion of those who can visualize immediate gains from trade restrictions.

It is probably the case that, no matter how large the country, those who gain from trade restrictions are less than a majority of producers. For that reason one would seldom expect the incentive of trade restriction to be sufficient to bring about federation. But the interests of these producers are intense, much more intense than consumers' interest in low prices. So, if one counts heads by the intensity of their feelings, it may well be that, in a large country, the sum of intensities in favour of trade restriction is greater than the sum opposed.

It is certainly true that the motive of trade restriction was an important, though secondary, incentive towards federation in many earlier instances, especially in those formed by constituent states themselves as against those encouraged by the colonial office of a dying empire. Thus, for example, the revision in 1787 of the United States from a peripheralized to a centralized federation was partially inspired by a desire to impose trade restrictions. One kind of trade restriction intended by the framers (but never subsequently adopted) was a Navigation Act, i.e. a statute that would prohibit foreign ships from picking up cargo in American ports. Another kind of trade restriction, perhaps not intended by most of the framers, but actually carried through by the first administration, was a tariff to protect infant industries. Yet the military motive appears to have been dominant. The framers wanted to create a government capable of managing foreign relations and fighting wars. Nevertheless, it is also unquestionably true that they wanted a government capable of imposing restrictions on trade. The framers' economic theories were mostly mercantilist and they consciously recognized the mercantilist advantage of the bigger government of a federation over the governments of thirteen fairly small states in generating internal oligopolies. Throughout the nineteenth century one main recurrent issue of American politics was the use of the federation to impose trade restrictions, mainly tariffs. It is no accident that the political party that chose to fight a civil war to preserve the Union was also the party of trade restriction. This fact alone reveals the close association between the big government of federation and the potential of generating gains for producers in the domestic market.

Similarly, the formation of the Canadian federation was certainly influenced by a desire to protect the infant industries of Upper Canada; the formation of the Australian federation was much influenced by a similar infant industries incentive; and the federation of imperial Germany was concerned with expansion of internally free trade balanced by the externally restricted trade of the earlier customs union. In none of these cases was trade restriction the primary motive, but the motive was present and contributed to the adoption of the federal constitution.

Today the question is: can this once secondary motive for federation become the primary motive that generates a federal Europe? In a world where trade is vastly more important than it was a generation ago, perhaps the answer is affirmative. But there are conflicting forces. There are increased opportunities for protected industries to gain from trade restriction. But the costs that these producers' gains impose on those domestic consumers who have no producers' gains are much more obvious than they were when foreign trade was a smaller proportion of national product. That is, the incentive for restriction is greater, but so is its visibility to those who are harmed by it. Thus, most Europeans now recognize that the European Union's restrictions on agricultural trade benefit, at great cost to everyone else, only a small proportion of the Union's population. Is it likely that the majority will fail to observe that additional restrictions on, say, automotive trade will greatly benefit a few hundred thousand metal-workers at great expense to everyone else? This increased visibility of the cost of trade restriction makes me sceptical of an affirmative answer. On the other hand, one must recognize the historical ability of producers to make their special interests appear to be the public interest of the federation. So it is unclear whether the motive of trade restriction is sufficient to replace the military motive in creating a European federation. Consequently, we look forward with intense curiosity to the struggles over European federation during the next decade.

BIBLIOGRAPHY

Davis, S. R., *The Federal Principle: A Journey through Time in Quest of a Meaning* (Berkeley, 1978).

Elazar, D. J., *Exploring Federalism* (Tusculoosa, Ala., 1987).

Forsyth, M., *Unions of States: The Theory and Practice of Confederation* (Leicester, 1981).

Franck, T. M., *Why Federations Fail: An Inquiry into the Requisites for Successful Federalism* (New York, 1968).

King, P., *Federalism and Federation* (Baltimore, 1982).

Riker, W. H., *The Development of American Federalism* (Boston, 1987).

Wheare, K. D., *Federal Government* (London, 1953).

3

The Political Theory of Federalism
The Relevance of Classical Approaches

MURRAY FORSYTH

European integration is a concept that embraces a very wide span of developments and institutions. The central core of the integration process, however, is usually, and with some justification, seen as running from the Schuman Plan through to the Rome Treaty, and from there to the Single European Act and the Maastricht Treaty on European Union. The degree to which this long, uneven process can or ought to be termed a federal one, and the relationship and relevance of federal ideas and practices to it, are matters which have been debated since its very beginning. In this chapter I wish to address certain aspects of this problem again. I wish to argue in particular that the older doctrines of federalism, while in no sense providing a blueprint for integration, do help us to understand what integration is, and to clarify the key issues that confront it now and in the future.

In order to make plain the relevance of the classical federal approach, I shall begin by considering the prevailing philosophy of integration, or, in simpler terms, the general assumptions that have predominated in the way in which integration has been prosecuted up till now. I shall then confront these assumptions with the characteristic and traditional concepts of federalism, showing how these serve to bring out certain less obvious features of integration. Central to the argument will be the tension between the technical-functional ideas that permeate so much of the structure and process of integration, and the federal-constitutional reality which has simultaneously grown up in—or been precipitated by—that process. The technical-functional approach, it will be concluded, has begun to show serious limitations, and a more explicit and determined recourse to federal-constitutional principles could help to rectify the lack of coherence and balance that has arisen.

1. THE UNDERLYING TECHNICITY OF EUROPEAN INTEGRATION

In the early years of integration, when the Schuman Plan had been launched and ambitious plans for a European Defence Community and a European Political Community were being debated, there seems to have been a widespread sense that integration was federalism in action, and that federal theory and practice were highly relevant to what was taking place. The impressive book *Federalism: Mature and Emergent*, edited by A. W. Macmahon, and published in 1955, stands as perhaps the best academic monument to this period and attitude. Largely the work of American scholars, it sought to bring the historical experience of federalism to bear on the events taking place in Europe. William Diebold's statement that 'at the basis of the Schuman Plan is a series of truly federal equations'[1] expressed the prevailing assumption of the authors.

With the collapse of the plans for the European Defence and Political Communities, the signing of the Rome Treaty, and the development of the European Economic Community, the prevailing assumption changed. There was still a strong and widely held belief that the Community was the preliminary to a federal system, but far less conviction that it was itself a species of federalism. The prevailing assumption of those who analysed and wrote about the Community, and indeed of those who worked in its institutions, was that it was an unprecedented form of organization, working according to a unique 'Community method', which involved the interaction of 'supranational' and 'intergovernmental' institutions, and that older theories of federalism had very little to tell one about this kind of body. 'On one point', wrote the British Commissioner, Christopher Tugendhat, 'all could agree. The Community represented a unique structure which could not be related to any known models of government, nor to any conventional theory of international relations.'[2]

As has been emphasized, there have always been many who believe that the Community, with its unique structures, is the preliminary to the creation of a federal system, and who urge that the transition to the federal end-point should be made as quickly as possible. An attempt was made to incorporate this idea of a federal end-point into the founding treaty of the Community at the Maastricht Summit in 1991, though it is worth noting how tentatively the aspiration was worded. Thus the Treaty establishing a European Union, as it was originally drafted by the Dutch Presidency of the European Council, prior to the Maastricht meeting, stated that 'This Treaty marks a new stage in the process leading gradually to a Union with a federal goal.'[3] In other words, the Community was to be transformed forthwith into a 'Union', which was later to be developed into a 'Union with a federal goal'. Even this tentative proposal failed, chiefly because of the strenuous opposition of the British Government. The final text reads: 'This Treaty marks a new stage in the process creating an ever closer union among the peoples of Europe, where decisions are taken as closely as possible to the people.'[4]

If the attitude of those for whom the existing process of integration is the preliminary to a federal system is reasonably clear, a word is needed about the perspective of those who are not convinced of the need to posit a federal end-point. For them integration remains simply a 'process', or as Andrew Shonfield put it, 'a journey to an unknown destination'.[5] The Community is regarded as a pragmatic 'going concern' that not only does not require to be seen as a means to a federal end, but does not require to be seen as being in itself federal. It is simply 'there', a unique and flexible mechanism, more tightly organized than a typical international organization, that accumulates new functions from time to time, when this is judged to be necessary by its members.

For most analysts and commentators, then, the development of European integration since 1957 does not represent a federal phenomenon, but rather a unique and unprecedented process, that for some is the preliminary to the creation of a federal structure, and for others is a cumulative functional phenomenon with no precise or definable end. This is not to say that there have not been those who have regarded and defined the Community as a federal or confederal body—and this view will be examined and expounded later in the chapter—but the predominant view has been a different one.

Let us turn now from the way integration has been viewed in

public debate to the assumptions that are embedded in the actual process itself. What is the political philosophy underlying the Schuman Plan, the Spaak Report, that provided the basis of the Rome Treaty, the Rome Treaty itself, and its two major amendments, the Single European Act, and the Maastricht Treaty on European Union? The most obvious characteristic common to all these texts is a determination to avoid overall constitutional matters, wherever possible, and to concentrate instead on the elaboration of concrete programmes of joint action by the signatory states in specific economic and social areas. Foreign policy and security objectives have, it is true, been added in the two most recent texts, but they are still secondary, in terms of the extent of the common action envisaged, to the economic and social ones.

Robert Schuman's words in his famous declaration of 9 May 1950 provide the leitmotiv of the whole approach: 'L'Europe ne se fera pas d'un coup, ni dans une construction d'ensemble: elle se fera par des réalisations concrètes, creant d'abord une solidarité de fait. . . . Le gouvernement français propose de porter immédiatement l'action sur un point limité mais décisif.'[6] The Spaak Report, it is true, moved from a *point* to an *ensemble* in the sense that it went beyond the sectoral approach to that of a common market, and we shall return to this important shift later. But it too was expressly 'un plan concret d'action' involving 'réalisations qui sont immenses, qui prendront du temps, mais qui peuvent commencer toute de suite'.[7] The Rome Treaty, in keeping with this emphasis, was a special form of treaty, a *traité-cadre* or 'framework treaty', and its later amendments also have this framework character. In other words, the Treaty and the amendments do not define completely and finally the obligations agreed by the signatories. Rather they set out a series of programmes for the future, involving the progressive elaboration of common policies, increasing cooperation, harmonization, and a whole host of other measures. The formulation of the various programmes in the Treaty and amendments is sometimes very precise and detailed, with stages and timetables and objectives clearly defined, and sometimes surprisingly general.

In keeping with this action-plan philosophy, the institutional framework established by the Treaty and amendments is emphatically a means, a mechanism, an instrument, for the elaboration and implementation of outline programmes. The Commission, to use the conventional terminology, is intended as the motor or propellant of integration, and the guardian of the Treaty. Created and appointed by the Member States, its prime task is to ensure that the programmes that they have mapped out and agreed to follow, are in fact implemented. It is, to use another metaphor, the artificially created conscience of the states, constantly reminding them of the promises they have made in their various treaties, but all too aware that, like the individual conscience, it only possesses a relative independence from the beings it tries to guide. Around the central push-and-pull interaction between the Commission and the Council, or between what are conventionally termed the supranational and the intergovernmental organs, are arranged the other major institutions of the Community—the Court, to ensure the legality of the process, and the Parliament, to ensure that it is in some sense democratically supervised. The latter are, as it were, the constitutional penumbra of something that at heart is not conceived of in a constitutional way at all. Finally, out of the continuous process of programme implementation emerges a steadily growing European administrative structure, centred, though by no means wholly concentrated on the Commission. What is being produced by integration is the regulatory or managerial framework of a European economy or society.

What one is confronted with, then, is a dynamic organization, which is technical in the sense that it is conceived primarily as a machinery or apparatus for implementing a set of action programmes. David Mitrany's concept of 'functionalism', conceived before the integration process began, still provides perhaps the best theoretical framework (better even than the neo-functional theories of his American followers) for understanding its technical nature. It is true that for Mitrany the function—that is, the concrete problem to be solved—determined the region of the organization established to solve it, and that he was therefore strongly critical of organizations that began, so to speak, from the wrong end, starting with a region—Europe, for example—and defining the problems to be solved in terms of the region. Mitrany was a true cosmopolitan, who sought via functionalism to transcend all territorial frontiers, rather than to create new ones. Having made this important reservation, however, it is possible to see in his doctrine of the functional organization of international relations a peculiarly apposite summary of the assumptions behind the integration process.

Mitrany's central contention was that economic and social developments in the twentieth century had made it imperative to move beyond the classical liberal notions of the nineteenth century. The latter were essentially static, formal, and constitutional, laying down hard and fast rules not only for sharply delimited national areas, but also for the separation of state and society, for the distinction between public and private, for the protection of individual—and in federal systems, of state—rights, and for the provision of such negative functions as law, order, and security. The modern economy, and modern society, by contrast, had given birth to a mass of ceaselessly changing and frequently convergent positive needs which cut across, and rendered largely irrelevant, these hard and fast distinctions. They called instead for a pragmatic, flexible and problem-orientated functional type of government, focused at those points within and beyond national or state boundaries where needs converged.

The whole modern trend, wrote Mitrany, 'is to organise government along the lines of specific ends and needs, and according to the conditions of their time and place, in lieu of the traditional organization on the basis of a set constitutional division of rights and powers'.[8] Further:

The function . . . determines the executive instrument suitable for its proper activity, and by the same process provides a need for the reform of that instrument at every stage. . . . Not only is there in all this no need for any fixed constitutional division of authority and power, prescribed in advance, but anything beyond the most general formal rules would embarrass the working of these arrangements.[9]

And again: 'Functionalism knows only one logic, the logic of the problem, and of a problem apt to be always in flux in its elements, its spread and its effects. Function is never still'.[10] Finally: 'The functional way is action itself.'[11]

Here it is worth pointing out that Mitrany's vision of the development of functionalism was as strongly influenced by what he had observed happening within particular states as it was by his observation of the international scene. He had witnessed at first hand the Great Depression and the New Deal in America and he had noted how, in the face of imperative social needs the constitutional division of powers between the federal government and the states had been largely bypassed, and concrete action had been taken which had created new types of administrative organs, such as the Tennessee Valley Authority, whose sphere of responsibility cut across state boundaries. 'The significant point in that emergency action was that each and every problem was tackled as a practical issue in itself. No attempt was made to relate it to a general theory or system of government.'[12] For Mitrany the hard and fast constitutional boundaries implied by federalism were as outmoded as a means of dealing with social and economic demands within the state as they were as a means of dealing with such demands across state boundaries.

Mitrany's ideas have been cited here at some length because they articulate so succinctly many of the unspoken assumptions lying behind the integration process in Europe, and because they bring out so sharply the antithesis between these assumptions and the idea of constitution-making, particularly federal constitution-making. The modern, no-nonsense, down-to-earth, technical, activist, and programmatic approach to politics here finds full expression, and starkly confronts the 'old-fashioned' constitutional approach. His words compel one to ask not only whether federal theory and practice has any relevance to the process of integration that has so far taken place, but also whether it can or should have any relevance in the future. Is it indeed outdated? It is to these questions that we must now turn.

2. THE FEDERAL COMPONENT OF THE INTEGRATION PROCESS

Federalism has a long, rich, and diverse history and encompasses a wide variety of political forms. This is worth stressing at the outset, because it is all too easy to move from the correct assumption that federal structures are more than international or technical structures, and inevitably have a constitutional aspect, to the false conclusion that there is only one model of a federal constitution. As Henry Higgins, one of the speakers in the debates leading up to the constitution of the Australian Federation, rightly said:

(T)he hon. gentleman treats federation as if it were an Athena sprung ready armed from the head of Jupiter—that it was something absolutely defined from its first inception. But I take it that 'federation' is a word used to indicate a number of devices which have, as their general object, the relegating of certain subjects to the central government, and the leaving of other subjects to the state governments.[13]

Higgins's words cannot be too frequently recalled in the European context.

A historical survey of federal institutions immediately reveals contrasting types, and a brief account of some of these types will help to create a realistic way into the subject. First, let it be said that every federal system establishes or incorporates a union, and that the concept of union is a federal one through and through. But while all federal systems embody a union, there is considerable variation between federal systems in terms of the depth and strength of the union. The distinction between confederation and federation was invented in the nineteenth century to try to discriminate precisely between strong and weak forms of union, and is still used widely today. Unfortunately this distinction, which began as a useful instrument, has tended to become frozen into a rigid antithesis, and it is widely assumed that with the help of a few simple criteria all federal systems can be popped into two separate pigeonholes. In practice it is not as simple as this, and preoccupation with the antithesis has the unfortunate effect of deflecting the eye from the common union element in federal systems, and also from the more subtle gradations in the strength and weakness of unions.

Walter Hallstein, the first President of the Commission, demonstrated how a rigid adherence to the confederation–federation antithesis caused the Community to disappear from the federal map. If, he argued, a confederation was defined, in the customary way, as a body which does not possess legislative powers that directly affect the individual members of the union, then the EEC was more than a confederation. On the other hand, the EEC was clearly not a state, and hence was also not a federation, according to the customary definition of the term. What was the Community then? Hallstein was wary of calling it a federal body, and preferred to refer to it simply as a 'Community', but he also interestingly termed it a 'union of states'.[14]

Rather than dwell on the distinction between confederation and federation, it is probably better to focus on a few concrete turning-points in the history of federal unions, which illuminate their differing levels of intensity. Thus the change represented by the drafting of the American Constitution in 1787 is real and profound. For the first time, as both the protagonists and the opponents of the new Constitution argued, a fully articulated and firmly based government was created at the centre of a federal union, alongside the governments of the member units. This feature, as John C. Calhoun wrote, was 'new, peculiar, and unprecedented'.[15] The American Civil War provides another illuminating turning-point: here a trial of strength determined that in the last resort the power and right of the central government of a federal union was superior to that of the members. Already we can distinguish at least three levels of intensity of a federal union: one in which the central organs have not been deliberately welded into a fully fledged government; one in which they have been so welded, but remain co-equal rather than superior to the member governments; and one in which the central government has a status and power superior to the members. All these systems remain federal, but there are plainly wide differences between them.

Another profound difference between federal systems relates to the degree to which the people forming the member units of the union are ethnically and/or linguistically homogeneous. All the early federal unions in Europe and America were homogeneous in one or both of these senses. Not until the nineteenth century do federal systems emerge in which the constituent member units are ethnically and linguistically diverse—namely the renovated Swiss Confederation and the Canadian, or British North American Confederation. This heterogeneity plainly has an impact upon the division of powers and the development of the union. There will always be, in any genuine federal system, a push and pull between the member units and the centre, between nation-building at the centre and province-building at the periphery, but in a heterogeneous federal system there will be an additional, natural, built-in limit on the nation-building capacity of the centre, whereas in a homogeneous system the sense of being one people can conceivably develop to the point where the federal system itself is seen as an unnecessary restraint on the expression of national unity. The Netherlands, after all, was a federal union for two centuries, but then became, and remains today, a unitary nation-state.

Finally, there is a marked difference between federal unions between states in which the executive branch of government is traditionally powerful, whether because of its accepted role as the legislative pacemaker within a parliamentary system, or because of

strong monarchical, princely, or bureaucratic traditions, and between unions between states in which the legislative power is seen
as being co-equal with or even superior to the executive. It is
natural and inevitable that federalism will be more executive in
structure in the former than in the latter, though it is by no means
inevitable that executive federalism will always manifest itself in the
same way, or that it will not appear in some form in systems with
a more legislative bias. The profound difference between the history and development of the American Senate and the German
Bundesrat is a sufficient example of this contrast.

These diffferences not only illustrate the variations within
federalism, but are clearly relevant to European integration when
viewed from a federal perspective. Not only is Europe highly diverse, ethnically and linguistically, but the position of the executive
(or the government) *vis-à-vis* the legislature, in most of the leading
European states, is an exceptionally strong one. It is very unlikely,
therefore, that a federal system in Europe would resemble that of
the United States of America, which is so often taken as the exclusive model for such a system.

The theory of federalism requires to be treated with the same
discrimination as federal unions. It is possible to distinguish at least
three streams of federal thought that can be dignified with the name
of theory. The first may be identified with Kant's doctrine of a
gradually expanding federation contained in his famous essay on
Perpetual Peace. It is founded on the idea that war is the greatest
evil, and that the possibility of war is inherent in the co-existence of
independent states. It therefore advocates the construction of an
ever-widening federation between states, as the most appropriate
means of abolishing this evil throughout the world. It is not unfair
to call this a moral rather than an authentically political theory of
federalism, and Kant defined its starting-point succinctly when he
wrote: 'Now, moral-practical reason within us pronounces the
following irresistible veto: *There shall be no war*, either between
individual human beings in the state of nature, or between separate
states . . . For war is not the way in which anyone should pursue his
rights.'[16]

A second stream of federal theory sees federal arrangements as
the correlate or superstructure of the idea of popular self-government, or of democracy in the classical, participatory sense. This
vision has historically had a great variety of exponents, including

Rousseau, Proudhon, the so-called 'integral federalists' of the twentieth century, the advocates of subsidiarity, and even those who, in America, opposed the tighter union of 1787 (the so-called Anti-Federalists, who actually saw themselves as being loyal to the federal idea). Expressed somewhat crudely, the fundamental argument common to these diverse groups is that those forms of power and authority that are closest to the people, or in which the people participate most directly, are *ipso facto* the most legitimate. It follows that only as little power as is necessary should be delegated upwards to higher levels, which are by definition less participatory, and that the higher levels themselves should be organized as loose federal unions of the lower units, which are by definition more participatory. The word 'loose' needs to be stressed here. This form of federalism cannot logically allow a strong federal centre to emerge; it must insist on the dependence of the centre on the democratic parts. If confederation is taken to mean a loose federal union, then this theory is essentially a theory of confederation. Its ethos was well summed up by the American 'states righter' James Jackson Kilpatrick when he wrote in 1957: 'I hold this truth to be self-evident: That government is least evil when it is closest to the people. I submit that when effective control of government moves away from the people, it becomes a greater evil, a greater restraint upon liberty.'[17] This approach is, of course, reflected in the Maastricht Treaty's stipulation that in the new European Union decisions are to be taken 'as closely as possible to the citizen'.[18]

The third theory of federalism may be called the classical political theory of federalism. It is concerned with federalism, not as the path to world peace, nor as the correlate of participatory democracy, but in itself, as a phenomenon produced by the pulls and pressures of the political world, with its own logic distinct from that of the unitary state or the world of international relations. Here, federalism is the ensemble of structures and processes whereby a union of states or a union of polities is created and sustained, whether such a union results from a unitary system disaggregating itself, or from a number of political units coming together, or from a simultaneous movement in both directions. Classical federal theory is typically concerned with expounding the nature of such unions, explaining why they are established, and examining their strengths and weaknesses.

Such a classical tradition may be said to have started with *The*

Federalist, the series of papers produced by Alexander Hamilton, James Madison, and John Jay, to promote the adoption of the Constitution drafted at Philadelphia in 1787. Though not purporting to be theory, the skill and sophistication with which these papers expounded and justified the principles of the new Constitution make it appropriate to see them as such. To be sure, there had been some speculation about the nature of federal systems before this, but nothing so sustained. Alexis de Tocqueville, in his *Democracy in America*, published in 1835, introduced the ideas of *The Federalist* into European political thought, adding some insights of his own.

The pre-Civil War debates in America on the nature of the Union provide another landmark in the development of the classical theory. In particular the writings of John C. Calhoun represent a radical rethinking of the principles of the American federal system which was every bit as thorough and sustained as *The Federalist*. Calhoun's German contemporary, Friedrich List, deserves to be noted here too, for he elaborated the main features of what may be called an 'economic' federal union, that is to say one whose content was concerned primarily with economic rather than security matters.[19]

The founding of the federal German Empire of 1871 stimulated a rich flowering of writing in German about the nature of federalism, mostly by constitutional lawyers. One thinks, for example, of the works of Georg Jellinek, Heinrich Triepel, and the 'Bavarian Calhoun', Max von Seydel. Mention should also be made of Karl Renner's systematic efforts, during the same epoch, to devise a federal order (what he termed the *Nationalitaets Bundesstaat*) to accommodate the ethnic diversity, and the competing national aspirations, within the Austro-Hungarian Empire.

During the inter-war years the tide of analytical writing about federalism seems to have subsided, though by no means completely. Carl Schmitt, for example, had some characteristically incisive things to say on the subject. Then after the Second World War, Kenneth Wheare's study of *Federal Government*, first published in 1946, inaugurated a steadily increasing number of works that have appeared since the Second World War, not least in the United States of America, Canada, and Australia, that have carried forward the classical tradition up to the present day.

Having provided a brief outline of the classical tradition, we may now ask how far the kind of analysis characteristic of it assists our understanding of European integration. It does so, I believe, in two ways. First it enables one to see how far the technical, programmatic process of integration has—almost in spite of itself, precipitated or deposited a rudimentary federal structure. In other words, it enables one to detect the fundamental, constitutional changes that have been brought about by a movement which has, as we have seen, focused resolutely on the non-constitutional. Secondly, it enables one to understand why, and to some extent also how, the rudimentary, implicit constitutional structures of integration should be rendered coherent and explicit.

To substantiate this contention, it is necessary to develop a little further the notion of 'union'. It has already been emphasized that the concept of union is a federal one through and through—the very use of the word in bold capitals in the first paper of *The Federalist* is perhaps sufficient proof of this. All federal systems are unions. What then is the classical notion of union?

A union signifies above all that a certain threshold of intensity has been reached in the relationships between states. In a provocative essay, Carl Schmitt argued that the political aspect of any human grouping or arrangement related not to its ostensible ends or objectives (religious, economic, ideological, etc.), but to the intensity of the tie between the members.[20] The closer the bond came to a friend–enemy relationship, the more it was political. A federal union is a political body in this sense. It means an arrangement in which a firm line has been drawn between 'us' and 'them', between insiders and outsiders. At the minimum—in a union whose content is economic—it means a body in which systematic preference is given by insiders to insiders within an enclosed economic space. At the maximum, it means a body capable of conducting war—the most intense form of the friend–enemy relationship. It always signifies a spatial entity with a boundary, and not a point in the Mitrany sense. It also implies permanence. A temporary arrangement is not a union; it has no distinct political existence. Hence a union goes beyond a co-operative arrangement, or an alliance, or a common arrangement to resolve a particular problem.

A union is represented—in the old classical sense of 'made present'—by a set of institutions, which enable it to act as one within the boundaries of the union, and as one *vis-à-vis* outsiders. This classic concept of institutions representing the union can be made clearer by contrasting it with the provisions of the Maastricht Treaty which say merely that the European Union will be 'served by a common institutional framework'. There is a world of difference embodied in such terminology.

The establishment of these representative institutions, and their endowment with the right and power to act internally and externally, is the constitution of the union. Hence constitution does not mean the creation of a technical agency capable of carrying out certain joint tasks, it is an act by which reality is given to a common political will, the creation of a distinct political personality. It is an act emphatically in the present tense, which changes the status of the partners. The basis of a union is thus always more than a conventional treaty, it is a constituent treaty.

The union does not abolish the constituent members, but rather exists alongside them. In other words, the right and power of the constituent members to act internally (and often externally too) is retained in certain spheres. There must always be, as Calhoun stated with particular clarity, 'reserved' powers in a union. The 'right and power to act internally', to which reference has been made, means essentially the right and power to make law, or to act, at discretion, in a directly binding manner within the boundaries of the union. A union implies the co-existence of two such discretionary legislative powers, one at the centre, one in the parts. It necessarily implies the supremacy of the laws of the centre in those spheres in which it is entitled to act. The right and power of law-making (which may fairly be referred to as sovereignty), assigned to the union's representative institutions, is the core of a union when viewed internally. The delimitation of the spheres in which this discretionary right and power may be exercised is a secondary thing, a matter of circumstance, though still, of course, of great importance.

This sketch of the key features of a federal union, according to the classical concept, helps us to understand the federal elements which exist within the present European Union as well as those that as yet do not. As regards the former, a resumé may be helpful. The decision made in 1957 to go beyond the sectoral approach and to create a common market, subsequently defined more precisely as an 'internal market' or an 'area without internal frontiers', is clearly in keeping with the idea of union, and makes the European Community a political entity in the sense outlined above. It draws a boundary between insiders and outsiders, and establishes a far-reaching form of internal preference. The distinction between inner and outer has been deepened by subsequent amendments to the Rome Treaty, such as the programme for monetary union, and the creation of a common citizenship for the individual members of the Community—one of the few genuinely constitutional ingredients of the Maastricht Treaty.

Secondly, the Community is intended as a permanent body; the Rome Treaty was concluded 'for an unlimited period'.[21] Thirdly, the Community's institutions possess the power to make directly binding laws within the spatial boundary of the Community, over a wide range of matters. These laws take precedence over the laws and the constitutions of the member states, and national judges are obliged not to apply a state law which conflicts with a directly effective Community law. The Community's Court of Justice has played a most important role in drawing out the full 'federal' implications of the Community's law-making power, most notably in the three cases of *van Gend en Loos* (1963), *Costa* v. *ENEL* (1964), and *Simmenthal* (1978).

At the same time, the European Court, while emphasizing the real, direct, sovereign powers possessed by the Community's institutions, has conspicuously refrained from saying expressly that this marks the Community out as a federal body. With understandable caution it has restricted itself to saying that the Community is not 'an ordinary international agreement' but has involved the creation of 'a new legal order' coexisting with the legal systems of the member states.[22] The German Federal Constitutional Court has gone slightly further. In the late 1960s it stated:

The institutions of the EEC exercise sovereign rights which the Member States have renounced in favour of the Community they have founded. This Community itself is not a State, nor is it a Federal State. It is a Community of a special kind . . . to which the Federal Republic of Germany—like the other Member States—has transferred certain sovereign rights. By this fact a new public authority has been born, which is autonomous and independent in relation to the public authority of the individual Member States. Its acts do not, therefore, need to be ratified by the Member States, nor can they be repealed by them.[23]

The political theorist, however, has no need to be restrained by the caution of the legal profession. To the student of federalism the features of the Community expounded by the European and the

German Courts are quintessentially federal. It may be true that the Community is not a 'state' or a 'federal state' but this does not prevent it from being a federal union, that is to say a permanent linking together of states to form a corporate entity with a distinct boundary *vis-à-vis* the outside world, and possessed of two coexistent structures of government, one at the centre, and one at the level of the Member States.

Viewing the Community through the lens of classical federalism hence enables us to see the federal structure encased in the technical-functional apparatus. It also permits us to view the institutions in a different light. The conventional approach is to see supranational organs confronting intergovernmental ones, the former being the motor and guardian, the latter, for example the Council of Ministers, being a kind of resistant mass, requiring to be cajoled and pushed forward. In the federal perspective this is a misleading categorization. Intergovernmental bodies such as the Council should not be seen as secondary bodies, or as a regrettable brake on progress. Rather they express an authentic federal principle, which is realized in all federal unions, whether in the form of diets, congresses, senates, or even conferences of premiers, namely the representation of the member units at the centre of the union.

3. EMPHASIZING THE FEDERAL-CONSTITUTIONAL SIDE OF THE INTEGRATION PROCESS

Our thesis may be summarized by saying that two souls or spirits dwell within the European integration process, as it has developed so far. The most immediately apparent, indeed the dominant one up to now, has been the technical-functional, or the programmatic. Alongside this is the federal-constitutional spirit, manifesting itself less directly, often masked by the technical-functional language of the official texts, but none the less there, and not a mere fiction or aspiration for the future. Familiarity with the classical tradition of federal thought is valuable precisely because it enables one to identify the less obvious federal component in the present system.

The juxtaposition of the two approaches, the tension between them, and the curious ambiguities that can emerge when the attempt is made to express them both simultaneously, can be seen very clearly in the Maastricht Treaty on European Union. On the one hand, the very title suggests a fundamental constituent act, of the kind that was described earlier. The first sentence of Article A of the Treaty does not disappoint this expectation: 'By this Treaty, the High Contracting Parties establish among themselves a European Union.'[24] This has the true ring of a constitutional decision. So has the wording of the later Article 8 of the amended EEC Treaty, which states: 'Citizenship of the Union is hereby established.' Unfortunately the clauses and articles in between, and many of the subsequent ones, lack any such constitutional character, and the nature of the Union itself quickly becomes blurred and obscure.

Thus the second sentence of Article A (cited earlier), weakens the definitive nature of the act, by stating that the Treaty marks a new stage in the process of creating an ever closer union. Then the third (the nearest to a definition) states: 'The Union shall be founded on the European Communities, supplemented by the policies and forms of cooperation established by this Treaty. Its task shall be to organize, in a manner demonstrating consistency and solidarity, relations between the Member States and between their peoples.' The first sentence introduces ambiguity: is the Union founded by the Treaty of Maastricht? Is the Union already in existence? Or does Union consist of an accretion of policies and co-operation? The second sentence could scarcely be more general and insubstantial. In the next Article we are told that the Union 'shall set itself' certain objectives, including the establishment of economic and monetary union, and, more remarkably, the assertion of its identity on the international scene. Then it is stated that the Union shall be 'served by a single institutional framework' and that the European Council will provide the Union with 'its necessary impetus for development'. The great bulk of the succeeding articles elaborate new 'policies' and 'forms of cooperation' to be added to the tasks of the existing EEC, renamed the 'European Community'. We are back in the world of programmes.

Faced with this curious mixture, one must inevitably ask whether the existing structures have been genuinely reconstituted so that a new political entity has come into existence, a union in the classic sense of the term. Or does the resounding opening phrase merely paper over an organizational adjustment, an extension of the technical and programmatic functions of the existing apparatus? On balance the second alternative seems the most accurate.

It may be objected here that there is no need to make a choice between the technical-functional and the federal-constitutional, and that the two impulses can go on coexisting in the work of integration in the future, as they have coexisted hitherto. A little of one, a little of the other, as time and circumstances dictate—is that the way forward? This is the question which finally has to be addressed.

There can be no question of denying the achievements of the technical-functional approach, nor of retrospectively arguing that some other course should have been chosen in the 1950s. It is one of the lessons of history that few, if any, federal unions have been constituted *ex nihilo*; the states or polities concerned have always been linked together by some pre-existent bond. The technical approach has created a whole host of bonds, and in this sense has not contradicted but prepared the ground for a European federal union. At the same time the technical approach, as it progresses, reveals defects which cannot be ignored.

The first and most obvious defect is that its persistent application eventually creates a dense and opaque mass of structures and policies, embracing a plethora of different procedures for dealing with specific areas of economic and social life, with which the citizens of the nation-states find it virtually impossible to identify. Not only this, but the treaty base of the whole technical edifice gradually expands into an immense tract not unlike a legal code, that mixes the fundamental with the secondary, the general with the highly specific, and which is as such incapable of attracting the loyalty of those whose destinies it so markedly affects. In place of the general discretionary powers, within broad circumscriptions, which a genuine constitution contents itself with allocating, we have endlessly repeated formulae for dealing with a multitude of specifics. Moreover attempts to insert some form of democratic control into this mass of procedures only seem to make the system even more complex and impenetrable.

Secondly, the very nature of the technical apparatus at the centre makes it almost inevitable that it will seek to extend its activities unnecessarily. In other words, the Commission, the motor of the Community, whose authority rests on relatively shallow foundations, has a vested interest in expanding its activities into every area, however trivial, to which the wording of the Treaties and their amendments offers the excuse of opportunity.

Thirdly, the open-ended, programmatic character of the Community, and the lack of a comprehensive and definitive allocation of powers to the centre makes it simultaneously difficult to make a clear definition of the powers retained by the Member States. In the beginning, to be sure, this was scarcely seen as a problem; the imperative was to effect a derogation of power by the states, not to guarantee them. However, as the manifold programmes have been put into action, and the in-built tendency of the centre to expand its activities has begun to accelerate, so the need to differentiate reserved and delegated—and concurrent—powers inevitably becomes more acute. The steps taken in the Maastricht Treaty to reassure the Member States and their component units, and to insert some kind of brake on the expanding powers of the Community's institutions—namely the express declaration of the principle of subsidiarity, and the various provisions stating that the Union and the Community must respect the identity and the cultural diversity of the Member States—are indicators of a growing anxiety, but such statements of principle and intent seem feeble indeed when compared with the differentiation of powers typical of an authentic federal constitution.

Finally, and linked to this, it may be argued that the technical spirit of the integration process produces a tendency to underestimate the importance of factors which are not susceptible to a precise, quantitative calculation, namely cultural factors. By this one does not mean, of course, the production or preservation of works of art, but the attachment of the citizens of the European states to their own ways of life. The emphasis that has been placed by the Community on the establishment of a single market with no internal frontiers has been unusually intense when compared with the priorities of other federal systems around the world, and is perhaps ironic when the exceptional cultural diversity of the European continent is borne in mind. It is admittedly difficult to guarantee the individuality of member states in a federal constitution (as the Canadian experience has illustrated), but without some form of guarantee there is a real danger that the single-minded pursuit of economic homogenization will produce some kind of ethnic or nationalist backlash.

In view of these problems and dangers, therefore, there is good reason at this moment, and in the coming years, to place a much greater emphasis on the federal-constitutional approach to integration, and to apply it more openly and thoroughly than has been done in the past. It is not a question of establishing centralization but of establishing a just balance. More precisely, the task is to create a genuine and explicit union in place of the confused and incoherent one that has so far emerged, and to replace proliferating technical mechanisms and programmes with organs clearly constituted to represent a body politic, and capable of acting with discretion within delimited spheres of competence. To adapt Robert Schuman's words, the task is to concentrate on the *ensemble* as much as, if not more than, the specific. As I have tried to indicate, the classical tradition of federal thought is by no means irrelevant to this task.

Notes

1. W. Diebold, 'The Relevance of Federalism to Western European Integration', in A. W. Macmahon (ed.), *Federalism: Mature and Emergent* (New York, 1955), 455.
2. C. Tugendhat, *Making Sense of Europe* (Harmondsworth, 1986), 73.
3. *EUROPE/Documents* No. 1750/1751 (Brussels, 1991), 3.
4. *Treaty on European Union* (Luxembourg, 1992).
5. A. Shonfield, *Europe: Journey to an Unknown Destination* (Harmondsworth, 1973). Shonfield's phrase is endorsed and adopted by Tugendhat, *Making Sense*, 73, 185.
6. Cited in H. Brugmans, *L'Idée Européenne* (Bruges, 1965), 272–3.
7. Comité Intergouvernemental créé par la Conference de Messine, *Rapport des Chefs de Delegation aux Ministres des Affaires Etrangères* (Brussels, 1956), 10.
8. D. Mitrany, *A Working Peace System* (London, 1944), 20.
9. Ibid. 35.
10. D. Mitrany, *The Functional Theory of Politics* (London, 1975), 258.
11. Mitrany, *Working Peace System*, 55.
12. Ibid. 21.
13. Cited in G. Craven (ed.), *Australian Federation: Towards the Second Century* (Melbourne, 1992), 42.
14. W. Hallstein, *Europe in the Making* (London, 1972), 38–40.
15. R. K. Cralle (ed.), *The Works of John C. Calhoun* (New York, 1853), i. 163.
16. H. Reiss (ed.), *Kant's Political Writings* (Cambridge, 1970), 174.
17. Cited in R. B. Dishman (ed.), *The State of the Union: Commentaries*

on *American Democracy* (New York, 1965), 41.

18. *Treaty on European Union.*
19. For a further account of List as a contributor to federal thought, see M. Forsyth, *Unions of States: The Theory and Practice of Confederation* (Leicester, 1981), 169–75.
20. C. Schmitt, *Das Begriff des Politischen* (Berlin, 1963), *passim.*
21. *Treaty establishing the European Economic Community*, Art. 240.
22. Cited in T. Sandalow and E. Stein (eds.) *Courts and Free Markets: Perspectives from the United States and Europe* (Oxford, 1982), i. 14.
23. Cited ibid. 112.
24. This, and all succeeding citations, from *Treaty on European Union.*

4

The Constitutional Arrangements of Federal Systems
A Sceptical View from the Outside

CHERYL SAUNDERS

1. INTRODUCTION

Federalism has been defined as combining self-rule with shared rule.[1] In a system of government, self-rule usually involves a territorial base and always requires a degree of autonomy, or final responsibility, for each level of government. This feature in particular distinguishes federations from decentralized unitary systems and can be used to advantage where a federation is working well. Each of the governments between which rule is shared operates directly on individual members of the community. In contrast, in confederal systems, the direct relationship is likely to lie between the central government and the member states.[2]

Whether viewed as a bargain between participating jurisdictions or as a technique for the diffusion of public power, federalism relies on rules, institutions, and practices which normally derive their authority from a written constitution or other formal instruments. This chapter considers the nature and content of federal constitutions as a particular type of precondition of federal political systems. In doing so, it canvasses some issues for the design of federal constitutional systems which are of current relevance in countries around the world.

There is no single or obvious model for federations or for their constitutional arrangements. While the discussion that follows assumes some common features in the institutions of federal systems and their operating principles, it also reveals a wide variation in the forms which exist. While it may readily be agreed that it is possible to have too many constituent units for a workable federation or too few, and that ideally units should be roughly comparable in size, wealth, and influence, most federations depart from these norms, in one direction or another. And while considerations of defence or economic advantage generally play some part in decisions to enter into or maintain a federal form of union, each federal-type system is subject to a variety of other influences and pressures which dictate the form it takes and which may themselves change over the time-span of the federation.

Nevertheless, the potential for argument about the character of a system which is federal in form but highly centralized or decentralized in practice throws further light on the nature of federalism and the preconditions for it. Federalism is not established by institutions and rules alone, but also depends on attitudes to the process of government, whether derived from political culture or from force of circumstance. Thus, in some cases, the effects of federalism may be obtained in the absence of fully federal constitutional arrangements. In other cases, which are apparently federal in form, key benefits of federation may be missed, representing the worst of both worlds. The significance of the will to make a federal system work, underpinned by appropriate constitutional concepts and principles, is evident from the experience of all federal-type systems.

Some of the principal benefits of federation, from the standpoint of any system, flow from the effects of union. Most obviously they include the advantages of economic union through the creation of a larger market and the elimination of unproductive competition, but they may have social, environmental, and political dimensions as well. Other benefits are associated with the retention of a degree of regional autonomy in federal systems; typically, an encouragement to diversity, greater responsiveness of government, and an opportunity for broader citizen participation in public affairs than would otherwise be the case.

The potential for conflict between these two types of benefit requires a balance to be struck for each federal system lest the benefits become costs through undue centralization or decentralization. The historical experience of federations, however, suggests that an appropriate balance is neither easy to achieve nor likely to last for long. One consequence is a preoccupation with direct and indirect methods of constitutional change. Further costs of federation notoriously include complexity, a tendency to detract from public accountability, rigidity or at least some loss of flexibility, and impediments to quick and efficient government decision-making.

The weight attached to these various costs and benefits depends on the circumstances of each federal system, including the practical importance of union and the alternatives to union in federal form. Where the principal alternative is disunity or disintegration, the federation is likely to be decentralized.[3] The potential for increasing centralization will be perceived as a cost, with less emphasis placed on complexity and delay. By contrast, where the alternative to federation is unification, so that the advantages of union are no longer at risk, the tangible burdens of fragmented public power tend to overshadow the more subtle benefits of diversity and self-rule. While the contest may be more equal in systems with an established tradition of checks or other kinds of government action, including separation of powers or constitutional guarantees of individual rights, these federations may be expected to mount less resistance to centralization.

These different perspectives have implications for the constitutional design of different systems, to maximize the potential benefits of federation and to minimize its costs. The next part of this chapter examines some of the key features of federal constitutional arrangements: the status of the constituent instrument; the division of powers between the centre and the regions; the scope of economic union; regional disparity; and the relationship of federalism to the rest of the system of government.

2. A CONSTITUENT INSTRUMENT

Federal systems require a formal, written, constituent document, usually but not necessarily called a constitution,[4] which has the status of fundamental law, overriding other laws or executive acts. There is no dispute about this requirement, in theory or in practice. It is generally assumed to be a logical consequence of a system not controlled by any particular level of government that a document is needed to prescribe the limits of each level. The assumption persists, despite a tendency for the actual operation of older federal systems to differ dramatically from the formal constitutional text, through judicial interpretation or political practice or both. The United States is a case in point, with Australia not far behind. Two aspects of the status of federal constitutions which reveal a range of different approaches and raise some of the most important current problems are the amending procedure and methods of enforcement: these are examined below. This section concludes with a consideration of the distinction between constitutions and treaties as constituent instruments for federal-type systems.

Amendment

The same logic which requires an overriding constitution as the basis for federal arrangements suggests that the constitution should not be able to be amended by a single level of government. The principle is not universally applied. In Germany,[5] Austria,[6] India,[7] and Malaysia,[8] for example, the constituent federal document can be amended by special majorities in the federal legislature. The analysis is complicated, however, where the constituents of the federation are effectively represented in the organs of the central government. Germany is again a case in point.[9] Even where unilateral amendment is the norm, there may be exceptions requiring some form of state involvement in amendments with particular implications for the federal structure,[10] or overall inhibitions on amendment of certain federal provisions.[11]

Federal systems with a peculiarly federal amending procedure include the United States,[12] Canada,[13] Australia,[14] and Switzerland.[15] All deal with amendment differently, with procedures ranging from approval of proposals, once initiated, by a proportion of state legislatures[16] representing a proportion of the people,[17] by specially constituted conventions,[18] or by the electorate.[19] Initiation procedures also vary, although initiation by the federal legislature is the most usual.[20]

Common to all of those countries, with the possible exception of Switzerland,[21] is the relative difficulty of constitutional amendment.[22] On this score, there is little to choose between their procedures. Other values may also be relevant, however. This may be illustrated by contrasting the Australian and Canadian experiences.

In Australia constitutional amendments are required to be passed by the federal parliament and, following Switzerland, put to referendum and accepted by a majority of voters overall and in a majority of states. The record of success is not impressive. Only eight out of forty-two referendums have passed in almost 100 years, and the proportion of affirmative votes has been remarkably low in recent attempts.[23] In consequence, in some quarters, constitutional change has become a preoccupation bordering on an obsession. On the other hand, recourse to the electorate to amend the Constitution may be considered appropriately democratic and consistent with a federalist philosophy.[24] There is an alternative view that problems of constitutional amendment in Australia are at least equally attributable to the politicization of the process that inevitably accompanies the passage of an amending bill through the federal parliament.[25] In any event, for better or for worse, the constitutional referendum is now firmly established in the Australian political culture and its removal would be fiercely opposed.

More consistently with the traditions of parliamentary government, the formal Canadian procedure involves approval of amendments by the Parliament and a proportion of provincial legislatures.[26] While theoretically easier to use, one disadvantage of this mechanism became apparent in the criticism of the Meech Lake Accord as an agreement to amend the Constitution hammered out · by governments behind closed doors.[27] Meech Lake eventually failed when several of the original adherents did not control their legislatures at the critical time.[28] A subsequent reform round which culminated in the even more sweeping proposals of the Charlottetown Accord of 1992 was highly consultative but failed to proceed when a nationwide referendum was lost, by an overall majority and by majorities in seven of the ten provinces. Although the referendum neither was nor is a constitutional requirement, the results on this occasion may make future governments wary of proceeding with constitutional change before testing the support for it.[29]

Enforcement

The constituent instruments of most federal systems, with the notable exception of Switzerland, provide for or assume enforcement through judicial review. In reality, however, the picture is rather more complex. All systems necessarily rely to a degree on self-policing by the legislative and executive branches of each level of government.[30] All courts are reluctant to intervene lightly to find

unconstitutionality, particularly where the validity of federal legislation is at stake. At the extreme point of this development, under
current doctrine, the Supreme Court of the United States rarely
intervenes at all, on the grounds that the federal distribution of
powers is already adequately protected by political forces within
the other branches of government.[31]

Judicial review affects the substantive operation of federal constitutions and is considered in that context below. Two structural
issues may be mentioned at this point, however. The first is the use
of specialist courts or tribunals to consider constitutional questions.
Federations in the civil law tradition—including Germany,[32]
Austria,[33] and Belgium[34]—have created such courts. Common law
federations—including the United States, Canada, Australia, India,
and Malaysia—generally resolve constitutional disputes through
the jurisdiction of the ordinary courts. Even in these countries,
however, constitutional cases tend to occupy a major part of the
work-load of the highest court, to the point of conferring a *de facto*
constitutional specialization on it.

The second issue concerns the relationship to the several levels of
government of the court or tribunal which determines federal constitutional questions. Typically, such bodies lie within or at the
apex of the federal court structure, with their members appointed
by federal authorities. This arrangement may be considered unsatisfactory by sub-national units of the federation, and in both
Canada and Australia there has been pressure for regional involvement in appointments to the court with final constitutional jurisdiction. In Australia, this culminated in a weak legislative requirement
for federal government 'consultation' with the States over High
Court appointments.[35] Recent Canadian proposals would have
committed the Government of Canada to support a constitutional
amendment to require Supreme Court appointments to be made
from 'lists of nominees submitted by provincial and territorial
governments, the individual appointed being acceptable to the
Queen's Privy Council of Canada'.[36]

Constitutions and Treaties

The evolution of the European Community towards structures and
attitudes which are increasingly federal in appearance invites

characterization of the Treaties as a form of constitution and raises questions about the distinction between framework treaties devised for supranational arrangements and the constitutions of federal states.

This striking illustration of the convergence of international and public law has been discussed extensively in the literature.[37] Clearly there are some similarities between the Community Treaties and the constitutions of federal states, including their status as overriding law, their function of providing a framework for the institutions of government, and their enforcement through judicial review. Dissimilarities include the manner in which powers are allocated to the Community and the goal-oriented approach which the Treaties take to Community action.

The very success of the Community in advancing its goals has given rise to concerns about the adequacy of the Treaties as a constituent instrument for the future. Particular criticisms include the weakness of the Community's democratic structures and mechanisms for accountability and the apparent extreme flexibility of the limits of Community power. In these circumstances, there is a temptation to draw comparisons with more traditional federal constitutions in which these matters are or appear to be dealt with more directly.

The irony is that the approach of the Community Treaties, as interpreted by the courts and implemented through Community action, has been a source of inspiration and some admiration for older-style federations as well. The concept of subsidiarity, the techniques of mutual recognition, the institutionalization of qualified majority voting in intergovernmental meetings, and a modern definition of a common market in a federal-type system are all likely to be enduring contributions of the European Community to federal constitutional arrangements elsewhere in the world.

3. DIVISION OF POWERS

Which Powers?

Older forms of federalism assume that each level of government has the capacity to function as such including, at least, the capacity to make and administer law.[38] The implications of this assumption for present purposes is that not only legislative powers but also other types of governmental powers must be allocated under the constitutional arrangements. In most cases, this may follow automatically from the division of legislative power, but confusion is possible unless express provision is made.

There is a question whether this analysis applies to the judicial power, to the extent of requiring each level of government to have its own court system. Where separate court systems exist, it is assumed that judicial power should be divided between them consistently with the rest of the federal arrangements. Existing federal systems offer a range of judicial models. In Germany, the court system is unified.[39] Common law federations would, by contrast, tend to make provision for courts at both levels of government, although in Canada the provincial judges are appointed by the federal government.[40] In some countries, of which the United States is an example, the court systems are completely separate. In others, including Canada and Australia, they are united at the apex by the highest federal court. The Australian Constitution also enables the State courts to be used for federal purposes, holding out the possibility, which was ultimately missed, that separate court systems might be avoided.

The practical difficulties created for litigants by the existence of two separate court hierarchies, each with limited jurisdiction, sparked a debate in Australia in the 1980s over whether it would be practicable to establish a single court system, attached to neither level of government, to adjudicate over all disputes without distinguishing between their federal or State character.[41] The suggestion foundered, ostensibly on the unwillingness of politicians to surrender their powers of patronage to appoint judges. A more fundamental question, raised at a late stage in the debate, is whether it was desirable in any event to disturb the delicate balance of the system of government at either level by removing the courts from it.[42] In the end the inconvenience to litigants was eased, at least in the short term, by co-operative arrangements designed to ensure that each court could deal with the whole of the dispute before it.[43]

Method

The traditional method for the division of legislative powers, employed under the older federal constitutions, is by reference to subject-matter or vertically. Even amongst federations of this kind, however, different models exist. Some, like the United States,[44] Switzerland,[45] and Australia[46] allocate specific powers to the centre, either exclusively or concurrently, leaving an unspecified residue to the states. The Canadian Constitution, by contrast, uses two lists, allocating powers to the centre and the provinces respectively, generally on an exclusive basis, although again with the residue reserved to the centre.[47] In a further variation, a third list is included in the Constitutions of both India[48] and Malaysia,[49] specifying powers able to be exercised concurrently by either level of government. Where powers are concurrent, conflict in their exercise is usually resolved in favour of the federation, although there is room for some judicial creativity in determining whether a conflict exists.

The tendency of all federations towards centralization is even more pronounced under a vertical distribution of power where there is a single list of federal powers, enforced by judicial review. The experience of both the United States and Australia suggests that the brief statement of federal power itself offers little effective limit to its scope in the absence of competing powers expressly assigned to the states. Thus in the United States the commerce clause extends to activities with a 'substantial effect' on interstate commerce, raising questions about the existence of any judicially enforceable limits on it.[50]

There is some commonality between these federations in the particular powers assigned to the federal level of government. Federal power usually, although not invariably, extends to defence, foreign affairs, immigration, matters physically transcending state boundaries, and key aspects of economic activity for which uniform regulation is deemed important, including currency and postage. Beyond these, however, the allocation of powers reflects the history and values of the polity and the purposes of its federation. A national preoccupation with equity or equality, as in the case of Australia, tends to be reflected in the assignment of power to the federal level of government or in other mechanisms designed to achieve the same result. And the experience of the European Community demonstrates how the objective of perfecting an internal market can create consequential pressures for uniformity or harmonization in different but related areas including social policy, industrial relations policy, and the environment. Similar chain reactions can be detected in the structure and operation of any federal-type system.

A central problem of a vertical distribution of power in a federal-type system is its assumption that the subjects of government activity can be isolated from one another, to the point of being regulated by different and competing levels of government. In practice, the consequences are alleviated in various ways: a generous interpretation of federal power by the courts; intergovernmental co-operation; and referrals of power between governments or parliaments.

A different approach, tackling the problem at its source, is taken in some of the continental European federations, including Germany and Austria. Both the German Basic Law[51] and the Constitution of Austria[52] allocate a much wider range of legislative power to the federation, but also confer a general right of administration on the *Länder*. The potential of this technique for achieving national standards while leaving some flexibility in their implementation and administration at the regional level is potentially of interest to federations grappling with the restrictions of the older-style vertical distribution model.[53] The concentration of federal power in Germany, however, is integrated with and balanced by *Land* participation in the *Bundesrat*, and there is some doubt whether the German combination could be translated successfully to federations with different political structures and parliamentary traditions. Another feature of the German model which might prove more adaptable is the provision for federal framework legislation in Article 75 of the Basic Law.

Even where constitutions are not apparently centralized, the experience of most federations suggests that central power is likely to expand, at the expense of the powers of the regions. The impression that the European Community structure is unusually flexible in this regard is somewhat misleading.[54] In the United States[55] and Australia,[56] concern about this process has led to debate in some quarters about different constitutional arrangements which might stem the tide, through explicit constitutional protection of particular state powers or groups of powers. For the same reason, there has been some interest, at least in Australia, in the concept of subsidiarity as developed by the European Community as a counterweight to a formal increase in federal power, and to inhibit its unnecessary exercise.[57]

In all federal systems, the constitutional distribution of power is altered by co-operative arrangements of various kinds. Some are designed to simulate as nearly as possible the effects of an exercise of federal power, and in this case may be a substitute for the transfer of power to the centre. Others are directed towards co-ordination or harmonization or the implementation of common standards with flexibility on matters of detail. Devices in common use include conditional grants, intergovernmental agreements, uniform legislative schemes, regular ministerial or officials' meetings, and joint executive agencies. While there is a tendency to regard such arrangements as a second-best alternative to federalization or as embellishments which detract from the system design, experience suggests that intergovernmental co-operation is both an inevitable and a desirable feature of all federations, which should be regarded as central, rather than peripheral to their operation.

Some intergovernmental arrangements have a basis in the Constitution itself. Examples are the provision for joint tasks in Germany,[58] for inter-State compacts in the United States,[59] for conditional grants[60] and agreements on borrowing in Australia,[61] and the Council of the Federation proposed for Canada in 1991.[62] For the most part, however, these arrangements have developed outside the constitutional framework, have uncertain constitutional and legal effect, and avoid the traditional mechanisms for the accountability of executive government. An important question facing many federations is the extent to which a modern federal constitution should recognize and regulate arrangements of this kind.

4. ECONOMIC UNION

Economic advantage is a principal motivating force for most federal-type systems. Typically, it is sought through a customs union, a larger internal market, and a regulatory framework more conducive to economic development and international competitiveness. Traditional mechanisms to achieve these results include an exclusive federal power to impose customs duties and to secure a common tariff policy; guarantees of internal free trade; and conferral on the federation of power over most major commercial regulatory functions. Inevitably the assignment of commercial powers in the older federations has become outmoded as changes have taken place in approaches to the regulation of business, with consequences which have been relieved in part by a bold use of existing power sanctioned by judicial review.

A host of issues arise, only several of which are selected for elaboration here. They are the features of an internal market, the appropriate balance of power and responsibility between a federation and its constituent parts in the interests of economic development, and the relationship between these considerations and the federal financial framework.

An Internal Market

The scope of the concept of an internal market changes over time. The original emphasis on freedom of movement of goods has changed, and the concept now embraces services and capital as well. The contribution of an efficient transport system and other forms of infrastructure to the internal market is recognized. A multitude of sophisticated devices have become identified as harmful to an internal market, to be eliminated if market conditions are to be maintained.

The difficulties potentially caused by this moving target will be obvious. They raise a question of how the internal market can and should be secured in the constituent federal document. A common solution is a declaration of the freedom of inter-state trade, generally or by reference to specifics.[63] It may be coupled with a prohibition on action by one or both levels of government which transgresses the guaranteed freedom or with a positive federal power to legislate to protect it.[64]

One hazard of such statements, particularly where they take the form of a prohibition, is the tendency for the text to assume a life of its own, obscuring the broader goal of an internal market. The Australian experience is illustrative. Section 92 of the Australian Constitution provides that 'trade, commerce and intercourse among the States . . . shall be absolutely free'. Over more than ninety years since federation, it has been one of the most litigated sections of the Constitution. Until recently, the successive phases of its interpretation revolved almost exclusively around the words of the section and the previous case-law, rather than the role which the section was fulfilling in the constitutional system. There is nothing surprising about this from the standpoint of the courts: these are the usual tools of statutory interpretation under the common law. Notably, however, successive governments were no more purposive in their approach, with the result that there was no attempt to redefine and articulate the broad economic goals of Australian federal union for most of Australian federal history. When the change came, in 1988, it was led by the High Court, with a reinterpretation of section 92 in the light of the purpose it was intended to serve.[65] The particular purpose identified, however, was that of the framers of the Constitution in the 1890s. Section 92, as now interpreted, protects inter-State trade from discriminatory burdens of a protectionist kind and has an old-fashioned air about it. Again, blame does not lie at the door of the Court, which is not equipped to fashion afresh modern economic goals for the Australian federation, and would undoubtedly be criticized if it attempted to do so. On this occasion political leaders took up the task, with efforts which showed early promise but which may not now be realized.[66]

Economic Development

The perception of the roles which the respective levels of government can and should play in economic management and in promoting economic development varies between federations, with significant consequences for the system as a whole. Matters on which it is likely to have a particular influence include the degree of latitude allowed to the states to encourage local economic development, at cost to the internal market; the extent of state fiscal powers over taxation for their own purposes, expenditure, and borrowing; and the existence of arrangements for the co-ordination of government policies in the interests of the economic management of the entire polity.

There is a subtle but important difference between the concept of economic management in federal and unitary states. Techniques used for the purpose in federal states demand a greater degree of sophistication and self-restraint in government, but may be capable of achieving results which are more satisfactory in the long run. Experimentation with such techniques is still in its early stages. Innovative proposals which emerged in Canada in 1991 would have broadened the common market clause,[67] conferred power on the federation to make laws 'for the efficient functioning of the economic union' with a specified proportion of provincial consent, and introduced procedures for the co-ordination of the fiscal policies of the respective governments.[68] Other models which were discussed in the period leading to the European Community's intergovernmental conferences on economic and monetary union also added to the range of theoretical options for dealing with these issues.[69]

Fiscal Federalism

The financial arrangements between a federation and its constituent parts for taxation, grants, expenditure, and borrowing are intertwined with the issue of economic union at several levels. First, even minimum demands of economic union will undoubtedly influence the allocation of taxing powers to a degree, if only by withdrawing from the regions power to impose customs duties between each other and against the outside world. Secondly, in federations where the prevailing philosophy demands a high degree of central capacity for economic management, there is likely to be opposition to significant state autonomy in taxation and possibly in borrowing as well.

A wide variety of approaches is taken on this issue across the existing federations. They range from the United States on the one hand, where both levels of government have very considerable freedom to impose most forms of taxation, to Germany, where all taxation is centrally raised but distributed in accordance with constitutional requirements.[70] Most other federations lie somewhere between these two models, sometimes mixing the techniques of each.[71] The European Union differs from all other systems in this regard, because of its lack of a central tax-raising capacity.

Tending towards the more integrated end of the spectrum but with little by way of constitutional framework or underlying principle is Australia. The Australian federal financial arrangements have developed through a combination of political practice, economic circumstance, and judicial review over the decades since federation to the point where the States impose a range of minor taxes but no major ones;[72] are heavily dependent on the Commonwealth

for general and specific purpose funds;[73] and are controlled in their
borrowings as well, through complex and antiquated arrangements
which have long since lost touch with their legal base.[74] In law,
Australian fiscal federalism appears comparable to that of the
United States. In practice it is closer to the German system, without
constitutional recognition of this arrangement of convenience, with
consequences for the accountability of both levels of government.

5. REGIONAL DISPARITY

There are important philosophical questions about the degree of
disparity between regions that is acceptable in a federation and how
it should be alleviated. Federation contemplates diversity and,
within limits, regional autonomy. Continuing compensation for
natural disadvantages also raises efficiency considerations.[75] On the
other hand, large differences in economic circumstances between
regions are likely to threaten the social cohesion of the federation,
and to distort federal policy-making and the operation of the internal market. On one view it is incompatible with the very concept
of a federal system of government.

These issues tended to go unrecognized when the older federations were formed and are largely unreflected in their formal constitutions. Most federations have some equalization arrangements,
however. Again, a wide range of differences can be seen, both in
approach and degree. In the United States, for example, equalization is only built in to selected conditional grant programmes, to
the extent that it takes place at all. India[76] and Australia,[77] on the
other hand, have elaborate fiscal equalization procedures effected
through general revenue redistribution.

Amongst the host of questions raised by the current range of
different systems are the following. What types of disparities should
be subject to equalization? Should categories of additional expenditure needs be considered as well as revenue-raising disabilities?
Should equalization be directed to specific goals or projects? Or
should it take the form of an untied transfer, in the interests of
regional autonomy? And by whom should decisions about the
methodology, level, and purpose of equalization programmes be
made?

An associated question concerns the obligations of the federation towards individual states, particularly in fiscal and economic matters. At one level there is argument for a principle of legal rule that requires the central government to treat all the constituent units of the federation equally in the sense of preventing it from having favourites. Thus the Australian Constitution requires federal bounties to be uniform and prohibits the federation from discriminating between states in taxation and from giving preference to one state over another in matters of trade, commerce, or revenue.[78] The Advisory Commission on Intergovernmental Relations in the United States publishes annual tables of federal expenditure in the respective states, which presumably leads to some form of political action if gross discrepancies appear.[79] Principles of this kind may cut across other values, however, particularly if they are constitutionally entrenched. In particular, they may inhibit appropriate federal action to equalize disparities in regional economic conditions. Possibly for that reason, the Australian constitutional guarantees have so far received a narrow, literal interpretation which is easily and frequently evaded.[80]

6. THE REST OF THE SYSTEM

The discussion so far has focused almost exclusively on federal elements of systems of government, to the exclusion of other institutions and principles. But all parts of any system of government are necessarily interwoven. The practical operation of federal constitutional arrangements is significantly affected by the rest of the system.

A familiar characteristic of federal systems of government is the reflection of the federal principle in the organs of government, particularly at the central level. In most federations, an upper House of the federal legislature represents the regions or is constituted by reference to them. In Germany, the *Bundesrat* is a critical component of the federal machinery.[81] The United States,[82] Switzerland,[83] and Australia[84] each have upper houses comprising an equal number of members from each of the regions. Pressure in Canada for 'an elected, effective and more equitable Senate' which would, amongst other things 'provide for much more equitable provincial and territorial representation than at present' may well surface again, despite the failure of the Charlottetown Accord.[85] An issue in each case is the extent to which such chambers are likely to play a genuine federal role in the central legislature, particularly where national party politics becomes the dominant interest.

Federal influence in the central organs of government is by no means confined to upper houses. Popular representation in lower houses may also be state-based, in the sense that constituencies are formed within state limits, rather than using the entire geographical area of the federation as a starting-point.[86] Moves in Canada and Australia for regional involvement in appointments to the court which adjudicates in constitutional matters were noted earlier. Regional representation is usually a factor in the constitution of the federal executive government, in practice if not as a requirement of law. And the amending procedure for a federal constitution is likely to provide an opportunity for the expression of views on a regional basis.[87]

There is a question whether there are particular principles or structures of government which must or should be present in association with a federal system. Consideration of the range of past and present federations suggests that while some combinations of federal and other types of constitutional arrangements are more natural, or more workable, than others, none is necessary or inevitable. Thus while federalism is historically or characteristically associated with democracy, it is theoretically possible to create a working federal system in a polity which is not otherwise democratic. Similarly, the association of federalism with a separation of powers and with constitutional guarantees of individual rights, for which the United States provides the paradigm, makes sense, but is not essential. They are conceptually consistent with each other, and therefore work together well, because each assumes the value of limitations on absolute government and the need for negotiation and consultation in government.

As the existence of most modern federations shows, it is possible to incorporate federal principles into a system of government which lacks a formal separation of powers or a bill of rights or both. A practical difficulty which they also suggest, however, particularly where federalism is combined with a parliamentary system along Westminster lines, is that attitudes formed by the traditions of parliamentary sovereignty and executive domination of the formation and implementation of policy are not particularly conducive to federalism. The problem is not insuperable, but requires a genuine commitment to the concept of federalism, usually in response to other influences, if it is to be satisfactorily overcome.

The interaction between federalism and other aspects of the system of government are relevant to the federal structures themselves in two further ways. First, to the extent that the likely consequences of a particular combination of features can be predicted, provision should be made for them when the original system is designed or in any movement for wide-ranging reform. For example, the phenomenon of executive federalism and its effects in systems otherwise based on the parliamentary model are well known. There may be a need for additional, innovative governmental structures in such systems, to compensate for the loss of accountability and openness in government which executive federalism tends to produce. Secondly, deficiencies in other parts of a system of government may reflect adversely if unreasonably on the federalist components, which tend to be both more visible and more recent. Thus, in Australia, suggestions that are made from time to time that one level of government should be abolished appear to be influenced in part by dissatisfaction with the political process generally.

7. CONCLUSION

The latter part of the twentieth century is a time of great fluidity in the concept and practice of federal government. While there is, as might be expected, a marked similarity in the issues with which all federal constitutional arrangements must deal, there is surprisingly wide and growing diversity in the mechanisms and principles through which this is done. This is evident, for example, in the manner in which powers and responsibilities are divided between centre and regions, in the procedures for enforcement of federal constitutions, in the extent of economic integration, in the mechanisms of constitutional amendment, and in the very approach to the articulation of rules in the constitutional instruments themselves.

By definition, the constitutional arrangements of all federal-type systems seek to achieve a balance between unity and diversity. The experience of each is that a satisfactory balance is likely to be achieved only temporarily in the formal constitution, if indeed it is achieved at all. Thereafter, the system will be reliant on the evolution of the constitution, whether through judicial review, political understandings, or constitutional change. All federal-type systems exhibit a tendency to centralization, which constitutional mechanisms are likely to be only partially successful in overcoming.

The variety of federal constitutional arrangements suggests that no single model is correct or any particular feature indispensible. It also provides an impressive range of options on which individual systems might draw. Nevertheless, any such exercise must be conducted with caution. Federalist elements are closely interlinked with other aspects of the system of government. They are likely to work differently, although not necessarily unsatisfactorily, when separated from them, or even from the historical, political, and economic setting in which they were developed.

As important to a federal system as its formal constitutional arrangements is a commitment to making federalism work. Inevitably, that commitment is greater when driven by necessity, or by the acceptance of federalism as the most palatable alternative. An important adjunct is a tradition of limited government in other aspects of the system. Another is a degree of diversity in the society, although not to such an extent as would threaten unity. The experience of Germany suggests that the operation of the system is also assisted by the development of a concept of the common interest or the 'whole state'[88] which is owned by neither level of government; to which, ideally, all levels should have an opportunity to contribute.

Much of the innovation in thinking about federal constitutional arrangements in recent years is due to the European Community, in its progression from supranational to quasi-constitutional body. Ironically, the Community or now Union is itself looking wistfully at other federal-type models, to resolve some of the problems of its uneven growth. It remains to be seen whose debt to whom will ultimately be greater.

Notes

1. Elazar, D. J. (ed.), *Constitutional Design and Power-Sharing in the Post-Modern Epoch* (Lanham, Md., 1991), xii.

2. Ostrom, V. 'A Conceptual-Computational Logic for Federal Systems of Governance' in Elazar, *Constitutional Design*, 10; Frenkel, *Federal Theory*, Centre for Research on Federal Financial Relations (1986), 77. J. Frenkel identifies two other points of distinction: a confederation is based on a treaty between member states and the states retain independent status in international law.

3. An opposite reaction to these circumstances, sometimes employed to effect, is unification, reflecting a concern that self-rule may provide a springboard for sole rule, or for fragmentation along undesired lines. Indonesia is one example. For similar reasons, the particular present circumstances of South Africa may cast doubt on whether federation would be an appropriate form of government there.

4. The principal exception amongst federal nations is the Basic Law of Germany. A Basic Law, rather than a constitution, was originally implemented in 1949 in recognition that the consent of the whole German people could not be obtained for it: E. Klein, 'The Concept of the Basic Law' in C. Starck (ed.), *Main Principles of the German Basic Law*, 1st edn. (Baden-Baden, 1983), 15, 25. Reunification in 1990 in fact took place under the Basic Law (through accession under Art. 23), although questions remain as to whether the Basic Law should ulti-mately be replaced by a constitution: M. Schroder, 'Strengthening of the Constitutional Law: Efforts and Problems' in C. Starck (ed.) *New Challenges to the German Basic Law*, 1st edn. (Baden-Baden, 1991), 25, 40.

5. Basic Law, Art. 79(2).

6. Federal Constitutional Law, Art. 44, subject to a requirement for a referendum in the circumstances set out in Art. 44(2).

7. Constitution of India, sect. 368.

8. Federal Constitution of Malaysia, sect. 159.

9. An amendment to the Basic Law requires an affirmative vote of two-thirds of the members of the *Bundesrat* as well as the *Bundestag*: Art. 79(2). The *Bundesrat* in turn comprises members of the *Land* Govern-ments which appoint and recall them: Basic Law, Art. 51(1).

10. Art. 161 E of the Malaysian Constitution requires the concurrence of the Yang DiPertua Negeri of the State in amendments which affect certain safeguards for State matters. Art. 368 of the Constitution of India also requires amendments changing the representation of the States in Parliament to be approved by at least half of the State legislatures.

11. Art. 79(3) of the German Basic Law renders amendments affecting the division of the Federation into *Länder* or the participation in principle of the Länder in legislation 'inadmissible'. The Supreme Court of India has held that there are 'fundamental features' of the Constitution, including federalism, which are beyond the reach of the

amending power: *Kervasananda* v. *State of Kerala* AIR 1973 SC 461.

12. Constitution of the United States, Art. V.

13. Constitution Act 1982, pt. V.

14. Commonwealth of Australia Constitution, sect. 128.

15. Federal Constitution of the Swiss Confederation, ch. III.

16. One of the two amending procedures for the Constitution of the US involves ratification by the legislatures of three-quarters of the States: Art. V.

17. Canada Act sect. 38(1) requires resolutions of the assemblies of at least two-thirds of the Provinces that have in aggregate at least 50 per cent of the population.

18. The other US amending procedure requires ratification by conventions in three-quarters of the states.

19. Both Switzerland and Australia require approval of constitutional amendments at referendum, by overall majorities and majorities in a majority of cantons or states.

20. Constitutional amendments in Switzerland may be initiated by popular initiative: Arts. 120, 121. In the US two-thirds of the state legislatures may initiate constitutional change: Art. V.

21. C. Hughes, 'Switzerland (1875): Constitutionalism and Democracy', in V. Bogdanor (ed.), *Constitutions in Democratic Politics* (Aldershot, 1988), 277, 279.

22. There have been 25 amendments to the Constitution of the US, including the original ten which followed closely on its introduction. The Canadian Constitution has not been amended since the introduction of the new procedure in 1982, despite the major attempts at amendment following the Meech Lake and Charlottetown Accords. The Australian experience is dealt with in the text.

23. In the four referendums held in 1988, the highest 'yes' vote was 37.6 per cent and the lowest 30.8 per cent.

24. J. Crawford, 'Amendment of the Constitution', in G. Craven (ed.), *Australian Federation: Towards the Second Century* (Melbourne, 1992), 177.

25. The Constitutional Centenary Conference held in April 1991 supported a search for additional ways to initiate proposals for change, including a specified proportion of electors, or a specified majority of State parliaments: 'Statement of the Constitutional Centenary Conference 1991', *Public Law Review*, 2 (1993), 153.

26. Constitution Act 1982, sect. 38(1)(*b*).

27. R. Macdonald, '... Meech Lake to the Contrary Notwithstanding', *Osgoode Hall Law Journal*, 29 (1991), 253, 268.

28. Manitoba and Newfoundland: see generally, *Amending the Constitution of Canada*, Federal–Provincial Relations Office (Ottawa, 1990).

29. Courchene, T., 'Death of a Political Era', *The Globe and Mail*, 27 Oct. 1992.
30. For this argument in relation to the United States see Fisher, L. *Constitutional Dialogues: Interpretation as Political Process* (Princeton, NJ, 1988). The role of administrative agencies and the Federal President in constitutional review in Germany is discussed in J. Ipsen, 'Constitutional Review of Laws' in Starck, *Main Principles*, 134–7.
31. *Garcia* v. *San Antonio Metropolitan Transit Authority* 469 US 528 (1985).
32. The Federal Constitutional Court: Basic Law, Arts. 92, 93.
33. Federal Constitutional Law, Arts. 137–48.
34. Court of Arbitration: Belgian Constitutions, Arts. 92, 93.
35. High Court of Australia Act 1979 (Cth), sect. 6.
36. Government of Canada, *Shaping Canada's Future Together*, Sept. 1991, pt. 2.3.
37. See in particular J. T. Lang, 'European Community Constitutional Law: The Division of Powers between the Community and Member States', *Northern Ireland Legal Quarterly*, 29 (1988), 209; 'The Constitutional Principles governing Community Legislation', *Northern Ireland Legal Quarterly*, 40 (1989), 233; 'The Development of European Community Constitutional Law', *International Lawyer*, 25 (1991), 455.
38. The force of this characteristic is modified in the German and Austrian federations, which employ a horizontal as well as a vertical distribution of power.
39. D. Kommers, 'The Judiciary' in C. Schweitzer, D. Karsten, R. Spencer, R. Taylor Cole, D. Kommers, and A. Nicholls (eds.), *Politics and Government in the Federal Republic of Germany: Basic Documents*, (Leamington Spa, 1984), 85.
40. Constitution Act 1867, pt. VII.
41. For an early stage in this debate see C. Saunders, 'Owen Dixon: Evidence to the Royal Commission on the Constitution 1927–29', *Melbourne University Law Review*, 15 (1986), 553.
42. Report of the Advisory Committee to the Constitutional Commission, *Australian Judicial System* (Fyshwick, 1987), 37–9.
43. Jurisdiction of Courts (Cross-Vesting) Acts 1987 (all jurisdictions).
44. Constitution of the United States, Art. 1, sect. 8, amendment X.
45. Federal Constitution of the Swiss Confederation, Art. 3.
46. Commonwealth of Australia Constitution, sect. 51.
47. Constitution Act 1867, sects. 91, 92.
48. Constitution of India, pt. XI, 7th schedule.
49. Federal Constitution of Malaysia, Art. 74, 9th schedule.
50. *Perez* v. *United States* 402 US 146 (1971).

51. Pt. v. For a recent discussion, see U. Leonardy, 'The Working Rela-
    tionships between Bund and Länder in the Federal Republic of Ger-
    many', in C. Jeffery, and P. Savigear (eds.), *German Federalism Today*
    (Leicester, 1991), 40.

52. Arts. 10–15.

53. The concluding statement of the Constitutional Centenary Conference
    1991 in Australia, for example, referred to the need to examine 'new
    models for the allocation of powers' (key issue 9).

54. J. T. Lang, 'European Community Constitutional Law: The Division
    of Powers between the Community and Member States', in *Northern
    Ireland Legal Quarterly*, 39 (1988), 209.

55. In the United States the debate was a reaction to the decision in *Garcia
    v. San Antonio Transit Authority*. For an examination of a range of
    options for change, see Advisory Commission on Intergovernmental
    Relations, *Reflections on Garcia and its Implications for Federalism*,
    M 147, Feb. 1986.

56. In reaction to the expansion of the external affairs power in the
    Franklin Dam case op. cit. n. 55 there was some discussion in
    Australia of the utility of two lists of powers, on the Canadian model,
    as a means of preserving particular State powers. See generally, Con-
    stitutional Commission *Final Report 1988*, ii. 743–4 (rejecting the
    proposal).

57. The 'subsidiarity principle' was one of four principles identified by the
    State Premiers and Territory Chief Ministers as a basis on which a
    reconsideration of the respective roles of the levels of government
    should occur, following their meeting on 22 Nov. 1991: *Intergovern-
    mental News*, 4/1 (1991), 2.

58. Basic Law, Art. 91*a*.

59. Constitution of the United States, Art. 1, sect. 10.

60. Commonwealth of Australia Constitution, sect. 96.

61. Commonwealth of Australia Constitution, sect. 105A.

62. Government of Canada, *Canada's Future*, proposal 28.

63. e.g. Federal Constitution of the Swiss Confederation, Art. 31; Com-
    monwealth of Australia Constitution, sect. 92; Constitution of India,
    sect. 301; Constitution Act 1867 (Canada) sect. 121; Federal Consti-
    tutional Law, (Austria), Art. 4.

64. e.g. Basic Law Art. 73(3), Constitution of the United States, Art. 1,
    sect. 8.

65. *Cole v. Whitfield* (1988) 165 CLR 360.

66. The Special Premiers' Conference efforts to modernize the Australian
    federal economic union became entangled with the struggle over the
    federal leadership in late 1991. Progress continues to be made, but
    more slowly and with less coherence.

67. Constitution Act, 1867, sect. 121.
68. Government of Canada, *Canadian Federalism and Economic Union— Partnership for Prosperity*, elaborating the specific proposals in *Canada's Future*.
69. 'Intergovernmental Conferences: Contributions by the Commission', *Bulletin of the European Communities*, suppl. 2/91.
70. Basic Law, Art. 106.
71. e.g. Belgium, in which some tax sources are apportioned, and others are joint or shared. See generally R. Senelle, *The Reform of the Belgian State*, v, Ministry of Foreign Affairs, External Trade and Cooperation in Development (Brussels, 1990), 212–15.
72. They are precluded from imposing taxes on goods by the exclusive Commonwealth power over duties of excise in sect. 90 of the Constitution, as interpreted by the courts; and from income taxation by political arrangements which were originally sanctioned by judicial decisions: *South Australia* v. *Commonwealth* (1942) 65 CLR 373; *Victoria* v. *Commonwealth* (1957) 99 CLR 575.
73. C. Saunders, 'Fiscal Federalism—General and Unholy Scramble', in G. Craven (ed.), *Australian Federation: Towards the Second Century* (Melbourne, 1992), 101.
74. Borrowing is ostensibly governed by the Financial Agreement of 1927, which derives its force from sect. 105A of the Constitution.
75. Commonwealth Grants Commission, *Issues in Fiscal Equalisation*, (Melbourne, 1990).
76. See the provisions for the Finance Commission in the Constitution of India, sects. 280, 281.
77. Allocations are made through the political process, on the recommendations of the statutory Commonwealth Grants Commission, using the grants power in sect. 96 of the Commonwealth of Australia Constitution.
78. Commonwealth of Australia Constitution, sects. 51(ii), (iii); 99.
79. Advisory Commission on Intergovernmental Relations, *Significant Features of Fiscal Federalism* (successive years).
80. Constitutional Commission Final Report 1988, 814–17.
81. Basic Law, pt. IV.
82. Constitution of the United States, Art. 1, sect. 3.
83. Federal Constitution of the Swiss Confederation, Arts. 80–3.
84. Commonwealth of Australia Constitution, sect. 7.
85. *Canada's Future*, 23.
86. Commonwealth of Australia Constitution, sect. 24.
87. See nn. 12–15, above.
88. Leonardy, 'Working Relationships'.

PART II

Federal Arrangements: Costs, Benefits, and Preconditions

5

The Political Dimension, German Practice, and the European Perspective

UWE LEONARDY

1. INTRODUCTION

Public discussion on the political dimensions and implications of federalism in Europe currently suffers substantially from what can rightly be termed a confusion of perceptions, notions, and conclusions—and even sometimes of hostile misinterpretations. At least the emphases of what is considered to be the essence of federalism in the debate preceding and following the decisions on Political Union in the European Community differ widely. In France, for example, the nucleus of the federal idea seems to be linked to a stronger role for the national parliaments. In Germany federalism certainly does not mean a strengthening of the nation-states of Europe, whilst in Britain allegations against federal structures go so far as to equate them with what in Germany is felt to be their exact opposite, i.e. with centralism.

Facing this almost Babylonic confusion it would be neither hopeful nor helpful to try to approach the subject by defining the central elements of federalism in a purely abstract way. At the same time, a discussion of necessarily abstract costs and benefits of federalizing Europe would hardly carry us very far on its own. Bearing in mind these inherent limitations on its chances of success, I will nevertheless attempt just such a discussion in the first main part of this chapter. However, standing alone it would certainly run a double risk in this context. In the first place, at a level of abstractions such as 'uniformity' versus '*e pluribus unum*' it would lead to the boredom of truisms. Secondly, for British readers in particular, a discussion of the subject by way of the assessment of abstract costs and benefits would only tend to make it all the more suspicious as an alien domain of an alien continental lawyer.

For these reasons (and no less because of my role as a practitioner among academics in this volume) an approach will also be attempted, by pointing out some of the major lines of institutional developments and constitutional terms in the German system and by hinting at their potential applicability or non-applicability to Europe. This will produce mental associations of similar problems between a national federal scenario and the European one with the objective of reaching solutions at the EU level. Offering such solutions merely by way of theory would be less convincing than pragmatic analysis on empirical grounds of an existing federal system within a Community emerging into a Political Union.

2. POLITICAL COSTS AND BENEFITS OF FEDERALIZATION IN GENERAL

Lack of Uniformity versus Diversity through Identity

After moving residence from one political sub-unit of a federal system to another, citizens in such systems frequently complain about the difficulties of adjusting to different legal or economic conditions in various fields of their own or their families' day-to-day lives. Curricula or other school standards might impose burdens on their children (as they often do in Germany), hitherto unknown tax regulations (for example in the United States) may cause additional trouble in adapting to a new job environment, or the organization of local government authorities may be found confusing because it is not the same as the one which the citizen had been accustomed to. Accumulated anger about such complications is sometimes expressed politically in demands for more uniformity, which a centralist system could offer more easily and more widely. Demands of this nature were quite frequent and strong in Germany during the first post-war years after the revitalization of the federal form of government.

Such personally irritating effects for the individual citizen and their political implications do occur in any federal system. However, when confronted with the ultimate consequence of sacrificing his or her own politically organized regional identity (whether old or new) as the price for uniformity in the centralist sense, the same citizen has preferred diversity of identity rather than changing over to the centralist camp. Opinion polls in Germany since 1949 have shown a constantly growing popular acceptance of the federal system[1] in spite of migration within the Federal Republic and the consequent anger about personal experiences of regional differences, particularly when masses of war refugees from the East had to be accommodated in the various parts of the country over a long period of time. It would thus appear that the costs of less uniformity could be compensated for by the political benefits of a diversity rooted in regional identity. A corresponding multiplicity of economic, political, and cultural centres would consequently seem to be perceived as the necessary and safest possible protection against any excessive uniformity imposed by a single strong centre. Thus a federation would appear to be best qualified to house different identities of political salience.

It is obvious, however, that this requires the creation of political structures and processes which have to be aimed at regional equilibrium. This logic lies behind the fact that the achievement and maintenance of equivalent living standards is one of the basic challenges for any federal system. As will be shown below, it may even be embodied in the constitution.

Complexity versus Vertical Separation of Powers

Federal political systems are, by definition, more complicated than centralist ones. Not only do they divide legislative competences between at least two levels of government, but they may also attribute independent structures of public administration to their constituent parts, as they do in the concept of the dual state in American federalism. Even when they do not do so, by leaving administrative responsibility mainly with their sub-units, the need for co-ordination does not disappear. On the contrary, it may be even stronger here, resulting in a large number of institutions which tend to complicate administrative affairs. Moreover, the need for constant executive co-operation may become so strong as to seriously prejudice parliamentary decisions at the lower tier, if institutional precautions are not yet or not yet adequately organized. The present constitutional structure of the European Union would seem to be at a stage at which complexity might prevent both transparency for, and acceptance by, the individual citizen. Clearly, not only this quasi-federal system but also all genuinely federal systems face this danger.

However, facing it does not necessarily mean having to be harmed by it. Though organized at three different levels, the working structures of German federalism, for example, have up to now proved to be not only efficient but also politically acceptable. This is because the public feels convinced that the addition of a vertical dimension of the separation of powers between federation and states to the horizontal one between the legislative, the executive, and the judicial branches of government contributes vitally to the protection of democracy. Thus, the costs of complexity are counterbalanced by the benefits of an additional system of checks and balances which do not exist in a centralized state. Moreover, the acceptance of complexity is substantially enhanced by the much larger and much more numerous opportunities for political participation.

The extent to which these benefits of federalization may serve as effective counterparts to the costs of complexity would seem to be dependent on the number of sub-units within the specific federal structure. If this number is too large, the needs for interaction may strain both the federal and the democratic processes too heavily.

Blurred Accountability versus Proximity and Competition

The complexity of federal structures is also responsible for political costs in another field. The task of achieving and maintaining not only political but also financial and economic regional equilibrium requires particularly close executive co-operation and also co-financing between the national and the sub-national tiers, especially in crucial areas of regional economic development. The network of interaction and compromise arrangements under the pressure of inadequate financial means may tend to disguise and even to blur political accountability if responsibility for decisions and their impact in these fields can no longer be clearly located. Centralized states would thus appear to distribute accountability more clearly than do federal states in such areas of policy-making.

Again, however, centralization has severe disadvantages in exactly the same fields. The closer the responsible political tier is to the problem, the earlier and more easily it is able to discern it and respond to it. Moreover, the population concerned will naturally entrust its regional problems more readily to its own elected representatives rather than to those in a distant political centre. Proximity both to the citizen and to the task at hand is thus one of the indisputable benefits of any federal system. It is closely coupled with the incentives stemming from competition between the regional units organized as constituent parts of the federal structure. Needless to say, competition between them is not confined to economic standards. It also applies to creativity in offering solutions in all other fields of state competence, such as schools, local government, social services, and the maintenance of law and order. A single-centred system will hardly be able to offer a comparable process of mutual stimulation and of reciprocal learning by trial and error.

Still, the perils of blurring accountability and undermining the inner balance between the centre and the periphery will always remain on the agenda of any federal system. They will be all the stronger if there are large differences between the administrative and financial capacities of the component parts at the state level. A balance between the political costs and benefits in this field will, therefore, strongly depend on the capacity of such a system not only for crisis management but also for reforming its own constitutional structures if necessary. Flexibility of response, however, would rather appear to be one of the strengths of federalism as compared with centralization.

Time-Consuming Procedures and Friction versus Avoidance of Mistakes

Political and legislative processes in federations are not infrequently criticized for generating friction and because of that, for tending to waste valuable time in solving urgent problems. This must be the case in constitutional structures in which federal and state levels force each other into deadlock for long periods of time. Then, indeed, the costs of federalization may be high, compared with the apparent capacity for quick action in centralized systems.

In assessing their apparent relative strength, however, it should not be overlooked that the latter may also run into the same dilemmas of time and friction if they have a bicameral national system with a powerful (non-federal) second chamber politically opposed to the first chamber. Moreover, speed of decision-making and lack of friction are not intrinsically beneficial. Both systems are always in danger of making serious mistakes by neglecting factors which can only be properly evaluated close to the problem to be solved. Here, again, the advantage of proximity inherent in a federal constitution comes into play. The nearer the level of decision-making or at least participation to the task to be fulfilled, the higher will be the probability of avoiding mistakes in finding a solution. The balance of interests will also be better secured if the legitimately interested regional units have a substantial chance of taking part in the process of shaping the decision, even if they disagree. Even if the decision reached does not in the end meet optimal standards, friction and participation in the decision will have a much stronger peace-making effect than if it had been imposed by a central institution without any obligation to take regional implications into account.

Whether or not costs and benefits can be balanced given the time limitations and background of friction will strongly depend on the constitutional arrangements for the legislative process. Where the federal institution within it is, to a considerable extent, bound by a system of deadlines for its decisions (as in the case of the *Bundesrat* in Germany),[2] the risk of time-wasting by friction and deadlock will be relatively small compared with the dangers of over-hasty law-making.

High Costs of Political and Administrative Structures

Federations are often said to cost more money by having to maintain constitutional organs and administrative authorities not only at the national but also at the state level. This is indisputably true regarding political personnel and their immediately attributed services, as there are obviously more members of parliaments and more ministers at two levels than there are in one legislature and one cabinet at the national level in a centralist state. The assumption becomes very doubtful, however, if it includes ministerial personnel and administrative bodies. Thus, a high degree of centralization in the United Kingdom requires ministries in London which employ far more civil servants and other staff than the total of all German Federal ministries plus many of the *Land* ministries. If the number of employees in the territorial branch offices of the British ministries outside the capital is added to those in London, it may well be equal to, if not even higher than, the total number of staff numbers in all Federal and *Land* ministries in Germany. Exact figures are rather difficult to determine in this field because the administrative organization and the division of functions between ministerial and non-ministerial tasks differ widely between the two countries.[3] Yet, even if the total number of ministerial personnel were the same or slightly higher in Germany (leaving aside the question of its larger population) this would not in itself involve a more expensive administration after taking into account organizational costs and benefit rules.

The degree of functional devolution to bodies within a self-governing structure is, therefore, considerably higher in a federal system, with all its ensuing effects of closer intra-organizational control coupled with closer proximity to the administrative task itself. The financial effects of these advantages taken together certainly outweigh the (relatively small) higher costs of the political structure in a federation as compared with a centralist state. Thus, all in all, the allegation of higher costs for the federal system as such cannot be justified. It may be the most popular allegation against it, but it is the most obviously false one, so that there is no need to discuss countervailing benefits matching detrimental effects which are non-existent.

3. CHARACTERISTICS AND CRUCIAL FIELDS OF A FEDERAL STATE: THE CASE-STUDY OF GERMANY[4]

Three Levels of Working Structures

In the current structure of German federalism the bulk of legislation is enacted at the federal level, while the *Länder* are constitutionally the main administrators, even in the field of federal legislation. The development of the system has left only a fairly small number of legislative powers for the *Länder*, while the administrative powers of the Federation are classed more as exceptions than as the rule by the Basic Law.

In conjunction with the historical and functional role of the *Bundesrat* as an intergovernmental organ, these characteristics have produced working structures which may be categorized at three different but interwoven levels:

• The whole state (*Gesamtstaat*), comprising institutions in which the Federation and its constituent parts are represented on terms of equal status, allowing no room for majority decision-making;

• the federal state (*Bundesstaat*), covering the constitutionally organized structure of relationships between *Bund* and *Länder* institutions in which decisions are subject to majority voting rules;

• the so-called third level (*Dritte Ebene*) of horizontal co-ordination between the *Länder* themselves on which, again, decisions must be unanimous.

At the level of the whole state, the Conference of the Heads of Government of *Bund* and *Länder*, the co-ordinating bodies of the political parties, and inter-parliamentary co-ordination are the main co-operative institutions. At the level of the federal state, the *Bundesrat* is at the centre of the structure with a double role in a double field, being both a co-legislator (with the *Bundestag*) and the representative of the *Länder* in their function as administrators of federal legislation. The other major institutions at this level are the Committee of Mediation (in cases of conflict between *Bundestag* and *Bundesrat*), the Missions of the *Länder* to the Federation and the bodies of 'co-operative federalism' (such as the Financial Planning Commission). At the third level the Conference of Minister-Presidents and various *Land* Departmental Ministers Conferences organize horizontal co-operation between the *Länder* both in their own affairs and in the preparation of business in the federal field.

Within and between all the three levels, various bodies with a party-political orientation serve as coordinating machineries, particularly in the relationships between the federal structure and the parliamentary party fractions in the Bundestag, if and whenever issues of potential party-political controversy arise.

The German Länder in a Doubly Federalized Structure

Participation by the *Länder* in European affairs has now been shifted from the third level (where it partly resided earlier) to that of the federal state, by incorporating EU business fully into *Bundesrat* procedures, since the Statute of Ratification of the Single European Act 1986 and the new Article 23 of the Basic Law in 1992 substantially strengthened *Bundesrat* and *Land* rights in this field. This meant that the implications for Germany of the European power changes effected by the Single Act led the *Länder* to the conclusion (confirmed by the European Union) that they should ban the principle of unanimity which governs third-level procedures in favour of applying the majority rule fully in EU matters. Simultaneously, the *Bundesrat*'s position in this field was firmly consolidated by the following factors:

- the obligation of the Federal Government to take into account *Bundesrat* comments on draft European legislation, inasmuch as its subjects touch upon the exclusive legislative or administrative competences or on the 'essential interests' of the *Länder*;
- the need for the government to specify its reasons in cases of EU-bound deviations from this obligation;
- the right to send *Land* representatives as members or even as speakers of the German delegation to all negotiating bodies of the Commission and the Council if and whenever subjects or interests of this kind are under discussion.

In addition, the institutional structure for EU business, which had previously consisted of the *Bundesrat* Committee for EC Affairs (since 1957) and the Permanent Observer of the *Länder* at the EC (also from 1957) was widened by the creation of the EU Chamber of the *Bundesrat*, empowered to act on behalf of the *Bundesrat* under special standing orders in cases of urgency or confidentiality. In addition, the *Länder* set up individual and direct liaison offices in Brussels with both economic lobbying and political reporting functions, the Office of the Permanent Observer was reinforced, and, finally, information was provided to the state legislatures by their Governments on specifically relevant projects of European legislation. Until the end of 1992 this institutional network led to the consideration of more than 6,000 documents of draft European secondary legislation and other EU projects in the *Bundesrat*.[5]

Besides this, the negotiations of the EU Governments' Conferences on Political Union and on Economic and Currency Union resulted in the creation of a Commission on Europe (Europa-Kommission) of the *Länder* Cabinet Offices, which was succeeded by the Conference of the *Länder* Departmental Ministers in charge of European affairs after the completion of the Single Market at the end of 1992. So the German *Länder* have so far been fairly successful in securing the internal part of their role in the doubly federalized structure of German participation in EU policy-making.

The Crucial Issues of Political Costs and Benefits in the German System

The current system based on these main elements certainly works in Germany, at least in terms of executive efficiency. It would seem less clear, however, whether it provides for an adequate constitutional relationship between *Bund* and *Länder*, whether it adequately fulfils democratic requirements, and (most importantly at present), whether it is capable of supporting the burdens of German and European Unification with their political, economic, and constitutional consequences.

Though there have always been substantial elements of co-operative federalism within the German system, there has at all times also been a strong doctrine that *Bund* and *Länder* have a separate but equal relationship. Together with the problems it incorporates, this constitutional doctrine is reflected in two main areas: first, in the requirement of the Basic Law 'that the *Länder* by their size and capacity are able effectively to fulfil the functions incumbent on them' (Article 29) and, secondly, in the further constitutional requirement for the whole system to guarantee equality in living conditions throughout the entire federal territory in order to ensure an 'equivalence of living standards' (misleadingly termed a 'uniformity of living conditions' in Articles 72 and 106). These two principles were already the crucial components of German federalism when Unification came onto the political agenda rather unexpectedly and as European Political Union approached.

Considering the requirements described above together with the effects of the addition of the five new *Länder* to the federal system, territorial, functional, and financial reform will have to be the main fields for constitutional revision in the area of *Bund–Länder* relations. Territorial reform will have to aim at a reduction in the number of the *Länder* combined with an improvement in the balance between them both individually, as compared with one another, and collectively between them and the Federation. Such reform is needed because the constitution requires guaranteed equality of standards in living conditions, whilst the performance of the individual *Länder* in achieving this goal is grossly uneven. The German federal system thus includes a strong constitutional demand for comparability among its component parts and their political, economic, and social capacities which is, nevertheless, far from being achieved.

The notion of functional reform in Germany covers a multiplicity of postulates related mainly to the division of legislative powers between *Bund* and *Länder* and to the procedural position of the *Bundesrat* in legislation. The most important of these is a revision of the clause which requires an evaluation of the necessity for concurrent legislation (in Section 2 of Article 72 of the Basic Law[6]). Its implications are closely related to the problems of subsidiarity which German federalism thus partly shares with Europe.

Financial reform will have to focus on the creation of 'powerful *Länder* as sustainers of a viable federalism'. It will also have to concentrate on securing future coincidence of legislative power with responsibility for the financial consequences of legislation. Particularly under the impact of the needs for massive federal subsidies to the new *Länder*, constitutional safeguards against the abuse of the 'golden lead' by the Federation will have to be included as a high priority among the revisions to the Basic Law. The ironic and, in German politics, frequently used notion of the 'golden lead' refers to the fact that in the fields of co-financing the Federation feels inclined and in many instances even compelled to interfere in policy areas which are constitutionally the domain of the *Länder*. This is predominantly due to the financial inability of the *Länder* to provide their proper contribution towards the task of achieving and maintaining equivalent living standards. Similarities between these and the European problem fields of convergence, cohesion, and the structural funds are obvious. If territorial and financial reform fails after unification, German federalism will have to face the danger of a gradual and possibly even accelerating disintegration in favour of a centralized system in substance though not in appearance. In the process of European federalization the equivalent emphasis would seem to be on functional and financial reform.

These hints at similarities between German and European problems might suggest that, first, the need for reform of one specific federal system does not undermine the case for federalism as such, and, secondly, the innate complexity of all federal systems necessitates constant review of their institutional structures under changing political conditions but within certain guiding principles. Some of these principles with specific relevance to the political dimensions of costs and benefits of federalization at the European level will be briefly discussed in the following sections.

4. SUBSIDIARITY: THE KEY NOTION IN THE POLITICAL DIMENSION OF FEDERALISM

Subsidiarity is not identical with devolution or delegation. While the latter two are devices for the transfer of powers from a higher level to lower ones at the discretion of the higher, the idea of subsidiarity presumes that, in principle, political power should reside at the lowest possible level unless and until it is shown that, for the common purpose of the whole, it would be better exercised at the higher tier. It would seem to be only natural that this concept should be more difficult to understand in traditionally centralized than in federally organized states. However, the growing complexity of public functions and the interdependence of their performance at several institutional levels, even on the international scene, tends to encourage its acceptance.

The misunderstandings or misconceptions of the term have— unwittingly or deliberately—influenced its definition, which was in dispute during the negotiations on European Political Union. While 'the approach from above' marked the centralist camp, the protagonists of federalism rightly defended 'the approach from below'. As a result, subsidiarity is now embodied in the Maastricht Treaty on European Union as one of its basic principles by Article 3b in Article G in such a way as to allow the federalists to justly claim that at least it satisfied their main demands. In the first place, it refers to the criterion for deciding whether or not the aims of a particular measure not within the exclusive competence of the Community can be adequately achieved at the level of the Member States, thus attributing competence to the Community only in so far as these aims can be better achieved at its level because of their scope or their effects. In addition, Section 2 of Article 3*b* in Article G limits such measures of the Community to the extent necessary for the achievement of the aims of the Treaty. Although this nevertheless leaves the field rather wide open, the verbatim inclusion of the principle of subsidiarity in the Preamble to the Treaty in immediate connection with the guideline of proximity[7] would appear to emphasize its power-restricting function. The dispute about its adequate understanding and application suffered and will certainly continue to suffer severely from an incorrect equation between the essentials of competence distribution in a federal state on the one hand and the structural principles of task assignment in an international organization on the other. While federal constitutions distribute legislative power on the lines of defining policy fields, international organizations serve the purpose of achieving specific aims laid down in the treaties which created them. Political aims, however, have the inherent tendency of absorbing many more 'implied powers' than do clear-cut definitions of attributed policy fields. Though being a supranational organization, the EU was created with the structures and task assignments of a traditional international body. Particularly after Maastricht, its supranational elements are now, however, approaching a quantity which necessitates the conclusion that it has already obtained the quality of a federal body in large parts of its substance while neglecting this fact in its structures.

Consequently, its functions and their limitations *vis-à-vis* the Member States and their sub-units should no longer be defined by aims and programmes of action to their achievement but by competence for policy fields adequate to, and necessary at, Union level. Otherwise, the process of the piecemeal 'zoning-up' of powers allegedly or even correctly 'implied' in the needs of fulfilling widely defined aims as again repeated in the Treaty of Union will continue indefinitely.

Even after the inclusion of the principle of subsidiarity in EC constitutional law by the Maastricht Treaty, pressure continues to limit the chances of the application of this principle substantially at EC level in cases of conflict, as the jurisdiction of the European

Court would tend to demonstrate. As this fact, however, is due largely to an inadequate method for the distribution of powers, it is not subsidiarity but this method which ought to be questioned.

Further reform of the Community towards 'an ever closer Union'[8] in terms of a federal structure will, therefore, have to concentrate on moving away from the attribution of politically defined aims in favour of a legally defined distribution of legislative competences. Whether this can best be achieved by laying down strictly conceived competence catalogues of the Community or Union alone, while leaving all non-enumerated fields of legislation to its constituent parts (as in Germany),[9] or whether a double set of competence lists for both parts of the system should be developed (as in Canada),[10] will have to be examined carefully in this process. The risks of rigidity and of overlapping zone conflicts connected with double lists would certainly have to be taken into particular account within such an approach. But the nature of the solution would appear to be of minor importance compared with the need for the abolition of the present system of attributing to the Union almost irresistible powers to absorb competences under a regime of constantly expanding political aims. As long as this regime inherent in the original structure of the EC continues, the effectiveness of the concept and the application of subsidiarity as passed by the Edinburgh Summit of December 1992 is, and will remain, doubtful.

However, under the rules of a federal distribution of powers by way of defining competences instead of aims, subsidiarity remains a principle which can be protected by legal sanction only in cases of extreme and obvious violation. The jurisdiction of the German Federal Constitutional Court on the comparable clause of need in concurrent legislation[11] clearly defines its application as a political question.[12] Nevertheless, this does not render subsidiarity irrelevant as a central guideline of federalism. On the contrary, if and because its application and observance are an essentially political matter, its safeguards must and can be political, too.

Federal Loyalty (Bundestreue): Not Lyrics but Law

The political dimension of federalism cannot be properly evaluated without referring to mutual loyalty (or comity) as the basic obligation by which all components of a federation, the union as well as its parts, are bound together. After all, both the word 'federalism' itself and its historic roots are derived from *foedus* (agreement) in close connection with *fides* (trust) as the nucleus of maintaining reliable relations between states, their allies, and, at a later stage, their constituent autonomous parts. In Germany, the Federal Constitutional Court applied this principle of *Bundestreue* in one of its first decisions,[13] and thus made it a legal standard, obliging both *Bund* and *Länder* to conduct their affairs in a manner sympathetic to the idea of federation (*bundesfreundliches Verhalten*). This principle covers the entire field not only of federal–state, but also of state–state relations, and it governs not only the substance but also the style of conduct.

One of its constitutionally most relevant expressions was the dictum of the Court that 'a federal state can exist only if *Bund* and *Länder* in their relations with each other take into account that the standards under which they make use of formally existing competences are governed by mutual considerateness'.[14] There appears to be no reason why this should not also apply to a quasi-federal or federalizing structure such as the European one. However, the effects of the principle should not be misinterpreted as being merely legal ones: they also shape political conduct in negotiations under the requirement to arrive at solutions which do not violate or weaken the federal concept as such. The lines from here to the observance of subsidiarity as well as of solidarity (*bündisches Einstehen füreinander*, in the term of the German Constitutional Court) would appear to be obvious. The fact that they are, nevertheless, at risk of being disregarded does not undermine the principle. On the contrary, it stresses its need as a rule of law.

The European Court of Justice has often been criticized for protecting the rights of the Member States and their sub-units less than those of the Union. However, as long as *Bundestreue*, with its fully mutual obligations, is not a guiding principle of an EU still lacking genuine federal structures, the Court can hardly be blamed for that. This would appear to support the case for federalizing Europe substantially in the interest of the Member States and their component parts.

Comparability and Homogeneity: Relative Terms

It has been maintained that federalizing Europe would be inappropriate until the Member States of the Union are more comparable with one another and more homogeneous as a group. In so far as this refers to the political dimension (the economic and the cultural ones being the subject of other chapters), only general comments can be made about this allegation, as the terms in question are rather relative. Admission to the EU has always been, and should remain, conditional on the basis of commonly shared principles concerning respect for human rights and democratic constitutions.[15] Thus great heterogeneity cannot be discerned in this respect.

Complete homogeneity in the constitutional structures of the component parts has never been a postulate of federalism. Otherwise federalism would mean uniformity and thus the abolition of identity. In fact, it means the exact opposite within the framework of commonly acknowledged convictions. In so far as this refers to institutional structures, the Constitutional Court in Germany has made it quite clear that it belongs to the central domain of the *Länder* to determine their own constitutional organization within the rather wide terms of the so-called homogeneity clause of Article 28 of the Basic Law. As to the territorial basis of federal systems, the comparability of their constituent parts in terms of size, and their consequent political and administrative capacity, there are no generally applicable rules. As has already been noted, the German Constitution includes a strong demand for such comparability. However, although this is far from being accomplished, it nevertheless represents a federal structure. The only possible generalization would be one to the effect that the more there is of such comparability, the more balanced and thus more stable the system is likely to be.

Since it is totally unrealistic to suggest that the smaller Member States at the European level would have to be done away with, or the bigger Member States would have to be dissolved into smaller units merely for the sake of comparability before federal principles could be applied, stability must here be secured by other means. The constantly growing cohesion and the resulting stability of the EU, even within its present structures, would seem to demonstrate that there are no serious obstacles to achieving that goal. No doubt these structures would be further improved should the principle of federal loyalty (*Bundestreue*) become applicable.

Regionalism within Federalism: Heterogeneity versus Practicability?

The concept of the 'Europe of the Regions' requires clarification. As reasonably understood it does not involve a breaking-up of the Member States in favour of a restitution of what are termed the 'Old Nations of Europe'. Such a proposal would mean a severe weakening of the Union in a phase of history in which the EU is challenged by important new tasks within a greater Europe. However, this does not mean that the component parts of the EU in the next century will, of necessity, have to be identical to its present Member States. But to propagate a general dissolution of the Member States in favour of a direct EU-membership of the regions would not involve a dilution of federalism in favour of regionalism. Rather, it would result in a dilution of both in favour of an extreme European centralism, as the number of constituent parts in a European Union of this kind would be far too large to be immune to the powers of divide and rule vested in the centre of such a structure. The further existence of the national states as the basic component parts of the Union is thus not only a prerequisite of federalism but also a protective condition for regionalism in Europe.

Consequently, the concept of regionalism can only be interpreted as a means of securing or encouraging internal autonomy within the Member States against encroachment either by the Union itself (as in the case of the German *Länder*) or against impediments imposed by the structures of the Member States (as in almost all other cases). Thus, the concept would rightly result in a regionalism within European federalism equivalent to a doubly federalized system. This would obviously imply the use of the term of a Europe *with* rather than *of* the Regions when pursuing the concept further.

At present, however, only a few elements capable of elaboration in this direction can be discerned. Nevertheless, these few should not, and some of them even cannot, be neglected. This applies particularly to the German *Länder*, which, being part of a functioning federal system, will not agree to be sacrificed for the sake of European federalism, while at the same time decidedly favouring European Political Union. Along these lines and under the pressure

of subsidiarity, plus appropriate structural standards of regionalism, the *Bundesrat* openly threatened not to ratify the Treaty on
European Union (in a unanimous resolution of 8 November
1991[16]) unless these demands were met satisfactorily. The reasons
for doing so would appear to be obvious, and not only from a
German perspective. The consequence of legitimate regionalism can
only be to open up the institutional structure of the Union to direct
participation by constitutionally organized regions, such as the
Länder, wherever they exist or come into existence, and to encourage their creation elsewhere. Otherwise the case for European
federalism at the level of the Member States would undermine the
case for federalism at the level below them. However, it would be
unwise to assume that organized regionalism could be achieved at
a stroke. In particular, the Germans will have to be (and are) aware
of the suspicion that they might be trying to export their federalism
to the rest of Europe for their own ends. But this cannot be shown
to be the case, as the previously quoted *Bundesrat* Resolution
clearly demonstrates.

The creation of the Regional Committee by Articles 198*a*–198*c*
in Article G of the Maastricht Treaty immediately poses the question of how representative institutions can be built in regions which
have so far not been organized constitutionally (which means in the
majority of them). The reason for this self-fulfilling prophecy is
embodied in the practical problem of legitimizing the individual
members of the Committee. It seemed to be obvious from the
beginning that even if appointed by the Council of Ministers,[17] they
could not be instructed by their national governments, because the
Regional Committee would then be nothing other than a duplication of the Council. In the case of Germany there is the added
complication that the *Länder* would never have accepted such a
concept. The Committee members will necessarily, therefore, have
to be politically responsible to some kind of regional authority or
body as distinct from the national government. The provision of
Article 198*a* Section 4 in Article G of the Treaty, defining their
position as an independent one, is by no means a contradiction of
this. On the contrary, it rather emphasizes the essential fact that
instructing them by the national governments will not be in compliance with the Committee's legal bases.

That in turn will necessitate the creation of electing authorities or
bodies by the Member States themselves. If democratic standards

are to prevail in this branch of EU organization, this will, however, mean the need to build up responsible representation throughout the regional map of the Community—at least in the foreseeable future.

Not taking these needs into account would also simultaneously involve trying to do away with the obvious heterogeneity in the status of the regions throughout Europe. Any attempt of this kind would, however, misapply the concept of regionalism as distinct from that of federalism. While federalism is basically defined by homogeneity in status and tasks of the constituent parts of its system, regionalism is distinguished by a high degree of differentiation and thus heterogeneity in precisely those fields. Trying to ignore this fact would, therefore, result in abolishing regionalism as such with all its potential for adapting different historical developments to practical needs for autonomy (as, for example, in Spain).

Nevertheless, for the purpose of including regionalism in the institutional structure of the European Community or Union, there are limited needs for a diminution of heterogeneity such as those outlined for the creation and composition of the new Regional Committee. Compared with these indispensable diminutions of heterogeneity for very practical reasons, all other problems connected with this institution at the EU level would seem to be of limited importance. These problems include

• The rights and powers attributed to the Regional Committee in detail (although the right of determining its own subjects of concern—now secured by Article 198c in Article G of the Maastricht Treaty—is certainly of essential importance).

• Its status as an independent quasi-organ or as one administratively attached to the Economic and Social Committee (although its being organizationally twinned with this Committee by a joint secretariat[18] will be bound to cause problems).

• The inclusion of local government representatives in the Committee (to which the reshaping of the Commission's Advisory Council of Regional and Local Government Bodies into a distinct institution for them would have been a better alternative because it would have preserved a clearer function for the Committee of the Regions as the nucleus of a doubly federalized EU Structure).

Due to the prevailing very wide heterogeneity in the status of the regions, the powers of the Committee will be relatively weak, at least in the beginning. Still, initiating this change is not only profitable but necessary—despite all the problems connected with it. However, during this fairly weak first phase the German *Länder* would have to face the risk of endangering their only recently widened share of internal German EU policy-making. They would need to be protected against such a development by the appropriate constitutional safeguards which have now been created. Realizing this risk, they had already launched a scheme to counter it by drawing up recommendations in the *Bundesrat*'s Commission for Constitutional Reform which were designed to secure substantial amendments to Article 24 of the Basic Law in 1991.[19] They have now secured a new Article 23 which ensures that *Bundesrat* comments on EU legislation touching on exclusive *Länder* competences will be binding for the Federal Government in the Council of Ministers, and that in such matters Germany will be represented in the Council by a *Land* Minister nominated by the *Bundesrat*.

As its powers grow and develop the regional institution will have to ensure that it cannot be abused as part of a strategy of divide and rule at the cost of either the European Parliament, the Member States, or the regions themselves. Their large numbers could easily invite such a political game which is, after all, traditional. It would result in exploiting regionalism against federalism, and it would thus tend to strengthen neo-centralist tendencies rather than to diminish them. Last but not least, the Regional Committee will have to be careful not to allow predictable tendencies to shift it into an alibi function. To avoid this the Committee will rapidly have to develop efficient lines of internal cohesion. It remains to be seen to what extent these lines will emerge on patterns of common interests between groups of regions and to what extent such a process of grouping will be influenced by factors of party and/or national alignments.

Federalism and the Democratic Deficit

The debate on federalism in a European context, with all its complexities of power-sharing between several levels, should not conceal the fact that the origin of the discussion on Political Union is the issue of the democratic deficit in existing EU structures. It is the lack of genuine legislative powers of the directly elected European Parliament *vis-à-vis* the intergovernmental preponderance of the Council of Ministers that has pushed the federal train forward—and not vice versa. Regrettably enough, this gap has not been satisfactorily reduced by the outcome of the Maastricht Conference.

All attempts to strengthen the federal idea in the EU's political dimensions must, therefore, take into account that it would be counterproductive to the federal case itself if it were pursued in isolation to the detriment of the central representative institution. Speaking in more concrete political terms, this would certainly apply to projects advocating a direct European share of the national legislatures under the cover of a 'parliamentary federalism' (as obviously favoured in parts of the French political arena), as well as to potentially strategic ideas of favouring the regional concept simply because it could be developed into a tool against the European Parliament (as apparently exists in Britain). Criticizing the lack of democratic control over the Brussels bureaucracy and at the same time denying the need for stronger powers for the European Parliament can hardly go together. If the emergence of a new centralism in Europe is to be checked effectively for the sake of federalism (or whatever the preferred term may be for the protection of national and regional identities) then this will certainly need a strong European Parliament.

The genuine issue between the European Parliament and the federalists must thus lie in the recognition of the fact that any federal system needs intergovernmental processes, and the extent of these. Due to the origin of the EU as an international organization, the weight and power of such processes has surely become too heavy at the expense of democratic supremacy in a supranational structure, which is now developing into a federal one. But intergovernmental co-operation is also an essential element of federal systems, as is evident from the German example. However, its *status quo* and the needs felt for its reform also provide ample proof of the fact that intergovernmentalism and democracy can and must be continually brought into new balance.[20] At the European level that need would appear to be the strongest. In this context it should be noted that for the *Bundesrat*, as an intergovernmental organ, the improvement of the EU balance in substantial favour of the European Parliament is one of the essential elements of Political Union.[21]

5. CONCLUSION

The political dimension of the costs and benefits connected with federalization can only be properly evaluated under the actual conditions of a given historical situation. Thus, British impressions that the American system is a centralized one because the authors of *The Federalist* papers[22] argued for a strong Union, seem to neglect historical facts about the need at that time for a strong appeal to the electorate in the face of reluctance in several States to establish a Union at all despite imminent foreign danger. The result cannot be seriously classified as a centralized structure. Perceptions of it from the outside should take into account that the concept of *e pluribus unum* has certainly not diluted the vertical separation of powers between the Union and the States in American federalism.

To discuss federalization in the European context at the end of the twentieth century certainly does not require recourse to the magic notion of sovereignty. In the preceding discussion there was not even any need to use this term. The reason for this is the plain fact that the concept of sovereignty, in the sense of an unlimited power in national decision-making, has faded away as a constantly growing net of international obligations and interdependencies has made it obsolete.[23] Even within the field of constitutional law this fact is on the way to becoming formally acknowledged: in Germany, for instance, the new Article 23 of the Basic Law focuses on defining the place of the country and its institutions in a European Union within the central constitutional landmarks of human rights, democracy, and federalism. This by itself presupposes the disappearance of the notion of sovereignty in the traditional sense. So, too, does the new provision, by extending the rules for constitutional amendments, requiring the consent of two-thirds majorities in both Houses (including for the Union's treaty law), and thus binding national and European sovereignty into an identical legal frame work.

The end of the East–West conflict has not ended the need for a concentration of Europe's political potentials wherever possible without infringing legitimate national and regional identities. On the contrary, the rebirth of such identities in the former East clearly shows that an alternative must be quickly built up to counter the rise of a new wave of nationalism with all its devastating illusions of an independence which is no longer possible. Though admittedly complex in its institutional manifestations, the federal concept offers the only such alternative that can be discerned. If gradually but not reluctantly combined with adjusted forms of regional autonomy, both outdated separatism and new nationalism may be avoided through the concept of a 'Europe with the Regions' resulting in a doubly federalized structure.

The European Union is the only political structure which can provide this example of reconciling the democratic rights of majorities with the ethnic and other regional rights of minorities. Its transformation into a political union will, therefore, have to move away from the assignment of aims which marked its existence as an international body in favour of a distribution of legislative powers to the appropriate levels following the guidelines of subsidiarity which distinguish a federal structure. Otherwise a process will continue which results in the development of a 'competence on competence' at the European level. This would be the precise opposite of any even rudimentary federal system. Needless to say, it would thus also severely infringe the rights and status of the national parliaments, regardless of whether or not they individually approve of federalism.

A federal structure for the EU would be dangerously incomplete without the inclusion of policy areas which have so far (up to now and after Maastricht) only been subject to more or less institutionalized intergovernmental co-operation, such as in particular foreign affairs, defence, international crime and migration.[24]

Much of the confusion in the political debate on European federalism, which in part even equates it with its opposite of centralism, would seem to have its roots in the confused picture offered by the Union itself. While, on the one hand, representing a 'crippled federation' lacking sufficient powers in the policy fields mentioned above, it simultaneously creates the impression of a dinosaur with an enormous appetite, by legislating on matters of detail which could better be left to decision-making bodies at lower levels. Further reform after Maastricht will therefore have to concentrate on a double strategy: the principle of subsidiarity will not only have to limit central powers, but also to return powers of the Union to lower levels; at the same time, however, the very nucleus of the principle of federalism will have to shift powers, such as those referred to above, to the level of the Community as it develops into the Union. Steps in that direction would appear to be of special urgency in the face of the impending enlargement of the Union which will hardly be possible without a preceding widening and deepening of its constitutional form. In this perspective it might seem even more important to analyse the costs and benefits of *not* federalizing Europe[25] rather than those of the opposite. The aim of the 'ever closer Union of the peoples of Europe', as laid down in Article A of the Treaty of Maastricht, will inevitably necessitate the taking into account of these categories. Under its implications it would appear to be of little relevance whether or not federalism is called by its name in this Union's founding treaty.[26] The federalization of Europe will emerge as of necessity. Within democracy there is no other way of making our continent's future manageable.

Notes

* This chapter has been updated to 31 December 1992, following the consent of the *Bundesrat* to the Act of Ratification to the Treaty on European Union (TEU) on 18 December 1992, and the German constitutional amendments necessitated by it, as passed by the *Bundestag* on 2 December 1992. The chapter reflects the personal views of the author and it should thus not the identified with the *Land* of Lower Saxony or its Mission to the Federation in Bonn, in which he works as Head of the Constitutional and Legal Division.

1. See Bundesrat Press Release No. 2/76 of 10 Jan. 1977 ('Bundesrat und Föderalismus im Meinungsbild') and No. 4/89 of 30 Jan. 1989 ('Fast jeder kennt den Bundesrat. Starke Befürwortung des Bundesstaates—auch in einem geeinten Europa').

2. See Arts. 76–8 of the Basic Law (BL).

3. In the German Federal Budget 1992 the total number of all public employees (civil servants, employees under contract, and manual workers) in all Federal ministries (thus excluding the Federal Presiden-

tial Office, *Bundestag*, *Bundesrat*, Federal Constitutional Court, and Federal Audit Office) added up to 21,349 (*Bundeshaushaltsplan 1992*, i. 54–61). According to information given by the British Embassy in Bonn, the equivalent number for all British ministries is 553,200 (excluding 9,800 not in ministerial branches of government, e.g. HMSO). Accumulated corresponding figures for all the German *Land* ministries are not available; they would have to be extracted and added for each of the sixteen *Land* budgets, which was not possible within the available time-span. However, it is certainly a correct estimate that their total number is far below the difference between the British national and the German federal total of 553,200 − 21,345 = 531,851.

4. This part is based on the author's chapters 'The Working Relationships between *Bund* and *Länder* in the Federal Republic of Germany', and 'Into the 1990s: Federalism and German Unification', in C. Jeffery and P. Savigear (eds.), *German Federalism Today* (Leicester and London, 1991), 40–62, 138–48, which provide a more detailed analysis and further references.

5. *Bundesrat* (ed.), *Handbuch des Bundesrates für das Geschäftsjahr 1992/93* (Munich, 1992), 293: 5572 up to December 1990, to which a further 336 have to be added up to 15 August 1992.

6. Art. 72, Sect. 2 BL is the equivalent to the principle of subsidiarity in the German constitution. It reads: 'The Federation shall have the right to legislate in these matters [of concurrent powers] to the extent that a need for regulation by federal legislation exists because: 1. a matter cannot be effectively regulated by the legislation of individual *Länder*; or 2. the regulation of a matter by a *Land* statute might prejudice the interests of other *Länder* or of the people as a whole; or 3. the maintenance of legal or economic unity, especially the maintenance of uniformity of living conditions beyond the territory of any one *Land*, necessitates such regulation.' Conflicting concepts for reform have been developed by the *Bundesrat* Commission on Constitutional Reform and by the Joint Commission of the *Bundestag* and *Bundesrat* on the same matter. While the *Bundesrat* favours a political solution with itself evaluating the need for such legislation, the Joint Commission wants to call in the Federal Constitutional Court in cases of conflict (BR-Drucksache 360/92 Rd Nru 53–65 and Decisions of the Joint Constitutional Commission on Legislative Competences of 15 Oct. 1992).

7. For this guideline see also Art. A, Sect. 2 TEU.

8. Art. A, Sect. 2 TEU.

9. Arts. 30 and 70–5 BL.

10. See M. Burgess, *Canadian Federalism: Past, Present and Future* (Leicester and London, 1990).

11. See n. 5, above.
12. For more details: P. Blair, 'Federalism, Legalism and Political Reality: The Record of the Federal Constitutional Court', in Jeffery and Savigear (1991), 68–9.
13. *Bundesverfassungsgericht. Amtliche Entscheidungssammlung (BVerfGE)*, i. 299 ff. at 315.
14. *BVerfGE*, iv. 115 ff. at 141.
15. *See* Art. F TEU.
16. *BR-Drucksache* 680/91 (*Beschluß*).
17. Art. 198a, Sect. 3 in Art. G TEU.
18. Protocol regarding the Economic and Social Committee and the Committee of the Regions attached to the TEU (No. II 16 of the Final Act to the Treaty).
19. *Kommission Verfassungsreform BR and Sten Prot 2. Sitzung* (17 Oct. 1991), pp. 8–12, 55; *BR-Drucksache* 360/92 Rd Nru 3–17; *BT-Drucksache* 12/3896 and *Br-Drucksache* 809/92 (*Beschluß*), 18 Dec. 1992; details of its history and content in U. Leonardy, 'Federation and *Länder* in German Foreign Relations: Power-Sharing in Treaty-Making and European Affairs', *German Politics*, 1 (1992), 119–35.
20. See above.
21. See the resolution quoted in n. 16 and also the resolution accompanying the consent of the *Bundesrat* to the Act of Ratification of the Treaty on European Union, 18 Dec. 1992 (*BR-Drucksache* 810/92 *Beschluß*; ibid., No. 22).
22. A. Hamilton, J. Madison, and J. Jay, *The Federalist Papers*, ed. C. Rossiter (New York, 1961).
23. With similar conclusions: V. Bogdanor and G. Woodcock, 'The European Community and Sovereignty', *Parliamentary Affairs*, 44: 481–92.
24. See Arts. J–J II and K–K-9 TEU.
25. Impressively done by European Parliament (ed.), *Report in the name of the Institutional Committee of the EP on the Institutional Consequences of the Costs of a Non-Europe* (Rapporteur: Sir Frank Catherwood, 7 Apr. 1988 with an addendum of 27 Apr. 1988), EP-Document A2-39/88, PE 118.040/final.
26. As it is now out of semantic favour in terms of the definition of aims politically agreed on in the quoted formula of Art. A.

BIBLIOGRAPHY

Beyme, K. von, 'West Germany: Federalism', *International Political Science Review*, 5/4 (1984).

Bulmer, S., 'Territorial Government', in G. Smith, W. E. Paterson, and P. H. Merkl (eds.), *Developments in West German Politics* (London, 1989).

—— *The Domestic Structure of European Community Policy-Making in West Germany* (New York, 1986).

—— and Paterson, W., *The Federal Republic of Germany and the European Community* (London, 1987).

Burgess, M., *Federalism and European Union; Political Ideas, Influences and Strategies in the European Community, 1972–1987* (London, 1989).

—— (ed.), *Federalism and Federation in Western Europe* (London, 1986).

Davis, R., *The Federal Principle: A Journey through Time in Quest of Meaning* (Berkeley, Calif., 1987).

Forsyth, M. (ed.), *Federalism and Nationalism* (Leicester and London, 1989).

—— *Unions of States: The Theory and Practice of Confederation* (Leicester and London, 1981).

Gunlicks, A. (ed.), *Publius: The Journal of Federalism*, 19. *Federalism and Intergovernmental Relations in West Germany: A Fortieth Year Appraisal* (1989).

Her Majesty's Stationery Office (ed.), *Treaty on European Union* (London, 1992). (German text in Presse- und Informationsamt der Bundesregierung, Bulletin No. 16/1992, 12 Feb. 1992, 113–84: Vertrag uber die Europäische Union.)

International Institute of Administrative Sciences, Research Committee I (ed.), *Appraisal of National Policies of Decentralization and Regionalization*, Hochschule für Verwaltungswissenschaften (Speyer, 1989).

Jeffery, C. and Savigear, P. (eds.), *German Federalism Today* (Leicester and London, 1991).

—— and Sturm, R. (eds.), 'Federalism, Unification and European Integration', *German Politics*, 1/3 (1992).

Johnson, N., *State and Government in the Federal Republic of Germany: The Executive at Work* (Oxford, 1983).

Katzenstein, P. J., *Policy and Politics in West Germany: The Growth of A Semisovereign State* (Philadephia, 1987).

Kling, P., *Federalism and Federation* (London, 1982).

Knott, J., *Managing the German Economy: Budgetary Politics in a Federal State* (Lexington, Mass., 1981).

Press and Information Office of the Federal Government (ed.), *Basic Law of the Federal Republic of Germany* (rev. trans.; Bonn, 1992).

Rosolillo, F., 'Federalism and the Great Ideologies', *The Federalist*, Year 31 (1989), 7–34.

Rousseau, M. O. and Zariski, R., *Regionalism and Regional Devolution in*

Comparative Perspective (New York, 1987).

Scharpf, F. W., 'The Joint-Decision Trap: Lessons from German Federalism and European Integration', *Public Administration*, 66 (1988).

Schweitzer, C. C. and Karsten, D. (eds.), *Federal Republic of Germany and EC Membership Evaluated* (London, 1990).

——Karsten, D., Spencer, R., Taylor Cole, R., Kommers, D., Nicholls, A. (eds.), *Politics and Government in the Federal Republic of Germany*, Basic Documents (Leamington Spa, 1981).

Wessels, W. and Regelsberger, E., *The Federal Republic of Germany and the European Community: The Presidency and Beyond* (Bonn, 1988).

6

An Economic Perspective

DIETER BIEHL

1. INTRODUCTION

The purpose of this chapter is to stress that economic method, adequately designed in order to deal with political phenomena, is capable of presenting a full approach to an understanding of the costs and benefits of federal systems. It is organized as follows. First, an extended-cost approach is presented that may be used as a sort of frame of reference for evaluating existing constitutions and designing new elements of a (written or unwritten) constitution. With the help of this approach, the actual financial constitution of the European Community is then analysed in order to identify possible deficiencies. A final section draws conclusions from this analysis as to a blueprint for reform.

2. THE EXTENDED-COST APPROACH

It seems obvious that a traditional economic approach, based on resource costs and benefits, will not be able to make a significant general contribution to the issue of the constitution of a federal system. A broader perspective implies that the notions of benefit and cost have to be greatly expanded. One of the seminal contributions in this context is the book by James M. Buchanan and Gordon Tullock, *The Calculus of Consent: Logical Foundations of Constitutional Democracy*, published in 1962. The authors state in their preface that they aim 'to analyse the calculus of the rational individual when he is faced with questions of constitutional choice' (p. vi). Their analysis is based on what they call 'methodological individualism' which they claim to apply in a 'reasonably *wertfrei*' sense.

Their basic approach may be summed up by stating that it is possible to transform all benefits into reduced costs so that the whole analysis can be in cost terms only. These cost terms are to be understood in an extended manner. The authors summarize their approach in their famous cost diagram, a modified version of which is presented as *Fig. 6.1*. Total cost is said to represent 'interdependence cost', a term that is the aggregation of what they call 'decision-making costs' and 'resource costs' (RC), as decision-making involves resources (time, effort, use of human capital as a decision-making resource, information, etc.) that could also be used for market activities. 'External costs' could create possible misunderstandings, as this notion seems not to be equivalent to what is usually understood by this term. If, for instance, traditional external costs are internalized, they will disappear, but not Buchanan–Tullock external costs, since they also involve the consequences of the decisions of others on the perceived welfare of the individual considered. Therefore, I suggest the term 'preference costs' (PC) or 'frustration costs'. The latter term, 'frustation costs', is taken from Pennock (1969), who used it in analysing the implications of majority decisions in an election. His use of 'frustation' makes clear that this is an immaterial consequence of decisions taken by others.

These two new terms, although representing an extension of the original Buchanan–Tullock approach, capture the basic idea of their cost-based analysis, which requires that there are (at least) two countervailing cost functions, and that it is due only to these countervailing properties that a U-shaped total cost curve (TC) is obtained. The argument is quite straightforward: if only decision-making costs in the sense of using resources for arriving at a decision are considered, one might argue that these costs are zero or at least at a minimum, if only one person makes all political decisions. In this case, all others will not have to devote time, effort, and other resources in order to participate in political decision-making. These resource costs will increase to the extent that additional members of the group or society participate in the political process. With the increasing number of group members (N), the RC function therefore rises from left to right. The opposite cost curve has its minimum equal to zero at Ñ, i.e. members of the society

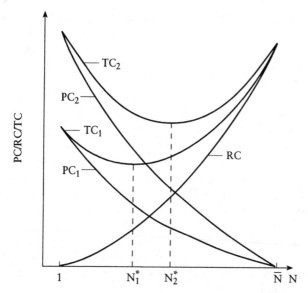

F IG. 6.1. The extended-cost concept

considered. If they all participate in decision-making, and if the rule of unanimity is applied, then all have the same chance to bring in their preferences, thereby minimizing frustration. This prevents political decisions that are based on the preferences of one person or group that may not be in line with those of the other members to the extent that their welfare will be negatively affected. The extended-cost approach also has consequences for the interpretation of the Musgravian triad of allocation, distribution, and stabilization (Musgrave, 1959; 5 ff.):

1. The allocation function will have to include all types of resource cost, particularly those of creating and maintaining institutions and of decision-making, in the meaning already discussed.[1]

2. The extension of the distribution function now includes those aspects of equity that are linked with the distribution of private property rights to individuals and public competences to levels of government. The well-known principle of separation of legislative, executive, and judicial powers will then be a part of the distributional function. The fragmentation of government power is clearly in contradiction with the allocation function that would require

minimizing political decision-making costs with the aid of a powerful single decision-making centre, whereas the distribution function
will consider it as just and fair to reduce government power in order
to avoid abuses by separating the three horizontal powers. With
this extension of the distribution function, in principle the same
type of goal conflicts can arise between the extended-allocation and
the extended-distribution function that is already typical in traditional economics for these two functions, i.e. efficiency v. equity in
interpersonal income distribution. The classical horizontal separation of power issue can then be viewed from this economic perspective as implying that a given society prefers higher resource costs in
political decision-making in order to obtain a less powerful government to protect the members of the society against abuse of government power.

3. The stabilization function will also have to be extended
in order not only to cover stabilization of economic cycles,
but also to include the stabilization of the society and the institutional and political system.

The extended Buchanan–Tullock diagram demonstrates that political decision-making will always have a positive total cost. On the
basis of their methodological individualism, therefore, the authors
argue that these costs of collective action will always have to be
compared with the costs of private action. To this effect, they
present a model with six different cases of which only two are
potential cases for replacing collective or government action by
private action (Buchanan and Tullock, 1962: 49 ff.). It seems quite
plausible to assume that a given society, consisting of free individuals, would never choose to transfer, for example, the provision of
a private good to a public authority as long as they are able to
provide this good on the basis of their free decisions at lower cost,
i.e. without the collective decision-making cost. However, market
provision of these private goods will be efficient only if the public
sector exists and has already provided the appropriate number and
types of human action and property rights. Markets will be inefficient if they have to deal with scarce goods for which no property
rights exist. The example of environmental rights clearly illustrates
this point: so long as air and water were 'free' goods, it would have
been inefficient to create property rights for these goods. However,
as these goods have become scarce, environmental property and
action rights have become necessary, and without these rights that

help to internalize the external effects of the use of these goods, the market economy would now be inefficient. As a consequence, the efficiency of markets always presupposes an adequately designed and protected system of action and property rights. The preceding considerations lead to the conclusion that there should be a clear separation between two basic areas or functions of decision-making: a constitution function and a (goods) provision function.[2]

The constitution function (CF) comprises the institutions and the decision-making rules considered by the society concerned to be necessary in order to produce and to maintain private action and property rights on the one hand, and public rights ('competences') of government levels on the other. Accordingly, CF represents the framework for private and public activities. It can also be considered to provide the higher-level public goods.

The second, provision function (PF) is subordinate to CF and represents the area where individuals use their private action and property rights in order to produce and consume private goods at minimum cost, and where the different types of government offer and finance public goods in the traditional sense (e.g. defence, social security, basic education, etc.). The role to be attributed to the market as the organizational structure of private goods provision on the one hand and to governments as the providers of public goods in the traditional sense on the other will, therefore, also depend on the perceptions and preferences of the majority of that society concerned.

Viewed from this perspective, what is normally called the 'public sector', always has two clearly separate functions: to create and maintain the institutional and decision-making framework as far as the production and control of private property rights and of competences are concerned on the one hand; and to create and maintain the area in which traditional public goods are provided and financed within this constitutional framework on the other. This strict separation is necessary in order to obtain decisions on a constitutional level that, due to the 'veil of ignorance' (Rawls, 1972; 136–42) can be taken without always being able to antici-pate costs to the decision-makers in later day-to-day policy-making within this constitutional framework. If this separation is not possible, any decision at the constitutional level would clearly be influenced by the expected costs of the decision-makers concerned when these rules are applied to themselves. Only if the constitutional rules fulfil the same function as the rules for a game, i.e. to be pre-established and not to be modified during the course of the game, representing a certain fair mixture of chances and controls, will it be possible to speak of efficiency and equity in the area of private and public goods provision.

3. PRINCIPLES OF FISCAL FEDERALISM

In order to be able to use the extended-cost approach as a sort of framework of reference to evaluate and to compare existing systems of government and to develop blueprints for new systems of government (for example, that of the European Union), the constitutional function has to be made more operational. This can be done by trying to develop principles of fiscal federalism. The term federalism is here used in a very broad sense, covering the full range of unitary versus federal government. Should only the horizontal separation of powers be considered to be necessary for a given society, this society would have a unitary government structure with a state level and with regional and local levels of government.

If the extended distribution function is considered to be very important to members of the society, they may decide to add to the horizontal separation of powers a vertical one and, in particular, to subdivide the state level of government into two entities: a federal government level and a state government level in the meaning defined in the US Constitution (the analogy in other federal countries would be the provinces of Canada, the cantons in Switzerland, and the Länder in Germany). But nothing in this structure is pre-determined. All will depend on the perception and the evaluation of the costs, especially the preference or frustration costs involved, by the members of the respective society. These considerations also apply in cases where a new, additional level of government, such as that of the European Union, is to be created or extended. A number of crucial issues, especially linked to the Single European Act of 1986 and the Maastricht Treaty are clearly determined by the different perceptions and assessments of the preference and resource costs involved. The basic extended-cost model is, however, too general to be helpful in understanding institutional systems and in identifying possible deficiencies. In order to make the approach more operational, it is proposed to derive a number of principles or criteria that can be used to assess existing and develop new financial constitutions.

The Principle of Optimal Assignment of Competences

If one starts from Buchanan's idea of an 'economic club' (1965), one might think of creating such a monofunctional provision organization for each type of non-private good. If, however, each club has to be endowed with the necessary institutions according to the separation of powers requirements, we would end up with a cost-maximizing system. This situation can be improved if all clubs whose servicing areas are more or less identical (the principle of congruence of servicing areas), are merged in order to obtain multifunctional territorial organizations or governments. If one adopts the suggestion by Albert Breton (1965) that all public goods can be ranked according to the size of their servicing areas, ranging from local to regional to national and to international, the result is a system of multi-level governments that is much less expensive. From an allocative efficiency point of view, these governments should be allocated all those competences that have roughly the same servicing areas.

The Subsidiarity Principle

This old principle has attracted new attention in the context of the ongoing discussion of European Political Union; it is explicitly referred to in Article 3B of the Maastricht Treaty. However, it is not always clearly defined. From the point of view of the extended-cost approach it can be characterized by stating that it corresponds to the extended equity distribution function. If a distribution of competences according to the efficiency-oriented principle of optimal assignment of competences would lead to too many competences being attributed to higher levels of government (for example, to the federal or EU level compared with the Member-State level, or to the Member-State level compared with the regional or local level), subsidiarity would favour the lower or smaller governments to the effect that they should keep or receive more competences than would be justified by efficiency criteria. The basic argument is that political decisions should be taken as close as possible to the citizens concerned and with as much political participation by citizens as possible.[3] Subsidiarity also has a second meaning: that the lower or smaller governments should be subsidized by the higher and larger ones in order to be able to carry out their functions in so far as their fiscal capacity is insufficient compared with their expenditure needs. A combination of own taxes and grants—in short: a more decentralized and differentiated *Finanzausgleich* system—would be the outcome of enhanced subsidiarity.

This solidarity aspect of subsidiarity is closely linked with fair burden-sharing and fiscal equalization.

From the extended distributional point of view, the number of competences attributed to non-central levels of government could even be increased if, for example, the society concerned places a high importance on the separation of powers and, therefore, establishes, in addition to horizontal separation, a vertical separation of powers to the effect that the central level of government is divided into a federal level and a Member-State level. If a well-balanced system of checks and balances is to be created, the Member-State level of government could then be given more than the competences derived from the efficiency assessment so as to make this level politically stronger than it otherwise would be. The decision as to which competences and how many of them to allocate to a level of government would then be the result of both an allocative (optimal assignment of competences) and a distributional (subsidiarity) evaluation.

The Optimal Differentiation of Competences

There are two aspects to this principle. First, competences may be assigned as full ones or may be divided into sub-competences, and the latter may be attributed to different levels of government. Second, competences may be exclusive or concurrent or competitive. The decision as to what type of differentiation should be used depends again mainly on preference cost elements. If, for example, a multi-level system of government is desired which consists of strong and independent units, then only full competences should be distributed. The result would be some sort of competitive federalism. If, on the other hand, legislative competences, for example, are mainly distributed to the federal level, but administrative competences to the Member-State level (cantons, provinces, or *Länder*), the system will have an in-built tendency towards co-operative federalism, as no level would be able to act independently of the others. The same is true for splitting up tax and expenditure competences. Concurrent or competitive competences are those that are in principle allocated to the Member-State level, but where the federal level has the right to withdraw them and use them for itself. If the conditions to be fulfilled by the federal government are not very strong, the result might be a tendency towards a 'unitary federal state' (*or unitarischer Bundesstaat* as this tendency was usefully characterized by Konrad Hesse for West Germany in 1962). The reason for taking this path is to try to obtain greater 'uniformity of living conditions' (*Einheitlichkiet der Lebensverhältnisse*) as stated in two clauses of the German Basic Law. Again, the attribution of concurrent or competitive competences will tend towards co-operative federalism, whereas using more exclusive competences will lead to competitive federalism.

The Correspondence Principle

This principle, which can be traced back to Breton (1965) and Oates (1972), is also based on the requirement that governments' territories should be congruent with the servicing areas of the public goods for which they are given responsibility. In particular, correspondence also includes the claim that the decision-makers are residents of those servicing areas and should be so chosen that they represent both tax-payers and expenditure beneficiaries. If tax-payers are overrepresented, the level of public services offered will be too low. If, on the other hand, expenditure beneficiaries have the majority, the result would be oversupply and too high a budget. The correspondence principle also implies that the political decision-makers should decide simultaneously on tax burdens and on expenditure benefits, because it is only under this condition that budgetary discipline can be obtained.

The Principle of Fair Burden-Sharing

Public goods are characterized by shared or joint consumption. In principle, therefore, it is possible to apply the benefit principle of taxation to the group or collectivity that are citizens or residents of the territorial servicing areas. The problem consists in designing criteria for distributing total tax burdens and for fixing individual contributions. If the public dimension is not too high, benefit taxes and fees could be used. In general, public goods have a high degree of 'publicness', so only taxation based on ability to pay, independent of benefits received, can be applied. According to spatial distribution of resources within a country and of preferences for the different types of taxes, national tax systems vary considerably. Fair burden-sharing implies that first, the appropriate financing instruments are used and, second, that the total tax burden is distributed fairly. This has implications for the choice of direct or progressive taxes versus indirect or regressive ones. Fair burden-sharing also has implications for the use of debt financing. According to Musgrave's pay-as-you-use principle, the capital cost of public investments is to be distributed to the members of the respective user generations. It is, therefore, not only admissible, but also both an efficient and equitable form of financing to use debt for this part of public expenditure.

The Principle of Fiscal Equalization

Fair burden-sharing can also be applied to governments. If a certain minimum or otherwise defined level of public services is to be provided to all members of a collectivity, and if distributional equity is to be secured, people with a significantly lower capacity to pay should be charged at lower tax-rates in order to finance this minimum or average supply. As a consequence, local, regional, and state governments with too low a tax capacity are to be entitled to receive grants from other units with a higher tax capacity. In unitary states, fiscal equalization takes place mainly through the national government budget, whereas federal countries rely more on explicit vertical and horizontal fiscal-equalization schemes. The choice of redistributive intensity again depends on the extended-cost approach, in particular on the degree of solidarity which, in turn, reflects preference cost. If transfers are too generous and if no matching rules are applied, there will be an incentive to waste public funds; if transfers are too low compared with the disparities in income and employment, excessive migration will be the result. In addition, intergovernmental transfers are not only pure solidarity-based gifts of the richer governments to poorer ones. As the MacDougall Report (EC Commission, 1977) has shown, the richer regions within a country are at the same time net exporters and net payers in the respective national finance systems, whereas the poorer regions are normally both net importers and net receivers. This coincidence can be attributed to the fact that the richer regions within a common market benefit from the fact that the poorer ones do not protect their markets and so offer the possibility for gains from trade for the richer net exporter regions. The latter then retransfer a part of their gains from trade to those regions from which they have originated, if the national public finance system is sufficiently progressive. This retransfer can be explicit or implicit, i.e. it can take place through higher spending by the richer regions or the higher-level government.

4. IDENTIFYING THE DEFICIENCIES OF THE CURRENT FINANCIAL CONSTITUTION OF THE EU

In what follows, the principles of fiscal federalism formulated in the previous section will be applied to the actual financial constitution of the EU in order to identify possible deficiencies.

Given the political preferences expressed in the EU-Treaty as amended by the Single Act of 1986 and the statements as to the desirability of a Political Union, and last but not least, the Treaty of Maastricht, the principle of optimal assignment of competences seems to be violated. First, the number of full or partial competences is not high compared with what a federal-level government in other existing federations would enjoy. Admittedly, the EU is not yet a federation, and the history of the Community Union shows that there has always been only a gradual transfer of competences. However, the institutional and decision-making capacity of the Union is large enough to deal with more competences, and with a more intensive utilization of existing competences. As there are competences which could be more efficiently used at the EU level currently, there exists a certain underutilization of the EU decision-making capacity. On the other hand, democratic control of these competences is not yet adequately secured at the EU level, as the most powerful legislative body is the Council of Ministers, implying that members of the (national) executive branch of government control themselves. In addition, there are structural distortions in the EU financial constitution: the Union does not yet have its own tax competence. In fact, although, its budget is officially financed from its own resources (e.g. the revenues from the common external tariffs and from the agricultural levies), these revenues cannot really be designed so as to make them financing instruments. Their use is restricted by foreign-trade policy and GATT in the case of customs duties, and by the EU agricultural price policies and their relation to world market prices in the case of the levies. The third main revenue category, VAT revenues, which, in principle, could be used as an unrestricted financing instrument, represents more a sort of tax-sharing arrangement than a true own resource and is regressive. In addition the EU has a GDP levy as a fourth revenue source. However, to increase these two latter categories of revenue requires not only decisions of the EU institutions, but also ratification in all Member States.

The lack of an autonomous tax authority also violates the correspondence principle. On the one hand, EU politicians can decide on how much to spend for the competences they do have, but are not allowed or obliged simultaneously to decide on the taxes needed to finance these expenditures. As a result, there is an in-built incentive to spend too much; there is no fiscal accountability. This is especially true for agricultural spending for which the EU has a full competence for the common agricultural market. On the other hand, it is the national politicians who have to defend, for example, the actual tax-rates of VAT despite the fact that 1.4 per cent of the VAT-base (roughly the same in percentage-point national tax-rates) has to be transferred to the EU treasury. That overall EU spending has not been excessive during the last few years is due to the fact that, after a number of financial crises in previous years, the medium-term budget planning for 1988–92 strongly restricted expenditure increases by imposing yearly maximum spending limits, by freezing CAP expenditure, and by restricting the revenues as well. (The admissible increase over 1988–92 in terms of the percentage of EU GDP was from 1.15 to 1.20 for all revenues taken together, corresponding to an absolute increase from 45.3 bn. ECU to 52.8 bn. ECU see EC Commission, 1989: 101.) The *Financial Perspectives* for 1993–7, that the Commission originally suggested should be increased to 1.37 per cent of the EU GNP ('Delors II'), were reduced by the Edinburgh Summit so as not to exceed 1.27 per cent in 1999, meaning an increase to 84.1 bn. ECU.

Another violation of the correspondence principle consists in the fact that one of the most powerful groups of national spending ministers, the agriculture ministers, have practically been allowed to serve their clients in an almost closed-shop fashion, fully protected from the competition of other spending ministers. It has only been during the last few years that, due to the very strict budgetary ceilings and the freezing of agricultural prices, CAP spending has been increasing more slowly from a planned 27.5 to 29.6 bn. ECU in 1988–92 (see EC Commission, 1989: 101). As a share of total expenditure, agricultural spending is even planned to go down from 60.7 per cent to 55.9 per cent during this period. According to Delors II, the CAP share should have decreased to 45.3 per cent of total EU expenditure in 1997 (Zangl and Groutage, 1992: 9); according to the Edinburgh Summit decisions, it will reach 45.6 percent in 1999.

The subsidiarity principle is always violated if at the EU level, on the basis of already transferred competences, detailed uniformizing decisions are taken only from the point of view of whether intra-EU trade could be affected. Even the President of the Commission cites as examples the Six VAT Directive that harmonized the VAT-base and a number of too detailed regulations such as the elaborated lawn-mower case (Delors, 1992: 171, 169). These (and other) cases illustrate the unitarizing and federalizing tendencies which parallel the application of the Interstate Commerce Clause in the USA. From the point of view of the German *Länder*, more significant cases are the intervention of the EU in the fields of education and culture, a competence that according to the German Constitution belongs with the *Länder*. Here the *Bundesregierung* participated in decisions at the European level; something it would not have been allowed to do in the German context. It was not surprising, therefore, that the *Länder* pressed the *Bundesregierung* and the *Bundestag* to agree on a modification to Article 24 of the Basic Law that allows the *Bund* to transfer competences to international institutions. The main claim is that whenever decisions are to be taken in Brussels that may affect *Länder* competences, representatives of the *Länder* have to be a part of the *Bund*'s delegation. Article 3A of the Maastricht Treaty seems to restrict the application of the subsidiarity principle to non-exclusive competences and to Community actions. This could restrict its effect to already transferred competences.

The principle of optimal differentiation of competences is also partly violated. This is again due to agricultural problems. CAP represents one of the few full competences attributed to the EU from the outset. The idea was that a true common policy should be based on uniform prices for agricultural products, independent of comparative advantage. Some (forced) price differentiation has taken place in the past due to the need to increase prices in countries that devalued and to decrease them in countries with a revaluation. However, the adjustments were asymmetrical, as the countries which devalued were not prepared to let prices go up fully, nor were those that revalued prepared to let them go down. But there was no room, as far as the market policy is concerned, to allow national or regional price differentiation.

Horizontal differentiation of competences exists in the EU in a very peculiar way: the separation of expenditure into one group called 'compulsory' and another called 'non-compulsory', together with the rules for budgetary procedures (the so-called Inter-institutional Agreement), implies that it is the Council of Ministers that had the last word about the first group, and the European Parliament about the second. This also represents a violation of the budgetary principles of a uniform and comprehensive budget. The undesirable consequence was that this categorization created an incentive for each part of the double budget authority to maximize spending in a sort of competition (the Council, for example, in the previous years for agricultural spending, and the Parliament for Structural Funds spending).

The principles of fair burden-sharing and of fiscal equalization have also faced some violations. The major critique applies to the regressivity of the overall financing system: in general, the poorer member countries pay relatively more than the richer ones. This is due to the fact that, especially the agricultural levies and VAT in general, cause a higher burden on persons and families with a low income who will face a greater relative increase in their cost of living having to spend more on consumption than those with higher incomes. Compared with the actual situation, the original financing system with national GNP had a rather more proportional burden. The step towards own resources in the form of customs duties and levies was a correct one; the addition of VAT revenues appeared as a first step towards the granting of a tax authority to the Union. However, these hopes were never realized. In the mean time, it was decided to endow the EU with a new revenue instrument, which is also related to GNP. In addition, a maximum limit to the VAT percentage of national GNP of 55 per cent was introduced which reduced the undesirable regressivity of the VAT system for Ireland and Portugal, but also for rich Luxembourg, and increased the payments from all other member countries. The UK would also have benefited from this maximum limit; but as its contribution is already reduced by another special mechanism (the so-called 'Fontainebleau mechanism'), the net effect was zero (Messal, 1991: 164).

As far as fiscal equalization is concerned, the extended-cost approach, in particular the preference-cost function, explains why there is not yet a fully developed explicit scheme. From the point of view of the richer potential net payers, there is not as yet sufficient homogeneity of preferences and rules for them to be sure that unconditional transfers will be spent in accordance with generally accepted standards. The EU, therefore, has only an implicit system of resource transfer which, however, is not fully in line with the principle of fiscal equalization. This is due to the net financial flows generated by the CAP. As high amounts are to be paid by a country such as the UK because of its high imports on the one hand and low exports on the other, this country is a net payer. Given that it has an income per capita that is slightly above the EU average, a net payer position, in principle, is not incompatible with fair burden-sharing. This argument does not appear to be decisive, but at any rate, in order to obtain a full picture, all other elements of the EU budget will have to be considered. In general, the Structural Funds cause transfers in the right direction as the sums spent in the poorer member countries are larger. Again, however, it is not possible to transform all EU policies into those that are geared to create positive net flows for the poorer countries. All these pros and cons require a very careful and differentiated analysis. Such analyses have been presented by Rüdiger Messal (1991) and Shackleton

(1990). However, they cannot be reproduced in one single set of figures. The general impression is that the EU financing system is not yet in line with fair burden-sharing.[4]

CONCLUSIONS FOR THE REFORM OF THE EU FINANCIAL CONSTITUTION

The arguments for reforming the EU financial constitution are not to be misunderstood in a way which suggests merely that principles should not be violated and, therefore, these violations have to disappear. The basic argument is rather that if these violations are not corrected they will continue to work as in-built incentives so that in the future, distorted decisions may be expected. One type of such distortion is that if the majority of member countries continue to be net receivers, then the net payers will remain a minority, without the power to prevent certain budget-maximizing decisions. Only if there is a somewhat more balanced representation of net payers and net receivers can one expect rational decisions. Only then will it be possible to get rid of some artificial rules, such as the distinction between compulsory and non-compulsory expenditure items, and of the maximum rate of increase of expenditure rule of article 203 of the EU-Treaty that is only an artificial substitute for normal budgetary discipline. It is from this perspective that the following proposals for reform should be seen.

1. In order to remedy the most serious violations of the fiscal federalism principles, the EU has to be endowed with a tax authority of its own. Only if the same decision-makers have to take the responsibility both for spending and taxing will there be normal democratic budgetary discipline. In addition, endowing the EU with a progressive revenue instrument will also contribute to an EU financing more in line with revealed preferences in the Member States. On average, indirect (regressive) and direct (progressive) revenues each represent 50 per cent. To replace 50 per cent of the actual revenues by a progressive source can, therefore, be considered to be in line with revealed preferences. However, to wait until preferences and structural conditions within the EU have become so homogeneous that a true European income and corporation tax will become possible will take too long. A possibility for the next

fifteen to twenty years would be to apply a progressive surtax to the existing national income and/or corporation taxes according to a two-stage procedure that first distributes 50 per cent of the tax burden among member countries according to their income per capita, and then transforms each national burden into an equivalent surcharge percentage (Biehl, 1991a; 1991b). This percentage is to be shown on individual tax bills, so that each tax-payer knows how much he or she has to pay for financing the European budget. As it is not possible to justify scientifically one and only one progressive tax rate, the proposal contains a lower and a higher rate of tax progression in order to show a band of possible solutions. Figure 6.2 presents the main results of this proposal for the lower and the higher progressive levels in comparison with the actual tax burden and a proportional one without progression for all Member States in ECU per capita. This presentation is based on the assumption that 50 per cent of the EU revenues would already have been replaced by the progressive surcharge by 1987. Member States would have paid only half of their actual VAT transfers, so that they could have used the other half in order to cut national taxes.

2. An EU autonomous tax authority requires that the actual intra-budget borders between compulsory and non-compulsory expenditure should be abolished in order to put an end to expenditure competition. This involves joint responsibility by the Council and the Parliament for the whole budget and for both the revenue and expenditure sides. The budgetary authority would thus have to become a sort of bicameral system in which conflict between the two parts would have to be resolved as is usual in those systems: with the aid of a conciliation body, consisting of members of both chambers. If this is achieved, the maximum spending increase rule may also be abolished.

3. The practice by which special councils of ministers, such as the agricultural ministers, decide on their own expenditure (or revenues) should also be abolished. Only council meetings at which spenders and tax-payers, i.e. the ministers of finance or their representatives, are present should be allowed to make budgetary decisions.

To carry out a reform like the one proposed here is certainly not possible without a sufficiently long period of discussion and consensus-building. Despite the efforts of the European Parliament,

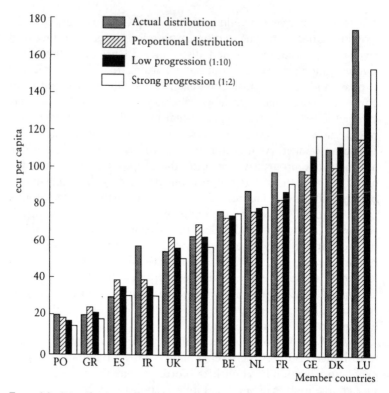

F IG. 6.2. Distribution of 50 per cent of EU own resources per capita in 1987 according to hypothetical progressive financing, with the aid of an EU surcharge on national income taxes

of the (former) responsible member of the Commission, Peter Schmidhuber, and of many economists working in this field, it seems unlikely that there will be any advance for some years to come. At the Edinburgh Summit, it was only decided to continue with a new Financial Perspective for the next seven years 1993–9, with a moderate increase in the Community budget from 1.20 per cent of EU GNP in 1993 to 1.27 per cent in 1999, but basically retaining the old financing system. A positive aspect is that implicit fiscal equalization through the Structural Funds and the new Cohesion Fund will be improved. Compared with the 2.5 per cent of the EU GNP mentioned by the MacDougall Committee in 1977 for a significant step forward towards a pre-federal European Union, there seems to still be a long way to go. It may be that a budget of

1.27 per cent of GNP is still too low in order to mobilize sufficient political support for a more progressive system of EU finance. It is also understandable that, given the prevailing overall economic difficulties, the governments of the Member States are too preoccupied with their national problems. The very ambitious aim of the Maastricht Treaty, to realize full Monetary Union by 1996 or at the latest 1999, may also explain why a big step forward to Public Finance Union at the same time may be too demanding. If one considers that the first plan for a Monetary Union was already developed in 1970 ('the Werner Plan'), after a long preparatory period, the prospects for Public Finance Union are not so bad. As this is a well-considered project it may well be successful.

Notes

1. For some economists, this will not be an extension of the allocation function, as they have always considered this to be a part of the allocation issue.
2. Buchanan and Tullock (1962) make a similar distinction between a 'constitutional phase' and an 'operational phase' of decision-making, but do not explicitly include the production and maintenance of rights in their first phase (See pp. 119–20). In his Nobel lecture of 1986, in comparing his approach with that of Knut Wicksell in 1896, Buchanan is more explicit in characterizing the 'constitutional choice' and the 'constitutional rules' level 'within which ordinary politics [are] allowed to operate' (Buchanan, 1992: 186 f.).
3. Unfortunately, Spinelli, in his otherwise very important endeavour to develop a true EU Constitution, seems to have placed subsidiarity too close to the efficiency issue (see Delors, 1992, who cites Spinelli's formulation. He, however, also stresses that subsidiarity means that decisions to realize a law ought to be taken as close as possible to those who are concerned; p. 173).
4. See Messal (1991), ch. 7: 'Horizontal Burden Sharing', pp. 149–72 and Shackleton (1990), pp. 24–47.

BIBLIOGRAPHY

Biehl, D., 'Financing the EEC Budget', in R. Prud'homme (ed.), *Public Finance with Several Levels of Government*, proceedings of the 46th

Congress of the International Institute of Public Finance (The Hague and Koenigstein, 1991*a*), 137–52.

—— 'Die EG-Finanzverfassung: Struktur, Mängel und Reformmöglichkeiten', in R. Wildenmann (ed.), *Staatswerdung Europas? Optionen fur eine Europäische Union* (Baden-Baden, 1991*b*), 355–91.

Breton, A., 'A Theory of Government Grants', *Canadian Journal of Economics and Political Science*, 1965, 31: 175–87.

Buchanan, J. M. and Tullock, G., *The Calculus of Consent: Logical Foundations of Constitutional Democracy* (Ann Arbor, Mich., 1962).

——'The Constitution of Economic Policy', in K.-G. Mäler (ed.), *Nobel Lectures in Economic Sciences 1981–1990* (Singapore, 1992), 180–9.

EC Commission (Commission of the European Communities) *Report of the Study Group on the Role of Public Finance in European Integration* ('MacDougall-Report'; Brussels), i. *General Report;* ii. *Individual Contributions and Working Papers.*

—— *The Community Budget: The Facts in Figures* (Luxemburg, 1989).

Delors, J., 'Le principe de subsidiarité' in J. Delors (ed.), *Le Nouveau Concert Européen* (Paris, 1992), 163–76.

Messal, R., *Das Eigenmittelsystem der Europäischen Gemeinschaft* (Baden-Baden, 1991).

Musgrave, R. A., *The Theory of Public Finance* (Ann Arbor, Mich., 1959).

Oates, W. E., *Fiscal Federalism* (New York, 1972).

Pennock, J. R., 'Federal and Unitary Government—Disharmony and Frustration', *Behavioural Science*, 1969, 4: 147–57.

Rawls, J., *A Theory of Justice* (Oxford, 1972).

Shackleton, M., *Financing the European Community* (London, 1990).

Zangl, P. and Groutage, C., 'Next Steps in EC Budgetary Policy' in H. Cowie (ed.), *Towards Fiscal Federalism* (London, 1992), 1–9.

7

The Cultural Dimension

PETER M. LESLIE

═══

Technology, which brings abundance and material happiness, presupposes an undifferentiated mass of consumers; it also tends to minimize the values that let a human being acquire and retain his own identity, values that I am grouping here under the vague term 'cultural'. The political order created by the state must struggle against this kind of depersonalization by pursuing cultural objectives.

Pierre Elliott Trudeau[1]

1. INTRODUCTION

This chapter explores how public support for the preservation or strengthening of national cultures observably affects processes of federalization. The discussion is cast in terms of costs and benefits, although that choice of terms—as will be argued—appears to imply an individualistic calculus or methodology that may be inappropriate in reviewing the cultural dimension of the federalization process. None the less, costs-and-benefits language is adhered to in the first part of the chapter, which reaches somewhat inconclusive results but still serves to open up the discussion, by bringing into focus three related questions:

• Is it possible to achieve, under federalism, economic benefits—and perhaps also security benefits—at only slight cultural cost to the national communities comprising the federation?

• Under what conditions does linguistic or cultural diversity create an impetus to the decentralization or even the fragmentation of states, both unitary and federal; and can a decentralized form of federalism provide an adequate response—and a stable solution—to internal conflict among ethnic, linguistic, or cultural communities, especially if regionally concentrated?

• What effects may processes of international economic and political integration have on the domestic politics and/or constitutional structure of linguistically or culturally diverse states participating in the integration process?

These three issues are directly addressed at the conclusion of the chapter, but are first explored through a review of some features of Canada's recent political or constitutional troubles (which seem likely to persist for some time to come).

2. FEDERALIZATION

Federalization is a process leading to a federal form of government for a given political community, or covering a given territory. Without attempting to explore the variety of constitutional forms that may sensibly be described as 'federal', the following characteristics appear as essential: the existence of a layered regime in which at least two orders of government exist, each with a significant set of powers and responsibilities, neither being subordinate to the other, and each (correspondingly) having its own electoral and fiscal base. Thus 'federalization' is a process tending towards a stated result—but from a starting-point that has not been specified.

Usually the context makes clear what the antecedent condition is, and therefore what kind of process is involved. Thus, if I write about 'the federalization of South Africa' it is clear that I am imagining a process of decentralization through which a set of autonomous and relatively powerful regional governments are created. On the other hand federalization can equally well refer to a process of centralization or political integration. For example, in writing about the aftermath of the American revolutionary war, federalization could only mean converting a weak confederal system into a much stronger federal one: a process binding the thirteen former colonies into 'a more perfect union'.

The phrase 'federalizing Europe', however, is mired in ambiguity. The most obvious meaning is the one that evokes the possible transformation of the European Union into a federation. Presumably that would involve political centralization. There would be an accelerated and perhaps open-ended process in which power was transferred from the governments of the Member States to Union institutions. However, more than increased centralization would be required to turn the EU into a federation. Indeed, Union competences are already quite extensive, and will be further extended under the Maastricht Treaty; but the structures and processes, even as envisaged in the Treaty, are still essentially confederal rather than federal. The EU's primary decision-making body remains the Council of Ministers or, intermittently, the European Council: Europe today is a Europe of baronies, not yet (as it were) of royal power. None the less, a great deal is accomplished within an institutional framework that offers multiple opportunities for deadlock, and where one might expect *immobilisme* to be the rule.

Notwithstanding the post-1985 dynamism of the Community, the present structures may soon prove inadequate. First, the frequently referred-to 'democratic deficit' (a non-elected Commission; a Council of Ministers that, at least hitherto, has met in secret) is becoming less and less acceptable as the activities of the Union expand. Second, a set of institutions designed for a six-member Community are subjected to added strains as the number of Member States increases. Under any further expansion of membership, the Council of Ministers could become too unwieldy to continue exercising its present functions. Third, the fiscal burdens of the Union may take a quantum leap, partly as a result of the building of 'social Europe', and partly as a result of economic assistance that the Union may be more or less forced to offer (for security reasons if no others) to several Eastern European countries. If the budget were to expand much beyond the present level of about 1.2 per cent of GNP, demands for more direct public control over, and participation in, Union decision-making could well become irresistible.

In the present European context, then, the creation of new central institutions—even more than the process of centralization—is arguably the essence of federalization. In other words, federalization should be seen as comprising not simply a drift of governmental functions to Brussels, but even more fundamentally, a process of democratization. Decisions applying across the whole territory of the European Union might, for example, become more effectively subject to popular control by placing the European Parliament at the centre of the legislative process and by transforming the Commission into a genuine political executive subject to far-reaching control by the Parliament. A complementary step would be to free the budget from the control of the Member States. In these ways institutions of the Union could become more solidly anchored in their own electoral and fiscal base. And that would, by definition, transform the present confederal structure of the Union into a federal one.

Adding that federalizing Europe could mean the devolution of powers and thus responsibilities to regional goverments, too, federalization has to be understood as a complex, multi-dimensional process. As noted, the following elements may play a part: the centralization of governmental functions on a supra-national basis; the simultaneous decentralization of existing national states (with the consequence that they lose power in two directions, both upwards and downwards); the drawing in of new states, not necessarily on a full-membership basis, resulting in the gradual or perhaps rapid accretion of territory; and the redesign, especially the democratization, of central political institutions. Presumably these elements create a dynamic, integrated process, and do not simply represent a set of parallel lines of development. Centralization, for example, may demand democratization; but equally, democratization, by legitimizing central authority, may facilitate or lead to greater centralization.

3. CULTURAL COSTS AND BENEFITS

A federalized Europe would be a Europe in which the process of economic integration continues along the track laid out in the Treaty of Rome and subsequent modifications to it, notably the Single European Act and the Maastricht Treaty. One fundamental purpose of the integration process is (as it has been all along) to realize the economic benefits flowing from the extension of markets—even though, as shown in the previous chapter, the extent to which aggregate economic benefits actually accrue will depend on the institutional design adopted. As was also shown there, the geographical distribution or redistribution of the benefits that may be achieved through integration will also be affected by the institutional structure. In both respects federalization may be instrumental to achieving desired outcomes, as a federal form of government presumably has a greater policy capacity than a confederal one. Also relevant, of course, is the fact that a decentralized form of government can operate more efficiently, and can better respond to citizens' preferences and needs, in respect of those governmental functions that can be effectively performed at the local level, and do not have significant neighbourhood or spill-over effects.

A new dimension to the costs-and-benefits calculus is opened up when one takes into account the role of government in giving expression to, and thus reinforcing, collective identities. Fundamental social values, as well as principles of inclusion and exclusion (drawing the boundaries of community, defining citizenship) are at stake here. The issues are qualitatively different from economic ones; they have to do with community and culture, or the emergence and preservation, development and decline, of national and ethnic communities.

Through most and perhaps all of Western Europe, the state has historically been the primary instrument through which national identities have been created. As the feudal order decayed, emerging nation-states incorporated within their boundaries a number of ethnic or cultural communities ('ethnies'), which eventually came to share common myths and historical memories, a common or mass culture, a common economy, and common legal rights and duties for all members. These, as Anthony Smith has noted, are the characteristics of nationhood. Smith writes:

Though most latter-day nations are, in fact, polyethnic, or rather most nation-states are polyethnic, many have been formed in the first place around a dominant *ethnie* which annexed or attracted other *ethnies* or ethnic fragments into the state to which it gave a name and a cultural charter [character?].[2]

If the instrument of this historical process has been the state, its agent has usually been what Smith calls a 'lateral ethnie', an upper stratum of society that initially consisted of a warrior class clustered around a ruling house, such as the dukes of Normandy. At a later stage of development, the lateral ethnie typically came to include an aristocracy, the higher clergy, high military officials, bureaucrats, and wealthy merchants. Through processes of administrative, economic, and cultural change, outlying regions and their ethnies

and middle and lower classes were incorporated into the dominant lateral ethnic culture through the agency of the bureaucratic state. The creation of secular, mass nations was ultimately the outcome of a vigorous programme of political socialization through the public, mass education system. But it was long preceded by the more gradual dissemination of an aristocratic ethnic culture and its transmutation into a more truly national culture: one that was civic as well as ethnic, and also socially inclusive, in line with the extension of civil and legal rights to wider segments of the kingdom.[3]

The process of cultural accretion, however, has a double aspect. As Walker Connor has insisted, nation-building is also nation-destroying: non-dominant ethnies have become ethnic fragments that have been subject to assimilation, whether through coercion, or attraction, or both together.[4] Some of these marginalized communities have disappeared entirely; others, while in a condition of passive subordination for a time, have subsequently been mobilized, both politically and culturally, under the leadership of artists and intellectuals. In these cases genealogy has been more important than territory as a defining characteristic of the (ethnic) nation, although its emergence or re-emergence has typically involved laying claim to a historic homeland, and identification with its 'sacred' forests and rivers, its mountains, lakes, and plains. However, notwithstanding the appeals of place, ethnic nations have been primarily communities of common descent, with a membership that has tended to be exclusive, non-voluntary, and in some cases all-pervasive.

The proto-typical ethnic nations—contrasting with territorial ones, built up around a lateral ethnie, but ultimately socially inclusive—have been non-European. However, to quote Anthony Smith once again:

Even in the West and the 'old, continuous nations' of Europe, ethnonationalism has renewed itself. Since the 1960s a third wave of ethnic movements for autonomy or separation has swept through much of Western Europe, reaching Yugoslavia, Romania, Poland, and the Soviet Union. Perhaps the earliest manifestations of this particular wave could be found in Canada, among the Quebecois [Québécois], and in the United States, among the Southern Blacks and later the Indians and Hispanics. On the other hand a good many of the European ethno-nationalisms (for example, the Catalan, Basque, Breton, Scots, Welsh and Flemish movements) were pre-war in origin, with cultural antecedents reaching back in some cases to the 1880s.[5]

Present-day movements for regional autonomy or separation call for the remodelling of the European state system to endow regionally concentrated ethnic minorities with an effective political instrument for their future development as communities with their own value-systems and institutions. Federalization of existing unitary states is one of the options, or a possible device. The autonomy that minorities thereby acquire may be all they need to follow the trajectory earlier traced by emerging territorial nations, in which the state was the essential instrument of nation-building. However, what cannot be known is whether the federalization of multi-ethnic unitary states would be a temporary pause along a route leading to eventual break-up, or a stable political arrangement giving the relevant communities adequate scope to develop as culturally distinct entities, while remaining in some respects an integral part of the territorial nation within which they have historically been encompassed.

From the perspective of those committed to the persistence of the existing state system (General de Gaulle's 'Europe des patries'), the federalization of Europe may seem doubly threatening. The downward or decentralization aspect of the federalization process may threaten eventual dismemberment of culturally or ethnically diverse states, while the upward or centralizing aspect will indubitably result in loss of national control over a wide range of matters hitherto subject to national decision. The latter effect, of course, is deliberate in some degree: partial 'pooling of sovereignty' is required for the integration of markets, which is presumed to bring economic benefits and thus a higher degree of economic specialization and correspondingly greater economic efficiency. The question, however, is: at what cultural cost? What erosion of national distinctiveness, what weakening of national institutions, what dilution of national values results?

'National', in this context, need not have anything to do with ethnicity—certainly not with race or genealogy, and perhaps not even with attributes such as language or religion. But 'national' does very much have to do with the existence of community and, in a democratic society, with shared citizenship. Common ancestry (actual or mythical), a common language, and common religious traditions may of course give rise to or may support a sense of community, but ultimately it is a shared value-system and a degree of social affinity or mutuality that is its defining characteristic. Equality of rights, entitlements, and obligations are the touchstones of such attitudes, and are the essence of a common citizenship.

Rights, entitlements, and obligations are the civic expression of a value-system that, together with characteristic modes of cognition and communication, make up a national culture. This is not to suggest that such rights, entitlements, and obligations concern uniquely the relationship between the individual and the state, or between the individual and the community through the state; rather, the whole institutional framework of the society supports these attributes of citizenship and the underlying value-system. An excellent example is the set of interlocking institutions and practices that establish a certain relationship between employer and employee, and indeed create a market society within which the categories 'employer' and 'employee' have a certain meaning and a specific set of status or role connotations. The culture defines the expectations that each has of the other; and the institutional framework for industrial relations—a framework that to some extent is created by law—codifies and perpetuates those expectations. Similarly, the system of social security (the means through which a society defines entitlements and obligations, setting up a relationship between the economically self-sufficient and the economically dependent) is a composite set of practices arising out of family ties, charitable and religious organizations, defined obligations of employer towards employee (minimum wage, attention to occupational health and safety, minimum notice of dismissal, retirement pensions), and collective measures for income support and social services: all these are implemented through or incorporated into law, which in turn reflects and shapes national values, or national cultures.

In sum, community values are embodied in and indeed nourished by a whole institutional structure, described by some as 'civil society', as if existing apart from and even in opposition to the state, but in fact also supported by—and to some extent an emanation of—government. It is thus axiomatic that political arrangements, including the location of national boundaries and the creation of linkages among political units (whether through treaty or federal constitution) will ramify through other social institutions, having significant cultural effects and implications. Being fully cognizant of this is the key to understanding, or estimating, the cultural costs and benefits of federalization.

In this light, let us consider the process of federalization within or across a given territory, and the cultural costs and benefits it may entail. As noted earlier, we shall have to distinguish upward from downward federalization—that is, to take account of antecedent political arrangements, whether these are (a) a unitary state, or (b) a grouping of independent states, or a confederal association of states. We shall also, consistently with the immediately preceding discussion, want to distinguish three quite different situations pertaining to the cultural attributes of the population; namely, whether the population is (a) culturally homogeneous (b) composed of distinct cultural communities distinguished by attributes such as ethnicity, religion, or language, or (c) encompassing various regional communities that are socially inclusive, even if regional attachments are supported by appeals to historical myth and, for most, common ethnic origins and linguistic traditions. While these distinctions are perhaps too schematic or lacking in detail and nuance, one may none the less obtain a first approximation of the cultural costs and benefits of federalization by constructing a matrix that classifies cases according to the two factors mentioned; namely, antecedent political arrangements and cultural attributes of the population. The matrix (see Fig. 7.1) represents the probable balance of cultural costs and benefits in the six types of case that our categories identify. In all cases, cultural costs and benefits are wholly subjective, and reflect perceptions of how the process of federalization bears upon the preservation, development, or attrition of the community that the individual person most strongly identifies with.

In the matrix, cell 1 may be empty. There may simply be no cases of a unitary state with a culturally homogeneous population where federalization is anything more than an abstract theoretical possibility. Italy may fall into this category. The case is ambiguous, given the importance of regional identities, regional dialects which are not mutually comprehensible, and regional differences in attitudes towards the state.[6] These cultural differences (non-homogeneity)

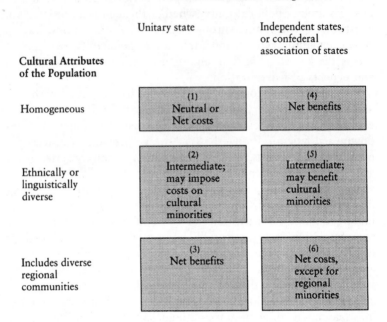

FIG. 7.1. Federalization: probable balance of cultural costs and benefits

suggest that it may not be at all appropriate to classify Italy as a 'type 1' case (unitary–homogeneous). On the other hand, cultural diversity appears to be less marked among the élite than at the popular level, suggesting that support for regionalization (and ultimately, perhaps, for federalization) is not culturally motivated and would have slight cultural effects or consequences. However, to the extent that such effects did occur as a result of federalization—or developments tending in that direction—it is likely that Italy's industrial north would tend increasingly to absorb or exhibit those cultural patterns that seem to typify the most economically advanced regions throughout the European Union, a sort of international European culture of entrepreneurship and the market. One could also imagine potentially corrosive effects on the traditional culture(s) of the rest of Italy, given that relatively wealthy, economically dynamic populations tend to exercise a degree of attraction over poorer, more conservative neighbouring populations, especially in the absence of language differences or other segregating characteristics. Hence, for type 1 cases, it is suggested that federalization would either be neutral as regards cultural effects, or would entail, potentially, some cultural costs (i.e. some loss of regional or national distinctiveness).

Cell no. 2 concerns unitary states that encompass two or more cultural communities—ethnic, religious, or linguistic. Belgium is an obvious example, with its three linguistic communities (Dutch and French, plus the much smaller German community); the communities live, for the most part, in their own well-demarcated regions, but overlap in the Brussels area, which makes up about 10 per cent of the population.[7] Such regional concentration, with mixed populations in border areas, is surely typical of multi-ethnic states, although of course in such states the geographic concentration or dispersal of the ethnies varies considerably from case to case. Thus the federalization of such states, if originally unitary, will create a set of regional units each of which will be, in all likelihood, controlled by a specific group or cultural community. As a result (but to an extent depending on the scope of governmental powers exercised by the regional units) these communities will be able to create and support a network of institutions consonant with their values or culture. On the other hand, the effect may be quite the opposite for regional minorities. To the extent that, in any region, a numerically preponderant group acted in an exclusionary or nationalistic manner—we are talking here of ethnic nationalism, not territorial nationalism—minority groups would pay a price, whether economic, or cultural, or both. However, this is not a necessary or inevitable outcome; federalization might come about in a form that provided effective guarantees of civil liberties and promoted widespread tolerance of ethnic and cultural differences. In fact, with different groups forming majorities in different regions, consociational-type[8] bargains might be struck among the élites, giving effective protection to all minorities, and encouraging a live-and-let-live attitude across the whole system. The possibilities are multiple. Thus type 2 cases have indeterminate cultural costs and benefits. Although that is a conclusion some may find unsatisfactory, it is none the less helpful, for it emphasizes the extent to which outcomes may depend on the particular form that federalization takes in any given case. The Belgian reforms of the 1980s, setting up both community councils and regional governments, each with a distinctive role and powers, are a particularly interesting example of institutional innovation to deal with the minorities issue.

Cell no. 3, like cell no. 2, concerns unitary states encompassing two or more cultural communities; but type 3 cases are ones where the communities are defined at least as much by territory as by ethnicity, language, or religion. Ethnicity and its attributes may facilitate the political mobilization of a regional community, even when non-cultural factors such as economic grievance apparently form the main basis for regional sentiment. Indeed, ethno-nationalism, with its strong emphasis on the possession of a traditional homeland, may be a significant force; but if so, the absorption of newcomers and the working out of a *modus vivendi* with cultural minorities are typical features. In type 3 cases, regionalism tends to exist as a phenomenon analogous to territorial nationalism, as a movement that is socially inclusive, and is built on a strong territorial identification that reflects a common history, and quite possibly expresses a (perceived) common economic interest. Examples would be Scottish, Breton, and Catalan nationalism. As a response to such peripheral nationalisms, the federalization of a unitary state may bring real cultural benefits to those groups that have felt sidelined by the emergence of nation-states; federalization may both accommodate and support the development of regional communities, as in 'the old, continuous nations' of Europe. (This may also be the appropriate perspective to take on regionalism in Italy; Italy may be a type 3—unitary–regionally diverse—case, rather than a type 1 case, which is unitary–homogeneous.) Be that as it may, the question arises whether, in such cases, there will also be costs associated with the process of federalization, and who will bear them. There may be diffuse cultural costs, as the over-mature nation-state is weakened by the reappearance of internal divisions; and there may be quite specific economic costs, borne by the fiscally weakest and most economically vulnerable regions, if the national market is disrupted and/or if interregional redistribution diminishes as a result of the dismantling of national policies for social welfare. But, if such costs can be kept in check by appropriate institutional arrangements, the federalization of an already regionalized society may be thought to bring net cultural benefits.

The remaining cases are ones of upward federalization, where either a grouping of independent states or a confederal association of states undergoes a process of political integration, making the transition to federalism.

Cell no. 4 represents cases where federalization brings together a culturally homogeneous population. The obvious example is the recent reunification of the former East and West Germany (though some would query the cultural homogeneity of these two entities after almost two generations of Communist rule in the former GDR). Whatever one may say of this, it is clear that the motive for reunification was to re-create a community forcibly kept asunder over four decades; and one must assume that most Germans, east and west, anticipated a net cultural benefit.

Cell no. 5 encompasses cases where several states, some of them—Belgium and Switzerland, say—containing distinct ethnies or cultural communities come together to form a federation; the states may, or may not, already be linked within a confederal association such as the present European Union. In the process of federalization, it is likely that both cultural costs and cultural benefits will accrue, though to different groups. To the extent that dominant groups are less able than in the past to shape or control a network of social institutions, the values and cultural patterns embodied in those institutions may be diluted. On the other hand, there may be real benefits for ethnic and linguistic minorities, which may find support for their collective rights through constitutional instruments and/or the spread of a political culture characterized by a high degree of tolerance of diversity and approval of bargaining and compromise as a mode of decision-making. In other words, within each of the states, the control of previously dominant groups may be somewhat diminished through their participation in a more complex political system that respects and guarantees minority (group) rights. All this is hypothetical of course: it depends on the form of federation that is brought into being, and on the political structures and political conventions that preceded it. Thus both the costs and the benefits of federalization may be small, or may be counterbalancing; the net effect is indeterminate. However, if there are any clear net winners, they are likely to be the minorities within each of the member states of the new or emerging federation.

The cases that are grouped into cell no. 6 are ones where diverse populations, each regionally concentrated and controlling its own state apparatus, are brought together within a federation.

• Some of the states joining together in a federation may be relatively homogeneous, exhibiting only slight regional diversity in cultural patterns, as (for example) in the case of Denmark and

Ireland. We may presume that the states (along with others) have agreed on federalization in order to achieve some combination of economic and security benefits, and have knowingly accepted some loss of control over policy formation and over the institutional structure of their respective societies. In other words, they have agreed to give up some of their capacity to do as they want, or to act consistently with their own preferences and values; they have implicitly acknowledged that in the federalization process, non-cultural benefits must be traded off against cultural costs.

• A more complex situation arises within those states, such as Spain and (arguably) the UK, that contain a number of distinct regional or regional/ethnic communities. In each of these states, the dominant group (if there is one) presumably agrees to incur some cultural costs from joining with other states in a new federal framework. In other words, one may posit that these groups anticipate reaping non-cultural (economic or security) benefits from union, and accept the need for (or inevitability of) the sort of trade-off just referred to. On the other hand, for other groups—the peripheral cultures, one might say—federalization promises considerable cultural benefits, as well as non-cultural ones. These groups may be able to bargain for or simply to assert substantial autonomy *vis-à-vis* the dominant group, without exposing themselves to military or security risks, and without losing the benefits of full integration within a large economic union. This, of course, is not guaranteed, or automatic; but the potential is there.

The federalization of Europe is represented by no single cell within our matrix, but by all of them together—except perhaps for cell no. 1, which (as discussed) may be empty. Three major conclusions may be drawn from considering the many facets of federalization as highlighted in the matrix and through the ensuing exposition of the situations typified by each of the cells.

First, it is almost certainly impossible to aggregate the costs and benefits of federalization (considering these in their cultural dimension), because costs and benefits are inherently subjective. One must always ask, 'Costs imposed on whom?', and 'Benefits accruing to whom?' When different groups are involved, the balancing of costs and benefits becomes impossible. This problem was underplayed in our discussion of net costs or benefits in each of the cells; it is a vastly greater problem when one must consider all situations (cells) together. There appears to be no solution to the problem of aggregation analogous to that provided by the concept of Pareto optimality in welfare economics. (Pareto optimality supplies the theoretical basis for assessing costs and benefits from an economics perspective—although even in this limited sense, its applicability has been questioned.[9])

Second, even if one could solve the problem of aggregation, it is evident that the cultural effects of federalizing Europe cannot be explored simply by examining what transpires within each of the categories that has been identified, and then adding them up. As has already been noted, federalization, at least in the European context, is a dynamic process involving a complex interrelationship between the downward federalization of unitary states and the upward federalization of existing nation-states. The matrix has explored some of the diversity within the two (or five or six) types of case; but in fact, there is only one case at hand, which is both historically situated and multi-faceted. One understands each aspect of the process by situating it in context with the rest.

Finally, the cultural costs and benefits of federalization do not differ only with reference to the variety of groups and situations involved, but according to the particular form of federal state(s) that emerge(s). For example, minority ethnic or linguistic groups will be affected by the guarantees of minority rights, both individual and collective, that may be included in a constitution or otherwise established, say through convention. In addition, the range of powers vested in, respectively, the central and regional-state governments will do much to determine the degree of control that the various cultural communities succeed in exercising over those policies and institutions that most pervasively affect their identities. And, to take a third example, the structure of central institutions—as well as the patterns of intergovernmental relations that are built up—will also have pervasive effects on the vitality of national, regional, and ethno-linguistic cultures.

The preceding discussion points more to the complexity of the situation we wish to review than to any sweeping generalizations about the cultural costs and benefits inherent in the federalization process. In fact our analysis suggests mainly that it would be desirable to reformulate the problem—not to abandon the exercise, but to adapt it. Rather than dwelling on the cultural benefits and the cultural costs that may be inherent in federalization, or even

asking how to maximize cultural benefits for some, while minimizing cultural costs for others, both the cultural costs and the cultural
benefits (for different groups) will usefully be seen in relation to
non-cultural issues. The most pertinent question becomes: what
features of a federal regime will go furthest towards realizing the
non-cultural benefits of a large state, while achieving (or retaining)
the cultural benefits of a small one? (Even here, one must take
account of the fact that for ethnic minorities within regionalized
states, participation in a larger political entity may be beneficial.)
Or, to address more specifically the present European dilemma: to
what extent is it possible to achieve through upward federalization
a set of non-cultural (primarily economic) benefits at minimal cultural cost, and to achieve through downward federalization a set of
cultural benefits without entailing non-cultural (economic and security) costs?

   In thinking about these questions, it may be helpful to draw on
comparative material from the Canadian case, for Canada illustrates in a particularly dramatic way the dynamics of federalism, a
form of government that everywhere appears to be evolving either
in a centralizing or decentralizing direction. If we can understand
better some of the forces at play in a case of especially rapid change,
it may help us understand better the federalization process in
Europe, in both its upward and its downward aspects.

4. FEDERALISM: COSTS AND BENEFITS—CANADA AND EUROPE

Canada presents the case of a federal state in danger of collapse, in
that Quebec—a province comprising about one-quarter of the
population, and the only province to have a French-speaking
(francophone) majority—threatens to secede. If it does so, the rest
of Canada could also splinter into several parts.

   For reasons that will be described below, Quebec governments
have been demanding greater constitutional powers since the early
1960s. In a 1980 referendum, 40 per cent of Quebec voters supported the objective of 'sovereignty-association', a formula under
which an independent Quebec would preserve its economic ties to
'Canada'. However, the referendum outcome was a defeat for the
Parti Québécois government; and, with the wind in its sails, the

federal government took the constitutional initiative. After intense wrangling it persuaded nine provinces—all but Quebec—to support a set of constitutional amendments (1982). The two major changes were: (a) 'patriation' of the constitution (that is, the transfer of the amending power to Canada, ending the British parliament's ultimate control over Canadian constitutional change—a step proposed by Britain in 1931, but never agreed to because of Canadians' inability to agree upon a suitable amending formula), and (b) the insertion of a Charter of Rights and Freedoms into the constitution. In both respects the precise terms of the changes were unacceptable to the PQ government, and indeed to the official opposition, the provincial Liberal Party. None the less, the changes were incorporated into a Constitution Act, 1982, the last set of constitutional changes in Canada to be passed by the British parliament. The irony was that Quebec had been able to put constitutional issues on the agenda, but was the only province to emerge from the process a clear loser.

In 1987, responding to demands put forward by a new (Liberal) Quebec government, the Prime Minister of Canada and all provincial premiers agreed on a package of constitutional amendments known as the Meech Lake Accord, reconciling Quebec to a modified constitutional order. However, ratification was not secured within the prescribed three-year time period, and the Accord collapsed.[10] Opinion polls in Quebec indicated that sovereignty—at least if brought about without causing rupture of the economic union—would have commanded majority support among the electorate. Under the pressure of Quebec opinion a new attempt at reaching federal–provincial agreement was made. However, this time the demands of other provinces, and of aboriginal peoples and other groups, were also reflected in a broad set of reforms. Unanimous agreement among First Ministers was reached in August 1992 (the 'Charlottetown Agreement'), but two months later the Charlottetown agreement was rejected by a wide margin, both in Quebec and in most other provinces, in a Canada-wide referendum. Constitutional reform has now, therefore, reached an impasse. Break-up is a real possibility, particularly in view of the fact that the present government of Quebec (the PQ) is committed to outright independence, although it still assumes that 'Canada' will have no option but to negotiate an economic union, essentially on Quebec's terms.[11] However, indefinite prolongation of the formal status quo—implying the continuing evolution of the federation within the existing constitutional framework—is not to be ruled out.

Enquiry into the background of these events, and into some of the issues arising in the constitutional reform process during 1965–92, may shed light on the question whether federalism can confer various benefits typically associated with political union, without entailing excessive cultural costs. This formulation of the issue accords with attitudes apparently widely shared within Quebec, where very few francophones endorse federalism as a politically superior form of government, or as a constitutional arrangement desirable on any grounds other than economic ones.[12] Those who are committed to the federalist option tend to argue that it is worthwhile for economic reasons alone, or even that it is 'profitable', while *souverainistes* argue that the political and cultural costs of federalism are high, and that its supposed benefits can be achieved by negotiating some form of economic association instead. Thus, at least among francophones, the perspective of *fédéralistes* and *souverainistes* is similar, but opinions differ regarding the trade-offs that must be made between economic and cultural objectives. Thus judgements on the desirability of federalism vary. The moderate nationalists—the dominant force within the Quebec Liberal Party—argue that federalism is, on balance, preferable so long as Quebec gains added power within the federal system; but most say the present federal structure is unacceptable.

The difficulty that Canada is now experiencing in containing secessionist forces in Quebec raises at least two interesting questions about the cultural dimension of the process of federalizing Europe. Both arise from the fact that Canada appears to be in danger of breaking up because of the discontents of the francophone majority in Quebec. The first question is: if cultural and linguistic diversity in Canada creates such difficulties for the federal system, would not the far greater diversity among the nation-states of Europe act to prevent the transformation of the EC into a federation? Or could a European federation be designed in such a way as to avoid all but the most minimal cultural costs, thus reducing opposition to the federalization process? The second question is: does Canada's experience of living at the knife-edge of dissolution suggest any lessons for individual European states that are experiencing demands for decentralization or federalization—and in particular, for Belgium, Spain, and Italy? (The issue here is whether comparative analysis helps one understand particular cases better, and whether Canada is a useful case for comparison.) With these two broad questions in mind, the following aspects of the Canadian situation will be reviewed:

• linguistic and cultural dualism, the rejection of dualism by many Canadians, and the bearing this has on pressures for decentralization or for Quebec's secession;

• the allocation of governmental roles and responsibilities between orders of government, and the feasibility of distinguishing social and cultural matters from economic ones;

• how Quebec's secession would affect linguistic and cultural minorities;

• American economic dominance as a potential cultural threat to Canada or for Canadians, and the relevance of this factor to the future of Canadian federalism.

Linguistic and Cultural Dualism

Québécois tend to see Canada as a political framework for the co-existence of two cultural communities, distinguished not only by language but by the multiple characteristics of an ethnie, of which language is the clearest identifier and the primary mobilizing force. There is historical justification for viewing Canada in dualist terms, but demographic change and shifts in public attitudes in 'English Canada' challenge this characterization. Conflict between dualist and more broadly pluralist perceptions of Canada is a source of political tension, and a major contributor to Canada's present constitutional difficulties.

Canada may well be unique in its origins as a federal state, in that the original step in the federalization process ('Confederation', 1867) involved both the partial unification of three formerly separate colonies, and also the division of one of them, the Province of Canada, into two parts (Quebec and Ontario): out of three British colonies was formed a four-province federation.[13] This nucleus was expanded shortly afterwards through the purchase of territory, most of which was subsequently carved up into new provinces or annexed to existing ones, and through the accretion of other British colonies. By 1871 the new Dominion stretched from the Atlantic to the Pacific, and upward to the Arctic Ocean; its present structure was completed through the subsequent addition of other British possessions in North America, most recently Newfoundland (1949).

For the French-speaking 'Fathers of Confederation'—whose active involvement was essential to the creation of Canada in its present form—Confederation was significant in cultural terms for two interrelated reasons. First, it conferred upon the Catholic, French-speaking majority in the future province of Quebec the capacity to develop as a self-governing community. Quebec became, of course, part of a federal union in which the central government controlled economic development and defence (with Britain, for a time, also retaining the power to make treaties); however, social and cultural affairs, including legislative jurisdiction affecting the institutions that pre-dated the British conquest of New France (1760), were provincial. Second, as a nation-building enterprise with explicitly transcontinental ambitions, Confederation held out the promise of the development of a bi-national state occupying the northern half of the continent. The descendants of the French settlers formed a substantial minority, though with only slight political influence, within the province of New Brunswick, which is located to the east and south of Quebec. More importantly, in the only significant settlement in the prairie region, in what became Manitoba, a racially mixed group (French–Indian, generally known as *métis*) comprised about half the population: it was hoped that this group would grow through the influx of settlers from Quebec, creating future prairie provinces in which the Catholic, French-speaking population shared equal rights and equal political influence with those of British origin. Thus, disregarding the aboriginal population (as was typical of the time), Canada was at its inception a federation that promised to develop as a dualist or bi-communal country—or so at least it appeared to its Catholic–French political leaders. However, as is well known, the Catholic–French population (or now, simply, the francophone community) flourished only within Quebec and, to a lesser extent, in the adjacent territory of New Brunswick and Ontario.

Today, about 80 per cent of Canada's francophones[14] live in Quebec, a province in which they predominate by a four-to-one margin. Of the other nine provinces, only New Brunswick has a significant proportion of francophones (about 30 per cent); Ontario, a much larger province, has an absolutely larger number of French-speaking residents, although they represent only about 4 per cent of the provincial population. Elsewhere the number and percentage of francophones are small and declining.

Since about the mid-1960s issues of language and culture in Canada have been partly about majority–minority relations, but even more about the relationship between the two linguistic majorities: the anglophone majority in Canada as a whole, and the francophone majority in Quebec. Federal language policy has laid great emphasis on protecting and extending the rights of official-language minorities (anglophones in Quebec, francophones elsewhere), but the thrust of federal policy has merely underlined the difference in perspective between the Government of Canada and the Government of Quebec. The latter has, within limits prescribed by the Constitution, pursued a policy of official unilingualism. It has also presented the language difference as simply the most visible element in a 'unique, original' Quebec culture, which makes Québécois want to shape their own future as a distinct society—as most provincial élites insist they will do, whether within Canada or outside it. The Quebec government declares that the distinctiveness of Québéc must and will be reflected in all aspects of policy, albeit within certain limitations, which are now the subject of the sovereignty debate. While some observers persist in seeing Quebec nationalism as a self-serving ideology to deepen the privileges of existing governmental and other élites, it is clear that for many Québécois the issue is assimilation: to succumb or to resist.

With every decennial census, the data indicate further linguistic polarization by territory, or the development of linguistically homogeneous communities. The official-language minorities are increasingly concentrated in shrinking enclaves. As a result of the large-scale influx of non-British, non-French immigrants, 'multicultural groups' now comprise (together with their descendants) a high percentage of the population in all major urban centres in Canada, including Montreal. In Ontario and all the western provinces these groups substantially outnumber those of French origin, let alone those who remain francophone. In addition, Canadians are now much more aware than in the past of the presence of aboriginal peoples, and of their desire to develop in culturally distinctive ways. For these reasons, Canadians outside Quebec are increasingly resistant to viewing Canada in dualist terms.

Quebec now comprises slightly more than one-quarter of the Canadian population. This percentage has been dropping steadily in recent years as a result of a falling birth-rate;[15] high rates of immigration, especially to Ontario, British Columbia, and Alberta, have also been a significant factor in altering the balance of regional forces within the federation.

These developments have tended to place Quebec on the defensive, or to renew fears of cultural assimilation as a result of its constituting a tiny minority, about 2 per cent, on the North American continent. In spite of demographic change, dualism remains for most francophone Québécois the essence of Canada. As their political weight within the federation appears to face decline, it becomes all the more important that dualism be reflected in constitutional structures. Simple majoritarianism on a Canada-wide basis, and a form of federalism in which Quebec is simply one province among ten, are a threat. Hence the claim to broader powers for Quebec, and (for many Quebecois, but clearly not all) to an equal say in Canadian decisions that, if made on a majoritarian basis, will override Quebec's interests every time. Without equality, arrived at through consensual decision-making—a Calhounian 'concurrent majority' rule, or a consociational form of democracy—Canada appears to some as a framework for domination, not partnership.

We return, in light of this situation, to our earlier question, whether Canadian experience suggests that the much greater cultural diversity among the EC states is likely to prevent its transformation into a federation. The answer appears to be no. There is obviously deep opposition to the homogenizing effects of economic and political integration through the Maastricht Treaty and other instruments, but linguistic and cultural diversity, as such, do not appear to be of greatest concern. It is not the persistence of specific ethnies but the continuing diversity of territorial communities or nation-states, that is evidently at stake. In any case, dualism—implying a majority–minority situation, and the potential for domination rather than pluralist power-sharing—is evidently not the relevant factor, as one considers the prospects for upward federalization. Member States (or their populations: those outside the ranks of the political and economic élites) may be worried about political autonomy, or the continued possession of sovereign powers; but there is a big difference between reduced autonomy and threatened linguistic or cultural assimilation. Assimilation is not an issue in a Community of twelve states with nine national languages, all with official status, and none coming close to being a majority language. The political dynamics of a twelve-member grouping are surely very different from those of a structure that, while containing ten provinces, tends none the less to be perceived by a quarter of its population in dualist terms.

On the other hand the relevance of the Canadian case, and the discontents of Quebec, may be much greater as regards downward federalization, or as regards the decentralization of some of the existing European states, whether or not federalization is envisaged at this time. Dualism and the bearing it has on political attitudes are evidently producing considerable difficulties for Belgium; inter-ethnic conflict may potentially create similar difficulties in Spain. These are matters explored in other contributions to this volume. In this chapter we note that the political fallout from ethnic differences points to another question of importance, where Canadian experience may be of relevance to the federalization of Europe. That is the question of the adaptation of institutional structures to accommodate linguistic and cultural differences, whether in a dualist pattern or a pattern characterized by a multiplicity of ethnies, regional communities, and nation-states.

The Allocation of Governmental Roles and Responsibilities

The Confederation settlement has conventionally been understood to have made a clear distinction between those matters which were of economic and military significance on the one hand, and those of cultural or social significance on the other; the former were allocated to the federal government, and the latter to the provinces. However, this pattern has not persisted. Both orders of government have expanded their activities, producing overlaps in federal and provincial roles, and resulting in supplementation, duplication, and conflict.

During or just after the Second World War, the federal government assumed a leadership position in creating the Canadian welfare state, relying mainly on its superior fiscal resources to do so. In the 1950s it began to offer fiscal support to universities and to various cultural organizations or arts groups. Its language policy, dating from the late 1960s, has supported the development of Canada as a bilingual country; and in 1982 minority language rights were written into the Canadian Charter of Rights and Freedoms, entrenched in the constitution in that year over the objections of Quebec (which feared the Charter's politically homogenizing effect).

These encroachments on areas of provincial responsibility have been resisted by Quebec and (less consistently) by other provincial governments. Until the Quiet Revolution of the 1960s, Quebec's stance was defensive. To protect the traditional culture of French Canada, provincial governments from the 1930s to the 1950s followed a strategy of withdrawal that involved affirming provincial autonomy within the Canadian federation even though, as Pierre Trudeau (not yet himself involved in electoral politics) polemically asserted, 'they [i.e. Quebec governments] barely exercised many of the powers given to them by the autonomy they so loudly affirmed.'[16] Thus, through the first half of the present century, Quebec governments restricted the growth of the Quebec state and sought to strengthen the social role of traditional institutions, notably the Roman Catholic Church—while at the same time acquiescing in anglophone (Canadian and American) control of the Quebec economy. However, this pattern ended after the Québécois began to recognize, during the 1950s, that a strategy of withdrawal could not be effective in counteracting the attractive power of a much wealthier, dynamic, and materialistic anglophone culture, dominant throughout North America.

Since about 1960, Quebec has become an aggressively materialistic, growth-oriented society, at first relying heavily on the role of an active Quebec state, and more recently on a class of entrepreneurs whose careers have tended to cross and re-cross the nearly invisible boundary between the public and private sectors. Quebec engineering and business schools are bursting at the seams, and Quebec entrepreneurs are increasingly oriented towards continental and global markets. Much of the support for the 1989 Canadian–American free trade agreement (FTA) came from Quebec, in contrast to Ontario, where public opinion was much more deeply divided and the provincial government was hostile.

Quebec nationalism is anything but inward-looking today; and

Quebec nationalists (which means virtually the entire francophone élite) are realistic enough to recognize that everywhere, including in Quebec, the capacity of government to shape the development of society is becoming more narrowly circumscribed as global markets and international trade regimes become more pervasive in their effects. However, the Québécois tend to argue that in these circumstances it is all the more important that the relatively few policy instruments which remain available to government should be wielded, to the extent possible, by Quebec rather than by a more remote federal government, which they perceive as being mainly controlled by 'English Canada'. There is, therefore, apparent consensus on the desirability of extending Quebec's powers to the greatest degree possible: this is true of *fédéralistes* as much as of *souverainistes*. The difference between them is mainly about the extent of the political concessions that must be made in order to achieve economic goals, and particularly in order to maintain Quebec's access to external markets. The provincial Liberal Party regards federalism as a necessary condition of maintaining the economic union, and perhaps for advancing Quebec's economic interests *vis-à-vis* the United States. The Parti Québécois denies this: it believes that the economic union can be preserved even after the political union is dissolved.

Even for most federalists in Quebec the strategic question is how much power the province can get without breaking up the federal system, entailing disruption of the Canadian market. The key point, at least in the context of the present discussion, is that the quest for new powers, or for exclusive control over policy fields currently shared with the federal government, has no clear boundary. Demands extend not only to obviously cultural matters such as education, broadcasting, and communications, support for the arts, and language policy (and making international agreements on such matters), but to the whole field of social security, where at present the federal government plays the fiscally dominant role, and to wide areas of economic policy. Immigration policy, with its consequences for demographic change, is also an area of particular concern to Quebec.

A review of areas of contention in these four broad fields reveals how difficult it is to make a clear distinction between subjects that have cultural significance and those that do not. First, in the most obviously cultural fields:

• The federal government does not challenge provincial control over education policy in any direct way, but does engage in activities that Quebec, in particular, regards as closely related to education, and therefore rightly in the provincial domain. Contested areas are workforce training or retraining (whether or not it is associated with unemployment insurance, a matter within federal jurisdiction), and support for research conducted in universities. The federal government also makes cash grants to provincial governments in support of post-secondary education, but does not attach any conditions to these grants.

• Control over broadcasting, including the licensing of radio and TV stations, is federal. Conditions, such as Canadian content requirements, are attached to licences. Quebec would like to control licensing operations, but agrees that technical issues such as the allocation of frequencies are appropriately federal. Other aspects of communications policy, for example regulation of the telephone system and fibre-optic networks, are a subject of contention for several provinces, including Quebec.

• Both the federal government and the provinces make grants to arts organizations. Quebec would like full control here, and claims that federal tax revenues spent in this area should be channelled to provincial governments instead, which would have the option of using these funds to support theatres, art galleries, dance troupes, and so forth.

• Language is a particularly contentious field. Minority language rights (French and English) in education are guaranteed in the Canadian Charter of Rights and Freedoms. Freedom of expression is also guaranteed in the Charter, but these guarantees can be overridden by express declaration of a provincial legislature, or, in the case of federal legislation, of Parliament. The Quebec National Assembly (legislature) has passed a law restricting the display of commercial signs in languages other than French, and has invoked a 'legislative override' clause of the Charter in order to validate the law. However, the province would like comprehensive and absolute control over everything to do with language, including the obligation to provide minority-language education (not at present subject under the Charter to override by parliament or by provincial legislatures).

A second area (besides these overtly cultural fields) where Quebec wants to be in control is social security, which comprises unemployment insurance, old age and disability pensions paid out of general revenues, earnings-related contributory pensions, family support, social assistance or welfare, and health care. As the social security system has developed over the years, it has become impossible to disentangle federal aspects from provincial ones. Unemployment insurance, by constitutional amendment in 1941, is exclusively federal. Pensions are a concurrent field, meaning that both the federal government and the provinces can enact the relevant legislation; but in cases of conflict, the provincial law prevails. In practice, though, the federal government is dominant in this field; both old age and disability pensions are provided by the federal government, and are linked to income tax. Contributory pensions, related to past earnings, are provided through the Canada Pension Plan in nine provinces, and in the case of Quebec through a Quebec Pension Plan that is broadly similar to the federal one, and integrated with it (benefits are interchangeable). Family support has been provided by the federal government since 1944, when a programme of family allowances (per-child cash grants to mothers) was instituted; it has now been replaced by a non-universal scheme integrated with the tax system. Social assistance, which is discretionary and is based on a needs test, is provincial, but is supported by federal cash grants to provincial governments. Similarly, health care programmes are designed and administered by the provinces, but are financially supported from the federal fisc—although at a level that has been declining since 1986. The federal grants have ensured that the provincial plans have some features in common, for example that benefits are portable among provinces, and that coverage is universal.

The point of this complex story is, precisely, its complexity. Quebec would like to gain full and exclusive control over the whole field of social security, arguing that all aspects of social policy reflect, express, and support its national culture, or the values of its distinct society. The province also argues that the social security system and the tax system should be designed together; in fact the two should actually be seen as a single, integrated tax-and-transfer system, which should be provincially designed—at least in the case of Quebec. Such a change would, however, have widespread ramifications for the rest of Canada, for at least three major reasons. First, the income tax is mainly designed by the federal government, which administers it on behalf of the provincial governments in every province but Quebec; a provincialized and therefore more fragmented tax system would make the task of economic management much more difficult and would interfere with the economic union. Second, the federal government keeps for itself almost two-thirds of the revenues from the personal income tax; this major revenue source enables it to fund the social security system—in income security, about four dollars of expenditure out of every five are federal—and to make fiscal transfers to the provincial governments. Both forms of transfer are highly redistributive among provinces (with Quebec being a net recipient, although to a lesser degree than the four Atlantic provinces, or than Manitoba or Saskatchewan). Third, the field of income security is increasingly difficult to distinguish from economic policy, as the forms and conditions of unemployment insurance and other transfers to persons obviously affect movement in and out of the job market, and may facilitate or impede economic adjustment. On top of all this, there is the additional fact that public support for federal government, that is, for federalism and Canadian unity, is presumably based in part on a sense of national citizenship entitlements, and wholesale transfer of responsibility for social security to provincial governments might fatally weaken the national fabric.[17]

In economic policy, the third broad field considered here, most powers are exclusively federal under the constitution; but in practice the role of provincial governments is extensive and has been growing. For Quebec, provincial control over economic development has a particular significance, in that economic equality between anglophones and francophones in the province, with francophone ownership and control of major enterprises, has been seen as a precondition for gaining cultural security. Regional development and control over the resource industries has been important to Quebec, as has been true of other provinces also, but that is not all. Quebec has been unique in the extent of its ambitions to control the provincial economy; as one aspect of this policy thrust, it has sought to establish a network of financial institutions controlled within the province, and by francophones. For this, the establishment of the (contributory) Quebec Pension Plan in 1965, with its large fund of investible dollars, was essential. The agency established to administer the fund has become the largest shareholder in Quebec and has been an instrument of economic restructuring, and a device for supplying francophone entrepreneurs with the capital and the credit needed to create major firms and industrial consortia.

Other public corporations, notably the giant Hydro Québec (electricity) and its subsidiaries, as well as agencies empowered to grant public subsidies to domestically controlled firms, have played a complementary role in creating what has been called 'Quebec Inc.' (by analogy with 'Japan Inc.'), an interlocking network of francophone-controlled industries, financial institutions, and public agencies.[18] Any federal policies that might interfere with or restrict the activities of these firms or agencies would be strongly resisted by Quebec, which in this case has powerful allies among the other provincial governments. Thus the federal government has been successfully pressured to abandon planned policies in the fields of competition policy, regulation of financial institutions and securities markets, and ownership of firms engaged in interprovincial transportation. Federal environmental regulation is another area in which provincial resistance, not just from Quebec, has been strong, because federal regulations at times interfere with development projects supported by the provincial governments.

Finally, in the field of immigration policy, Quebec wants to gain control, and indeed has been successful in obtaining new powers under administrative agreements with the federal government. This field is important to Quebec, and to a lesser extent to other provinces as well, given the impact of immigration on demographic patterns. Again, though, Quebec's concerns are unique: it wants to ensure that immigrants will integrate culturally with the francophone majority, even though most immigrants prefer to speak English, the language that gives them the greatest opportunities in North America. To counter this tendency, Quebec wants to have the decisive voice on the selection of immigrants, and exclusive powers regarding programmes for the integration of immigrants (language and citizenship training). Its goals in this field have largely been met, although the illogicality of having provinces control immigration even though, once on Canadian soil, any immigrant can freely move to any other province,[19] has not been addressed.

This review of federal and provincial powers and responsibilities in several major policy fields demonstrates that, whatever may have been thought at the time of Confederation, today no clear distinction can be made between economic and cultural affairs, or between policies with economic effects and those with cultural ones. That is because we live in the era of the mixed economy and the positive state—the state that accepts a range of social and economic responsibilities that were not contemplated in the nineteenth century, or much acted upon until the second half of the present one. Notwithstanding the recent growth of a market ideology that aims to dismantle the mixed economy and to reassert the leading role of private enterprise in promoting the public welfare, it is clearly not realistic to imagine a return to the *laissez-faire* style of nineteenth-century liberalism, and in Canada hardly any one would wish to do so. In these circumstances, and given Quebec's desire to develop, whether within Canada or outside it, as a distinct society, there is no obvious staging-post on the road to increased policy control, or the extension of the powers of the Quebec State.

This is an observation that appears to have considerable relevance to the potential federalization of Europe, in both its upward and its downward aspects. Canada was created as a federal state 128 years ago, with a federal or central government possessing powers that it could exercise independently of the provinces; this it has increasingly been doing in competition with them. The two orders of government are both rivals and partners, as to some extent appears to be true also of the relationship between the EU (particularly the Commission) and each Member State. But Canada has travelled much further along the road to political integration than the EU, with a federal government fully capable of engaging in policy wars with provincial governments, sometimes all at once. By contrast, in the EU, except in the case of treaty provisions which have direct application, the Member States control Union institutions; indeed, through the Council of Ministers and the European Council they are the Union. However, under the hypothesized transformation of the EU into a federation, the central authorities would necessarily (or by definition) gain greater policy control, and could more easily rival the Member States. No matter where or how the line is drawn between Union competences or powers, and those remaining to the states, there will be a grey area where the location of jurisdiction or responsibility is unclear or gives rise to overlaps and thus to conflict.

What Canadian experience seems to suggest with regard to the EU is that, the more the Union moves into fields such as social policy, environmental regulation, and the control of immigration, the greater the potential for conflict between its central institutions and its Member States, and among the States themselves. It is understandable that the Union will be drawn into these fields, and indeed that it will do so under the impulsion of some of the states (which ones, will depend on the policy fields in question). This process has already been visible for some time, and was highlighted by the controversy over the Maastricht Treaty. What the Canadian case appears to show is that, unless public opinion is so strongly committed to centralization as to render the states incapable of effective resistance—as has happened in both the United States and Australia—the shift of governmental power and functions can be expected to generate substantial conflict over a long period of time. Further (and this is perhaps the key observation), Canadian experience appears to indicate that linguistic and other obvious cultural differences, including well-developed historical memories, are likely to intensify and perpetuate the conflict. Conflict, presumably, is the outward manifestation of subjectively felt cultural costs, which will only be borne to the extent that economic goals (and perhaps security objectives) demand it.

With regard to the downward aspect of the federation process, involving the decentralization of existing unitary states, Canadian experience is all the more obviously relevant. Here the forces at play may be a mixture of ethnic and territorial nationalism, as in Quebec. Language differences, if not the source of decentralizing pressures, no doubt powerfully assist the political mobilization of regional ('sub-national': forgive me!) groups. The initial focus of demands for autonomy may be cultural in the most obvious sense, involving policy fields such as language and education. But if I am correct in asserting that the Quebec case shows there is no easily identifiable staging-post on the road to increased policy control, in Europe existing nation-states may reasonably be concerned about starting along that road, or, if already embarked on the journey, may understandably want to resist pressure to go very far.

Federalism, Cultural Openness, and Minority Rights

The case that Pierre Trudeau built for federalism prior to his entry into politics in 1965 was primarily philosophical (rationalist) and cultural. At its simplest and most strongly polemical, it scarcely moved beyond vehement repudiation of ethnic nationalism, support for which he described as 'the new treason of the intellectuals'.

Citing Lord Acton's famous essay on 'Nationality' (1862), Trudeau wrote, a century later:

It is not the concept of *nation* that is retrograde; it is the idea that the nation must necessarily be sovereign. . . . The moment the sovereign state was put at the service of the nation it was the nation that became sovereign—that is to say, beyond the law. It mattered little then that the prosperity of some meant the ruin of others. . . .

. . . The nationalists [in Quebec]—even those of the left—are politically reactionary because, in attaching such importance to the idea of nation, they are surely led to a definition of the common good as a function of an ethnic group, rather than of all the people, regardless of characteristics. This is why a nationalistic government is by nature intolerant, discriminatory, and, when all is said and done, totalitarian. A truly democratic government cannot be 'nationalist', because it must pursue the good of all its citizens, without prejudice to ethnic origin.[20]

Trudeau makes no allowance here for the development of a form of Quebec nationalism that is socially and ethnically inclusive, although that has clearly been the objective of some of the leaders of the independence movement. Both the Parti Québécois and the provincial Liberal Party have a mixed record on this. Both have, on the one hand, guaranteed and extended the provision of public services (education, health) in English, and have made a serious and evidently genuine effort to incorporate minority groups into the governing councils of their respective parties. On the other hand, both have enacted restrictive language laws giving priority to French for official purposes, and limiting freedom of choice in language use (education, municipal councils, public signs) so that newcomers to Quebec will become francophone. The PQ has said that Quebec must become 'as French as Ontario is English'; Trudeau, by contrast, proposed in 1965 'a constitutional amendment granting French minorities in other provinces, as well as in Ottawa, the same rights and privileges as the English minority in Quebec,'[21] and made it a priority, over the ensuing twenty years, to bring this about.

As this discussion has shown, the official-language minorities—anglophones in Quebec, and francophones in other provinces—are the groups most vulnerable to the potential collapse of federalism in Canada. The interests of these groups are protected to some extent by the Charter of Rights and Freedoms, but even more fundamentally by political coalitions and a political culture exhibiting strong support for diversity. The break-up of Canada would gravely weaken and perhaps virtually destroy the political power or influence of the official-language minorities.

On the other hand, how break-up would affect other groups is less clear. As already noted, the image of Canada as a country characterized by linguistic or cultural dualism is increasingly contested today. The dualist image ignores the position of the aboriginal peoples, 'visible' (i.e. racial) minorities, and 'multicultural groups', or non-English, non-French immigrants and their descendants. All receive a degree of rights protection under the Charter. However, it is not clear whether their interests, or their rights, are fundamentally at odds with those of official-language minorities (for dualist perceptions of Canada tend to undervalue those who do not belong to the 'two founding races' [sic]),[22] or whether, on the contrary, the political compromises required to accommodate linguistic dualism tend to generate additional sensitivity towards other groups as well, and augment support for policies that serve their interests.

The final point to be made about the likely cultural costs of break-up focuses on the group that supposedly would benefit: the francophone majority in Quebec. In raising this possibility we challenge the basic premiss of Quebec nationalism, that sovereignty would bring cultural benefits, though arguably at some economic cost. Again, Trudeau is a useful reference-point; and here we draw on the more positive side of his argument for federalism:

Precisely because they are such a tiny minority in North America, French Canadians must refuse to be enclosed within Quebec. I am opposed to what is called 'special status' . . . [because, among other reasons] in the long run this status can only tend to weaken values protected in this way against competition. Even more than technology, a culture makes progress through the exchange of ideas and through challenge. In our Canadian federal system, French-Canadian cultural values have a good balance of competition and protection from a fairly strong state . . . In a great number of vital areas, and notably those that concern the development of particular cultural values, Quebec has full and complete sovereignty under the Canadian constitution. . . . It is not at all certain that were Quebec to find itself isolated on the North American continent, it would find the game any easier, or its rules any more favourable.[23]

Today, few Québécois are inclined to ask whether Quebec might be better able to preserve and develop its institutional structures and public policies as part of the Canadian federation than it could do as an independent state. The issue here—alluded to also in the passage quoted at the beginning of this chapter—is the extent to which market integration, conducive to the economic power of multinational corporations and (in Canada's case) strengthening the influence of an economic giant on one's doorstep, may turn formal political sovereignty into a sham. This is the banana republic phenomenon. No Québécois wants to think of an independent Quebec as a banana republic, or perhaps a wood-pulp republic (a 'hewer of wood and a drawer of water' is the Canadian phrase); but it is prudent, if unflattering, to consider what *de facto* gains in power Quebec would make by declaring itself independent. In Trudeau's judgement, the gains would be negative.

This sort of *realpolitik* argument implicitly rests on assumptions about value similarities and differences, as revealed by comparing Quebec, the rest of Canada, and the United States. Here one is on treacherous ground, but it would be a mistake, too frequently committed, to imagine that culturally, or in terms of values, Quebec is fundamentally different from the rest of Canada, which in turn has close cultural affinities with the United States. Linguistically, of course, this is true; but in political and social values, attitudes, and behaviour patterns, the story is more complex. In some respects, Quebec appears to be at least as Americanized as other parts of Canada, while in others—if one can judge from apparently divergent policy preferences—Quebec shares values with the rest of Canada that are distinct from those south of the border. The more this is true, the more Quebec gains culturally from being part of the Canadian federation, that is, the more advantages it reaps from being a politically powerful entity within a state of 28 million as opposed to being, on its own, a state of 7 million.

On the basis of this and preceding arguments, the case for federalism is cultural as well as economic. The separate states option is explicitly rejected as being inimical to the interests of ethnic minorities, even the francophones who reside in Quebec and form a sizeable majority there. The case, though tendentious, supports the idea of a decentralized state with political arrangements that encourage tolerance and support diversity. As such, it applies not only to Canada, but to the idea of federalizing Europe.

The arguments and perspectives reviewed in this section have particular relevance to the design of a federalized Europe: they suggest the desirability of decentralizing political authority to the extent feasible, both within individual states and across the EC as a whole. In other words, they support the principle of subsidiarity. But they also appear to indicate that to press decentralization to the point where existing states, especially multinational ones, are dismantled, could be highly detrimental to cultural minorities. The problem would be especially severe to the extent that movements for 'national' independence are ethnically exclusive. This is one qualification to be imposed on the principle of maximal decentralization; the other is that minorities may gain protection from upward federalization, provided it is not limited simply to achieving the integration of markets. The further progress of political integration in Europe may reasonably involve the development of non-discrimination rules that apply not only to individuals, but to collectivities or national minorities.

Continentalism and Canadian Values

Any attempt, therefore, to view the current constitutional crisis in Canada uniquely in terms of cultural conflict between Quebec and the rest of Canada is simplistic. Quebec's constitutional demands are the outgrowth of fundamental social and cultural changes that appeared during the Quiet Revolution of the 1960s, when traditional institutions and values were challenged and overturned. A society that was more confident of its ability to take control of its own future, but also less sure of the characteristics that distinguished it from the rest of North America, laid claim to additional political instruments or powers to shape its economic, social, and cultural development. The conflicts thereby engendered were, to a considerable extent, internal to the province, as different elements in Quebec society struggled to take control of the reform process in education, labour relations, and social policy, and as the previously dominant anglophone economic élite was, in part, displaced. One could even say that social and cultural change was driven by the transformation of the economy, or the non-viability of the old ways; certainly there was close interaction between economic and social-cultural change. Be that as it may, one outcome was Quebec's shopping-list of demands for expanded constitutional powers.

The constitutional issues that Quebec placed on the Canadian political agenda had a different resonance elsewhere in Canada. Controversies arose not only over the Trudeau government's objectives in language policy, but also over the role of the federal government in income support and social services; the extent of federal powers over the economy, as well as the use made of those powers; and the thrust of federal economic policies—posing, as throughout Canada's history, but in ways already being affected by globalization of the world economy and steadily increasing American control of Canadian industry, the question of protectionism and Canadian economic nationalism versus continentalism.

From the mid-1960s onwards, Canada's relationship with the United States changed considerably, as American control of Canadian industry steadily increased, as cultural bombardment from American TV intensified—and also as American protectionism notched upwards, reflecting economic pressure from Europe and Japan. Canadians became more anxious to assert their independence of the US, but at the same time became increasingly aware of the costs entailed by resisting the continentalist embrace. The 1970s were a decade of economic nationalism; the 1980s, a decade of increasingly close ties, culminating in the Free Trade Agreement that came into force in 1989.

These changes in attitudes towards the United States coincided with changing perceptions of 'what Canada is all about'. The emergence of a serious independence movement in Quebec at first induced non-Quebecois to take dualism seriously; but the mood wore off after the Quebec electorate rejected sovereignty in a 1980 referendum. Today very few anglophone Canadians are, it seems, prepared to have the public agenda shaped to any large degree by issues of language and (in a dualist sense) racial or ethnic equality. Economic issues are generally regarded as more real and certainly more pressing; and the cultural issues that come to the fore are those of Canadian values. In both respects Canada's relationship with the United States causes much more concern than relations between Quebec and the rest of Canada. Interestingly, one source of resentment towards Quebec in some regions, mainly in Ontario and the Atlantic provinces, is the enthusiasm of francophone business élites for closer economic ties with the US. In fact, the

English Canadian Left reproaches the Quebec Left for not sharing or supporting Canadian nationalism (always defined in relation to the United States). Left-wing anglophones are mindful of the fact that without the votes of the Québécois, the 1989 Free Trade Agreement would not have been ratified.

Quebec is thus involved in a wide range of Canadian political controversies of a nationalist-cultural character in which the position or status of that province is not actually the object of controversy. Accordingly, the cultural aspect of the country's current constitutional difficulties is scarcely distinguishable from the economic aspect. Perhaps paradoxically, Quebec, being linguistically distinct from the United States, appears to be readier than much of the rest of Canada (except Alberta or British Columbia) to buy into economic continentalism. Relations between Quebec and the rest of Canada are thus intertwined with the relations of both to the United States.

The interlocking of cultural and economic issues can scarcely occur in Europe in quite the way it does in Canada, simply because the American presence requires (as Canadians tend to be aware, if only dimly) a central government that is strong enough to resist US economic and cultural domination. Obviously, there is no analogue to this situation within the boundaries of the EU. In Europe there is evident concern that Germany may come to dominate, especially economically; but as a member of the EU it cannot unilaterally set the rules for its relationship with its trading partners, as Canada fears the United States will do, even under the FTA. The crucial point is that no EU state has, on its own, the power to take control; at least politically, the influence that each is able to exercise depends on coalition-building within the Union. In that sense, the main issue raised by the prospective transformation of the Union into a federation is inherently political, not economic or cultural.

On this, it is significant that we may be witnessing the formation of a dominant political bloc within the EU, a grouping of states that is sufficiently cohesive and sufficiently powerful to force the pace of economic integration, and to extend market relations into ever-broader spheres of activity. A less powerful grouping of states may try to resist, without, however, being able to stop the momentum. Such a polarization into a dominant bloc and an acquiescent grouping of states tagging along could very well reproduce some of the political effects of dualism that are easily visible in Canada, even though in Europe the dualism would not be based on language differences. None the less, the social, or value-laden, or broadly cultural implications of rapid change are obvious, and could be pervasive. Thus economic integration, by partially erasing the boundary between the economic and the cultural spheres of human action (and government policy), could generate very intense conflict. The faster the pace of change, the more likely that fissures within the Union would become wider and deeper, perhaps ranging the more highly industrialized, wealthier countries against the less industrialized, poorer ones. And if federalization becomes a codeword for forcing the pace of change, its costs would be high. But it is not clear that the costs would be specifically cultural.

5. CONCLUSION

The idea of the nation-state is increasingly coming under scrutiny, both as a desirable form of political organization and as a historical reality. Europe, which saw the birth of the nation-state, may also pioneer its demise. The most obvious alternative, indeed the only alternative that emerges from existing state forms and could thus be constructed by building upon and adapting what already exists, is a federal structure that encompasses existing states while allowing for (and indeed supporting) the radical decentralization of at least some of them. Thus the federalization of Europe, if it occurs, may be a double process that involves both upward and downward movement, or centralization and decentralization. This chapter has explored the cultural costs and benefits of such a bi-directional process, in part by examining some aspects of the present crisis of federalism in Canada. Let us now draw the argument together by re-stating the three questions posed at the beginning of the chapter.

First, is it possible to achieve, under federalism, economic benefits—and perhaps also security benefits—at only slight cultural cost to the national communities comprising the federation? Presumably the way to reconcile these objectives, or to attempt to do so, is to allocate only economic powers (and, if desired, security-related powers) to the centre, while preserving the independence of the states in policy areas more directly related to culture or national values, such as social policy. This is what was aimed for in Canada under the 1867 constitution, but the distinction proved impossible to sustain as the role of government expanded, creating the positive state.

The European Union appears now to be embarking along a course similar in some respects to that traced earlier by Canada, with the building of 'Social Europe' as a principal goal. Those states with a relatively advanced level of social protection want to make sure that others, with lower standards, cannot compete for investment by promising employers exemption from the social (and environmental) obligations they would have to assume elsewhere. The slogan for this is to prohibit social dumping. At present the mechanism for dealing with it is bargaining among Member States, through the essentially confederal processes of the Union. However, federalization would involve the creation of new institutions and processes of governance establishing a more direct relationship between Union decision-makers and European citizens. This could lead to a considerable expansion of the role of the Union, drawing it into policy areas having quite obvious cultural implications. No doubt this process would be resisted by existing national states. In that case, tensions that have already arisen within the Canadian federation would presage similar conflicts in the EU—but for reasons having relatively little to do with ethnic or linguistic diversity, and a great deal to do with the interlocking of economic and cultural issues.

The distinction between the economic and the cultural would become even less clear if redistribution of the benefits of economic union is made, through some bargaining process, a precondition of further integration. An EU that was induced to expand its budget and to get deeply into the realm of social policy in a fiscal as well as a regulatory sense—as the Canadian federal government has done—would considerably curtail the autonomy of Member States. Of course, the shift of power to Brussels has been going on rather intensively since the mid-1980s anyway, but with extensive redistributive policies, the Union would cross a new threshold, bringing it ever deeper into the range of government activities that have evident cultural or value-laden implications. And disputes over redistribution could easily mean that those differences would become an even more fecund source of tension than has so far been revealed in the already acrimonious debate over the Social Charter.

It appears, then, that the transformation of the EU into a genuinely federal system could well intensify homogenizing pressures on national cultures, to the extent that the Union expanded its activities into the field of social policy and into other 'flanking' areas such as environmental protection. If the broadening of the Union's policy role becomes a quid pro quo of further economic integration, such homogenization, which will undoubtedly be reckoned a cultural cost by those having to adapt to it, will lead to heightened conflict, exacerbated by conflicts over redistribution. The question, then, is whether federalization would lead ineluctably in that direction. If that is what is anticipated, public support for the preservation or strengthening of national cultures will surely not only slow the pace of federalization, but halt the process altogether.

Second, under what conditions does linguistic or cultural diversity create an impetus to the decentralization or even the fragmentation of states, both unitary and federal; and can a decentralized form of federalism provide an adequate response—and a stable solution—to internal conflict among ethnic, linguistic, or cultural communities, especially if regionally concentrated?

Decentralist forces may gather strength for a variety of reasons that are both too numerous and too uncertain to attempt to catalogue here. Among the reasons most pertinent to our present argument, however, is that an ethnic minority that is concentrated within a particular territory may become more aware of its own cultural characteristics and its own history, may feel threatened with assimilation, may come to resent more keenly a long-standing condition of political subordination and/or cultural and economic discrimination, or may consider that external conditions (removal of a military threat, opening up of new economic opportunities) are more favourable than in the past. For any combination of these and other reasons a more militant spirit may catch hold, generating demands for new powers of self-governance. In this chapter we take those demands as given. Our problem is to discover under what conditions federalism, perhaps in a highly decentralized form, will satisfy those demands for self-governance, accommodate linguistic and cultural diversity, and provide a stable solution to ethnic conflict.

Part of the answer has to do with constitutional structures and with government policy, especially in culturally sensitive areas such as language policy and education. It may be necessary that in such matters the states be given free rein to impose fairly restrictive policies (e.g. unilingualism), if that is what they judge necessary in order to lessen the danger of assimilation, or to offer cultural security. The difficulty, perhaps not fully resolvable, is to reconcile this with recognition of, or guarantees for, minority rights. Another element of a solution may be to prohibit all forms of discrimination based on factors such as language, ethnicity, or religion, through constitutional instruments and legislation. Equitable power-sharing arrangements, especially through central institutions or in federal politics, may also help stabilize the system.

A second part of the answer has to do with balancing the supposed cultural benefits to be obtained through self-governance, against the anticipated costs of break-up or separation. If on cultural grounds alone, independence appears desirable, secessionist tendencies may none the less be restrained by fear of economic penalties, by external military threat or foreign support for the regime, or by threat of force internally (including the potential for disorder or, ultimately, civil war). Any combination of these factors may establish an equilibrium between centralizing and decentralizing forces, and thus create a stability of sorts.

However, such an equilibrium is provisional at best: it will presumably be maintained only so long as the status quo yields a subjectively satisfactory balance between economic and other benefits, and cultural costs. If cultural costs are felt, subjectively, to rise (say, as fears of assimilation mount, or a decline of political weight within the federation is anticipated), the balance may be tilted in favour of independence. The same may be true if there are changes in the external environment: the anticipated economic costs of independence may diminish, or a foreign military threat may become less great. Either of these factors could upset a previously, but provisionally, stable political structure.

For this reason one might argue that a third part of the answer to the question about the viability of federal arrangements under conditions of linguistic or cultural diversity is the most important one. Stability is best assured when and if existing arrangements are thought to provide cultural advantages as well as economic and/or security-related ones. A precondition for this is probably that the cultural communities making up the federation should share similar value-systems, systems that are compatible with each other and are mutually supporting, especially in relation to the values of neighbouring states. Under such conditions a single state, whether federal or unitary but decentralized may be more effective in counteracting the homogenizing effects of transnational market relations and the price system. Here relative size, or critical mass and considerations of *realpolitik* are crucially important.

Third, what effects may processes of international economic and political integration have on the domestic politics and/or constitutional structure of linguistically or culturally diverse states participating in the integration process? This question, perhaps the most important one in the context of a federalization process that is both upward and downward, is relatively easy to answer in light of the preceding argument. In states where cultural or linguistic differences give rise to separatist tendencies, but economic considerations restrain them, the integration of markets internationally may reduce the anticipated economic costs of break-up. In other words, external events may alter the calculus of cultural costs versus economic benefits. A small state could become economically viable in a federalized Europe, in which regions within existing states became Member States in their own right. If Denmark, Luxembourg, and Ireland, why not Wallonia, Catalonia, or Scotland? An analogous argument is certainly being used by Quebec *indépendentistes*, who claim that because of US free trade, the Canadian political union no longer has the economic significance it used to, and that Quebec is no longer dependent on federalism to preserve its access to the Canadian market. Such calculations, which seem to take too much for granted in the Canadian/Quebec case (it is assumed, gratuitously in my view, that the FTA could be restructured without substantive change to accommodate an independent Quebec, and that 'Canada' would have no option but to preserve the economic union anyway) are perhaps more credible in the European context.

In this situation, however, the arguments about critical mass and *realpolitik*, alluded to above, come fully into play. So does the issue of compatibility or tension between the values of the cultural communities at present contained within the boundaries of a multinational state. If the values are basically similar, notwithstanding linguistic differences or other identifying characteristics, it may be advantageous to all to retain existing state boundaries, in order to better defend and advance the interests of their respective populations in a federalized Europe. For example, if Scotland and England tended, as a rule, to support each other within a European Union, they might speak more powerfully with a single voice than with two weaker ones. Would they want to act together? What of Wallonia and Flanders, or Catalonia and a truncated Spain? Speculation on these matters may be misplaced, but the questions do seem, in light of the preceding argument, to be pertinent ones. Others, who know these cases better, may provide more authoritative answers.

Notes

1. *Federalism and the French Canadians* (Toronto, 1968), 28–9.
2. A. D. Smith, *National Identity* (London, 1991), 39.
3. Smith, *National Identity*, 52–3, 61.
4. C. Walker, 'Nation-Building or Nation-Destroying?' *World Politics*, 24 (1972), 319–55.
5. Smith, *National Identity*, 125.
6. I am grateful to my colleague Grant Amyot for a discussion of the Italian case.
7. On the cultural communities, each endowed with a governing council for the most culturally sensitive policy areas, and regional governments for regional economic policy, housing, environmental matters, and other matters not interfering with the operation of the Belgian economic and monetary union, see ch. 12, below.
8. A. Lijphart, 'Consociational Democracy', *World Politics*, 21 (1969), 207–25. See also Lijphart's *Democracies: Patterns of Majoritarian and Consensus Government in Twenty-One Countries* (New Haven and London, 1984).
9. Pareto optimality solves the problem of interpersonal comparisons by putting forward a reason for avoiding making them. Pareto optimality is a condition in which no one can be made better off without making someone else worse off. However, it has been shown that a Pareto-optimal situation cannot be arrived at unless one assumes some particular distribution of incomes in society. It has been maintained that this fact vitiates the concept of Pareto optimality altogether. For a general review, see E. J. Mishan, *Introduction to Political Economy* (London, 1982).
10. The province of Manitoba never ratified the Accord, while Newfoundland ratified it but later revoked its supporting legislative resolution.

Opinion polls outside Quebec indicated that a substantial and steadily increasing majority rejected the proposed amendments, a situation which contrasted with the state of public opinion regarding the Constitution Act, 1982. However, in terms of government agreement, 'Meech' met a far more rigorous test than the 1982 reforms. Only the absence of a constitutionally prescribed amending formula in 1982—and the willingness of the British parliament to do as it was asked—permitted this anomalous result.

11. Former Prime Minister Pierre Trudeau is an obvious exception. There remains a wing of the federal Liberal Party that is committed to his views, but none have his penchant for the exposition of a political philosophy, or the intellect and inclination that would enable them to carry one through.

12. The PQ government promises a referendum on independence in 1995, but says that Quebec will propose an economic association, and also a form of political association, with 'Canada'. The proposal looks uncannily like the European Union, or (one might say) 'Maastricht for two'.

13. The colonies of Lower Canada (the southern part of present-day Quebec) and Upper Canada (the southern part of present-day Ontario) had been united in 1840. The British government attempted in this way to destroy the political power of the French-speaking population—the descendants of the inhabitants of New France, conquered in 1760)—and ultimately to assimilate it. But in practice the united colony had operated as a quasi-federation, requiring (by convention) concurrent majorities of the legislative representatives in both regions to pass laws. This tended to produce deadlock, from which Confederation, which divided the territory but also retained its unity for economic and defence purposes, provided an escape. The two colonies of New Brunswick and Nova Scotia, in effect, adhered to the political settlement negotiated between the political leaders of 'the Canadas'; the financial terms of the Confederation agreement went part way to meeting the needs of the two maritime provinces, although 'better terms' remained a rallying cry for years to come.

14. Defined as those whose primary language at home is French. Data on ethnic origins (British, French, other) do not exactly match data on home language; the difference reflects assimilation patterns. In 1981 every province but Quebec had more French-origin Canadians than francophones. In New Brunswick 31.4 per cent were francophone, as ·compared with the 36 per cent who were of French origin. In Quebec 80 per cent were of French origin, and 82.5 were francophone. In all other provinces, more than half those of French origin were no longer francophones; in most cases the ratio was 4 or 5 to 1.

15. Quebec used to have one of the highest birth-rates in the world.

However, during the 1960s, as a result of changing life-styles and the sharply diminished influence of the Roman Catholic Church in Quebec, this situation was reversed. For several years, Quebec had one of the lowest birth-rates in the world—according to some, absolutely the lowest, but there has recently been an increase, with a relatively high percentage of births to older women.

16. Trudeau, *Federalism*, 139. This book is a collection of essays; the one from which this passage is drawn was written in 1961. Trudeau continues: 'as a result, social and cultural legislation was the product of the central government over which the French-Canadian electorate had no absolute control.' A little further on (140–1) he writes: 'Central government encroachments, which are accepted in other provinces as matters of expediency, cannot be so viewed in Quebec. For French Canadians are not in any important sense represented in the Canadian power élite, whether governmental or financial.' The latter statement, of course, pertains to the time the article was written (1961); when Trudeau entered politics in 1965, he made it a primary objective to involve French Canadians fully in all aspects of Canadian life; and in this he largely succeeded. This has always seemed to Trudeau a far preferable option for French Canadians than to develop within Quebec, as within a self-contained enclave.

17. K. G. Banting, *The Welfare State and Canadian Federalism* (Kingston, Ont, 1982), 176–8.

18. T. J. Courchene, *Quebec Inc.: Foreign Takeovers, Competition/ Merger Policy and Universal Banking* (Kingston, Ont., 1990).

19. A mobility rights clause in the Canadian Charter of Rights and Freedoms guarantees this right.

20. *Federalism*, 151, 161–2, 169. A footnote citation from Lord Acton's essay, in *Essays on Freedom and Power* (Glencoe, Ill. [1862] 1949), 184, clearly indicates the origins of Trudeau's thinking on this subject.

21. *Federalism*, 32.

22. The Royal Commission on Bilingualism and Biculturalism, established in 1963, was assigned the task of recommending 'what steps should be taken to develop the Canadian Confederation on the basis of an equal partnership between the two founding races, taking into account the contribution made by the other ethnic groups to the cultural enrichment of Canada and the measures that should be taken to safeguard that contribution', Canada, Royal Commission on Bilingualism and Biculturalism, *Preliminary Report* (Ottawa, 1965), 151.

23. *Federalism*, 32–3, 35.

PART III
The European Experience

8

German Federalism and the Challenge of Unification

GERHARD LEHMBRUCH

The institutional framework of a future European federal system is, quite obviously, to a large degree prefigured by that of the present European Union. It will therefore be very much unlike the familiar American model of federalism. The emerging European federalism obeys a rather different institutional logic. However, some of the salient institutional properties of the European Union find close parallels in the federal system of Germany. Most conspicuously, the development of German federalism was characterized by a preponderance of government bureaucracies and of inter-governmental relationships very similar to the European Community. Not surprisingly, therefore, there are interesting parallels between inter-governmental policy-making in Germany and in the EU.[1]

The Unification of the two Germanies that were divided for more than four decades is an appropriate test-case to illustrate the specific institutional logic of German federalism. Unification is, after all, a process of far-reaching rapid institutional and social transformation. This puts the adaptability of German institutions to a serious test.[2] And as Unification has taken the form of inserting new states into an existing federal framework,[3] it is above all a test-case for the adaptability of German federalism to a challenge that is far from routine in politics. This process of adaptation is often on the brink of crisis. But at the same time it is also characterized by some innovative muddling through. Quite naturally, it first employs established routines and reproduces the established structures of the old Federal Republic. Nevertheless, enough vested institutional positions and distributive patterns of West German society are jeopardized, and new cleavages and alliances have emerged correspondingly.

Ostensibly, intergovernmental relations (vertical and horizontal) are the crucial mechanism of German federalism. It is therefore not surprising that recent political science research on German federalism has focused largely on their development.[4] This includes, of course, the important and complex problems of fiscal federalism. They are also at the centre of current controversies over how federalism might cope with the problems of Unification.

Yet this focus on executive federalism should not lead to premature judgements about the performance of the system as a whole. Authors who analyse Unification from an intergovernmental perspective sometimes tend to emphasize the dysfunctional effects of the federal structure on the process of political integration of the two Germanies. These are certainly of a serious nature. But for a balanced judgement on the potential contribution of federalism to the integration of this still-divided society two other important dimensions should be also considered: the linkages between executive federalism and the party system; and the 'systemic' impact of federal institutions on the structuration of societal cleavages.

1. THE INSTITUTIONAL LOGIC OF GERMAN FEDERALISM

I have already indicated that German federalism obeys a specific institutional logic distinguishing it from other federal systems. From an institutionalist perspective, the scope for political action is to a considerable degree determined (and restricted) by the institutional framework of state and society. This framework has, since the early phases of the process of state-building and through long processes of social learning, shaped the strategic and procedural repertory employed by political actors when they find themselves confronted by new issues. Hence, if we want to comprehend the impact of federalism on the integration of the Germanies, it is helpful to understand the genesis and transformation of this framework. This should help us to develop grounded hypotheses about possible paths of future development.

The Formation of an Intergovernmental Bargaining System

In a narrow sense, the formation of the modern German federal state dates back to the foundation, under the guidance of Bismarck, of the *Norddeutsche Bund* (North German Confederation) in 1867. Four years later it was enlarged by the accession of the South German states to what now took the historical name of the *Deutsche Reich*. This formative period is crucial to an understanding of the institutional dynamics of German federalism. But some fundamental institutional patterns were also inherited from the pre-modern federal system of the Roman Empire of the German Nation, in particular from its late phase after the Westphalian treaties (1648).

For in Germany the formation of the 'modern' bureaucratic state (in Max Weber's sense) was distinct from the building of the nation-state: it took place not on the level of the Empire but of the larger territories—most notably, Austria and Prussia. This process was largely completed before the unification of the smaller German states by Bismarck. Since the Napoleonic conquest of Germany, the statehood of the territories was strengthened by their rise to the status of largely sovereign subjects of international law (which they lost in 1867–71). But a much more lasting imprint was left by the far-reaching administrative reforms which some of the major states (not only Prussia but also Bavaria, Baden, and Württemberg) undertook under the impact of the Napoleonic model. The situation was thus different from that found by Cavour in some of the major Italian states (Naples, the papal state), where such a modern administration was largely absent. Bismarck not only had to take account of dynastic traditions; although he preferred to define the *Reich* as an alliance of princes (and hence not based on democratic representation), he also faced the important restriction of the resilience of autonomous bureaucratic traditions in the major member states of the *Reich*.

Hence German federalism essentially originated from a process of institutional strengthening of inter-governmental relationships. Bismarck conceived this executive federalism as a barrier against the development of parliamentary responsibility for the executive that had existed in the system of the *Deutsche Bund* (German Confederation) of 1815.[5] As a logical consequence, the national parliament (the *Reichstag*) remained outside the intergovernmental arena. This pattern was of course modified by the parliamentarization of the central and *Länder* governments after the downfall of the dynasties in 1918. But even later parliaments were never involved in the intergovernmental relationship. And in the Federal Republic since 1949 the executive preponderance in the intergovernmental subsystem has been progressively strengthened. The increasing complexity of the intergovernmental network, particularly since the institutional reforms of the grand coalition government of Christian Democrats and Social Democrats (1966–9), has also contributed to this trend. The autonomous political influence of state parliaments (the *Landtage*) has declined correspondingly.

The importance of the bureaucratic traditions of the member states led Bismarck to the construction of the *Bundesrat* (Federal Council) as a sort of federal executive of the *Reich*. As an ambassadors' conference, the *Bundesrat* continued an institutional tradition dating back to the 'permanent diet' of 1663 (located at Regensburg).[6] Through the *Reichsrat* of the Weimar constitution, the present *Bundesrat* is the direct heir to these bodies. Repeated attempts (in 1919 and 1949) to replace it with an elected parliamentary chamber after the model of the US senate proved futile. This institutional continuity since the seventeenth century forms a striking contrast with the discontinuity of most other German political institutions. It illustrates the remarkable strength of the traditional pattern of intergovernmental bargaining and accommodation. (Remarkably, this pattern finds its modern parallel in the Council of Ministers of the European Community).

The administration of the *Reich*, in Bismarck's federalism, first developed out of the Prussian executive. Only in the following decades did it acquire an autonomous weight as the centre of gravity of policy formation. But intergovernmental relations remained important for policy formation at the level of the *Reich*. Bismarck himself had begun his diplomatic career as the Prussian minister to the confederal *Bundesrat* at Frankfurt. And he was eager to preserve the characteristic diplomatic style of intergovernmental relations, a legacy of the German Confederation of 1815–66. He did this with the double aim of easing the integration of the member states into the *Reich* and, at the same time, of keeping the *Reichstag* out of the intergovernmental arena. As a consequence, German federalism has always been characterized by strong elements of bargaining and quasi-diplomatic accommodation on the executive level. Although Prussia was in a position to exert a hegemonic influence on the *Reich* administration and might always have mustered a majority in the *Bundesrat*, Bismarck and his successors developed a practice of seeking the preliminary agreement of the major states (notably Bavaria) for all major initiatives.[7] In this way a tradition of intergovernmental bargaining developed, which has been maintained up to the present.

Moreover, the constitution left the responsibility for policy implementation in most fields to the member states. Hence, the central government had to co-operate with the state governments and their bureaucracies, and increasingly so with the growth of the welfare state. This resulted in a distinct interdependence of federal and state bureaucracies.

Politics and Policies: Federal Unitarization

This formative period is important because it helps to explain the peculiar German combination of institutional decentralization and procedural integration. It is certainly correct to characterize Germany as a decentral state.[8] Yet it is important to add that the decentralized actors do not have a wide scope for autonomous action but are strongly dependent upon each other. Under these conditions, we observe the emergence of a characteristic relationship between politics and policies, between the institutional framework and the procedural and strategic repertory of political actors: the public prefers the homogenization and uniformity of policies throughout the federal system. And its expectations are met (and at the same time kept alive) by decentral, but strongly interdependent executive authorities. The institutional autonomy of these actors is limited by their integration into a multilateral bargaining system. And the manifest *raison d'être* of this interlocking relationship is the production of homogeneous policies.

Closer inspection reveals two different strategies in the history of modern German federalism, centralization and unitarization.[9] The concept of centralization must be qualified in this context: it refers to central rule-making but neither excludes participation by the *Länder* in this process nor their continuing importance in rule implementation. Against this strategy of centralization, the more recent strategy of unitarization through substantive and procedural harmonization is based on horizontal co-ordination between the *Länder* alone, or co-ordination between the *Länder* and the *Bund*. Such 'interlocking politics' (*Politikverflechtung*) links different governmental actors in the process of policy formation but largely safeguards their organizational domain and organizational autonomy.

The centralizing strategy meant that, much more than in US or Swiss federalism, the states progressively lost their autonomy in large areas of legislation. This was the consequence of the rule that *Reich* legislation superseded the laws of the member states (Article 2 of the constitutions of 1867 and 1871). For German liberals, the foundation of the *Deutsche Reich* meant the fulfilment of their aspirations for a unitary national state. Therefore the national-liberal majority in the *Reichstag* in the early 1870s was particularly eager to introduce uniform legislation in order to promote the economic integration of Germany. In consequence, commercial, civil, and penal law and the organization of the judiciary were successively unified in the final decades of the nineteenth century. This strong unification drive certainly owed a lot to the impact of the French model of the national state on the political conscious-ness of the German liberal bourgeoisie. But Bismarck—notwith-standing his fundamental conservatism—was not immune to the temptation to adopt a centralizing strategy if it fitted his political design. The beginnings of the German welfare state are the best illustration: unlike Switzerland or the United States, where impor-tant innovations in social policy were first developed on the level of some progressive member states, in Germany the introduction of social security in the 1880s was explicitly conceived by Bismarck to underline the protective functions of the *Reich*. Finally, however, even this strong leader gained acceptance only for a strongly decen-tralized version of his original plans.[10]

Since its beginnings, then, the German variety of the European national state combined a strong tendency towards uniformity of rules with federally decentralized rule implementation. To be sure, the inter-war period saw a progressive centralization of legislative and administrative responsibilities. After the defeat in the First World War, the resulting crisis of public finance led the Weimar Republic to centralize fiscal administration in 1920. The Nazi regime later continued to introduce uniform administrative stand-ards. This centralizing trend was reversed after the defeat of 1945. But remarkably, the political decentralization that went along with the Allied occupation and with their influence on the constitution of 1949 did not lead to an overall resurgence of administrative hetero-geneity. Rather, state bureaucracies found it in their interest to further uphold uniform standards through (informal and formal) harmonization.[11]

In the Federal Republic, therefore, as far as centralization continued, it increasingly assumed a controlled character. In some important domains the *Länder* were indeed prepared to surrender parts of their original jurisdiction to the *Bund*. But as a rule they insisted that, as a counterpart, the legislation remained subject to the consent of the *Bundesrat*. This enlargement of the Federal Council's veto power (*zustimmungspflichtige Gesetze*) had the advantage of preserving at least part of the organizational domain of the state bureaucracies.

But this aim was still better met by the alternative strategy that became characteristic of post-World-War-II federalism. This is unitarization through the progressive harmonization of administrative rules and standard operating procedures. Conferences of state ministers, of which the Standing Conference of Ministers of Education (*Ständige Konferenz der Kultusminister der Länder*, KMK) is the best-known example, are the most important instruments for such policy homogenization. The strategy of unitarization permitted the further promotion of the overriding imperative of homogeneity of living conditions. But as an alternative to outright centralization it safeguarded the organizational domain and organizational autonomy of the *Länd* administrations.

Some exceptions from these generalizations are in order. There are some important fields where the new decentralization led to heterogeneous solutions, most notably, the organization of local government, the regulation of the media, and the educational system. In local government, different approaches of the occupation powers led to a new diversity of institutions. And such diversity was later maintained, although only because it was in the obvious political interest of state party organizations to preserve newly established patterns of locally vested interests. Similar trends characterized the regulation of radio and television. In primary and secondary education, on the other hand, party ideology was the driving-force behind the re-emergence of contrasting patterns of organization. But even in these fields, harmonization of standard operating procedures was always strongly valued and encouraged. Here too, contemporary German federalism is thus characterized by a strange combination of decentralization of autonomous bureaucracies with substantive harmonization of policies and highly developed procedural uniformity.

The Integration of Public Finance in Fiscal Federalism

In a parallel development, fiscal federalism has become a strongly integrated revenue-sharing system. The idea of a clear separation of fiscal powers never took root in Germany because of strong vested institutional interests in the entanglement of fiscal responsibilities.[12] In a striking contrast to doctrines of fiscal equivalence as they are professed in the economic theory of federalism, the constitutional requirements for the system of revenue-sharing include 'achieving a fair adjustment' and 'safeguarding the homogeneity of living conditions on the federal territory' (Art. 106, 3). In German federalism, this postulate of homogeneous living conditions is central to the evaluation of policy outcomes. It is therefore not surprising that the *Länder* have virtually no competence to raise their own taxes. Rather, most major taxes are levied on the basis of federal legislation, and their yields are divided in fixed proportions between the federal and the *Länd* governments (*Steuerverbund*).[13] Fiscal resources of the member states are partially levelled out through complex formulae for horizontal transfers governed by federal legislation (*Länderfinanzausgleich*).

All this, however, does not signify a hierarchical preponderance of the federal level. The rules for revenue-sharing are subject to approval by the *Bundesrat* and hence have to be agreed—in always extremely laborious negotiations—between the *Bund* (the federal level of government) and the *Länder*. The functioning of federal decentralization is thus strongly dependent on the system of revenue-sharing. And on this issue the larger West German *Länder* have a veto position in the *Bundesrat*.

Since the foundation of the Federal Republic, the federal government has increasingly intervened into state policy—notably in economic and social areas—through grants-in-aid to the weaker *Länder*. The resulting *Mischverwaltung* ('mixed administration') was often criticized on constitutional and political grounds. In the late 1960s and 1970s the (hitherto para-constitutional) practice of federal grants-in-aid was therefore transformed into a complex system of jointly administered federal–state programmes.[14] This integration of policies and polities between the different levels of government (*Politikverflechtung*) sprang from the enthusiasm for systems politics, so typical of the late 1960s, just as the design for an integrated system of budgetary planning developed at the same time. However, many of the hopes that were originally placed in these schemes were disappointed, and the 1980s saw a return to decentralization with autonomous action for the *Länder* in areas such as industrial and social policy.[15]

2. FEDERALISM AND THE ORGANIZATION OF SOCIAL AND POLITICAL CLEAVAGES

A Polycentric or a Centralized Society?

In his analysis of the (old) Federal Republic of Germany as a 'semi-sovereign state', Peter Katzenstein argues that 'the dispersion of state power contrasts sharply with the concentration of private power in large social groups'.[16] This apparent coexistence of a decentralized state and a centralized society is, however, less paradoxical if we take the peculiar institutional logic of German federalism into account. As it has emerged since Bismarck, it has blended the federal heritage of the *Deutsche Bund* with the unitary aspirations of the liberal bourgeoisic. As I have already pointed out, the German state, although it is decentralized, produces largely uniform policies. As a logical consequence of this co-operative unitarization, social groups concerned by these policies co-ordinate their activities through concentrated forms of organization.

A significant instance of this reactive centralization of society is the system of industrial relations. Students of cross-national labour relations have often ranked West Germany as a case characterized by (at best) medium-level centralization.[17] Not only does the German Labour Union Confederation (*Deutscher Gewerkschaftsbund*) not have any authority over collective bargaining, in a majority of the industrial unions collective bargaining formally takes place not on the national but on a regional level. However, this formal organizational distribution of jurisdiction is overestimated in the above-mentioned cross-national rankings. They neglect the pervasive trends toward co-ordinated settlements. If we take the most important industrial union, the *Industriegewerkschaft Metall*, typically a wage agreement reached in one district of the metal industry is then adopted in a more or less similar form in all other districts. Often it even sets the pace for the other industrial unions. There are good reasons to assume that this characteristic 'pattern bargaining' (as it is called in the United States) is the result of concertation between the large industrial unions normally considered as wage leaders (the metal workers, public sector, and chemical workers unions).[18] Still more remarkable is that—in spite of repeated calls from segments of the employer community for a greater regional spread of wages—the employer organizations have usually acquiesced in this homogenization of wage levels. In the public sector there is even a nationwide collective agreement for white-collar employees (*Bundesangestellten-Tarif*) with uniform wage levels. It is periodically renegotiated between the public-sector unions and a coalition of employers from the federal, state, and local governments (*Tarif-Gemeinschaft des Bundes, der Länder und Gemeinden*) led by the Federal Minister of Interior.[19] It thus appears that the postulate of homogeneity of living conditions has become a fundamental social norm which is internalized by collective actors in the private as well as in the public sector. And it is implemented— just as in intergovernmental relations—through bargaining among formally decentralized organizations.

Another example of this blend of decentralization and unitary policy outcomes is the organization of public television. According to the jurisprudence of the Federal Constitutional Court, broadcasting belongs to the jurisdiction of the *Länder*. Public radio corporations are therefore mostly state-wide institutions, or they cover two or more states on the basis of inter-state compacts.[20] Television was first organized by these state radio corporations. But they also formed a syndicate (Arbeitsgemeinschaft der Rundfunkanstalten Deutschlands, ARD) for tasks such as the joint production of nationwide newscasts and the establishment of an international network of correspondents. Later through an inter-state compact the *Länder* established a second, nationwide TV channel (*Zweites Deutsches Fernsehen*, ZDF). Therefore, although broadcasting continues to be formally decentralized, the public has been confronted by public nationwide TV newscasts, and these form a distinct contrast to the polycentric organization of the private print media.

Hence, in Germany the centralization of society has no resemblance with that found, for example, in France. So far in the Federal

Republic there has not been one centre that one might oppose to the periphery. Rather, the strong organizational position of the *Länder* has resulted in the maintenance of a plurality of centres. German society, notwithstanding its powerful peak associations, thus mirrors the decentralization of the state with its strongly polycentric organization.

This polycentric structure can be traced back to the pre-modern Roman Empire of the German Nation. As I mentioned already, in Germany the process of state-building was based not on the national but on the territorial level. This also had important consequences for the organization of German society.[21] Thus, Germany had no capital city as a dominant centre before the foundation of Bismarck's *Reich* in 1867–71. Even during the eight decades when Berlin was the German capital it did not really gain the same overwhelming preponderance which Paris and London had acquired over many centuries.[22] This polycentrism was increased when, with the division of Germany after the Second World War, Berlin lost its function as the German capital. While the federal parliament and government were established at Bonn, many other federal agencies were dislocated throughout the Federal Republic.

In post-war West Germany, this polycentric organization of society has had a remarkable impact on the spatial growth patterns of the economy. Whereas centralized societies in a strict sense are often characterized by strong inter-regional economic disparities between the centre and the peripheral regions, the decentralized political organization of the Federal Republic strengthened the polycentric regional policy networks. These structures served to mitigate tendencies towards spatial concentration of economic activity. Characteristically, although ordo-liberal polemics against industrial *Strukturpolitik* (as supposedly incompatible with the social market economy) found broad public acceptance, this verdict never impaired the legitimacy from which regional economic policy benefited in the Federal Republic.

The Regionalization of Policy Networks

Institutional regionalization also has strong roots in German history. The downfall of monarchical semi-constitutionalism in 1918 resulted in the parliamentarization of *Länd* governments. Thus

state bureaucracies, being now controlled by regional party coalitions, became the focal points of regional inter-organizational
networks linking state administrations to the regional society.

And this polycentrism of regional policy networks linking state
and society was further increased after the Second World War.
Under the occupation regime, together with the central government
the central networks of interest articulation and intermediation
disappeared. Instead, new regional policy networks emerged
around the West German *Länder*, including the successor states to
former Prussian provinces, like North Rhine-Westphalia, Lower
Saxony, or Hesse. Important interest associations adopted a decentralized regional organization. Even after the foundation of the
Federal Republic, these regional units remained important because
of the salience of the *Länder* for the implementation of federal as
well as state policies.[23]

But it was not only the governmental functions that were dislocated from Berlin. With the division of Germany, many leading
firms and associations moved away from Berlin to the major centres
of West Germany: thus the big banks made their headquarters in
Frankfurt, now the seat of the Federal Bank. Equally, labour union
headquarters were dispersed across different West German states.
Siemens—originally a leader in the drive originating from Prussia,
and increasingly from Berlin, towards making Germany a first-rate
industrial power—moved to Munich, and here it established close
linkages with the Bavarian government and the governing regional
party, the CSU. Bonn, of course, became a central target for lobbying, and many associations established their federal headquarters in
the region. But, apart from its administrative and political importance, Bonn remained a second-rank city compared with the
larger West German state capitals. An important aspect of this
regionalization is the organization of finance. On the one hand,
there are of course the well-known national finance institutions,
such as the three big private banks. But an important part of the
banking system is constituted by the public regional institutions
(*Landesbanken*) that head the organization of savings and loan
banks.[24] Similarly, the organization of co-operative banks (for agriculture and small business) is strongly decentralized. Even the private regional banks have strong informal links to the respective
state governments.[25] Such linkages strongly underpin the economic
policies of the *Länder*, sometimes labelled as 'neo-mercantilist'.

The controversies about *Land* neo-mercantilism referred in particular to the policies of conservative South German state governments. These governments employed their influence in regional policy networks to promote developments, e.g. in technology policy, not only through regional public financial institutions, but also through direct intervention in the formation of strategic alliances and the merger of important firms.[26] At the federal level, where the *Grundsatzabteilung* of the Federal Ministry of Economics always acted as the guardian of the pure doctrine of the social market economy,[27] this interventionist policy of state governments was often met with disapproval. Nevertheless, one can argue that in functional terms federal ordo-liberal orthodoxy at the macro level and state interventionism at the meso level resulted in quite a successful policy mix. But, as I will argue below, these traditional differences in economic strategies proved fatal when the federal government assumed strategic leadership during the process of Unification.

3. FEDERALISM AND PARTY GOVERNMENT

I have already indicated that, after 1918, regional parties became autonomous political players beside the *Länd* bureaucracies. During the Weimar Republic, however, their political weight was often inferior to the Berlin party headquarters. This predominance of national party organizations did not reappear in the Federal Republic. In particular the CDU and the FDP emerged as loose federations of regional party organizations, and the regional *Landesfürsten* (princes) played key roles in the federal party organization. The SPD was originally characterized by the antagonism of state party leaders and the federal party headquarters under Schumacher and Ollenhauer. But after Willy Brandt, then mayor of West Berlin, assumed the party leadership, the influence of regional organizations on the federal party became stronger. Today, thanks to social democratic control of the government in eight out of ten West German states, this regionalization of party leadership has reached its apex.

The symbiosis of federalism and party government has ambiguous consequences. At the federal level, it meant that party conflict had a strong impact on the *Bundesrat*, because an adverse *Bundesrat* majority can greatly complicate the task of a *Bundestag* majority. The anticipation of this interdependence by the first federal chancellor, Konrad Adenauer, opened the way for a tradition of federal coalition politics spilling over to influence elections and the formation of governmental majorities at the state level.[28] During the period of the social-liberal *Bundestag* majority (1969–82), the Christian Democrats held a majority in the *Bundesrat*. Since 1990 this situation has been reversed, with SPD-led governments controlling the majority of the *Bundesrat*. Similar constellations force the federal government to negotiate compromises with the opposition over all legislation that needs a *Bundesrat* majority.

It has often been asserted that state parliaments have lost most of their political influence because of the increased importance of co-operative federalism and *Politikverflechtung*. And indeed, the *Kontaktprivileg der Exekutive* (the bargaining role of the executive) exists at the expense of state parliaments. However, it should not be overlooked that state bureaucracies are now closely controlled by the governing parties.[29] And since state parties enjoy considerable political autonomy from the federal party organization, party government at the *Land* level is an important potential source of political diversity and of political innovation originating from the regional party organizations.[30] Thanks to this autonomy of state parties, it appears justified to speak of a revival of policy diversity at the state level since the late 1970s, in spite of the persistent trend towards inter-administrative unitarization.

4. FEDERALISM AND THE UNIFICATION OF GERMANY

Students of German federalism often view its future in the united Germany in a rather gloomy light. Arthur Benz, for example, considers the federal structure as being fundamentally impaired and asks whether in consequence the conditions for the efficacy and the adaptablity of German federalism have been lost.[31] I have already indicated that such sceptical observations mostly focus on the executive and fiscal dimension of federalism. Indeed, fiscal federalism is now subject to a severe crisis of redistribution that may greatly affect the federal balance.

The impact of Unification on federalism is, however, a more complex issue. Among the aspects that have to be considered is, first, the strategic leadership which the federal government assumed in the process of Unification. Since, as I have argued elsewhere,[32] the collapse of communist rule in the GDR took West Germany's political actors by surprise, their initial reactions oscillated between perplexity and short-term improvisation. Chancellor Kohl's strength in these circumstances was that he resolutely took the initiative, first to consolidate his contested leadership position, and then to maintain strategic leadership in a situation where most of the normal patterns of policy formation appeared paralysed.

It is particularly striking that during this formative stage of the Unification process the attitude of state governments remained largely passive. It was almost exclusively dominated by a defensive posture, motivated by concern about the protection of their distributional position and their vested interests. This situation was exacerbated by the cirumstance that the *Bundesrat* had recently fallen under social democratic majority control. The *de facto* leader of this majority, Saarland's prime minister Oscar Lafontaine, did not hide his scepticism about Unification. And since on the other hand Kohl was interested in keeping the social democrats as far out of the strategic deliberation processes as feasible, this further impaired the influence of the *Länder* on the Unification process. Moreover, Kohl's bargaining partner in the East, the new democratic government of the GDR, was still strongly guided by the habits of centralist policy formation inherited from the past and unaware of the intricacies of West German federalism.[33] As a result of this interplay of different factors, the federal government in a sense inherited and tacitly adopted some important elements of the centralist orientation of the GDR where this fitted its short-term objectives. This became quite apparent in the privatization policy aimed at the radical transformation of the East German economy.

The Restoration of the Five Länder

This interpretation may seem somewhat incongruous if we consider the restoration of the five East German *Länder* abolished in 1952.[34] The borders of these five states had been drawn by the Soviet military authority in the early post-war years, some of them as successors to former Prussian provinces.[35] As a historical process this was a close parallel to the concurrent developments in the Western occupation zones. However, the West German states newly created after the dissolution of Prussia had more than four decades to consolidate their organization and their popular legitimacy. By contrast, the continuity of East German federalism was broken after only seven years, and the five *Länder* were replaced by fourteen districts that lasted for more than a generation.[36]

Hence the point can be made that, paradoxically, this restoration constitutes a deviation from the historical path of federal development in Germany. Therefore it must be apprehended that it will in the long run weaken the strength of German federalism. Historically, as I pointed out above, the systemic singularity of German federalism was due to the circumstance that state formation at the territorial level pre-dated the foundation of the modern federal system. As a consequence, in all earlier instances of regime change in Germany (such as 1918/19 or 1945/6, and until the foundation of the Federal Republic in 1949, state administrations were the stable elements of the reconstitution of federal organization, against the unitarizing and centralizing trends in national politics. German federalism always rested on its 'bureaucratic support' (Theodor Eschenburg) that, in the upheavals of the past, had always served as an essential condition to maintain the functioning of *Land* institutions.

This pattern could have been maintained only if the GDR had acceded to the Federal Republic as its twelfth member state. This would not have been incompatible with the existing power balance of the federal system. After all, in 1989 East Germany had about 16 million inhabitants, slightly less than the state of North Rhine-Westphalia. Therefore the restoration of the *Länder* created in 1946 was regarded with mixed feelings by West German specialists of administration. Their concern was that, because of the sub-optimal scale of East German state and local governments, these are poor in financial as well as manpower resources and therefore have difficulties in developing efficient administrative structures.[37]

Thus the restoration of the former *Länder* was one of the most far-reaching decisions of the last GDR parliament, freely elected on 18 March 1990. Some prominent representatives of East Germany's public opinion—including leading members of the citizen protest groups of autumn 1989–have complained that the former GDR has been overrun by the wholesale transfer of West

German institutions.[38] But this certainly does not apply to some of the central constitutional features of the new East German system: the introduction of the parliamentary system as well as that of the federal structure were autonomous decisions of the new political élites of East Germany after the end of communist rule.

Given the short original lifespan of the East German *Länder*, it is striking that their restoration had such strong public support. The main reason was apparently that the centralized character of the communist regime had been widely resented.[39] Its downfall released strong popular desires for decentralization and for emotional identification with regional and local traditions. But, compared with the development of federalism in West Germany, these decentralizing developments had a certain anachronistic flavour. Among others the West German states, in the 1960s and 1970s, had reformed their systems of local government, notably by administrative consolidation of small communities into much larger units. But the communist rulers of the GDR did not need viable autonomous local units and therefore maintained a formal organization of local government characterized by its small scale. This is especially true of *Kreise* (counties) and *Gemeinden* (towns). The restoration of local self-administration in 1990 therefore took place within an organizational framework dating largely from the pre-industrial past.

Meanwhile, *Land* legislation has been passed with a view to creating more efficient administrative structures by the consolidation of the small lower-level units. As these were poor in resources they were not well prepared to resist such interventions, though some localized opposition to the new administrative map occured. It is different for the *Länder* themselves: obviously there is little chance that any of them can be persuaded to abandon their recently acquired political identity and to merge into a larger unit. Here, efforts at territorial reform will most likely remain as futile as they were in West Germany (except for the foundation of Baden-Württemberg early in 1952).[40]

The Dissolution of Administrative Traditions and the Role of West German Länder sponsorships

On the West German side, misgivings about the sub-optimal scale of the new *Länder* were finally neglected because of the apparent advantages in dissolving the political and administrative organizational structures of the GDR. Above all, it eased the task (on which West Germans had consensus) of firing the majority of public-sector personnel in East Germany. The public sector of the GDR was more than three times the size of that of North Rhine-Westphalia;[41] moreover it was thoroughly permeated by personnel recruited and trained on the basis of communist party loyalty. And, understandably, the West German leaders were still more eager than their new East German counterparts to get rid quickly of these former SED old boy networks, or—in a familiar West German figure of speech—'rope parties' (*alte Seilschaften*). It would obviously have been difficult to base large-scale political purification on collective criteria such as party membership alone,[42] and therefore the matter might be much simplified if the organizational structures of the former GDR became redundant as a consequence of Unification. Finally, one East German *Land* as the only successor to the GDR might eventually have become the rallying point for the affirmation of a distinct cultural GDR identity. This was something which West German leaders were eager to avoid: for average West Germans national cultural homogeneity had become a fundamental experience, and many secretly considered East Germany as a somehow alien culture. And it was expected that the cultural integration of East Germany might be eased by the dissolution of the organizational framework of the GDR.[43] The price to be paid for this was the institutional reconstruction of *Länder* that lacked any real administrative tradition and the viability of which was highly questionable.

If the small scale of the East German state and local governments is a congenital defect in terms of administrative efficiency, the problems were magnified, after Unification, by the impact of the extremely fast dissolution of the central and district administrations of the GDR. That decision was largely based on political convenience and aimed at dismantling the organizational networks on which the communists had based their power. But it left an administrative vacuum: because of the wholesale destruction of the administrative infrastructure of the GDR, new *Länd* (state) administrations had to be rebuilt practically from scratch. The new states not only lack financial resources but also qualified bureaucratic manpower. The nature of the qualifications required from public-sector personnel is now, moreover, defined by the West German tradition: it involves a complex system of legalistic rules and standard operating procedures which even experienced former East German administrators have difficulty coping with.

In the view of some West German observers, the problem with these people is simple: they are characterized by 'politicized incompetence'.[44] This judgement has of course some limited plausibility. But I am not sure whether it does full justice to the professionalization of important parts of the former GDR bureaucracy or to the skills often acquired informally. After all, what we observe is the difficult transition to a completely different administrative culture—where the difficulties are also largely due to the complexity and rigidity of the culture of the Western administration and its lack of tolerance for informality and diversity.

The transition was eased by a remarkable innovation in the system of co-operative federalism: West German *Länder* assumed sponsorship for East German states and assigned civil servants to help in setting up new administrative structures.[45] This sponsorship system certainly cannot compensate for the deficiencies of East German administrative structures, but its political importance should not be underestimated. It helps the new *Länder* to acquire a minimum of administrative autonomy, all the more since many of the assigned officials soon go native and tend to identify emotionally with their host state.

But the sponsorship system also serves the obvious interest of the Western *Länder*. After all, the only feasible alternative would have been to place East Germany under some sort of indirect federal administration, with federal civil servants serving in the East German state capitals. It is easy to imagine that this might have emptied the autonomy of the East German *Länder* of its very substance and thus considerably weakened the federal principle. Although West German state advisors do not always refrain from giving political as well as administrative guidance to their hosts, this does not result in the centralizing effects that would have necessarily been implied by a federal sponsorship. For among their important functions is the specific attempt to teach the East Germans how to defend their interests in negotiating with Bonn, on the basis of their own experiences, *Länder* sponsorships therefore contribute to the principle of decentral autonomy. And they have the additional effect of creating linkages, political alliances, and bonds of solidarity cutting across the East–West cleavage.

Quandaries of Fiscal Federalism

The major shortcoming of state sponsorships was that they constituted a relatively cheap form of federal solidarity.[46] In sharp contrast was the reluctance of the West German states to include their East German counterparts in the system of revenue-sharing.[47] This reluctance was quite understandable: under the present formula for the horizontal equalization of burdens, all West German states would become net payers in a large transfer of resources to the East German states. Although the Unification treaty stipulated the inclusion of the East German states in the system of revenue-sharing from 1995, it was doubtful whether the necessary revisions would be politically feasible and could be reached in time.

After all, the principal victims of a redistribution of revenue on the basis of the present rule would be the smaller and poorer West German states (including the crisis-ridden Saarland and Bremen). As a consequence of transfers to the (still poorer) East German *Länder*, their fiscal base would shrink so drastically that they would face enormous difficulties in maintaining services which their population has come to consider as vital. It was probably not by accident that some of the social democratic Minister Presidents from this group of (relatively) poor Western states—such as Oskar Lafontaine from the Saarland and Rudolf Scharping from Rhineland Palatinate—were considered as being particularly lukewarm towards Unification and integration with East Germany. In their resistance to a redistributive reform of revenue-sharing, the richer West German states therefore hoped to get, so to speak, the windfall profits from the resistance to change of the middle group of poor Western *Länder*.

However, some observers expected a different structure of alliance to emerge in the context of a larger constitutional redistribution of the respective tasks and burdens. In this picture, the (relatively) poor Western and the Eastern states might come to terms with the *Bund* over a centralizing settlement where some of the tasks of the member states, together with the corresponding financial responsibility, are taken over by the federal level of government. Both groups of states might be interested in the resulting budgetary relief.[48]

The possibility of a coalition of the small states was of course the nightmare of the larger, and mostly affluent, West German *Länder*. Until Unification, the four largest *Länder* together held more than a third of the *Bundesrat* votes and could therefore prevent any constitutional amendment that might hurt their interests. Under the existing constitutional rules, however, the accession of the small East German states would have deprived them of this veto power. Therefore, they successfully demanded that their representation in the *Bundesrat* be increased in a constitutional amendment included in the Unification treaty.

By and large, this defensive posture remained characteristic of the attitude of the West German states towards the process of Unification. A first improvised solution to the resulting financial problems was the establishment, in 1990, of an extra-budgetary Fund for German Unity for a five-year period, mainly financed by borrowing from the credit markets. Of its total volume of 115 bn. DM, the *Länder* agreed to guarantee and service the debt for 47.5 bn.; the rest was to be assumed by the federal budget. And since then the Western states have stubbornly refused to accept any further obligations.[49]

It soon became clear, however, that the initial arrangement would not be sufficient to satisfy the needs of the East German *Länder*. Consequently, there had to be a new round of *Bund–Länder* negotiations. In order to establish a more centralized management of Unification problems, the *Bund* sought to build a coalition with the new *Länder* and the richer West German states.[50] In return for a higher federal share (plus 5 per cent) of the turnover tax yields, the former were promised extra federal grants-in-aid amounting to an annual 32 bn. DM, whereas the latter could hope for a long-term reduction of horizontal transfers to their less wealthy neighbours. Quite obviously, this was a solution at the expense of the poorer West German states.

In spite of highly conflicting interests at the state level, the *Länder* managed to agree on a common position *vis-à-vis* the federal initiative. Cutting across party cleavages, conservative Bavaria and social-democratic North Rhine-Westphalia, bound by similar financial interests, successfully united the Western *Länder*. Brandenburg's key role as the only new *Land* run by a social democratic government finally helped to overcome the remaining East–West cleavage within the *Land* camp.[51] In February 1993 the federal government was confronted with a *Bundesrat* draft, which stood in stark contrast to its own vision: first, the *Land* share of the turnover tax yields was not to decrease but rather to increase by 8 per cent, which would allow horizontal equalization payments to continue along the conventional lines. Second, additional federal payments were to be granted not only to the new *Länder* but also, though on a smaller scale, to the poorer Western states.

To everyone's surprise, a closed meeting of the federal and *Land* heads of government and party leaders in March 1993 reached an agreement on the revenue-sharing issue in the context of the so-called Solidarity Pact, which was supposed to provide a comprehensive settlement of the financial consequences of German Unification. The compromise, which allows the East German states to join the system of revenue-sharing from 1995 without constitutional amendment, entails the following core items. First and foremost, the *Land* share of the turnover tax yields will rise from 37 to 44 per cent. *De facto*, these resources will be made available entirely to the new *Länder*, which are thus provided with a resource base similar to that of the poorer Western states. This was obviously the prerequisite for the inclusion of the new *Länder* plus Berlin in the traditional system of horizontal equalization payments. In addition, the East German states will receive extra federal grants-in-aid, so that in total the political goal of an annual West–East transfer of 36 bn. DM can be attained. This sum corresponds roughly with the resources presently transferred by the Fund for German Unity (34.6 bn. DM in 1994) with will end from 1995.

On top of this, the *Bund* agreed to assist the East German states in their task of catching up with West German standards by extra payments worth 20.6 bn. DM a year for a ten-year period judged sufficient for East German recovery. The federal government also made notable concessions to the poorer West German *Länder*, disproportionately hit by the inclusion of the new *Länder* in the system of horizontal equalization. They will receive federal grants-in-aid amounting to an annual 1.34 bn. DM limited to ten years from 1995 plus a substantial reduction of their debt services resulting from the Fund for German Unity. In addition, both Bremen and Saarland, the poorest Western provinces, are granted, from 1994 to 1998, an annual 1.7 bn. DM each for the purpose of budget consolidation. Finally, the *Bund* will also entirely guarantee and service, through the *Erblastentilgungsfonds*, the legacy of East German debts mainly accumulated by the *Treuhandanstalt*. In order to finance these heavy undertakings the *Bund* will, in addition to spending cuts, levy a so-called 'solidarity surtax' on income and corporation taxes from 1995 onwards.

The above settlement[52] is, quite obviously, very close to both the initial *Land* position and the traditional system of revenue-sharing. The *Länder* managed to frustrate the *Bund*'s intial strategy of divide and rule and to defend the status quo at the financial expense of the *Bund*, i.e. the problem of horizontal (West–East) transfers was solved by (just the necessary margin of) vertical redistribution.[53] One observer holds up the issue of revenue-sharing as a good example for a general status quo orientation of political actors in the process of German Unification. This orientation, so the argument runs, is not so much dictated by mental or institutional constraints but is rather to be interpreted as a rational choice in the face of uncertainty.[54]

As a matter of fact, the compromise struck between *Bund* and *Länder* illustrates the adaptive capacities of German federalism in the face of a daunting challenge, and apparently defies earlier expectations that a fundamental reform of public finance would be inevitable to cushion the financial consequences of Unification. However, the so-called 'Bonn agreement' of March 1993 does not address but rather postpones the fundamental problems of fiscal federalism. Already today, the financial arrangements agreed upon seem inappropriate to cope with the upcoming costs of Unification.[55] Largely due to the defensive posture of the Western states, the chance of an 'open window' for fundamental rearrangements was not seized.

Furthermore, to view the Bonn settlement basically as a victory both for the *Länder* and for the federal character of united Germany in general[56] could prove to be a premature judgement. The still important financial commitments of the *Bund* with regard to the new *Länder*, and the general consolidation of financial entanglement could reinforce the political importance of the *Bund* at the expense of the state level. The scenario of German federalism cut into a Western segment where, in principle, the status quo is maintained, and an Eastern segment with a much more centralist federal–state relationship, due to permanent dependence on extra federal grants-in-aid, cannot be dismissed so quickly.

The Nemesis of Unitary Federalism

The fiscal problems of Unification have been magnified by the choice of the unitarizing option in the negotiation process. It meant that most West German legislation would be introduced from the moment of the accession of the GDR. Originally, the GDR government favoured the maintenance of GDR legislation on the East German territory for a longer transitional period. And the leader of the West German delegation, minister of the interior Wolfgang Schäuble, a South German conservative with a realistic scepticism concerning the difficulties of administrative integration, sympathized with this position. However, he found himself isolated from all other West German government departments. And when, unexpectedly, the East Germans changed their position and opted for the fast introduction of the Western legislation, he was forced to cede, notwithstanding his secret concern about the almost total neglect of the serious administrative and fiscal implications of this decision.[57]

The motives behind the unitarizing option were complex. Among the most important was the avoidance of conflict over bureaucratic routines.[58] But West German interest groups also played an important role: business wanted to base investment decisions on West German legislation, and medical associations strongly and successfully lobbied for the destruction of the nationalized public health system of the GDR.[59] And environmentalists were concerned that the stringent West German procedural requirements in the planning process for public projects, such as environmental impact assessments for road construction and multiple judicial safeguards, might be sacrificed in favour of administrative expediency.

The choice of the unitary option for Unification, however, is not limited to government and administration. As I have argued earlier, unitarization as a rule for federal conflict management is fully internalized not only by the bureaucratic élites but by most societal élites as well. For all of them, the homogeneity of living conditions has become a fundamental goal. The resulting dilemma is that homogenization can only be obtained by improving the conditions of disadvantaged groups, since redistribution at the expense of vested political interests would be a too costly alternative. As a consequence, the unitary option turns into an extremely expensive Unification strategy, not only for the federal budget.[60]

This is immediately apparent in the powerful move towards the equalization of income levels in East Germany. From the outset, labour unions were eager to organize the East German workforce, and their aggressive wage strategy was certainly helpful in this effort. Moreover, they—and the compliant employer organizations—could justify it on the basis of the need to keep the qualified workforce from migrating to the West in order to preserve the industrial basis of East Germany. Many public-sector employers faced a similar dilemma: nurses were leaving *en masse* for better paid jobs in the West, and if public hospitals were to be kept running, it was inevitable that salaries would have to be raised much faster than the financial situation of the East German authorities might otherwise have allowed. And since a considerable spatial uniformity of wage levels is accepted in West Germany, it is difficult for all actors involved to adopt a completely different strategy in the East.[61]

The dysfunctional result, however, is that a downward equalization also takes place. In the educational system of the GDR, for example, pupil–teacher ratios were much more favourable than in the old Federal Republic. Now, West German finance ministers insist that the transfers needed to pay the salaries of East German teachers are accompanied by massive lay-offs in order to get that ratio down to the levels prevalent in the West German states. Similarly, many other—often quite remarkable—achievements of the East German welfare state have had to be abandoned in accordance with the unitary logic of German federalism.

Towards a Peripheralization of the New Länder?

No administrative strategy of integration can, however, compensate for the deficits that appear in the institutional and organizational infrastructure of East German society and hamper the reconstitution of the new *Länder* as viable social entities. Not only does the public sector lack qualified administrative personnel. In addition, the organization of civil society is still heavily underdeveloped. In particular, the economic actors that, in the West German states, form the symbiotic structure of regional policy networks, are either still lacking, or they are inexperienced in the subtle rules of the public–private interplay so characteristic of West German state polities.

This deficit is accentuated by the strategy chosen by the federal government for the institutional reconstruction of East Germany's economy. Its main actor is the *Treuhandanstalt* ('trust establishment') that was originally established by the 'reform communist' transition government of prime minister Hans Modrow in order to reorganize the socialist economy according to market principles. Following the election of a democratic government, this objective was redefined to become a transition to a private economy. Finally, after Unification, the *Treuhandanstalt* was transferred into the jurisdiction of the federal minister of finance, and privatization became the clear priority in the definition of goals.

This priority was questioned by many of the actors involved in the reconstruction process. But the organizational status of the *Treuhandanstalt* had its own logic that in a paradoxical manner made it the heir of GDR centralism. One may regard it as a sinister symbol that it had made its headquarters in the building of the former GDR State Planning Commission. More significant is the fact that its management was organized on industry lines, not unlike the former GDR economic administration. Therefore it naturally also tended to neglect regional economic inter-dependencies and the resulting potential economic and social synergies. Moreover, since investors could in practice only be found in the West, the critical organizational environment for a strategy of privatization was located outside the region. One typical conse-quence is that East German firms were acquired by investors who most often kept their headquarters in the West and remained physi-cally much less integrated into the civil society of East Germany. Even if these firms are more than simply the extended workbenches of their Western owners, they tend to form part of a periphery dependent upon the economic centres in the West.

The political preponderance of the federal government in the reconstruction of the Eastern *Länder* contributes further to this latent peripheralization. The anti-interventionist perspective of fed-eral economic policy tends to keep the upper hand over the eventual neo-mercantilist leanings of advisors from West German state governments. This new imbalance in the federal power relationship might thus signify that the counterforces against the much-dreaded *mezzogiorno* syndrome could remain weak.

Party Government and the New Pattern of Federal Alliances

So far, the impact of federalism on political cleavages and their organizational linkages with society has been neglected. If these are taken into consideration, future trends may have to be assessed in a more nuanced perspective. The emergence of a system of party government in the new states could prove an important counterweight to the dysfunctional effects of unitary federalism in the Unification process. To be sure, state parliaments suffer from the lack of experienced political personnel (and a non-negligible number of state MPs relinquished their seats after accusations of collusion with the former state security services). And the organizational continuity of the Eastern CDU and FDP—who, as subordinate allies of the ruling communists, were parts of the power structure of the former regime—is a rather ambiguous element in the formation of an East German party system. However, the net result is an increase in diversity within the parties that promises to contribute to innovation and might to some degree facilitate the adaptation of the German political system to the challenges of Unification.

The emerging structure of alliances and conflicts has ambiguous implications. Initially, the federal political majority had its counterpart in four out of five East German *Länder* and in the two affluent South German states of Bavaria and Baden-Württemberg. The social democratic opposition, for its part, had increasingly come to dominate West German state politics. But its chances of influencing federal policy depended on its East German partners, notably Brandenburg. In a controversy over an increase in VAT, the opposition strategy failed precisely because the SPD leaders overlooked the financial dependence of Brandenburg on federal subsidies. Recent elections allowed the social democrats to end or neutralize the christian democratic dominance in all Eastern *Länder* except Saxony. But as the Brandenburg case indicates, specific *Länder* interests in the East might well overrule party loyalty again and hence frustrate opposition strategies. If the social democrats aspire to regain control of the federal government, they will have to develop a more convincing East German strategy. But the problem of party cohesion has also arisen in the West. In a current controversy on a federal tax bill (*Jahressteuergesetz*), social democratic Lower Saxony and Schleswig-Holstein have threatened to step out of party lines in order to safeguard their own financial interests.

After all, the federal structure of the united Germany is a potential organizational basis for horizontal alliances that cut across the (vertical) East–West cleavage. Given the potentially destabilizing impact of distributional conflicts along this cleavage, the formation of cross-cutting alliances and conflicts (as they are actually observed, for example, in the sector of energy policy) might serve as an important factor aiding political integration of the two divided German societies.

Notes

* I am indebted to Burkard Eberlein who updated relevant facts and figures and revised the section on fiscal federalism after Unification.

1. This was pointed out most explicitly by F. W. Scharpf, 'Die Politikverflechtungs-Falle: Europäische Integration und deutscher Föderalismus im Vergleich', *Politische Vierteljahresschrift*, 26 (1985), 323–56.

2. For an overview of the problems of Unification see my articles: Die improvisierte Vereinigung: Die Dritte deutsche Republik', *Leviathan*, 18 (1990), 462–86; 'Die deutsche Vereinigung: Strukturen und Strategien', *Politische Vierteljuhresschrift*, 32 (1991), 585, 604 (an enlarged version was published as 'Die Deutsche Vereinigung—Strukturen der Politikentwicklung und strategische Anpassungsprozesse' in B. Kohler-Koch (ed.), *Staat und Demokratie in Europa*, (Opladen, 1992), 22–46; 'Institutionentransfer—Zur politischen Logik der Verwaltungsintegration in Deutschland', in W. Seibel, A. Benz, and H. Mäding (eds.), *Verwaltungsreform und Verwaltungspolitik in Prozess der deutschen Einigung*, (Baden Baden, 1992), 41–66; for a more recent perspective see 'Institutionen, Interessen und sektorale Variationen in der Transformationsdynamik der politischen · Ökonomie Ostdeutschlands', *Journal für Sozialforschung*, 34 (1994), 21–44.

3. Conveniently, in official semantics the popular phrase 'ex-GDR' is most often avoided by employing the locution 'the five new *Länder* (member states)'. (The more precise legal term is *Beitrittsgebiet*, i.e. 'territory of accession'. It includes East Berlin which is not, strictly speaking, a new state).

4. Central to the development of the theory of federalism in West Germany was the discussion initiated by F. W. Scharpf, B. Reissert, and F. Schnabel, *Politikverflechtung: Theorie und Empirie des kooperativen Föderalismus in der Bundesrepublik* (Kronberg/Ts., 1976).

5. This was already the dominant feature of the German Confederation of 1815. Bismarck successfully blended this institutional heritage with the aspirations of the liberal bourgeoisie for a unitary national state, for an excellent historical analysis, see H. Mommsen, 'Gouvernementaler

Föderalismus und Repräsentativverfassung in Deutschland und Österreich', *Casopismo Prawno-Historyczne*, 32 (1980), 117–54.

6. Even the numerical distribution of seats among member states was adopted, with appropriate modifications, from the successor institution of the old Imperial diet, the *Bundesrat* of the Confederal Act of 1815 (situated at Frankfort-on-Main).

7. H. O. Binder, *Reich und Einselstaaten während der Kanzlerschaft Bismarcks 1871–1890* (Tübingen, 1971), 142 ff; M. Rauh, *Föderalismus und Parlamentarismus im Wilhelminischen Reich*, (Düsseldorf, 1973). See also M. Weber, 'Bayern und die Parlamentarisierung im Reich', in *Gesammelte Politische Schriften* (München, 1921), 273 f.

8. P. J. Katzenstein, *Policy and Politics in West Germany: The Growth of a Semi-Sovereign State* (Philadelphia, 1987) 15 ff.

9. The distinction between (organizational) centralization and (substantive) unitarization has been introduced by a German constitutional scholar (and later constitutional judge), K. Hesse (*Der unitarische Bundesstaat* (Karlsruhe, 1962)). A recent analysis characterizes the Federal Republic as a 'unitary state in disguise': H. Abromeit, *Der verkappte Einheitsstaat* (Opladen, 1992).

10. Public health insurance funds, for example, are organized on a local basis (*Allgemeine Ortskrankenkassen*) and may set different rates although the benefits are uniform.

11. A salient case was the fiscal administration, where, in the early post-war years, high officials of the different *Länder* were eager to preserve the uniformity of standards that appeared jeopardized by the Allied policy of decentralization.

12. Again this pattern goes back to the time of Bismarck. Originally, the *Reich* depended on transfers from the member states (*Matrikularbeiträge*) because its own financial resources (customs duties and indirect taxes) were insufficient. After Bismarck's turn to protectionist trade policies (1878), the *Reich* seemed capable of achieving fiscal autonomy thanks to the growing yield of customs duties. The Centre Party in the *Reichstag*, however, obtained a capping of these resources (*Franckensteinsche Klausel*, 1879) in order to maintain the political leverage which the *Länder* had through the *Matrikularbeiträge*—and indirectly of the *Reichstag*, who voted for them. The First World War and German defeat definitely ended this period of fiscal dependence of the *Reich* on the *Länder*. But the integration of tax resources continued in a different way, now with the *Reich* in a preponderant position.

13. This *Verbundsystem* was first established at the beginning of the Weimar Republic (see preceding n.). The turnover tax and the income and corporation taxes were levied by the *Reich*, which then transferred

a fixed percentage to the *Länder*.

14. Scharpf *et al.*, *Politikverflechtung*.
15. On the autonomous industrial and technology policies of the *Länder*, see J. Hucke and H. Wollmann (eds.), *Dezentrale Technologiepolitik?* (Basel, 1989); U. Jürgens and W. Krumbein (eds.), *Industriepolitische Strategien—Bundesländer im Vergleich* (Berlin, 1991); and in a cross-national perspective: J. J. Hesse and A. Benz, *Die Modernisierung der Staatsorganisation* (Baden-Baden, 1990), 158 ff. On autonomous policies in Christian Democratic *Länder*, see J. Schmid, *Die CDU. Organisationsstrukturen, Politiken und Funktionsweisen einer Partei im Föderalismus* (Opladen, 1990).
16. Katzenstein, *Policy and Politics*.
17. See, e.g. D. R. Cameron, 'Social Democracy, Corporatism, Labour Quiescence, and the Representation of Economic Interest in Advanced Capitalist Society', in J. H. Goldthorpe (ed.), *Order and Conflict in Contemporary Capitalism* (Oxford, 1984), 165 (Table 7.6). For a recent nuanced discussion, see K. Thelen, *Union of Parts: Labor Politics in Postwar Germany* (Ithaca, NY, 1991), 38 ff.
18. This is, however, contested by an author close to organized labour: R. Seitenzahl, *Gewerkschaften zwischen Kooperation und Konflikt* (Frankfurt-on-Main, 1976), 105 ff.
19. The resulting wage rises are then also adopted, by federal legislation, for the salaries of civil servants at all levels of government.
20. *Südwestfunk* (Baden-Württemberg and Rheinland-Pfalz) and *Norddeutscher Rundfunk* (Niedersachsen, Bremen, Hamburg, Schleswig-Holstein plus the recently adopted Mecklenburg-Vorpommern).
21. For details, see G. Lehmbruch, 'Institutional Linkages and Policy Networks in the Federal System of West Germany', *Publius*, 19 (1989), 221–35.
22. Even the Hitler regime payed tribute to this tradition: in particular, Munich was named 'capital of the (Nazi) movement' and remained the seat of the party headquarters.
23. See W. Streeck, 'The Territorial Organization of Interests and the Logics of Associative Action: The Case of *Handwerk* Organization in West Germany', in W. D. Coleman and H. J. Jacck (eds.), *Regionalism, Business Interests and Public Policy* (London, 1989), 59–94; R. Mayntz, 'Organisierte Interessenvertretung und Föderalismus: Zur Verbändestruktur in der Bundesrepublik Deutschland,' in T. Ellwein *et al.* (eds.). *Jahrbuch zur Staats- und Verwaltungswissenschaft*, 4 (1990), 145, 156.
24. These are public institutions under the control of local governments.
25. To take one example, the supervisory board of the (private) Baden-Württembergische Bank, an important regional institution with a large clientele in medium-sized business, is traditionally chaired by the state

minister of finance. Among the members of this board is also the chief manager (Vorstandsvorsitzender) of the state-owned Landes-kreditbank.

26. A much-discussed example was the active co-operation of Baden-Württemberg's former prime minister Lothar Späth in the acquisition of several high technology (particularly air and space) firms by Daimler Benz. The common strategic aim was the diversification of this automobile firm with its dominant role in the regional economy. Although Späth fell over charges of collusion with private business, his successor Erwin Teufel has since then made clear that he intends to continue this strategic orientation.

27. On this subject, see G. Lehmbruch, 'The Institutional Framework of German Regulation', in K. Dyson (ed.), *The Politics of German Regulation* (Aldershot, 1992), 29–52.

28. For a detailed developmental analysis, see G. Lehmbruch, *Purteienwettbewerb im Bundesstaat*, (Stuttgart, 1976). See also E. Pinney, 'Federalism, Bureaucracy, and Party Politics in West Germany: The Role of the Bundesrat' (Chapel Hill, NC, 1963).

29. For the politicization of the civil service in West Germany, see R. Mayntz and H. U. Derlien, 'Party Patronage and Politicization of the West German Administrative Elite 1970–1987—Toward Hybridization?', in *Governance*, 2 (1989), 384–404. These findings are largely also valid for the state level.

30. See J. Schmid, *CDU*, and by the same author '*Bildungspolitik der CDU. Eine Fallstudie zu innerparteilicher Willenshildung im Föderalismus*,' in *Gegenwartskunde* (1990), 303, 313.

31. A. Benz, 'Die Entwicklung des Föderaliamus im Vereinten Deutschland. Möglichkeiten und Grenzen institutioneller Veränderungen' (paper presented at the 18th congress of the German Political Science Association, section 'State Theory and Political Administration', Hanover 10–11 Oct. 1991).

32. Lehmbruch, 'Improvisierte Vereinigung'.

33. This became clear when the GDR government abandoned complete control over the generation and distribution of electricity in East Germany to an oligopolistic consortium of West German electricity utility corporations.

34. The original 1949 constitution of the German Democratic Republic was still much indebted to the Weimar constitution and retained the federal organization. The major difference with the Bonn constitution was that it abandoned the *Bundesrat* model in favour of the senate model (that is, an elected second chamber). This model had originally been proposed by Hugo Preuss in his draft constitution for the Weimar National Assembly in 1919, but was then dropped because of the resistance of the new 'revolutionary' (i.e. party-controlled) state

governments. Earlier, in 1871, a similar suggestion from the liberal grand duke of Baden had been rejected by Bismarck.

35. Saxony has a historical continuity going back to the middle ages. The same is true of Mecklenburg, which was, however, merged with Western Pomarania (the remainder of the former Prussian province Pomerania west of the Oder). Brundenburg and Sachsen-Anhalt are essentially former Prussian provinces. Thüringen was created in 1920 from the territorial puzzle of the minuscule 'Saxon principalities', but the present capital, Erfurt, and the surrounding districts belonged to Prussia until the last administrative reform by the Nazi authorities in 1944. The case of East Berlin is distinct from the five new *Länder*: it was merged with the *Land* of West Berlin under the West Berlin constitution of 1950. It continues, however, to belong to the *Beitrittsgebiet* ('territory of accession') to which the special rules of the Unification treaty apply.

36. East Berlin retained a special status.

37. That most of the East German *Länder* are among the smaller states is clear from the following listing (number of inhabitants in million: East German states in italics): North Rhine-Westphalia, 17.104; Bavaria, 11.221; Baden-Württemberg, 9.619; Lower Saxony, 7.238; Hessen, 5.661; *Saxony*, 4.901; Rhineland-Palatinate, 3,702; *Berlin*, 3.410; *Saxony-Anhalt*, 2.965; *Thüringen*, 2.684; *Brandenburg*, 2.641; Schleswig-Holstein, 2.595; *Mecklenburg-Vorpommern*, 1.964; Hamburg, 1.626; Saarland, 1.065; Bremen 0.674.

38. For a discussion of the problem of transferring institutions, see Lehmbruch, 'Institutionentransfer'.

39. This became obvious with the preparations for the 750th anniversary of Berlin in 1987: the government ordered the districts to make an important part of their scarce capacities in the construction industry available for ostentatious reconstruction work in the capital city, and this aroused strong resentment from the periphery against the centre.

40. The only exception is the special case of the merger of Berlin with surrounding Brandenburg, which has recently been approved by the respective *Länder* parliaments.

41. W. Schäuble, *Der Vertrag. Wie ich über die deutsche Einheit verhandelte* (Stuttgart, 1991), 199.

42. Influential West German leaders understood early on that collective discrimination of communists as practised under the 'radicals decree' of 1972 could not be continued after Unification (after all, 2.3 out of 16 million inhabitants of the GDR had held SED membership). This position was explicitly affirmed by the Federal Minister of the Interior, the conservative Wolfgang Schäuble. Only the Bavarian Christian Social government clearly dissents from it.

43. These considerations played an important role in the dissolution of the

former GDR broadcasting system that had become a lively and progressive competitor of West German public broadcasting stations after 1989: see S. Hepperle, *Transformation und Integration des Rundfunks im Prozess der deutschen Einigung* (unpub. MS, Konstanz, 1991).

44. H. U. Derlien, 'Regimewechsel und Personalpolitik—Beobachtungen zur politischen Säuberung und zur Integration der Staatsfunktionäre der DDR in das Berufsbeamtentum' (Universität Bamberg, Verwaltungswissenschaftliche Beiträge, Nr. 27, mimeo: Bamberg, 1991), 42 ff.

45. Thus, North Rhine-Westphalia is the sponsor for Brandenburg, Lower Saxony for Saxony-Anhalt, Schleswig Holstein for Mecklenburg, Baden-Württemberg and Bavaria for Saxony, and Hesse for Thüringen. The smaller West German states are also involved to some degree.

46. Transfer payments from West German state and local governments to East Germany in 1991 and 1992 were approximately 5% of the total public transfers from West to East Germany (calculated on the basis of data from the Deutsche Bundesbank, cited in *Wirtschaftswoche*, 3 Apr. 1992, 30).

47. This appears to have been a central concern of the Western state representatives in the negotiations over the Unification treaty: see Schäuhle, *Vertrag*, 179 ff.

48. This scenario was developed by F. Scharpf, 'Entwicklungslinien des bundesdeutschen Föderalismus,' in B. Blanke and H. Wollmann, (eds.), *Die alte Bundesrepublik. Kontinuität und Wandel* (Opladen, 1991), 146–59.

49. This was repeatedly stressed by the leader of the West German delegation in his recollections of the negotiations on the Unification treaty: see Schänble, *Vertrag, passim*.

50. W. Renzsch, 'Föderative Problembewältigung: Zur Einbeziehung der neuen Länder in einen gesamtdeutschen Finanzausgleich ab 1995', *Zeitschrift für Parlamentsfragen*, 1 (1994), 116–38

51. Renzsch, 'Problembewältigurg', 122–7.

52. It was passed by both *Bundestag* and *Bundesrat* on 27 and 28 May 1993 as Sect. 3 of the 'Law implementing the federal consolidation programme'.

53. It should be remembered, however, that the deal struck best serves the defensive interests of the Western states, The financial position of the new *Länder* will only be improved by an annual 23 bn. DM from 1995, as compared with the present situation Renzsch, 'Problembewältigung', 138.

54. R. Czada, 'Schleichweg in die 'Dritte Republik'—Politik der Vereinigung und politischer Wandel in Deutschland', *Politische Vierteljahresschrift*, 35 (1994), 254.

55. Among others see R. O. Schultze, 'Der deutsche Föderalismus nach der Vereinigung', *Staatswissenschaften und Staatspraxis*, 4 (1993), 251.
56. This seems to be the viewpoint of Renzsch, 'Problembewältigung', 134.
57. For these controversies, see the details in Schäuble, *Vertrag*, 152 ff. Even later, Schäuble himself pleaded for a short period of transition in those exceptional fields where it was agreed that GDR legislation should provisionally remain in force. This included the legislation on abortion and put the cohesion of his own party—the CDU—under considerable stress (*Vertrag*, 194).
58. Thus the federal minister of labour, Norbert Blüm, is accused by Schäuble (*Vertrag*) of having pressed for this option because he wanted to introduce the social achievements of the West quickly regardless of the budgetary consequences.
59. For details, see Lehmbruch, 'Institutionentransfer'.
60. According to projections of the East German Institute für Angewandte Wirtschaftsforschung in 1992, the transfer needs of the new states would gradually rise from about 150 bn. DM in 1992 to more than 220 bn. in 2001 (*Wirtschaftswoche*, 20 Mar. 1992, 19).
61. In spring 1994, wage levels in the public sector, and in large parts of the private sector, are roughly at 80% of those in West Germany. The Berlin government recently promised full equalization for Eastern public employees by 1995.

BIBLIOGRAPHY

Abromeit, H., *Der verkappte Einheitsstaat* (Opladen, 1992).

Benz, A., *Föderalismus als dynamisches System. Zentralisierung und Dezentralisierung im föderativen Staat* (Opladen, 1985).

Blair, P. M., *Federalism and Judicial Review in West Germany* (Oxford, 1981).

Jeffery, C. and Savigear, P. (eds.), *German Federalism Today* (Leicester, 1991).

Gunlicks, A. (ed.), *Federalism and Intergovernmental Relations in West Germany: A Fortieth Year Appraisal* (*Publius*, 9/4).

Hesse, J. J. (ed.), *Politikverflechtung im föderativen Staat. Studien zum Planungs- und Finanzierungsverbund zwischen Bund, Ländern und Gemeinden* (Baden-Baden, 1978).

Hesse, K., *Der unitarische Bundesstaat* (Karlsruhe, 1962).

Katzenstein, P. J., *Policy and Politics in West Germany: The Growth of a Semi-Sovereign State* (Philadelphia, 1987).

Kisker, G., *Kooperation im Bundesstaat* (Tübingen, 1971).

Laufer, H., *Das föderative System der Bundesrepublik Deutschland* (Bayerische Landeszentrale für Politische Bildung, 6th edn., Munich, 1991).

Lehmbruch, G., *Parteienwettbewerb im Bundesstaat* (Stuttgart, 1976).

Mayntz, R., 'Organisierte Interessenvertretung und Föderalismus: Zur Verbändestruktur in der Bundesrepublik Dcutschland', T. Ellwein J. J. Hesse, R., Mayntz, and F. Scharpf (eds.), *Jahrbuch zur Staats- und Verwaltungswissenschaft*, 4 (1990), 145–56.

Merkl, P. H., 'Executive–Legislative Federalism in West Germany', *American Political Science Review*, 53 (1959), 732–41.

Mommsen, H., 'Gouvernementaler Föderalismus und Repräsentativverfassung in Deutschland und Österreich', *Czasopismo Prawno-Historyczne*, 32 (1980), 117–54.

Pinney, E. L., *Federalism, Bureaucracy, and Party Politics in Western Germany: The Role of the Bundesrat* (Chapel Hill, NC, 1963).

Rauh, M., *Föderalismus und Parlamentarismus im Wilhelminischen Reich* (Düsseldorf, 1973).

Reissert, B. and Schäfer, G., 'Centre–Periphery Relations in the Federal Republic of Germany', in Y. Mény and V. Wright (eds.), *Centre–Periphery Relations in Western Europe* (London, 1985), 104–24.

Scharpf, F. W., 'Entwicklungslinien des bundesdeutschen Föderalismus', in B. Blanke and H. Wollmann (eds.), *Die alte Bundesrepublik. Kontinuität und Wandel* (Opladen, 1991), 146–59.

—— 'Policy Effectiveness and Conflict Avoidance in Intergovernmental Policy Formation', in K. Hanf and F. W. Scharpf (eds.), *Interorganizational Policy-Making: Limits to Coordination and Central Control* (Beverly Hills, Calif., 1978), 57–112.

—— *Politikverflechtung: Theorie und Empirie des kooperativen Föderalismus in der Bundesrepublik* (Kronberg, 1976).

Schmid, J., *Die CDU. Organisationsstrukturen, Politiken und Funktionsweise einer Partei im Föderalismus* (Opladen, 1990).

Schreckenberger, W., 'Intergovernmental Relations', in K. König, H. J. von Ortzen, and F. Wagener (eds.), *Public Administration in the Federal Republic of Germany* (Deventer, 1983), 65–82.

Zimmermann, H., *Studies in Comparative Federalism: West Germany* (Washington, DC, 1981).

9

Austria: Has the Federation Become Obsolete?

REINHARD RACK

I

Article 2 Section 1 of the Austrian federal Constitution states: 'Austria is a federal state'.[1] A closer look at the Austrian federal Constitution shows that this statement is, at best, a half-truth. Austria is a federal state, but a weak one. Or, to be more precise, a country where the nine states comprising the Republic are not very strong and the federation is almost all-powerful.[2] In Austria, for instance, there is no real power-sharing between the federation (the *Bund*) and the states (the *Länder*). Articles 10 to 15, which is where the division of competences between the federation and the states is laid down, very quickly reveal that the federation has received the lion's share. Practically all that is worth having belongs to the federation. Not only external affairs, money, and the army, but also all civil and criminal law, all police powers, all matters pertaining to trade and industry, almost all traffic competences, mining, forestry, labour legislation, public health, most of education and science, and practically all taxation matters belong to the federation.[3]

When one looks into another significant area in terms of the federal nature of a federal state, the picture there is, if possible, even bleaker. There is very little co-decision for the states in federal affairs. Even though Article 24 maintains that 'the legislative power of the *Bund* is exercised by the *Nationalrat* [the national council] jointly with the *Bundesrat* [the federal council]', this is not really so. According to Articles 42 and 44, in matters of ordinary federal law the federal council is no real co-legislator. It does not even have a real veto power. The national council can simply override any federal council objection. The federal council does not have any say in budgetary matters,[4] and only in changing the Constitution to the detriment of the states does the federal council have the right of qualified co-decision.[5] Members of the federal council in Austria do not like to hear this but it is the case: the federal council is no second chamber, it is merely a second-rate chamber.

However, to put everything into proper perspective, in Austria the states are not weak in every respect. Or, more accurately, there is a particularity to the Austrian federal system which is quite important to the overall picture. This particularity is the so-called indirect federal administration, meaning that, according to binding constitutional provisions, in very many areas of federal competence it is not the federal administrative agencies that implement the law. The federation must make use of the states' administration. Thus it is the *Landeshauptmann*, the governor, and the state's administrative sub-structures that execute very many of the federal laws. Any political scientist will know that this situation gives real power to the governor, which means less power for the federation.[6]

II

There are many good reasons—and some that are not so good— why the Austrian Constitution has given only rather limited powers to the states. The most important of these reasons is that, in 1920, when the federal Constitution was created, the political authorities in Austria were divided in their opinions on federalism.[7] At the risk of over-simplification, the situation was that the Social Democrats were more or less strictly against real federal power-sharing between the federation and the states, and for a variety of reasons preferred a strong central government. Members of the so-called 'national camp' were not sceptical towards the idea of federalism as such but opposed it because they favoured the idea of Austria becoming an integral part of the Weimar Republic, and the sooner the better, and they foresaw technical problems for a federal state becoming a member state of a federal state. This left only the Christian Democrats who were strongly in favour of federalism.

Thus, it is not surprising that the Austrian Constitution of 1920, a *provisorium* to most of its founding fathers, settled on a luke-warm compromise on the matter of federalism. From the point of

view of costs and benefits, this precondition of the federal political
system in Austria was—to say the very least—suboptimal. There
seems to have been very little, if any, structural planning as to the
particular federal requirements of the Austrian situation. And there
was no long-term planning aimed at improving this situation.

However, Austria has a long tradition of *provisoriums* and
compromises, so it is not surprising that the provisional compromise of 1920 turned out to be a greatly cherished and long-lived
constitution. It survived the dark years from 1933 to 1938 and
through to 1945, and it also survived the critical times after World
War II, when Austria was offered the possibility of adopting a new
democratic constitution, a people's democratic constitution to be
more precise.[8] The Austrian federal Constitution not only survived
through these years, but became a living constitution, especially in
so far as federalism was concerned. Federalism became widely
popular with the people. The indicator of this acceptance of the
federal structure is the so-called *Länderbewußtsein*. Austrians
identify themselves first and foremost as Styrians, Tyroleans, or
Viennese, and a *Landeshauptmann* in Austria is a much more
central political figure than, for instance, a US state governor.
This is the case in the eyes of the people as well as in power
politics.[9]

The Austrian federal Constitution has also been a living constitution in another sense. It was never a permanent, rock-solid structure, and changes have always been easily made and therefore
readily carried out. Again, we note, with one central focusing point
of change, the imperfectly solved federal question. For years now
the states have presented the federation with a great number of
requests for change—more power to the states, more power to
the federal council, more power in financial matters and so on.[10]
From the point of view of costs and benefits practically all
Forderungsprogramme (demands made by the Länder in order to
improve and strengthen the federal principle of the constitution)
suffered from the very same problem that had made the Austrian
federal solution such an awkward one from the beginning. All
requested changes to the Constitution, those concentrating on the
acquisition of more and new competences as well as those intending
to improve (from a *Land* point of view of course) structural and/or
procedural rules, were never more than a collection of *ad hoc*
wishes or *ad hoc* practical needs of the *Länder*. Some of these

requested changes did come about, although the great break-through from the federalist perspective is still to be achieved.[11]

III

The *annus mirabilis* of 1989 brought about many changes throughout Europe. Above all, it was the beginning of the end of the geo-political division of Europe for the so-called reform countries. It was the beginning of new democratic structures, and possibly also, a new starting-point for the destructive forces of overbounding nationalism in Eastern and Central Europe. The year of 1989 was also an important one for Austria. On 17 July, long before the walls in Europe started to crumble and then to fall, Austria decided to apply for membership of the European Community.[12]

To some extent, the Austrian situation in 1989 and since has resembled that of 1920, however limited this analogy may be. As in 1920, Austria now wishes to become an integral part of a larger entity. It wishes to become a member of the European Union, and there federalism within federalism may cause problems.[13] It seems as though the Union is *Länder*-blind, i.e. that it does not really take into account the fact that Member States may be and are in fact federal states themselves. And this requires a three-tiered federal concept, or perhaps even a four-tiered federal concept if one takes local self-government into account too.

In this context one should not overlook the fact that, although the Union may ignore federal structures, membership of it does not seem have been an obstacle to the idea of federalism. Quite the contrary, Spain and Belgium have developed quasi-federal structures as members of the Community, and in Italy, in France, and even in the United Kingdom the idea of regionalism has gained some support, Community membership and Community structures notwithstanding.[14]

IV

Political life in Europe, centred around the European Community, has also given rise to a number of transnational organizations committed to the idea of regionalism and/or federalism within the Community or Union, as it now is, within the Member States, and even crossing the borders of the Community. There is, for example, the AER, the Association of European Regions, which nowadays comprises some 165 member regions from Strathclyde to the Moscow Region, from the new German *Länder* to the Canary Islands. There is also the so-called 'Conference: Regions of Europe', comprising constitutionally and economically strong regions such as Bavaria and Baden-Württemberg on the one hand and the region Lombardia and the Brussels region on the other. There are the so-called *Arbeitsgemeinschaften* or working groups, the ARGE Alp, the ARGE Alpen-Adria, composed of some 40 million people each. And, there are, finally, smaller organizations such as Euregio Basel and others.[15]

Last, but not least, there is a growing demand for subsidiarity and federalism within the Union. The Maastricht summit showed that these ideas have already taken root in European Union thinking. However, the results of Maastricht have also shown that these ideas might play only a limited part in developing the future architecture of the European Union.[16]

V

Assessing the overall picture of federalism in Austria an analogy comes to mind. It has to do with the hobby of growing orchids. Orchids bloom readily and richly only when they are raised under stress conditions. Himalayan orchids, for instance, do not bloom at all if you do not expose them to very cold, even to frost-like temperatures. And jungle orchids grow luxuriantly if fed well, but they bloom only when there is the danger of starvation or drying out. The case of federalism and European integration might require similar preconditions to these. Federalism will bloom if and when there is the danger of strong centralization. And the case of Austria seems to support that theory. Has the Austrian federation become obsolete? In a nutshell, definitely not. There is even a chance of improving the Austrian federal structures in the context of Austria joining the European Union, but there is much to be done (and changed) to make sure that Austria will remain a respected federal state in future years as a fully fledged Union member.

VI

This section examines the particular problems the Austrian states are faced with at the moment and what necessary and feasible changes could solve them. First the problems: one of the basic requirements of federalism, if not the most important one, is an autonomous regulating power, the authority to make one's own laws within one's own domain. In Austria, this hard core of federalism was never very strong. We have already noted the considerable federal law-making competences. Article 15 of the federal Constitution was at best a beautiful theory.[17] Section 1 of this article 15 reads as follows: 'In so far as a matter is not expressly assigned by the federal constitution to the (*Bund*) for legislation or also implementation, it remains within the states' (*Länder*) autonomous sphere of competence'. In reality, there were and there are very few residual powers left over after the federation has taken its share. A detailed account of these few state powers underlines this point: building laws, regional and local zoning laws, hunting and fishing, fire-fighting, and regional funding. And that is the complete list so far as the material competences of an Austrian state are concerned. It must also be stressed that there are very limited self-structuring powers given to the states by the federal constitution: the interior organization of the state and the structural provisions for local communities are both overtly predetermined by the federal Constitution.[18] Furthermore, there are almost non-existent autonomous powers of taxation.[19] Add to this bleak picture, however, the fact that the Austrian states do have a fairly good standing in all matters of law enforcement—once the indirect federal administration has already been invoked.[20]

For completion, the balance-sheet requires the not inconsiderable powers arising from the state's capacity to act as a 'holder of civil rights' according to Article 17 of the federal Constitution. This involves the capacity to spend state money like any other private undertaking and thus to be able to govern by funding and sponsoring.[21] This completes the overall picture.[22] However, the signing of the European Economic Area agreement and possible Austrian EU-membership calls all of this into question.[23]

If and when Austria as a whole, the federation as well as the states, has to abide by the Union's rules, this will mean that for money, if not for all of the above-mentioned state's law-making and law-enforcing powers, the tune will be called in Brussels and no longer, for instance, in Graz—the capital of Styria.[24] For the last years many Austrian civil servants have been checking and comparing the so-called *acquis* lists—the long lists of regulations and directives of the EU, that will form the basis for the common European Economic Area law—against Austrian state laws. It has been found that Austria had to change some seventy Styrian laws before the deadline of 31 December 1993. This may not sound much. After all, the Austrian legal order has been consistent with European requirements to a very large extent for quite some time. (This message was conveyed clearly by the *avis* of the Commission of the European Community which was prepared on the question of Austrian membership and presented to Austria in the summer of 1991).[25] Nevertheless, for a state that does not have many more legal competences than those involved in the adaptation process seventy laws is quite considerable number, because it represents nearly the total. And here we touch upon the first big problem: Austrian states will be reduced in a central prerequisite of federalism—in their autonomous regulatory power, i.e. their capacity for self-government.[26]

VII

Of course, this is a problem not only for the states. The federation will be faced with the very same loss of law-making powers.[27] In fact the federation will be an even greater loser. It will have to adapt around a hundred federal laws, to quote a recent figure, and there may be a few more than that.[28] And the federal laws involved will probably be even more important from a political point of view. But there is one important difference in the positions of the federation and the states. The federation will not only lose, it will also gain something. The federation will in the future be part of the European law-making structure (in different ways in the contexts of the European Economic Area and the Union law-making process) and thus will be adequately compensated.[29] This is the natural result of integration: some gains and some losses. But for the states there are no gains: will they simply have to resign themselves to their losses?

It can be argued that the states will not have to suffer these losses. They will have to look for adequate compensation—at the national level and at the Union level, and it appears that they will.[30] At the national level the federation and the states have agreed that there will be changes in the present balance of power between the federation and the states. At least there has been political and principal agreement on this point,[31] although the details will have to be worked out in detail. What do the states want? Briefly, the Austrian states want what the German states already have, and some further powers.[32] They want a complete redistribution of all regulatory powers, of all taxation powers, and others. They have presented the federation with a scientific study on this matter and a moderately specific catalogue of changes required.[33] It is an elegant study, concentrating on, among other topics, questions such as the costs and benefits of federation, and a very impressive catalogue of necessary reforms. One can be sceptical as to whether the states' wishes will be realized. Nevertheless, the study presented by the *Länder* is worth analysing. For instance, the states suggest changes to the system of the *Kompetenzverteilung* ('division of competences') as such. In the future they would prefer Article 11B-VG type power-sharing between the federation and the states, meaning that the federation ought to legislate; the states would then concentrate on the administrative side. The states also want changes in the present structure of indirect federal administration. Here, they suggest its abolition in favour of Article 11B-VG constructions, i.e. federal legislation and states' administration.

The states also suggest a more co-operative law-making and law-enforcing process. They want to conclude treaties with the federation on a number of co-decision schemes involving both the national and the state parliaments. And they want to lay down, in advance, common goals in planning matters. The states also recommend the creation of so-called *Gemeinschaftsaufgaben*, meaning co-legislation, co-finance, and co-administration in particular areas such as regional planning, environmental protection, and protection from catastrophes. Finally, and above all, the states suggest a new division of competences in the areas of finance and taxation. As yet no decisions have been made about the recommendations of the study. In addition, the states have also asked for a rather small number of structural changes in the national decision-making process, concerning the impact of European Area and Union law and the handling of the Austrian position *vis-à-vis* the making and breaking of Union law. The states want to be an integral and decisive part in shaping the national position where Union law is concerned. Some of these wishes, many but probably not all, will be granted to the states. In December 1991 the Council of Ministers decided to introduce constitutional legislation into the Austrian parliament that will grant to the Austrian states a number of participation rights in the handling of Austrian EEA and EC positions. In detail this draft paper for constitutional amendment—that has become constitutional law in June, BGBL 276/1992—provides for the following:[34]

A new passage in Article 10 sections 4–6 provides for the *Länder*—and to a lesser extent also the representative organs of the local communities—a full right of information in all areas affected by the integration process and relevant to either states' competences or otherwise relevant to states' interests. In matters of states' competences the states have been granted some sort of co-decision rights when these matters are decided upon at the European level. The states have been able to predetermine the Austrian position in these areas. The federation is bound—with very limited exceptions—by this position. In substance this constitutional amendment is more or less a copy of relevant German legislation introduced a few years ago in the context of the ratification of the Single European Act.

The constitutional amendment did have a second part. The states will, on the occasion of Austrian membership in the EEA agreement, be given all regulatory powers as far as the purchasing of land for house-building is concerned. It is a small but very important change in the present catalogue of law-making competences. It will also probably be the only change granted to the *Länder* (of the many they want), at least for the time being. It is the one change the states require to prevent the so-called '*Ausverkauf der Heimat*'—the sale of choice Austrian sites to well-to-do Union citizens.[35] In this area, the Austrian states, at least some of them, will want to do as the Danes did before acceding to the Community in 1972/3, that is, to restrict the purchase of land in special areas to permanent residents.[36] It is a necessary step to ensure that the very scarce land available for living purposes in some alpine regions where less than 10 per cent of the land is inhabitable, will be used in the best interests of the resident population.

VIII

What else is going to happen and must happen to give Austrian federalism a good chance of surviving the next few years of major change in Europe? The European Union and its legal order will have to be changed too. European Union law must provide adequate structures and adequate instruments for federal member states as well as for member countries structured in different ways. The future Union must no longer ignore the *Länder*. From the point of view of an Austrian federalist, the Union should even be one where our understanding of federalism ought to be one of the guiding principles for the architecture of the future European Union. It is hoped that what was decided upon in Maastricht in December 1991 will be a step in this direction.[37] However, we should not be naïve. The principle of subsidiarity may be a good thing, and as a specific provision in the revised Treaty of Rome it will be an even better thing. But drawing heavily on the author's professional experience as an Austrian constitutional lawyer it seems worth stating that good solid instrumental provisions and good solid substantive laws respecting the subsidiarity principle and giving it room to blossom would be much better.

A prediction should conclude this short contribution: federalism in Europe is currently a very much alive and lively idea, dear to the hearts of many Europeans. In the future it must be even more so. The European Union will be a multi-tiered federal union or there will be no union.

Notes

* Austria along with Sweden and Finland became a full member of the Union on 1 January, 1995. The promised package of the 'Bundesstaatsreform' has not yet materialized and will not become constitutional law for a rather long time. So the basic questions of federalism in Austria remain open.

1. See C. Kessler, *The Austrian Federal Constitution*, 2nd edn. (Vienna, 1983).
2. On federalism in Austria see L. Adamovich and B.-C. Funk, *Österreichisches Verfassungsrecht*, 3rd edn. (Vienna and New York,

1985), 122 ff; B-C. Funk, *Die Bedeutung gliedstaatlichen Verfassungsrechts in der Gegenwart, Veröffentlichung der Vereinigung der Deutschen Staatsrechtslehrer* (Berlin and New York, 1988), 46, 57–91; F. Ermacora, *Österreichische Verfassungslehre*, I (Vienna, 1970), 252 ff; F. Koja, 'Der Bundesstaat als Rechtsbegriff', in *Theorie und Praxis des Bundesstaates, Föderative Ordnung III*, (Vienna and New York, 1974); id., *Das Verfassungsrecht der österreichischen Bundesländer*, 2nd edn. (Vienna and New York, 1988); R. Walter and H. Mayer, *Grundriß des Österreichischen Bundesverfassungsrechts*, 6th edn. (Vienna, 1988), 64–6.

3. See Adamovich and Funk, *Verfassungsrecht*, 171; B.-C. Funk, 'Die grundlegenden Ordnungsprobleme im System der bundesstaatlichen Kompetenzverteilung', *Juristische Blätter*, 98/17–18 (1976), 449; H.-G. Ruppe, *Finanzverfassung im Bundesstaat*, (Vienna, 1977), 25; P. Pernthaler, *Kompetenzverteilung in der Krise, Voraussetzungen und Grenzen der Kompetenzinterpretation in Österreich*, (Vienna, 1989).

4. Compare with the situation of the legislative power in budgetary matters: P. Pernthaler, *Österreichische Finanzverfassung*, (Vienna, 1984), 65; Ermacora, *Verfassungslehre*, I. 285.

5. See Art. 44(2) Bundes-Verfassungsgesetz: Adamovich and Funk, *Verfassungsrecht*, 94, 127; Walter and Mayer, *Grundriß*, 88; T. Öhlinger, *Verfassungsrechtliche Aspekte eines Beitritts Österreichs zu den EG* (Vienna, 1988), 19–49; Koja, *Verfassungsrecht*, 51–2.

6. See L. Adamovich and B.-C. Funk, *Allgemeines Verwaltungsrecht* (Vienna, 1987), 331; P. Pernthaler, *Die Zuständigkeitsverteilung zwischen Bund und Ländern auf dem Gebiete der Verwaltungsorganisation* (Vienna, 1976); H. Schäffer, 'Aktuelle Probleme des Föderalismus in Österreich', *Österreichische Juristenzeitung*, 36/1 (1981), 1; R. Rack, 'Föderalismus also reformpolitisches Anliegen', *Österreichische Juristenzeitung*, 45/8 (1990), 225–31; M. Whelan, 'Grundsatzgesetzgebung und Ausführunsgesetzgebung', in E. Hellbling and T. Mayer-Maly (eds.), *Theorie und Praxis des Bundesstaates* (Vienna, 1974), 11.

7. For more about the federal constitution of 1920 see K. Kelsen, W. Froehlich, and A. Merkl, *Die Bundesverfassung vom 1. Oktober 1920* (Vienna, 1922); Adamovich and Funk, *Verfassungsrecht*, 71; Ermacora, *Verfassungslehre*, i. 10; P. Pernthaler, *Die Staatsgründungsakte der österreichischen Bundesländer. Eine staatsrechtliche Untersuchung über die Entstehung des Bundesstaates* (Vienna, 1979); E. Hellbling, *Österreichische Verfassungs-und, Verwaltungsgeschichte*, 2nd edn. (Vienna, 1974).

8. Compare with the rebirth of Austria; K. Renner, *Denkschrift über die Geschichte der Unabhängigkeitserklärung und die Einsetzung der provisiorischen Regierung der Republik* (Vienna, 1945); L. Werner,

'Das Österreich vom 13.3.1938 und vom 27.4.1945. Eine Untersuchung von Kontinuität oder Diskontinuität der österreichischen Rechtsordnung', *Juristische Blälter*, 68/1 (1946), 2; id., 'Das Wiedererstehen Österreichs als Rechtsproblem', *Juristische Blätter*, 68/5 (1946), 85, 105; id., 'Nachwort', *Juristische Blätter*, 69/7–8 (1947), 137, 161; H. Siegler, *Österreichs Weg zur Souveränität, Neutralität und Prosperität 1945–1959* (Bonn, Zürich and Vienna, 1959); K. Gruber, *Zwischen Befreiung und Freiheit*, (Vienna, 1953); R. Hiscocks, *Rebirth of Austria* (Oxford, 1953); A. Schärf, *Österreichs Erneuerung 1945–1955*, 7th edn. (Vienna, 1960); cf. W. Oberleitner, *Politisches Handbuch der Republik Österreich 1945–1960* (Vienna, 1960).

9. Cf. *Länderbewußtsein*; also R. Rack, 'Federalism: Making the Community more Attractive to Europeans: The Austrian Point of View', in C. Church (ed.), *Widening the Community Circle*, University Association for Contemporary European Studies (London, 1990); Motz M., / P. Pernthaler, 'Der Bundesstaat als staatrechtliches Instrument der politischen Konfliktregelung am Beispiel der österreichischen Bundesverfassung', in F. Esterbauer, G. Heraud, and P. Pernthaler, (eds), *Föderalismus als Mittel permanenter Konfliktregelung* (Vienna, 1977).

10. Adamovich and Funk, *Verfassungsrecht*, 96, 128–9; cf. P. Pernthaler, *Die Forderungsprogramme der österreichischen Bundesländer*, (Vienna, 1980); S. Morscher, *Land und Provinz, Vergleich der Befugnisse der autonomen Provinz Bozen mit den Kompetenzen der österreichischen Bundesländer* (Vienna, 1981); K. Berchtold, *Die Verhandlungen zum Forderungsprogramme der Bundesländer seit 1956* (Vienna, 1988).

11. For more about Austrian federalism and further discussion of the reform of the competences and functions of the states see B.-C. Funk, *Neuordnung der Kompetenzverteilung in Österreich* (Vienna, 1991), 61–72; P. Pernathaler, *Kompetenzverteilung in der Krise*, Schriftenreihe des Instituts für Föderalismusforschung, no. 46, (Vienna, 1989), 13–21, 69–86.

12. See 'Österreichische Außenpolitische Dokumentation', Texte und Dokumente, Bundesministerium für auswärtige Angelegenheiten, (Vienna, 1990), 7, 8, 9, 74, 76.

13. See S. Huber, and P. Pernthaler, *Föderalismus und Regionalismus in Europäischer Perspektive* (Vienna, 1988), 13; F. Ossenbühl, (ed.), *Föderalismus und Regionalismus in Europa* (Baden-Baden, 1990); Kinsky, R., 'Die Prinzipien des Föderalismus', in F. Esterbauer, and Hingerleitner (eds.), *Die Europäische Gemeinschaft und Österreich* (Vienna, 1977), 141; W. Burtscher, *EG-Beitritt und Föderalismus* (Vienna, 1990), 92; S. Schmidt-Meinecke, *Bundesländer und*

Europäische Gemeinschaft, 2nd edn. (Speyer, 1988); S. Magiera and D. Merten, *Bundesländer und Europäische Gemeinschaft, Vorträge und Diskussionsbeiträge* (Speyer and Berlin, 1988); G. Ress, 'Die Europäischen Gemeinschaften und der deutsche Föderalismus', in *Europäische Grundrechtezeitschrift* 13/19 (1986), S 549–58.

14. See M.-J. Chiner, *Landesbericht Spanien*, (1990), 167–98; L. P. Suetens, 'Landesbericht Belgien', 263–306; and A. Onida, 'Landesbericht Italien', 239–62 all in F. Ossenbühl (ed.), *Föderalismus und Regionalismus* (Baden-Baden, 1991); R. Senelle, *The Reform of the Belgian State*, no. 198, (Brussel S, 1990).

15. For further details on the ARGE Alp and ARGE Alpen Adria see J. Lausegger, 'Die ARGE Alpen Adria—ein Sonderfall grenzüberschreitender regionaler Kooperation', in S. Huber and P. Pernthaler, *Föderalismus* (Vienna, 1990), 125.

16. See R. Rack, 'D'rum prüfe, wer sich ewig bindet', *EG-Magazin*, 1–2 (1992), 24–6; U. Kalbfleisch-Kottsieper, 'Viel Fortschritt ist versäumt worden', *EG-Magazin*, 1–2 (1992), 12, 13; W. Wessels, 'Maastricht: Ergebnisse, Bewertungen und Langzeittrends', in *Integration* 1 (1992), 2–16.

17. See P. Pernthaler and K. Weber, 'Versteinerung von Landeskompetenzen? Ein Betrag zur Auslegung von Art. 15(1) B-VG' in H. Schäffer (ed.), *FS E. Melichar: Im Dienst an Staat und Recht* (Vienna, 1983), 149 ff; B.-C. Funk, 'Neuordnung der Kompetenzverteilung in Österreich', in *Bundeskanzleramt-Verfassungsdienst* (Vienna, 1990), 107–24.

18. See R. Novak, 'Die relative Verfassungsautonomie der Länder,' in R. Rack (ed.), *Landesverfassungsreform*, (Vienna, 1982), 35–50.

19. C. Smekal and E. Theurl (eds.), *Finanzrecht und Finanzbedarf von Gebietskörperschaften* (Vienna, 1990).

20. See in detail K. Weber, *Die mittelbare Bundesverwaltung. Eine verfassungs- und verwaltungsrechtliche Untersuchung der Organisation und Verwaltung des Bundes im Bereich der Länder außer Wien, zugleich eine Geschichte der Behörden der allgemeinen staatlichen Verwaltung in den Ländern außer Wien* (Vienna, 1987).

21. Compare with Art 17: R. Walter and H. Mayer, *Bundesverfassungsrecht*, 109–10; G. Holzinger, 'Die Zuständigkeit zur Regelung der öffentlichen Auftragsvergabe', in *FS Wenger; Beiträge zum Wirtschaftsrecht* (Vienna, 1983), 139–46; E. Thöni, *Privatwirtschaftsverwaltung und Finanzausgleich* (Vienna, 1978).

22. See in detail Funk, *Bedeutung*, 73–87.

23. See 'Föderalismus-Enquete 20 March 1991', F. Ermacora, P. Pernthaler, J. Jäger, C. Havranek, and R. Unkart (as reviewers); M. Strimitzer, W. Burtscher, H. Legtmann, H. Schreiner, R. Unkart, E. Pramböck, W. Hummer, N. Wimmer, T. Öhlinger, R. Rack, *et al.*, 'EG

und Föderalismus', *Parlamentarische Enquete des Bundesrates*, 20 June 1990, xvii, GP, Klagenfurt.

24. See R. Rack, 'Rechtsfragen aus der Sicht der österreichischen Bundesländer', *Economy-Fachmagazin*, 10 (1991), 249, and 11 (1991), 258; Burtscher, *EG-Beitritt*, 67; R. Rack, 'Landesinterne Interessenvertretung, in Die Steiermärkische Landesregierung (ed.),' *Der Jurist im steirischen Landesdienst*, 1 (Graz, 1991), 18 ff.

25. Compare with details of the *avis* in 'Österreichische anßenpolitische Dokumentation', special issue on *Stellungnahme der Kommission der Europäischen Gemeinschaften zum Beitrittsantrag Österreichs, Bundesministerium für auswärtige Angelegenheiten* (Vienna, 1991).

26. G. B. Oschatz, and H. Risse, 'Europäische Integration und deutscher Föderalismus', *Europa-Archiv*, 43 (1988), 9–16.

27. See R. Rack, 'Bundesländer und Europäische Integration', *Österreichische Monatshefte*, 8 (1989), 23 ff; id., 'The Austrian Application', in UACES Occasional papers 6, *Widening the Circle*, 31 ff.; id., 'Europäische Integrationspolitik—eine neue Querschnittsmaterie und ihr innerstaatliches 'handling', in P. Pernthaler (ed.), *Außenpolitik der Gliedstaaten und Regionen* (Vienna, 1991), 33.

28. See Richtlinie des Bundeskanzleramt-Verfassungsdienst, *Legistische Fragen der Rechtsreform im Zusammenhang mit der Teilnahme Österreichs am Europäischen Wirtschaftsraum*, GZ 671.804/28 V/8/91, (Vienna, 1991); Vierter Bericht über den Stand der österreichischen Integrationspolitik, 29 Oct. 1991, Beilage zu VST-2520/2 vom, 4 Feb. 1992 (Vienna).

29. See Burtscher, *EG-Beitritt*, 135 f.; A. Khol, *Aufgaben auf dem Gebiet von Bundesverfassung und Föderalismus* (Vienna, 1988), in P. Marboe (ed.), *Österreich und Europa, Bericht der Europakommission der ÖVP: Österreichs Beziehungen zu den Europäischen Gemeinschaften* (Vienna, 1988).

30. Cf. the *Gutachten des Bundeskanzleramtes/Verfassungsdienst. Verfassungsrechtliche und verfassungspolitische Fragen einer Teilnahme Österreichs am EWR*, GZ 671.810/204-V/8/91; W. Burtscher, *Auswirkungen einer allfälligen EG-Mitgliedschaft auf den bundesstaatlichen Charakter Österreichs*, (Vienna, 1988); *Schluß-bericht der Arbeitsgruppe für Fragen der Neuordnung der bundesstaatlichen Kompetenzverteilung vom 7.3. 1991*, VST 56/11.

31. See *Föderalismus und EG*, Bundeskanzleramt, Verfassungsdienst, GZ 672.80-5/10-V/5/89; *Verbindungsstelle der österreichischen Bundesländer, Strukturreform/Bund-Länder-Paktum, Beschluß der Landeshauptmännerkonferenz vom 29.11.1191*, VST-56/661.

32. See more about the situation about the German states by F. Esterbauer, *Nationaler Freiraum in der Europäischen Gemeinschaft* (Vienna, 1989), 52 ff.; R. Streinz, *Die Auswirkungen des Europäischen*

Gemeinschaftsrecht auf die Kompetenzen der deutschen Bundesländer 15; H. J. Blanke, 'Die Bundesländer im Spannungsverhältnis zwischen Eigenstaatlichkeit und Europäischer Integration', in D. Heckmann, and K. Meßerschmidt, *Gegenwartsfragen des öffentlichen Rechts*, (Berlin, 1988), 53–81; S. Magiera, 'Als Bundesstaat in der Europäischen Gemeinschaft, Einführung in das Tagungsthema', in S. Magiera and D. Merten (eds.), *Bundesländer und Europäische Gemeinschaft* (Berlin, 1988), 11–19; U. Leonardy, 'Gegenwart und Zukunft der Arbeitsstrukturen des Föderalismus: Status quo, "Europa der Regionen" und staatliche Einheit Deutschlands', *Zeitschrift für Parlamentsfragen*, 21 (1990), 180–200; Fuhrmann-Mittlmeier, D., *Die deutschen Länder im Prozeß der Europäischen Einigung* (Berlin, 1991); G. Ress, 'Die Europäischen Gemeinschaften und der deutsche Föderalismus', *Europäische Grundrechte Zeitschrift*, 3 (1986), 549–58; S. Schmidt-Meinecke, *Bundesländer und Europäische Gemeinschaft, Entwicklung und Stand des Länderbeteiligung im Europäischen Einigungsprozeß*, 2nd edn. (Speyer, 1988).

33. See Funk, 'Neuordnung'; *Schlußbericht der Arbeitsgruppe für Fragen der Neuordnung der bundesstaatlichen Kompetenzverteilung*, vom 7.3.1991, VST 56/11.

34. See in detail *Entwurf einer B-VG-Novelle betreffend die Mitwirkungsrechte der Länder und Gemeinden in Angelegenheiten der Europäischen Integration*, GZ. Nr 372 Blg Sten.Prot.NR XVIII GP; see also draft paper concerning co-decision rights of the states and local communities on European integration matters, 26 Feb. 1992, GZ. 671.805/29-V/8/92. See also the supplementary law on the Austrian federal Constitution, BGBL 276/1992; and the agreement between the federation and the states on the participatory rights of the states concerning European integration, BGBL 775/1992.

35. For more information see W. Hummer and M. Schweitzer, *Ausverkauf Österreichs*, (Vienna, 1990); W. Burtscher, 'Ausländergrundverkehr und EG-Beitritt', *Economy*, 8 (1989), 2–12; B. Eccher, 'Ausländergrundverkehr-EG, Verhinderung von Umgehungsgeschäften', *Economy*, 4/3 (1990), 2 ff; R. Rack, 'Grundverkehr in EWR und in der EG', *Economy* (1992).

36. See 'Das Netz des dänischen Grundverkehrsrechtes—ein Modell für Salzburg?' *Handelskammer Salzburg* (June 1991).

37. See R. Rack, 'D'rum prüfe, wer sich ewig bindet', *EG-Magazin*, 1–2 (1992), 24–6; W. Wessels, 'Maastricht: Ergebnisse, Bewertungen und Langzeittrends', *Integration* 1 (1992), 2–16.

10

Switzerland: The Model in Need of Adaptation?

DANIEL THÜRER

In a recent handbook about the federal systems of the world, Switzerland is described as being 'one of the three classic federations in the world along with the United States and Canada' and furthermore 'the oldest and probably the most fully federal in its political culture and structure'.[1] Is Swiss federalism—as one could legitimately ask—an outdated, anachronistic form of government without any relevance, is it even an obstacle for effectively dealing with present-day problems of public life, or is it a help in solving the challenges of modern society? Whichever is the case, it is worth considering the three questions set out in the following pages, namely: What are the particular features of the Swiss federal system? How does it adapt to the dynamics of European integration? Could the Swiss federal system be applied, in whole or in part, as a model for organizing and shaping Europe?

1. FEATURES OF THE SWISS FEDERAL SYSTEM

Alle diese, zum Teil fremden Gemeinden und Herrschaften wurden zusammengehalten durch ein vor Jahrhunderten gegebenes Wort.

Johannes von Müller commenting at the end of the eighteenth century on the origins and the evolution of the Swiss Confederation.

Rien n'est plus contraire à l'essence même du fédéralisme que l'esprit théorétique et les généralisations.

Denis de Rougemont

Origins and Political Foundation

No other country in Europe is split into so many small autonomous political units as Switzerland. As a middle-level of government structure only the Norwegian Fylkers are comparable with the Swiss cantons as far as the size of their population—if not their territory—is concerned; and only in France is the average size of local government areas smaller than in Switzerland. As such and in its essence the 'systemless system', the 'anarchic order' called the Swiss Confederation is a product of history. It grew out of a complex network of alliances between communities of different status, size, religion, ideology, and political orientation, and some vestiges of the communal state of the Middle Ages are still visible in its present-day political institutions and its mentality. Swiss federalism is, furthermore, the product of the varied topography and the linguistic and religious pluralism of the country. Federalism also appears to be a state of mind: 'un sentiment politique' as one constitutional lawyer observed.[2] It is not conceived as an end in itself but as a means to protect, above all, two basic values underlying this institutional order. These principles are the maintenance and strengthening of regional and local communities with their varied identities on the one hand, and the possibility of creating an optimal form of self-government and political freedom for citizens within those communities on the other. As such, the federal arrangements of government have evolved gradually and pragmatically and were not constructed rationally. They were based on the common political will of the citizens and yet they were not a product of deliberate choice. Napoleon rightly commented to a Swiss delegation in 1803: 'Les constitutions des petits cantons sont sûrement pas raisonnables; mais c'est l'usage qui les a établies. Quand l'usage et la raison se trouvent en opposition, c'est le premier qui l'emporte.'[3]

Constitutional Shape

By the Swiss Constitution of 1848, which was totally revised in 1874, the old Swiss Confederation was transformed into a federal state. In its basic structure it was modelled on the Constitution of the United States. As in the American constitutional system all powers not delegated to the federal government by the constitution or on the basis of the constitution were reserved to the cantons. Similar to the system of government in the United States a second chamber within the national parliament was created in which each canton is represented with two seats and every half-canton with one seat. As in the United States a relatively independent executive power has been established, but instead of a president, a collegial body of seven members is entrusted with the power of government. This Federal Council, composed according to a so-called magic formula, is thought to be highly representative of the various regions, opinions, languages, and creeds from all over Switzerland. Finally, as in the United States and other federal states, federal power was successively extended, mainly as a result of the growing financial resources of the central government. On the basis of a complex web of federal grants-in-aid, a highly integrated, non-transparent, and heavily overloaded system of intergovernmental relations emerged.[4]

As a result, in constitutional law and political and administrative reality, Switzerland gradually emerged as a somewhat more centralized system in which legislative power is concentrated to a large extent at the federal level, whereas it became one of the principal functions of the cantons to supplement federal legislation and to implement it in relation to its citizens. Thus, even though Switzerland has, in the course of history, gradually developed into a stronger and more compact state, psychologically it is still conceived by its citizens as a highly heterogeneous, pluralistic, barely visible set of units. Switzerland as a state of mind, as a 'sentiment politique', is not convergent with political reality; the 'pays légal' does not correspond with the 'pays mental, pays d'esprit'.

Unlike the situation in the United States, the Swiss Federal Court was prevented by the Constitution from becoming the guardian and arbiter of last resort for every aspect of federal–state relations. This is because a review of constitutionality of federal laws and international treaties is excluded by Swiss constitutional law.

Strengths and Weaknesses

In the course of its development Swiss federalism has proved to have strengths and advantages, but also certain weaknesses and disadvantages. Two examples within each category may illustrate the point.

(a) *Strengths and benefits.* One special strength of Swiss federalism seems to be a marked constitution-making capacity at the cantonal level. What is meant by this aspect of constitutional life? One of the outstanding features of modern Swiss constitutional history was the creation in 1976 of a new canton. After a more or less intense political struggle lasting 160 years between the Canton of Bern and some of its Jura districts, it became possible to carve a new canton out of the existing canton of Bern. The Republic and Canton of Jura, which became the twenty-sixth member of the Confederation, came into existence as a result of a set of complicated negotiations and diplomatic procedures of dispute settlement, in which all levels of the Swiss federal system were involved. The borders of the new canton were determined in a series of plebiscites. Throughout the history of self-determination it is hard to find another example in which the plebiscite method has been applied with such a degree of perfection as was the case in the efforts to define the people and the territory of the Canton of Jura.

As a new member of the Confederation, the Canton of Jura created a highly original constitution for itself. In addition, during the last two or three decades, in a great number of other Swiss cantons, constitutional assemblies have been elected and cantonal parliaments have been entrusted with the task of framing new constitutions. We now find, at the cantonal level, a colourful variety of old and new constitutions: progressive and conservative ones, limited and open ones, some more plebiscitarian and others more representative, some more ecologically and others more economically orientated. Each speaks with its own voice and gives expression in its own right to varying cantonal identities. The cantonal constitution-making capacity is certainly a sign of creativity and vitality within the Swiss federal system.

A second strength of Swiss federalism seems to be its regional openness in shaping trans-border relations with local or regional units of other countries. There is no space here to expand on the extremely intricate problems of municipal and international law which are involved in establishing trans-border institutions and functioning regional arrangements.[5] Let us briefly consider, however, as a particular feature of the Swiss constitution, that the

cantons are entrusted with a certain degree of international personality. Thus Switzerland does not appear in its external relations as
a monolithic unit. It leaves some—limited—room for the cantons to
appear as subjects of rights and duties under international law and
to deal and involve themselves with subordinate units of other
states within the scope of their competences, i.e. in areas such as
regional planning, pollution control, hospitals and schooling. This
potential for trans-border legal relations and informal contacts
should be even more fully exploited by the cantons and be more
generously acknowledged by the federal government than it is
today.[5a] In addition, efforts of the Council of Europe to facilitate
similar constitutional regimes in other and, above all, in neighbouring countries, should be supported. For this conception of European integration from the bottom can flourish only if legally
competent actors exist on both sides of the border.

(b) *Weaknesses and disadvantages.* Let us now turn to the drawbacks of the Swiss federal system. After all, the theme of the present
chapter is also to demonstrate the need for adaptation. In this
context the following two issues might be raised: the incapacity to
restructure federal–cantonal relations in a major and meaningful
way; and the difficulties encountered by Switzerland in adequately
finding its way within the process of European integration
which is conditioned, to a certain degree, by its federal system of
government.

With regard to the first point, the incapacity to redefine and
reorganize federal–cantonal relations, in the 1970s meaningful efforts were undertaken by commissions of experts and government
officials to redefine and reshape the federal system. This was with
the overall intention of restoring a certain degree of convergence of
public tasks and financial resources at each level of government and
thereby strengthening cantonal autonomy and responsibility in the
federal system. These efforts proved, in the course of political
events, to be futile. The same was true of the efforts to redefine
federalism in a new, totally revised federal constitution which included, for instance, as a guideline for federal co-operation, the
principle of federal loyalty (*Bundestreue*).[6] Too many conflicting
official, corporate, institutional, and private interests were involved
to make reform possible. In its present state Swiss federalism is, on
the whole, characterized by a highly defensive attitude from the

cantons.[7] It has been used, throughout the centuries, to keeping the federal government from intruding into the bastion of their traditional powers. But only infrequently have political initiatives and innovation of a lasting character had their origin in the cantons. Highly democratized methods of decision-making and competition with other cantons for obtaining financial resources prevented them, as a general rule, from becoming more active as partners in the federal compact.[8]

The second point of criticism of Swiss federalism concerns the fact that Switzerland is experiencing some difficulties in finding its proper place within the process of European integration. In a double sense the mechanisms, procedures, and traditions of Swiss federalism are, to a certain extent, the cause of these difficulties in adapting flexibly and in time to a changing European environment. In the first place, the system of government was, as a whole, conceived to keep government small, limited, and relatively powerless, in order to prevent it from taking action which might endanger individual liberty and regional autonomy. Special safeguards were introduced into the state structure in order to hinder the federal government from becoming committed on the international scene. So a double majority is required for the decision of adherence to the Agreement on the European Economic Area (EEA-Agreement) or membership of the European Union: the majority of the people and the majority of the cantons. Secondly, in a more indirect way, federalism tends to block the opening up of Switzerland to European integration. Federalism, cherished in Switzerland for centuries, seems to have strengthened and cultivated a sense of localism, introversion, and abstinence from international affairs. Local questions absorb a good deal of the political energy and imagination both of the authorities and of the people, and make it difficult for many citizens to think on a larger international political scale. However, in its true sense, federalism should, on the contrary, be a principle facilitating change and integration. Federalism as it exists today is itself a product of integration: of integration from the local to the cantonal and from the cantonal to the federal unit. Becoming a member of wider European institutions would, in this sense, merely involve placing a fourth circle around the federal system developed within the framework of the nation-state.[9] It is to be hoped that the dynamic force of federalism will be rediscovered and that in a non-defensive, open spirit new methods and mechanisms will be found in order to make Swiss federalism function effectively within a federally organized Europe.

2. SWISS FEDERALISM FACED WITH THE PROCESS OF EUROPEAN ORGANIZATION

Ein 'Bundesstaat im Bundesstaat' bedeutet auf der Ebene der technischen Organisation 'eine heillose Komplikation'.

Hans Kelsen, 1927

General Premisses

In May 1992 in Porto (Portugal) Switzerland, together with the six other EFTA countries, the twelve EC Member States, and the European Communities signed the EEA Agreement. This Treaty was subsequently adopted by the two Chambers of the Federal Assembly, but it was rejected on 6 December 1992 by the people and the cantons by way of a referendum. The future course of Swiss foreign policy is now uncertain, but a second vote on the EEA Agreement as a long-term aim of Switzerland's integration policy cannot be excluded and remains highly relevant as a subject to be discussed in this chapter. In the event of a possible future full membership of the EEA or the European Union, the Swiss constitutional order would become part of an autonomous supranational legal system which would have direct effect within the sphere of domestic law and be directly applicable to individuals and enterprises if its principles and rules were designed to and were capable of having such an effect.[10] Community law or EEA law as a whole (i.e. its primary and secondary norms) or EEA law would take priority over the national legal order including its constitution. From this perspective the question arises if and in what way would Swiss federalism be affected or its structure and working mechanisms be modified by being integrated into the larger supranational order. It therefore seems reasonable to analyse first the constituent elements of a federal system such as that of Switzerland, and then subsequently to examine if, to what extent, and in what way these basic principles would be affected or modified.

In his classic treatise on *Federal Government* Q.C. Wheare stated that:

Federal governments exist . . . when the powers of government for a community are divided substantially according to the principle that there is a single independent authority for the whole area in respect of some matters and that there are independent regional authorities for other matters, each set of authorities being co-ordinate with and not subordinate to the others within its own prescribed sphere.[11]

This description does not seem to conceptualize federalism in a complete and correct way. It was modelled on the traditional American doctrine of 'dual federalism'. But such a dualistic system of separate and co-ordinated 'sets' of governments has, as a matter of fact and of law, never existed, even under the US Constitution. It has been replaced in the literature and in public debate by the concepts and terms of 'co-operative federalism', 'intergovernmental relations', 'new federalism', etc.[12] All these theories and doctrines lay emphasis on the great variety of political, administrative, and financial links and interrelations at all levels of government as essential elements of federalism. Thus, in the light of the reality of the modern state it seems to be appropriate to start from the premiss that every modern federal system is constituted by the existence and interplay of three elements: first, the constitutional division of powers between the central and regional levels of government (including their constitution-making authority); second, the implementation by regional authorities of laws and programmes enacted by the central government and policies shaped by it; and third, institutions and practices enabling political authorities, professional bureaucracies, and people of regional (and local) areas to represent their values and interests and to influence, shape, and contribute to decisions made at the central level. The question is to what degree and in what form these three constitutive elements of Swiss federalism would be affected if in future Switzerland became a member of the EEA Agreement or of the European Union.

Intervention in Cantonal Autonomy

As far as the spheres of competence of the federal, cantonal, and local governments are concerned, it seems obvious that supranational law would first of all intervene at the federal level. Much of the economic and social legislation which, having been gradually built up over the years under the federal constitution in order to create a Swiss internal market, would be replaced by Union or EEA law intended to create an internal market within a larger economic and political framework at the European level. The federal government would thus—as far as the supranational character of integration law is concerned—appear to be the main 'loser' in the process of European integration. Important branches of federal law such as customs law, the law of aliens, and banking and insurance law would become inapplicable if and to the extent that they conflicted with Union or EEA law. Or they would have to be modified in order to fit into the *acquis communautaire*. New conflicting legislation would be barred in fields occupied by Union or EEA law.[13] The sphere of cantonal autonomy (or 'sovereignty' according to the terminology of the Swiss federal Constitution) would be affected far less extensively. Matters such as public education, public markets, professional regulations, and economic monopolies would be affected.[14] Legislation within these domains would only have to be adapted and not totally replaced. Finally, intervention of Union or EEA law in the domain of local autonomy, such as regulations on public employment and public procurement, would be of only a marginal nature.

Generally speaking, a rule of diminishing relevance of supranational law may be observed from the top to the bottom level of the federal order. Important consequences of this fact are clear as far as the institutions of direct democracy (popular initiative and referendum) are concerned. They, as has already been demonstrated, form an essential part and are one of the main legitimating bases of the Swiss federal system. At a federal level around 10 per cent of the popular votes could not have taken place at all and 20 per cent could have taken place only to a limited extent if Switzerland had already been a member of the European Community or the EEA Agreement over the last ten years. By way of contrast, within the cantonal sphere of competence, there are hardly any popular initiatives or referenda to be found which would have to be invalidated because of their conflict with supranational law. And within the sphere of local autonomy there would be hardly any effect on direct democracy at all.

Implementation of Union Law or EEA Law within the Federal System of Switzerland

One of the basic constitutional principles of the law of European integration is that it is shaped and regulated on the supranational plane and is implemented by the Member States. Within the broad framework of its constitutional provisions and by use of the instrument of Community directives rather than regulations (Article 189 EC Treaty), a large measure of discretion is often left to the Member States in completing the principles agreed upon at the Community level and adapting them flexibly. In this way they meet the special needs and traditions of each country and fit in with its established institutional structures. In this context the question naturally arises: what level of government is responsible for the discharge and implementation of integration law within a federal system? And: does a federal system built into and connected with a larger federal order result in a 'terrible complication' as Hans Kelsen said in a comment concerning the possible integration of Austria into the German Weimar Republic?[15]

When analysing and developing the basic conception of the Community constitution, the European Court of Justice decided in several cases that, as a general rule, Community law is addressed to the Member States as such. It is then a matter of national constitutional law to determine the level within its federal structure and the organs within the relevant community which are to be responsible for the implementation of Community or Union law.[16] The Union constitution is said to be *föderalismusblind*, as component units such as *Länder* or regions do not have a status of their own under its law. From the perspective of Swiss national constitutional law it would seem to be a sound principle of construction to distribute the authority to implement supranational European law along the general lines of the division of powers between the federal government and the cantons. European law would thus have to be developed or applied by the federal or cantonal authorities respectively if, as a matter of domestic legislation, it fell within the sphere of their competence. Of course, new methods of co-operative federalism (vertical and horizontal) would additionally have to be developed in order to enable the often very small Swiss cantonal units, with their limited personnel and financial resources, to discharge their functions under Union law effectively. In order to fulfil its respon-

sibility *vis-à-vis* the other Member States and/or the European
Union and to avoid legal procedures on the supranational plane
the federal government would, in the interest of the functioning of
the system as a whole, be entitled to step in and to act instead of the
cantons if they should refuse to implement the relevant principles
and provisions or fail to fulfil their responsibilities in an effective
and proper manner and within the set time limits.

Representative Federalism

Essential features of modern federalism seem to be the legal rights
and the *de facto* power of the constituent units to influence and
shape and to participate in the decision-making processes at the
higher level of government. Within the framework of Swiss constitutional law, institutions and certain consultative rights were designed to give status and voice to the cantons at the federal level.
For example, there is the requirement of a double majority—i.e. the
consent of the people and the cantons—for fundamental decisions
such as changes in constitutional law. To a much greater degree
than provided for in constitutional law, means and mechanisms
were created in practical political life for cantons to represent their
values and interests in the federal arena. Cantons and cities are
informally represented in Bern, in that many federal politicians
start their careers (*cursus honorum*) at the local or regional level
before taking up federal office. Additionally, the accumulation of
functions at different levels of government and a dense network of
personal and functional relations characterize the working mechanisms of Swiss federalism. Even city mayors and local public
officials go to Bern, due to the organization of private associations
which are intended to put pressure, as semi-official 'topocratic' and
'professional' lobbies, on the federal government.[17]

Obviously, as a result of integrating Switzerland into the framework of European institutions, representative federalism would
lose much of its object and its political potential, in that essential
powers of the national authorities of the federal system would be
shifted to the supranational level. New institutions would have to
be designed to enable cantons (and local authorities) to influence
and bring pressure to bear on the federal authorities charged with
the power to take part in European decision-making. In this

connection the proposal has been made to transform the Council of States (the Second Chamber) into a sort of *Bundesrat* as in the German or Austrian constitutions, in which the governments of the *Länder* are represented. But such a *Bundesratslösung* would hardly fit into the federal tradition and democratic value-system of Switzerland, especially considering the fact that the German *Bundesrat* functions more as a power instrument in the hands of *Länder* bureaucracies and a highly centralized party system than as a platform on which the diverging identities and political visions of regions and their peoples can be given adequate expression. In any case such a profound transformation of the institutional system would make sense only in the event of Switzerland joining the European Union as a full member and not in the case of the EEA Agreement in which no provision is made for supranational institutions. Rather than a possible transformation of the Council of States, the creation of a 'permanent inter-cantonal consultation organ', a 'Council of Cantons' would be sensible.[18] It could be given the power to influence the federal vote in the process of European legislation by giving the cantons the right to veto such projects by majority vote if, at the constitutional level, they fall within the competence of the cantons. But such an influence would be excluded by overriding considerations of foreign or European policy.[19]

3. SWISS FEDERALISM—A MODEL FOR EUROPEAN ARCHITECTURE?

Yet all the while there is a remedy which, if it were generally and spontaneously adopted by the great majority of people in many lands, would as if by a miracle transform the whole scene, and would in a few years make all Europe, or the greater part of it, as free and happy as Switzerland is today. What is this sovereign remedy? It is to recreate the European family, or as much of it as we can, and to provide it with a structure under which it can dwell in peace, in safety and in freedom. We must build a kind of United States of Europe.

Winston Churchill, speech at the University of Zurich, 1946

Switzerland was, on the whole, reluctant to open up its constitutional structures in order to participate in the process of reorganizing Europe by means of intergovernmental co-operation and supranational integration. It became a founding member of the Organization of Economic Co-operation in Europe (OECE) in 1948 and of the European Free Trade Association (EFTA) in 1960, but it entered the Council of Europe only in 1963. Like all other EFTA countries, it concluded a Free Trade Agreement with the European Communities in 1972, and signed the Agreement on the European Economic Area in May 1992.[20] But the majority of the voting citizens as well as of the cantons did not give their consent to the ratification of this Treaty. In 1992 the Federal Council had deposited a demand to take up membership negotiations in Brussels. But as things stand at present Swiss voters seem not yet ready to undertake this decisive and logical step towards European integration. The Swiss constitutional structure, which has in the past shown itself able successfully to cope with new forms of political challenges and demands, in this case proved to be an obstacle rather than a help in responding and adapting to a changing external environment in an effective and timely way. The institutions of direct democracy favoured an insular, highly localist view of politics: they were marked by a preference for little or administrative rather than statesman-like government, and stood in the way of developing visions and institutional designs for the establishment and strengthening of overriding schemes of an effective and modern European order. Similarly—and paradoxically— Swiss federalism was consequently unable to develop its potential in order to reach out flexibly and embrace this new dimension of interaction and co-operation. On the contrary, it supported a rather conservative, defensive attitude towards the demands of European and international solidarity. As far as security policy is concerned, Switzerland is not yet ready to give up its policy of military neutrality as long as no overriding, effective, and credible security system is established to protect its interests in an equal or better way. It is convinced that the will and capacity to keep its own house in order should also be considered as a contribution to strengthening security on an international plane.

Does Switzerland, despite its hesistance in joining in the process of European integration, have sufficient legitimacy to take part in the debate concerning a new European architecture? It should, in my opinion, endeavour to make its contribution, as many factors indicate that we will soon be entering a new phase of European institution-building in which federalism might, within a larger Community composed of many more small and medium-sized states, play a decisive role. Federalism, which used to be a predominant subject in constitutional debate in the late eighteenth and early nineteenth centuries, might again become the theme of the age in a much larger context including infranational, transnational, international, and supranational elements of construction. The chance of passing on the knowledge and practical experience gained by the fruitful cohabitation of a highly diverse population would be a strong motivating force for Switzerland to join or to follow other EFTA countries in their application for full EU membership. The country which never believed in the doctrine of absolute national sovereignty as proclaimed by Bodin and Hobbes would seem to be predestined to adopt and to follow the alternative, more relativist and empirical line of political philosophy developed by Althusius, Locke, and Montesquieu,[21] with a view to building up from the bottom a strong union consisting of stable, autonomous, and democratically governed composite units.

However, if one were to judge the will and the capacity of Switzerland to influence constitution-making in the sense just mentioned, there is no doubt that its federal system and the experiences incorporated within it do stand out as a possible model and yardstick with which European institutions as living realities as well as ideas and plans for reform might be compared. Let me briefly try to extract a few lessons from Swiss federalism which could be, like that of other countries,[22] a source of inspiration and a guiding principle in the endeavour to design European institutions in a more federal way. In this sense it seems to be true, as Denis de Rougement noted, that national constitutions with their specific characteristics should not be copied or exported but could well be considered as 'trustees of a political formula' which might be relevant at the international and supranational level as well.

Constitutionalism versus functionalism. Jean Monnet's philosophy of 'functionalism', which aims at gradually building up, from problem to problem, new supranational structures has proved, in practice, to create a highly technocratic, over-loaded, and complex system of inter-bureaucracy and inter-lobby relations.[23] The climax of this development was the Maastricht Treaty in which, hidden from the eye of public opinion, new constitutional structures were conceived in poorly drafted instruments by heads of states and their advisers. In contrast to this approach, the experiences of classic federal states indicate that political structures should be planned, debated, and created in an open process and should be based on broad principles. Functions should be designed as a consequence of constitutionally defined roles, and roles are not supposed to follow functions. To cope with spill-over problems on the basis of professional or technical skill alone does not seem a sound principle for shaping an economic and political organization of state-like dimensions, such as the European Union.

The subsidiarity principle versus a true division of powers. In the Maastricht Treaty the principle of subsidiarity is mentioned no fewer than three times (in the preamble, in Article B, and, *in extenso*, in Article 3*b* of the Community Treaty). It is conceivable on the basis of this principle that a Member State, in accordance with Article 173 of the EC-Treaty, might appeal to the Court of the European Communities in order to exclude Community action in a certain field as being *ultra vires*. In such proceedings the subsidiarity principle[24] would not prove to be a hard-and-fast rule of decision, but rather appear as one among differing arguments and guiding principles of judicial decision.[25] As part and parcel of the Maastricht agreement it seems above all, in the judgment of some observers, to have been introduced with the intention not so much of counterbalancing but rather of disguising a further round of centralization. Instead of this approach a better strategy of federal constitution-making would be to draw the line between the spheres of competence of the Community and the Member States in a clear and detailed way. In such a scheme, only those general powers should be attributed to the Community which are indispensable to safeguard the common interests of Member States as far as the achievements of a functioning internal market and some common goals and principles of the Member States in the field of internal and external politics are concerned. Furthermore, a system of impartial constitutional adjudication should be designed and put into practice in order to ensure that the dividing-line and an adequate balance of power between national and supranational powers is not transgressed.

Internal market versus regionalism. European and domestic constitutional law should be seen to be part of an emerging, comprehensive system. This overall structure has the purpose of creating, on the one hand, a uniform order guaranteeing to all involved the same economic rights and chances in competition without discrimination. On the other hand, there seems to be a real need to create, to develop, and to protect autonomous and democratic institutions on a regional basis in fields such as culture, planning law, and the preservation of nature, in which history can be preserved, new life styles can be developed, community life and identification would be possible,[26] and specific policy and economic advantages of small and flexible units could be pursued.[27] A truly federally inspired European order would be constituted as a whole by a dialectic tension or the countervailing forces of market uniformity on the one side and political as well as cultural diversity and competition on the other. As a principle of organizational construction it would not seem to be advisable to conceive of the regions as independent partners in a tripartite system, as envisaged by the European Parliament in the concept of *Europe des régions* but rather to let them communicate, as a matter of principle, with the European institutions through the authorities of the nation-states. This same construction principle of the 'Roman Fountain' underlies the Swiss, German, and Austrian Constitutions, in which the cantons or *Länder* are conceived as intermediate pieces in the federal architecture between local governments and the federal government: towns and villages are as a general rule considered, *vis-à-vis* the federal authorities, as integral parts of the cantons or *Länder*.[28] Similarly, European regions should be primarily developed within and not against the nation-state. The democratic nation-state does not seem to have outlived its purpose as a legitimate category of international order but should be transformed from the structure of highest order and last instance into a structure forming a part of a whole.

Solidarity versus democracy. Institutions strengthening solidarity among European nations and a full measure of democratic citizen participation are concepts which cannot both be fully realized at the same time.[29] For Switzerland, sacrifices of its direct democracy would inevitably have to be made if it decided to join the European Union. But the Swiss Constitution might also be considered as a model for the creation of government structures in a comprehensive sense which, like pyramids, are democratically broader at the base and narrower at the top. Both principles—solidarity among states and peoples as well as opportunities for grass-roots democracy as a potential for innovation originating at the lowest level—seem to be imperatives and challenges for organized modern life. They should be optimally balanced in a comprehensive system embracing all governmental institutions at a national, international and supranational level. In this context, the protection of a broad field of autonomy of regional and local communities which are best able to bring government really close to the people seems to be, as an overall principle of construction, more important than the problem of compensation for losses of their competence by including them in decision-shaping or decision-making processes at the higher level. This latter is at present the focus of the debate on supranational law and its implications for federalism in the Federal Republic of Germany, in Austria, and in Switzerland. But these compensations seem to serve the interest of local and regional governments and their bureaucracies rather than the true will of the people.

Alexis de Tocqueville criticized religious people 'qui adorent la statue, oubliant la divinité qu'elle représente'.[30] What is—we might ask and conclude—the true substance of federalism which is so often overlooked by technicians of political and economic efficiency? Two features seem to be relevant and might be kept in mind as possible lessons from the Swiss experience: the first is that there is, at the core of the system, a true political will on the part of all parties concerned, to co-operate within a broad constitutional framework,[31] and the second is that the powers of the centre be limited to the statement of general goals and principles whereas the integrity of the parts is otherwise preserved and protected in order to secure cultural diversity and free political choice on the basis of political autonomy and liberal democracy.

Notes

After the submission of this chapter, Swiss citizens rejected by a majority of 50.3 per cent and with the vote of 16 out of 22 cantons, the Agreement on the European Economic Area. Nevertheless, as a future second vote on the Agreement or on full EU membership is by no means precluded, I have not substantially altered the text of this chapter.

1. D. J. Elazar (ed.), *Federal Systems of the World—A Handbook of Federal, Confederal and Autonomy Arrangements* (London, 1991), U. 252.

2. J.-F. Aubert, *Droit constitutionnel suisse* (Neuchâtel, 1967), 203.
3. See S. Möckli, *Die schweizerischen Landsgemeinde-Demokratien* (Bern, 1987), 79.
4. See M. Frenkel, *Föderalismus und Bundesstaat*, 2 vols. (Bern and Frankfurt a.M., 1984/6); H. P. Fagagnini, *Föderalistischer Aufgabenverbund in der Schweiz* (Bern and Stuttgart, 1991); D. Thürer, *Bund und Gemeinden—Eine rechtsvergleichende Untersuchung zu den unmittelbaren Beziehungen zwischen Bund und Gemeinden in der Bundesrepublik Deutschland, den Vereinigten Staaten von Amerika und der Schweiz* (Berlin, Heidelberg, New York, London, Paris, and Tokyo, 1986).
5. For a more detailed analysis see D. Thürer, 'Föderalismus und Regionalismus in der schweizerischen Aussenpolitik: Zum Verhältnis von Bundeskompetenzen und kantonalen Kompetenzen unter veränderten Umständen', *Schweizerisches Zentralblatt für Staats- und Verwaltungsrecht* (1992), S. 49 ff.
5a. Meanwhile, in a general report of 1994, the Federal Council adopted a quite generous line of action; see Bericht (des Bundesrates) über die grenzüberschreitende Zusammenarbeit und die Mitwickung der Kantone an der Aussenpolitik vom F. März 1994, in: Bundesblatt 1994 Ia, 620 ff.
6. See P. Saladin, 'Bund und Kantone', *Zeitschrift für Schweizerisches Recht* (1984/II), 435 ff., 448 ff.
7. See D. Schindler, *Gemeinde Zollikon. Föderalismus und Gemeindeautonomie im Sog von Europa 92* (Zollikon, 1991), 26 ff.
8. See especially D. Schindler, 'Schweizerischer und europäischer Föderalismus', in *Schweizerisches Zentralblatt für Staats- und Verwaltungsrecht* (1992), 193 ff., 197 ff.
9. See O. Jacot-Guillarmod, 'Conséquences, sur le fédéralisme suisse, d'une adhésion de la Suisse à la Communauté européenne', in *EG-Recht und schweizerische Rechtsordnung, Beiheft zur Zeitschrift für Schweizerisches Recht* (Bern, 1990), 3 ff. See the reports of Helmut Steinberger, Eckart Klein and Daniel Thürer on the subject 'Der Verfassungsstaat als Glied einer europäischen Gemeinschaft', in *Veröffentlichungen der Vereinigung der Deutschen Staatsrechtslehrer*, 50 (1991).
10. See D. Lasok and J. W. Bridge, *The Law of Economics in the European Communities*, 4th edn. (London, 1991); B. Beutler, R. Bieber, J. Pipkorn and J. Streil, *Die Europäische Gemeinschaft—Recht und Politik*, 3rd edn. (Baden-Baden, 1987).
11. K. C. Wheare, *Federal Government*, 4th edn. (Oxford, 1964), 35.
12. See e.g. D. J. Elazar, *American Federalism*, 2nd edn. (New York, 1972); W. H. Riker, *Federalism: Origin, Operation, Significance* (Boston, 1964); W. B. Graves, *American Intergovernmental Relations*

(New York, 1964); M. Grodzins (ed. D. J. Elazar), *The American System* (Chicago, 1966); M. D. Reagan, *The New Federalism* (Oxford, 1972); M. J. C. Vile, *The Structure of American Federalism* (Oxford, 1961); Thürer, *Bund und Gemeinden*, 101 ff.

13. For details concerning the different fields affected see D. Schindler, G. Hertig, J. Kellenberger, D. Thürer and R. Zäch (eds.), *Die Europaverträglichkeit des schweizerischen Rechts* (Zürich, 1990).

14. See Kontaktgremium der Kantone, *Anpassung des kantonalen Rechts an das EWR-Recht* (Bern, 1991).

15. See G. Ress, 'Die Europäischen Gemeinschaften und der deutsche Föderalismus', in *Europäische Grundrechte-Zeitschrift* (1986), 489.

16. For more details of the whole problem see D. Thürer and Ph. Weber, 'Zur Durchführung von Europäischem Gemeinschaftsrecht durch Gliedstaaten eines Bundesstaates', *Schweizerisches Zentralblatt für Staats- und Verwaltungsrecht* (1991), 429 ff.

17. See Thürer, *Bund und Gemeinden*, 266 ff.

18. See R. J. Schweiter, 'Die Kantone vor der Europäischen Herausforderung', *Jahrbuch für öffentliches Recht* (1991), 59 ff.

19. On the composition and functions of such an institution see Jacot-Guillarmod, 'Conséquences', 26 ff.; D. Thürer, 'Schweizer Verfassungsordnung vor der Herausforderung durch die europäische Integration; Perspektiven, Prinzipien und heisse Eisen', *Zeitschrift für Schweizerisches Recht* (1992), 93 ff. From a German perspective see K. Hailbronner, 'Die deutschen Bundesländer in der EG', *Juristen-Zeitung* (1990), 149 ff.; P. Bohley, 'Chancen und Gefährdungen des Föderalismus', in K. Bohr, *Föderalismus—Demokratische Struktur für Deutschland und Europa* (München, 1992); H.-J. Blanke, *Föderalismus und Integrationsgewalt* (Berlin, 1991); D. Fuhrmann-Mittelmeier, *Die Deutschen Länder im Prozess der Europäischen Einigung* (Berlin, 1991); R. Hrbek and U. Thaysen (eds.), *Die Deutschen Länder und die Europäischen Gemeinschaften* (Baden-Baden, 1986); D. Merten (ed.), *Föderalismus und Europäische Gemeinschaften* (Berlin, 1990). From an Austrian point of view: P. Pernthaler (ed.), *Auswirkungen eines EG-Beitritts auf die föderalistische Struktur Österreichs* (Vienna, 1989).

20. See B. Spinner, 'Das Abkommen über den EWR im Lichte der schweizerischen Integrationspolitik', Conference of 8 May 1992. See, as forms of legal and political analysis (in alphabetical order): Th. Bruha, 'Verfassungsrechtliche Aspekte der Rechtsetzung im EWR', *Aussenwirtschaft* (1991), 349 ff.; O. Jacot-Guillarmod, 'Droit international et droit communautaire dans le futur Traité instituant l'EEE', *Schweizerische Zeitschrift für internationales und europäisches Recht* (1991), 59 ff.; J. Kellenberger, 'Switzerland in the New European Architecture', *Aussenwirtschaft* (1991), 299 ff.; A. Lombardi,

'Verfassungsrechtliche Answirkungen eines Beitritts der Schweiz zum EWR-Vertrag', *Schweizerisches Zentralblatt für Staats- und Verwaltungsrecht* (1990), 449 ff.; H. Seiler, *EG, EWR und schweizerisches Staatsrecht* (Bern, 1990); B. Spinner, 'Der Europäische Wirtschaftsraum: Ist das Völkerrecht der Herausforderung gewachsen?', *Schweizerische Juristen-Zeitung* (1990), 409 ff.; ders., 'Europäischer Wirtschaftsraum (EWR): Verhandlungsentwicklung bis Mitte Juni 1991', *Schweizerische Juristen-Zeitung* (1991), 237 ff.; D. Thürer, 'Auf dem Wege zu einem Europäischen Wirtschaftsraum?' *Schweizerische Juristen-Zeitung* (1990), 93 ff.; ders., 'EWR Vertrag— eine Form legalisierter Hegemonie?' *Nene Zürcher Zeitung*, 109, 14 May 1991, 23.

21. See T. O. Hüglin, *Sozietaler Föderalismus—Die politische Theorie des Johannes Althusius* (Berlin and New York, 1991), 244.

22. For a comparison with the model of the German Federal State see K. Hailbronner, 'Legal-Institutional Reforms of the EEC: What Can We Learn from Federalism Theory and Practice', *Aussenwirtschaft* (1991), 485 ff.

23. See M. Burgess, *Federalism and European Union* (Leiden, 1989).

24. See e.g. V. Constantinesco, 'La subsidiarité comme principe constitu-tionnel de l'intégration européenne', *Aussenwirtschaft* (1991), 439 ff.; J. P. Jacqué, 'Centralisation et décentralisation dans les projects d'Union Européenne', *Aussenwirtschaft* (1991), 469 ff. Generally see J. Isensee, *Subsidiaritätsprinzip und Verfassungsrecht* (Berlin, 1968).

25. See P. Pescatore, 'Die "Neue Europäische Architektur"—Maastricht und danach?', Conference at Solothurn, 1992.

26. See in this context J. J. Hesse and W. Renzsch, 'Zehn Thesen zur Entwicklung und Lage des deutschen Föderalismus', in J. J. Hesse and W. Renzsch (eds.), *Föderalstaatliche Entwicklung in Europa* (Baden-Baden, 1991), 29 ff., 36 f.

27. See F. W. Scharpf, 'Regionalisierung des europäischen Raums', in U. von Alemann, R. G. Heinze, and B. Hombach (eds.), *Die Kraft der Region* (Bonn, 1990), 32 ff.; R. Maintz, 'Föderalismus und die Gesellschaft der Gegenwart', *Archiv des öffentlichen Rechts* (1990), 233 ff.

28. See Thürer, *Bund und Gemeinden*, 290 ff.

29. See A. Auer, 'La Démocratie directe face à l'intégration européenne', *Semaine judiciaire* (1991), 374 ff.; C.-A. Morand, 'La constitution saisie par l'Europe', in *Mélanges offerts à la Société suisse des juristes pour son Congrès 1991 à Genève*; O. Jacot-Guillarmod, 'Les perspec-tives des relations de la Suisse avec la Communauté Européenne sous l'angle de la politique intérieur', in A. Riklin, H. Haug, and R. Probst, *Nenes Handbuch der Schweizerischen Aussenpolitik*, 2nd edn. (Bern, 1992, 513 ff); D. Thürer, 'Aussenpolitische Aspekte der künftigen

Beziehung der Schweiz zur Europäischen Gemeinschaft', in Riklin *et al.*, *Handbuch*, 531 ff. As far as the ethical and economic foundations of direct democracy are concerned see B. S. Frey and G. Kirchgässner, 'Diskursethik, politische Oekonomie und Volksabstimmungen', in: Analyse und Kritik (1993), 129 ff.

30. Quoted in M. Imboden, 'Die staatsrechtliche Problematik des schweizerischen Föderalismus', in id., *Staat und Recht* (Basel and Stuttgart, 1971), 183.

31. As an overall legal and philosophical analysis see P. Pescatore, 'La constitution, son contenu, son utilité', *Zeitschrift für Schweizerisches Recht* (1991), 41 ff.

11

Spain: A Federation In The Making?

JUAN JOSÉ SOLOZÁBAL

1. THE SOCIO-POLITICAL FOUNDATION OF THE SPANISH AUTONOMOUS STATE

The Spanish Constitution of 1978 established a model for territorial organization which may be considered to be midway between a unitary state and a federal one. Both politicians and constitutionalists have agreed on the terms 'autonomous state' (*estado autonómico*) or 'state of autonomous territories' (*estado de las autonomías territoriales*) to describe this model, although nowhere do these labels actually appear in the Constitution.

The socio-political dynamics operating in Spain when the new Constitution was drafted prevented its authors from considering any of the proven models of territorial organization, whether centralized or federal, as an option for Spain.

The Crisis of the Centralized State

The crisis of the Franco regime also reflected the crisis of the centralized model, of which it was certainly an archetype. The intensification of centralized power during the Franco regime resulted in the centralized model being equated with the abuse of power, despite the examples of the French and British centralized states (with the exception of English local self-government) in which this model is perfectly compatible with democracy. But other factors which contributed to this mistrust of centralized government must not be overlooked.

It might be implied that the centralized model of territorial organization had become exhausted in Spain, and that it had been incapable of serving as an instrument of renovation in the struggle against the *ancien régime* and as an agent of political and administrative rationalization, as it had done in other countries. On the contrary, the centralized system in Spain served further to consolidate out-dated structures and to reinforce the decaying institutions of the state.

This belief in the obsolescence of the centralized model, which was typical of but not necessarily exclusive to Spain, and which has been blamed for many of Spain's political failures throughout history, found support in academic, administrative, and political circles. All agreed on the advisability of bringing the centres of decision-making as close as possible to the individual citizen, closing the gap between the ruler and the ruled, and, in a new vertical division of power, ridding them of their impersonal dimensions. There was also agreement on the technical-functional arguments which insisted on the need to redistribute territorial power in Spain.

In effect, regional planning would facilitate a greater degree of institutional integration of regional economic and social forces, whose contribution in the design and execution of territorial policies is considered fundamental. Regional planning, in addition to demonstrating the inadequacy of the urban area in providing services within the city, underscores the need for a redistribution of territorial power. But, of course, the fundamental driving-force behind the transformation of Spain's centralized structure and its redistribution of power has historically come from the Basque and Catalonian communities, whose inclusion within the Spanish state has proved problematic since the early attempts at unification under the Bourbons in the eighteenth century. With the brief exception of the Second Republic, this process of integration has become increasingly difficult, especially as a result of the rise of nationalist sentiment. This sentiment was prompted by an awareness in these regions of their cultural and economic uniqueness during the Romantic movement and the Industrial Revolution. There were also the risks which these regions perceived in the corresponding process of modernization of the centralized Spanish state. For although the crisis of the centralized unitary system has been universal, affecting even its creator, France, in Spain the collapse of the centralized state has been accompanied by peculiar circumstances resulting from the secular pluralism which has surfaced within its borders and which has been particularly vehement as a result of the typically uniformizing attitudes of the Franco regime.

Perhaps reference should be made to the inadequate articulation of Spanish unity which has plagued many centuries of its history. Until the eighteenth century the organization of the Estates-based Spanish monarchy had the characteristics of a confederation, maintaining scrupulous respect for the political peculiarities of the diverse kingdoms in Spain. We might argue that the communication between these political units, the interchange of both men and merchandise, was minimal, and the absolute power of the monarchy did not even dare to suggest a common enterprise or the creation of a national market. The primacy of Castile, evident by virtue of its structural superiority, its large population, and its wealth, was oriented above all towards its role as leader in international politics. But Castile proved incapable of extending its institutions to the other kingdoms. Nor was it able to involve the élites of other regions in its international enterprises.

Olivares's attempts at integrating other regions, sharing with them positions of power as well as taxes, came at a time when, with the waning of the Spanish empire, the disadvantages of integration for the regions outweighed the advantages. The inhabitants of the Spanish kingdoms did, indeed, share a sense of belonging to a higher political entity to which a degree of loyalty and even affection was due, and this type of proto-national sentiment ran particularly deep among the political and literary élites. But this does not invalidate our thesis on the precariousness of this common link and the essentially Castilian character of the Habsburgs' political enterprises.

It was the Bourbons who were able to succeed where the Habsburgs had failed and, importing patterns of French absolutism, created a unitary and centralized state in Spain. The peculiar organizations of the parliaments of Aragon, Valencia, and Catalonia were done away with; the necessity of establishing a unified national market was pursued; and, to the extent possible, a centralized administration was created which functioned principally through intendants. In fact, it was, in the eighteenth century that a cohesive Spain gradually emerged, as opposed to the semi-universal Spanish monarchy of the previous period.

During the nineteenth century a series of developments affected the bases for integration of the different peoples of Spain. The war against the French invasion marked the high point of Spanish nationalism, providing it with its long-standing myths and references. However, this was also a period in which parochial regional expressions emerged—*Juntismo*—and when, above all, the concept of national sovereignty developed, requiring great efforts of homogenizing centralism. In the end, given the special conditions in which this was done and the policies of forced assimilation which it employed, it had just the opposite effect. Once the monarch as the agent of unity in the political community had been replaced, and his sovereignty transferred to the nation, a degree of homogeneity was considered imperative in order to ensure the nation's political viability.

But centralization, which in other countries functioned as an agent in favour of the liberal revolution and the abolition of feudal particularism, in Spain acted, on the contrary, as an instrument for consolidating the *ancien régime*. Thus centralization found enemies not only among the advocates of traditional particularisms, who rallied to the Carlist cause, but also among the numerous democratic groups and the *petite bourgeoisie*. These groups supported a type of federalism which defended a political organization for the state capable of limiting the centralized power which they considered to be monopolized by the *moderado* oligarchy then in government.

Also paramount in strengthening regional distinctions was Romanticism, which, as is well known, promoted an interest and a desire to make new discoveries in the expressions of popular thought, contributing towards the strengthening and re-evaluation of destructive features. The process of industrialization was also a decisive factor in unleashing nationalist sentiments in Spain's periphery: a potential for nationalism had been reconfirmed when, by virtue of Spain's economic *décalage*, the peculiarities of each group or region had become evident, or a national identity had manifested itself in regions questioning their own economic roots. In effect, industrialism, by questioning traditional modes of existence and/or fostering considerable economic distinctions, provided perhaps the best opportunity for manifesting nationalistic ideals.

The Unavailability of the Federal Model

If, indeed, these forces were operating against the continuity of a unitary organization of the state in Spain, at the same time, other

powerful currents were at work to oppose the adoption of a federalist system. This, after all, appeared as the logical alternative to the
unitary state among available models for the territorial organization of power. Working against the federal model was the rejection (which was widespread in many levels of Spanish society), of
a system associated, however wrongly, with the turmoil and
cantonalist movements of the First Republic during the nineteenth
century. This is the image that the Right held of federalism, as did
other groups, since regarding certain concepts in Spanish political
culture—for example, the concept of the unity of Spain—positions
vary only slightly along the whole political spectrum, and the idea
of a federalist state was particularly intolerable to the army and the
majority of the Spanish bureaucracy.

A second force hampering the acceptance of federalism was
the different degree of autonomous sentiment present in Spain's
various regions. It did not seem prudent from the onset to give
the same treatment with respect to powers and organizational
structure to regions with a high level of demand and a clear
desire for self-government as to other regions which seemed
satisfied with their current mode of integration in the Spanish
state, or whose level of dissatisfaction was quite low. In a further
complication, Catalonians and Basques decided to present their
nationalist demands from different standpoints. While the
Catalonian nationalists were content with a Constitution which
would guarantee them a framework in which to draft a Statute of
Autonomy similar to that which was in effect in 1932, the Basque
nationalists made demands based on their historical rights, interpreted as an expression of the sovereign power of the ancient
Basque people.

A third impediment to the introduction of a federal system in
Spain might be described as functional. With all its shortcomings,
the services provided by the central administration were not entirely lacking in efficiency and its personnel displayed a recognized
level of competence. The replacement of this central administrative
organization with another created *ex novo* or improvised from the
reorganization of centralized structures, based on criteria unknown
at present, could only be described as risky. It was thought that a
federal organization might be desirable for a newly created nation,
but its introduction in states with centuries of centralized existence
seemed ill-advised.

2. ORGANIZATIONAL AND LEGAL FEATURES OF THE AUTONOMOUS STATE

We should bear these factors in mind, since, without examining these political aspects, it is difficult to comprehend the character of the Spanish autonomous state. In Spain, the autonomous division of the state is not a simple formula for organizing power from the standpoint of technical perfection, in a distribution derived solely or principally from demands for efficiency or even as a means for bringing political decisions closer to the individual citizen. The Autonomous State cannot be considered as an original political variation from the standpoint of its vertical disposition of power nor due to its innovative constitutional design, but rather as a valiant if risky attempt to offer an institutional solution to the problems arising from political factionalism and peripheral nationalisms. This explains the originality of Spain's decentralized state, which does not reside so much in the uniqueness of its organizational features or in the peculiarities of the delimitations of powers which have been established between central entities and the Autonomous Communities, but rather in the nationalist tensions which justify its existence and which it seeks to address.

The Spanish Autonomous State is a state which is politically decentralized. Within it coexist, on the one hand, a central or general political organization with jurisdiction in the entire national territory (with a complete level of authorities: a parliament, a government, and a common court system); and, on the other, a level of regional authorities with their corresponding parliaments and governments. In the legal realm, there is a system of norms produced by central organs, and another seventeen territorial legal sub-systems of laws resulting from the normative activity of the corresponding regional organs.

It should be stated that, as in the political arena, the presence of a variety of political centres does not hinder the unity of the state as a common organization corresponding to the existence of a single Spanish people to which the Constitution in Article 1 attributes the sovereignty of the nation. In the legal arena, the central legal system and the territorial legal systems form a general type of super-system of norms which displays a certain degree of homogeneity, a consequence of the pre-eminent role which the Constitution plays in it, as the base for legal order as stipulated in Article 9-2, whose structural, organizational, and value principles apply throughout the system, and within which it plays a role in integrating the central state's legal order.

These are features which the Autonomous State shares with the unitary model, but we should not forget that, as opposed to this type of legal and political system, the entities comprising the Autonomous State (the Autonomous Communities), enjoy true legislative capacity to the extent that, within the jurisdictional framework outlined in the Constitution, the Parliaments of the Autonomous Communities may pass laws which have the same status and force as those of the state and which are barely distinguishable from them, although they are of doubtful justification from a constitutional standpoint. This is a reference to the fact that the laws of the Autonomous Communities, as opposed to general laws passed in the central parliament, are not required to be sanctioned by the King, although they are signed in the King's name by the President of each respective Autonomous Community. In addition, the central government, when appealing to an Autonomous Community law before the Constitutional Court, may suspend the law temporarily. In the reverse case, when an Autonomous Community challenges a law passed by the central parliament, this law is never subjected to suspension. Thus, while in a unitary state decentralization is merely administrative in nature, in the Autonomous State decentralization takes on true political significance, which is reflected in this attribution of legislative power to the Autonomous Communities.

The Second Chamber or Senate

On the other hand, the Autonomous State does not reflect many of the features of a federalist state. It is true that certain characteristics or 'federal instrumentalities' do exist (although they might be considered to be insufficient), which include the presence of a Senate. Perhaps improperly termed in the Constitution as a 'Chamber of Territorial Representation', the second chamber is granted a quota in the designation of members of certain constitutional organs, such as the Constitutional Court or the General Council of Judicial Power, as well as a capacity to authorize the government to intervene in cases of serious attacks on the constitutional order by the

Autonomous Communities outlined in Article 155. It also has the power to ask the government to adopt a draft law or legislative proposals from the Assemblies of Autonomous Communities before the central Congress of Deputies, or other acts involving information or suggestions, such as in the central parliament's elaboration of economic plans.

The differences between the Spanish Autonomous State and a federal state should not be overlooked and are based principally on the fact that in the Spanish system the Autonomous Communities do not possess real constitutional power, according to the true conception of the constitutional organization of the Autonomous State. There is a difference between sovereignty, understood as original and unlimited legal political power which belongs to the central state, and autonomy defined as the derived and limited power of the different regions and nationalities.

The norm which organizes the institutions of self-government in the Autonomous Communities and grants powers to the territorial parliaments and governments, within the framework of the Constitution, is the Statute of Autonomy. But this norm is not a true constitution of the Autonomous Communities and, contrary to the constitutions of the member states in a federation, is not ratified by the Autonomous Communities' parliament, but rather by the central parliament, since it has the rank of organic law.

In effect, the Statute of Autonomy is really two-dimensional in character, to the extent that, as stated in Article 147 of the Constitution, it is the basic institutional norm of the Autonomous Community which the state recognizes and upholds, as well as an integral part of its legal order. On the one hand, the Statute is formally just another norm in the overall legal system of the state, passed as an organic law, but whose content is the result of an agreement or pact between the Community and the representatives of the state. It represents a special type of organic law in that it cannot be modified by a norm of similar rank, but rather 'according to the procedures established therein'. Its amendment requires, in any case, the approval of the national parliament by means of an organic law. On the other hand, as the norm which organizes and grants specific powers to the Autonomous Communities, in accordance with the precepts of the Constitution, the Statute of Autonomy is the basic institutional norm of the Community. It is, thus, 'within the limits of the Constitution', the highest norm of the territorial legal order to which all other laws and regulations are subordinate, and it expresses the values and contains the sources of this order. The position of the Statute within the territorial legal system is clearly rooted in the principle of hierarchy and, in this sense, does not seem to present any major problems.

The Spanish Senate carries out only modest functions as the institution of participation of the Autonomous Communities in the formation of the will of the nation-state. In the first place, the powers of the Spanish Senate are not comparable with those exercised by an authentic lower chamber. Thus, with respect to its legislative function, any amendments or vetoes which the Senate makes to draft laws remitted to it by the Congress may eventually be overridden. And, in the second place, the government of the nation is not politically responsible to the Senate, in the sense that the Senate cannot exercise any extraordinary control over the government. In addition, the Senate lacks practically any authority in matters concerning the Autonomous Communities.

Furthermore, the origin of the members of the Senate does not differ significantly from those of the Congress, since only one-fifth of all Senators can be properly called Autonomous Senators, having been designated as such by the parliaments of their respective Autonomous Communities.

Variation in Power between the Autonomous Communties

This summary of the characteristics of Spain's Autonomous State cannot be considered to be complete without a reference to the problem of distributing powers between the central state and the Autonomous Communities. The powers assumed by the Autonomous Communities, defined as their ability to intervene in diverse sectors of public life, are outlined in the Statues of Autonomy which define and clarify those outlined in the Constitution. The latter lists those powers reserved exclusively to the central state (Article 149) and those which may be assumed by the Communities (Article 148). The powers assumed by each Community depend on the provisions of each Statute of Autonomy. The central state has a residual clause in its favour, which permits it to exercise any powers not assumed in the autonomy statutes; a prevalence clause, which provides for its regulation of or intervention in shared powers; and a supplementary clause, which declares in effect that the law belongs to the central state whenever a legal vacuum may exist.

In general terms, the state assumes exclusive powers in those matters concerning the protection of the unity and sovereignty of the state, including foreign policy, defence, customs, etc.; the guarantee of equality and the protection of the fundamental rights and liberties of all Spaniards; the regulation of the basic *corpus* of Spanish legal norms (civil, criminal, and trial law); and the powers which shape the state's economic policy. The Autonomous Communities may assume powers related to the development of their own institutions of self-government; the promotion of their economic well-being; the guarantee of their cultural identity; and powers relating to the preservation of public order. It should be noted that not all Autonomous Communities enjoy the same scope of powers, in the sense that there are some Communities which have an ordinary statute and others with a special one. But, in principle, this distinction is not definitive, since the Constitution allows for (but does not require) the modification of the statutes five years after their approval. And this difference between the Communities is neither qualitative nor essential (as in some cases there might exist a degree of administrative decentralization, and in others a situation of political decentralization), given the fact that, as we have stated previously, all of the Autonomous Communities have governments with authentic political power and complete legislative authority.

Perhaps the most outstanding feature of the Spanish Autonomous State is the absence of uniformity in its organizational structure, and, above all, in the distribution of powers among its members. The differences between Autonomous Communities having ordinary statutes and those having special ones reside in the manner in which they assumed autonomy and, consequently, in the elaboration of their statutes (the contents of the statutes of the Special Autonomous Communities were agreed upon previously and were subjected to a referendum in their respective territories). Above all, the differences lie in the powers granted in these statutes, which in the case of the ordinary Communities are limited to those outlined in Article 148 of the Constitution, while the special Communities exercise their powers in the much wider framework of Article 149.

The authors of the Spanish Constitution wanted to reserve the special status for the so-called historical nationalities within Spain: those territories with specific historical and cultural features, and especially those with their own language (which is the case in the Basque Country, Catalonia, and Galicia), as well as with some previous experience of self-government. Other regions were not excluded from this status, but their access to this degree of self-government was made more difficult. Thus, in addition to these three, Andalusia has also achieved a special statute, and in practice Navarre (which attained autonomy through a procedure based on its special historical status), and the Canary Islands and Valencia enjoy a level of powers similar to these, although not granted through an autonomy statute, but rather by means of an organic law. The eleven remaining regions of Spain have adopted ordinary status of autonomy.

The differences between these diverse Communities, which, as was previously stated, are in no case qualitative in nature have less relevance at an organizational level, since all share a similar structure. All of the autonomous political systems have a parliament, elected according to a proportional system, and a government or executive council. The parliaments of the Communities exercise legislative functions and political control. The parliaments of the Special Communities have fixed sessions (two, each lasting four months) while the duration of the parliamentary sessions of the other Communities may not, in principle, exceed a total of four months. Only in the first Communities which achieved autonomy (Catalonia, the Basque Country, and Galicia) does the president of the executive have the authority to dissolve parliament, although this capacity is not provided for in the statute, but rather established in a law passed by the Community.

3. THE ROLE OF THE CONSTITUTIONAL COURT AS GUARANTOR OF THE AUTONOMOUS MODEL

It is perfectly understandable that in a state with such a high level of political strife, in which well-supported demands for self-government exist, divided among nationalist ideologies, and with such a complicated distribution of powers between central and regional organs of power, there has been no lack of conflict which has required the mediating intervention of the Constitutional Court.

The decisions of the Constitutional Court have been especially decisive in questions relating to the workings of the Autonomous State because, while admitting the predisposition of politicians to accept the intervention of a court to arbitrate in conflicts between the central state and the Autonomous Communities in the exercise of their respective powers, the Court acts exclusively as a jurisdictional organ, without introducing criteria of opportunity or merit into the parameters determining its application of the constitutional norm.

As the great number of jurisdictional conflicts which it has resolved would indicate, the existence of the Constitutional Court in Spain is justified. This is a consequence of the implicit demands which underlie the logic of the normative idea of the Constitution, whose superiority in the judicial system demands the existence of a body which, in the exercise of its jurisdictional function, is capable of enforcing the pre-eminence of that norm over all others. But above all, the entire Spanish state required an organ which would assure throughout time a respect for the division of powers between the central state and the Autonomous Communities, while at the same time guaranteeing the unity of the legal system against fractionalizing tendencies and the persistence of the political and legal powers unique to each component of the state.

It is pertinent to analyse the image of Spain's legal order and the positions within it which both the central state and the Autonomous Communities hold, which can be derived from the jurisprudence of the Constitutional Court. We might think that the Constitutional Court does not support a balanced idea of the Spanish legal order, which is based on an adequate blending of sovereignty and autonomy, conceived as powers belonging respectively to the central state and the Autonomous Communities. On the one hand, the Court seeks to reduce the centrifugal tendencies resulting from the Communities' normative powers. This it achieves, first, by reminding them of the limits of their sphere of action, the most important of which is respect for the basic equality of all Spaniards (with respect to the limits imposed on the Communities in the exercise of economic power (see Decision 88/1986); and, secondly, by restricting the number and significance of their exclusive powers (see Decision 37/1981 and 5/1982), despite the specifications outlined in their Statutes). Above all, the Court has performed its tasks by attributing a structural function to national state law in the general legal order. This the Court has done, principally, by deducing the territorial power distribution from constitutional principles, whether explicit or implicit (thus, the unity of the national market in Decision 88/1986) or by taking advantage of the *vis expansiva* of some of the state's powers, such as in the establishment or co-ordination of economic planning or of civil and commercial legislation (Decision 15/1989). In this function the court has used the idea of basic legislation, which serves as the normative instrument by which the integration of autonomous law into the general legal system may be achieved, and which constitutes the ordinary means of normative collaboration between central and autonomous powers.

Spanish basic legislation is characterized by the establishment of the fundamental criteria which will assure an indispensable level of normative unity in the sector or activity being regulated: 'basic laws will reflect the objectives, goals and general orientation for the entire nation which the unity of the state and the basic equality of all of its members require.' Negatively, basic laws establish a limit which the autonomous legislator cannot transgress: 'the basic law constitutes a limit within which the organs of the Autonomous Communities may operate in the exercise of their powers' (Decision 25/1983).

But to understand the articulating role that the basic legislation of the central state plays, it must be appreciated that it cannot confer merely an auxiliary role on the autonomous bodies which would prevent them from developing their own normative system (with the consequence that collaboration between the central legislator and the autonomous body would resemble the underlying hierarchal relationship between a law and a by-law or executive order). The state's creation of basic laws cannot 'go so far as to leave the Community's correlative power void of content' (Decision 32/1981).

It is necessary to underline the fact that the Constitutional Court's insistence on the principle of unity within the Spanish legal order has been accompanied by a staunch defence of the pluralist features of the Spanish legal system. The Court's position in this matter is particularly well known, especially from Decision 76/1983, which underlines the constitutional guarantee of autonomy, prohibiting the central legislator from proceeding to redefine the limits of its powers. This task is reserved exclusively to the drafters of the Constitution or to the Statutes of Autonomy.

The Constitutional Court is also well known for its persistent attempts to underline the special character of self-government which autonomy confers, and more specifically, as we have stated earlier, the nature of the Spanish territorial communities' political power, which should not be conceived merely as a power to implement or interpret the decisions of the central state, but rather as the power to adopt their own political solutions.

4. REDUCING NATIONALIST TENSIONS

In conclusion, this chapter addresses two issues. The first consists in underlining the fact that a political system of autonomous organization has been established in Spain despite the transformation which this required of the traditional model of Spain's unitary and centralist state, and despite the fact that little more than ten years has elapsed since the Constitution of 1978 was passed. Thus, at present, the budgets of the Autonomous Communities make up 23.9 per cent of all public spending, the central state controls 60 per cent, and towns and local corporations control 16 per cent. The Autonomous Communities' 23.9 per cent represents 8 per cent of Spain's GNP. On the other hand, the different Communities employ well over 500,000 people, which represents 25 per cent of the country's civil servants.

The second issue refers to the system's capacity to consolidate the Autonomous State, as an institutional remedy for the sectionalist tendencies operating in Spain. This issue is of the utmost importance, since, as previously stated, the Autonomous State owes its origins to the problems which the presence of regional nationalisms presented for the acceptance of a common political framework, especially in the Basque Country and in Catalonia. The Autonomous State's integrative performance must be taken into account with respect to its possible transformation into a federal state.

With respect to the Autonomous State's capacity for consolidation, it is worth pointing out that, in general terms, the current regions' capacity to reduce territorial sectionalism is similar to the federal model's capacity to do so. Regarding the capacity of federalism to reduce tensions derived from territorial sectionalism, we should first note, as a word of caution, that the federal model is not the only answer to problems derived from territorial sectionalism, but rather is principally a technique of decentralization and distribution of political power. Without a doubt, the federal system's performance has been more satisfactory in the task which we might term the technical division of power, than as an answer to problems of a nationalist origin, principally because these problems are very difficult to solve without recognizing the nationalist communities' right to self-government. However, federalism seems to suit those situations in which different communities without exclusive nationalist sentiments are willing to accept, given their past experience or future interests, a superior political structure, that is, a common state, as long as their right to autonomy and their participation in government and in their common political culture has been guaranteed constitutionally. Thus, federalism's function in reducing pluralism depends, first, on an adequate constitutional framework which guarantees the constituent communities a margin or political manœuvring on two levels: in self-government and in their participation in the federal institutions. It depends, secondly, on the effective application of this framework by means of institutional practice capable of overcoming resistance to centralism and sectionalist tendencies and which ensures, by means of the appropriate instruments of control, a fair distribution of power and the generation of an atmosphere of mutual loyalty on the part of the federation as well as of the units or constituent states. The third essential element is a compatibility between the common or shared nationalism, defined as the acceptance of a superior institutional and also affective integration, and local or individual nationalisms. The political culture of a federation—its history, symbols, and so on—should have a shared, plural, non-obligatory character. But individual nationalisms must renounce their secessionist ideals.

The implication of these three stipulations should be highlighted. A good but inoperative constitutional framework, a nominal constitution which is not observed, has no value; but a good federal structure may compensate for constitutional inadequacies. Continual federal practice may assert conflicts arising from both general nationalism and regional nationalism and propitiate their co-existence and even harmony. What is the situation in Spain? Briefly, the country started with an inadequate constitutional framework, especially with regard to the Constitution's inclusion of the participatory part of the federal formula. These inadequacies have not been adequately compensated for on the political plane. This is demonstrated by the absence of mechanisms of co-operation and, above all, of the political will to co-operate. The result is the relative significance of the Senate, whose obvious constitutional limitations have not been compensated for by political means.

Secondly, the Constitutional Court has carried out the important task of accommodation by means of the balanced position of its jurisprudence, which, on the one hand, has reinforced the constitutional nature of autonomy and, on the other, has insisted on the limited character of autonomy. It has underlined the need to co-ordinate its function, above all by means of its interpreted integration in the general legal order, presided over by the Constitution, by attributing a shared nature to the majority of the powers of the Autonomous Communities, and by conferring the important task of co-ordination on the basic legislation of the central state. Finally, as to symbolic and common cultural considerations, one may observe the existence of a double resistance. First, central political forces are reticent in recognizing the pluralism of the nation. Secondly, peripheral nationalities refuse to give up their dreams of an independent state, although in practice (especially after the resignation of the first President of the Basque Autonomous Community) there has been a loyal acceptance of the present institutional framework and a recognition of the integrative capacity of the Crown.

5. PERSPECTIVES AND PROBLEMS OF THE AUTONOMOUS STATE

As previously stated, one of the basic features of the Autonomous State, which contrasts with the same features in a federal system, is the diversity of its members, especially with regard to the distribution of powers. For many, this diversity, a logical consequence of the principle of the free assumption of powers, is perfectly compatible with the pluralistic character of the Spanish nation and, more specifically, has facilitated the Autonomous State's integrative performance. Others consider that, in practice, the distinction between ordinary communities and special communities (and within these, between the privileged and less privileged ones) can be justified only temporarily. It is in itself discriminatory and a hindrance to the normal workings of the Autonomous State.

This problem carries with it a significant legal-technical dimension, since it must be determined whether the equal distribution of powers between the special communities and the ordinary ones will be carried out, as would seem logical, through a reform of their relevant Statutes of Autonomy in accordance with the provisions (not imperative stipulations) of the Constitution (Article 148–2), or whether this can be accomplished using a procedure to increase powers by means of the State's organic laws, which provide for the transfer and delegation of powers (as outlined in Article 150–2). The use of a reform of the Statutes would seem more in accordance with the constitutional concept of autonomy, as a true right of the nationalities and regions which the legal system recognizes, and whose exercise it regulates, but whose content in terms of powers cannot be determined at will by the central legislator, or submitted in its exercise by the Autonomous Communities to any other control but judicial. On the other hand, as stated earlier, there does exist a constitutional provision for reforming the statutes of the ordinary communities, five years after their coming into effect, a limit that has long since elapsed (the last Autonomy Statutes were passed early in 1983).

Apart from these arguments in support of the advisability of proceeding to increase the powers of the ordinary Autonomous Communities by means of a reform of their statutes, we should not overlook the advantages and disadvantages of distributing powers outside this statutory formula, as outlined in Article 150–2. To re-initiate at this date a semi-constitutional process of statutory reform may incur destabilizing risks, above all if it encourages the Special Autonomous Communities to request, at the same time, a revision of their statutes. The use of delegation to distribute new powers would, in practice, yield the same results as statutory reform, and it would not be exposed to the same risks, since it would permit the existence of certain formal distinctions among the diverse Autonomous Communities. There would be those which would exercise the powers delegated to them by means of their statutes, and those which would do so only thanks to powers delegated to them by means of laws which are still central state laws. Moreover, from a technical point of view, increasing powers by means of delegation cannot result in an abolition of the state's transferred powers, since a revocation of these powers can only be justified constitutionally in extreme cases. Any other case would be contrary to the protection of autonomy which is covered by means of the mechanism of institutional guarantee. In addition, this means that reserving certain instruments of control for the central state facilitates the co-ordinated functioning of powers, which ensures the greater functional efficiency of their application which is consistent with the necessary orientation of the Spanish Autonomous State and in line with co-operative federalism.

This last argument brings us to a preoccupation of the present autonomous system in Spain, in which many have observed significant inadequacies in the instruments of co-ordination between the central state and the Autonomous Communities. This is, first of all, a consequence of deficiencies in the institutional design itself (an example being the small integrative capacity of the Senate, as well as its composition, which is hardly deflective of autonomous forces). On the other hand, it would seem logical that, in the first phase of the operation of the decentralized state, and before concerning themselves with the co-ordination of the functioning of powers, the autonomous entities would be more interested in affirming their own existence and legitimacy. Hence, this period must needs be characterized by demands rather than co-operation.

The demand for the Senate to play a more significant role in the Autonomous State is supported by its being defined in the Constitution as a Chamber of Territorial Representation, and by recognizing that this is the role played by the senates in federal systems. But it is true that the Constitution itself, (and the composition and powers of the Senate which it establishes), does not contemplate for the Senate any territorial role other than that described in this chapter. The question arises as to whether a reform of the Senate in Spain should be carried out without modifying the Constitution, since initiating a constitutional reform would, in practice, re-open the entire constitutional process, and without there being serious motives to do so. Futhermore, and above all, the same level of agreement or the pact among all political forces (which was achieved during the drafting of the Constitution of 1978), is unlikely to be achieved again. The process, in practice, would entail considerable destabilizing risks.

This initial limitation would exclude, for example, the possibility for Senators to be elected by their entire Autonomous Communities (as an electoral district) rather than by their provinces, as stipulated in the Constitution, or that the entire Senate be designated by the Autonomous Parliaments or Territorial Governments rather than the approximately 25 per cent designated by them at present. Thus, reform of the Senate must be restricted to the possibilities open to its standing orders, which might involve the creation in the Senate of an autonomous commission to which all Senators designated by territorial parliaments would belong regardless of their party affiliation, or the appearance before the Senate of the presidents of the governments of the Autonomous Communities. Much criticism has been raised concerning the problems which Senate reform would involve. The inviolability of the Constitution is supported by a quasi-mythical conception of this fundamental law which ignores both its instrumental character and the truly conservative nature of all constitutional reform. On the other hand, it might be feared that any return to constitutional reform is in practice an expression of the refusal to grant the Senate any decisive role in the working of the Autonomous State, which could be achieved through a constitutional revision, but which does not necessarily require one.

Assigning to the Senate a role in Autonomous Community matters, regardless of whether or not this is achieved through constitutional reform, depends above all on the political will to do so. Thus, the intervention of the Senate in the working of the autonomous system would depend on, for example, the development of conventions by which the central government's autonomous policies could preferably be controlled by the Senate, or by the determination, in the phase of discussion of draft laws before the Senate, of the content of laws pertaining to basic legislation, or to the articulation of central and autonomous legal systems.

The demands for developing mechanisms of articulation in the working the Autonomous State are usually included within those demands derived from co-operative federalism, which is defined as a system of decentralization based on specialization and collaboration in the activities of the various territorial entities. It is not difficult to find a constitutional justification for this system in the principle of solidarity (Article 2) or in the demands formulated in Article 103 that the acts of public administration be measured by the criteria of efficiency. The problem lies in rendering the principle of co-operation operative, in the sense that it should not be reduced to a pious hope of aid, collaboration, and goodwill between the central state and the decentralized entities. This concern has resulted in the widespread conviction that it is necessary to proceed towards a certain formalization or legalization of this principle, in an attempt to define its scope and supervise its application, so that it does not remain at the mercy of informal practices and is not controlled exclusively by bilateral agreements between the central state and each individual Autonomous Community. This concern is essentially justified, since in 1989, for instance, over 200 agreements between the central state and Autonomous Communities were signed, but sectoral conferences (with a few exceptions concerning educational or economic matters) were practically non-existent. But we cannot overlook the fact that, on the one hand, the legal formalization of relationships between territorial entities and the state, the establishment of formal meetings (such as the Conference of Presidents, or sectoral conferences or meetings of ministers and councillors), as well as the determination of the rules for convoking and conducting these meetings, cannot in any case transfer the relevent institutional limits and powers outlined in the Constitution and in the Statutes, which are obviously binding on all. On the other hand, the institutionalization of vertical relations to which we are referring cannot ignore the fact that their political significance makes them especially susceptible to convention rather than to formalized practices.

Another matter which has been the object of reflection is the assessment of the workings of the autonomous parliaments. We may ignore those commentators who criticize in the ordinary Autonomous Communities a lack of presidential or executive power to dissolve the territorial legislative assemblies, which they consider upsets the institutional balance typical of parliamentary systems. The counter-argument used is the complication that this power might introduce into the overall political system, exposing the Autonomous Community, in practice, to a continuous electoral campaign.

Criticism of the efficiency of community parliaments has been contradictory. On the one hand, the small numbers of laws passed by the autonomous parliaments is usually cited, especially in the case of the ordinary Autonomous Communities, where the number rarely exceeds ten per year. But, at the same time, their implementation is criticized, above all because the content of autonomous laws tends to be subordinate in character, defining and delimiting state laws (since, due to their higher normative rank, they are not susceptible to appeal on the part of the citizens as is the case with by-laws and executive orders). Thus, critics suggest a weakening of the judicial guarantees which those affected by the normative activity of the public powers have at their disposal. Perhaps this paradoxical situation might be solved if the autonomous legislators were given the authority to increase their powers in certain areas which at present are beyond their jurisdiction, and to decide themselves whether to exercise these powers. In any case, we should note that the weakening of the citizen's judicial recourse against the normative activity of public powers is compensated for, in the case of autonomous laws, by his greater capacity to make his opinions known in the legislative process, due to the higher degree of representativeness of the autonomous parliaments compared with that of the central parliament.

Although suggestions have been made to give more generous recognition to popular legislative initiatives than is currently possible, the most severe criticism of the autonomous parliaments has been of the performance of their function of control *vis-à-vis* the executive of the Communities. The most serious objection concerns the level of functional and organizational imitation which exists, since the standing orders of autonomous parliaments tend to be simple copies of those of the national congress. With the exception of the Basque Community, this may be observed, for example, in the principle whereby individual members of autonomous governments are not politically responsible, or in the function of practical control which parliaments exercise over the governments, which is subject to the same legal obstacles and practical impediments that shelter the central government from the control of parliamentary opposition. Thus, the executive of an Autonomous Community may avoid debate on the replacement of one of its ministers, even though this may have great political significance. Thus, too, the reply to questions or to summons may not be handled with the expediency which the parliament's function of control would demand.

Spain's Entry into the European Community

The last problem which is worth examining is the effect of Spanish entry into the European Community on the structure of territorial autonomy. It should be noted that the problems arising from entry into the European Community are only one example of the general problems concerning both the implementation of international treaties signed by Spain within our internal legal system, and the application of the derived law of organizations to which state powers have been ceded.

The territorial decentralization of the political system does not affect the powers of the central organs of the state to negotiate any treaty, so long as its content is not contrary to the Constitution (in which case its ratification would require a previous constitutional amendment). Nor does decentralization affect the state's assumption of international responsibilities in the observance of these treaties. Obviously, in the carrying out of the obligations contracted by the state, when these affect matters over which the Autonomous Communities have jurisdiction, it is the autonomous bodies which must act, since any interpretation to the contrary would admit the possibility that international obligations could modify the distribution of powers established, fundamentally, in the Constitution and in the Autonomy Statutes (Decision 252/ 1988). The statement on the impossibility of implementing any part of the EEC Treaty or EEC derived law which would alter the territorial distribution of powers in Spain's Autonomous State cannot hide two facts. The first is that the Autonomous Communities' powers have been seriously eroded by the state's exercise of its *ius contrahendi* in matters concerning autonomous powers. In these matters, the Autonomous Communities have witnessed a weakening of their decision-making powers: when international obligations must be met, the central authorities must be recognized as having certain centralized faculties of control, surveillance, and even implementation by the central state, in the case of inactivity or default of the Autonomous Communities. Secondly, the implications of the ratification of international treaties and agreements for the internal distribution of powers between the state and the Autonomous Communities make it difficult to explain why the Communities have not been given additional powers (other than those related merely to obtaining information) in the negotiation of international agreements which may affect their own powers or which may oblige the state to enter into additional treaties. Nor does any law, at any level, provide for the presence of Autonomous Community representatives, observers, or commissioners in the institutions of international organs to which Spain belongs (i.e. the European Union) and whose decisions or norms may certainly affect the exercise of autonomous powers.

At present, the Spanish Ministry of Public Administration is preparing an agreement (its exact normative status is still unknown) with the Autonomous Communities, whereby an observer representing the Autonomous Communities may have a presence in Brussels. To date, the Autonomous Communities' participation in EU matters is channelled through the Sectoral Conference of the European Union, created in 1988 by the Ministry of Public Administration, after their having reached an agreement in relation to the Autonomous Communities' participation in Spanish cases brought before the European Court of Justice and in relation to the implementation of EU norms affecting free competition.

As stated previously, in the Spanish legal system only the state may assume obligations involving international law, and it alone is responsible for its implementation. Thus, the Autonomous Communities neither participate in the exercise of *ius contrahendi* nor are they responsible internationally for obligations which they have not assumed, by virtue of this lack of international jurisdiction. This does not prevent the Autonomous Communities from carrying out the obligations contracted by the central state, within the limits of their constitutional powers, which may be exclusive or shared, as previously noted.

This situation, if not involving a redefinition of the distribution of powers which would question the very constitutional basis for autonomy, does suggest a need to alter the balance of distribution, and for two reasons. First, the ratification of international treaties may affect matters in which the central state, in principle, lacks jurisdiction; and, secondly, the state's international responsibilities include, in any case, the functions of co-ordination, supervision, and replacement in the implementation of treaties or agreements, which implies that the central organs of the state will assume these additional powers. The Constitutional Court has invoked the need for collaboration (for example, in Decision 252/1988 of 20 December, cited previously) between central and autonomous organs, so that the implementation of EU law is carried out (notwithstanding the central state's responsibility), with respect for the Autonomous State's constitutional distribution of powers. The constitutional guarantee of state control of the observance of a certain uniformity in the content and timing of the implementation of treaties or of the derived law of organizations to which powers have been ceded (i.e. the European Union) must result in the central state's assuming an obligation to oversee these matters, or in the words of the Constitutional Court, power to give 'instructions and supervision.'

However, we cannot exclude the possibility that these instruments may be inadequate and that it may be necessary to create others. In the event of inactivity in the drafting of norms by the Autonomous Communities, a subsidiary regulatory provision may be necessary, based on Article 149–3 of the Constitution, which outlines in general terms the subsidiary character of central state law in relation to the Autonomous Communities. Our present constitutional system lacks a provision similar to Article 16 of the Austrian Constitution or Article 13 of the Catalonian Statute of 1932 (whereby the normative intervention of the Government of the Republic was envisaged in those cases in which the *Generalidad* did not exercise its powers with reference to international treaties). In cases where the Autonomous Communities fail to comply with already established norms, a judicial control may be instituted. Thus, by virtue of its higher normative status and the immediate effectiveness of derived European law, the ordinary courts will refuse to apply autonomous legal norms and the administrative courts may declare null and void any regulations which are contrary to European Union law. The possible intervention of the Constitutional Court in these conflicts would present special problems, unless an Autonomous Community law which is contrary to an EU law can be considered unconstitutional, by virtue of its lack of jurisdiction as outlined in Article 93 of the Constitution. Even more problematic would be the use, in these cases, of the instruments of intervention known as 'laws of harmonization' as outlined in Article 150–3, especially in the light both of the restrictive interpretation which the Constitutional Court has assigned these laws in Case 76/1983 and of the State's co-action regulated in Article 155, which due to judicial and political consideration, would surely be difficult to implement.

FURTHER READING

The most complete and systematic treatment of this subject may be found in S. Muñoz Machado, *Derecho Público de las Comunidades*

Autónomas (Madrid, 1982), although the original exposition of this material appeared in E. Garcia Enterria, *Estudios sobre Autonomías Territoriales* (Madrid, 1985). See also E. Aja, E. Tornos, T. Font, J. Perulles, and E. Alberti, *El sistema jurídico de las Comunidades Autónomas* (Madrid 1985). See also the collective work, Comunidades Autónomas (eds.) *Organización territorial del Estado* (Madrid, 1984), and J. Leguina Villa, *Escritos sobre Autonomías Territoriales* (Madrid, 1984).

On the problem of distributing powers between the central state and the Autonomous Communities, see C. Viver y Pi-Sunyer, *Materias competenciales y Tribunal Constitucional* (Barcelona, 1989); A. Alonso de Antonio, *La Organización Territorial del estado en la Constitución española de 1978* (Madrid, 1985); S. Martin Retortillo (ed.), *Pasado, presente y futuro de las Comunidades Autónomas* (Madrid, 1989); L. Lopez Guerra, 'El reparto de competencias Estado—autonomías en la jurisprudencia del Tribunal Constitucional' in *Comunidades Autónomas y Comunidad Europea* (Valladolid, 1991).

On the jurisprudence of the Constitutional Court, see F. Tomas y Valiente, *El reparto competencial en la Jurisprudencia del Tribunal Constitucional* (Madrid, 1988); P. Cruz Villalon, 'La Jurisprudencia del tribunal Constitucional sobre Autonomías territoriales', *Revista Jurídica de Castilla–La Mancha. 3–4 (ed.* J. J Solozabal), as well as J. J. Solozabal, 'Estado Autonómico y Tribunal Constitucional' *Revista de Estudios Políticos.* 73 (Madrid, 1991) and 'Sobre los Supuestos jurídicos de la cobertura institucional del pluralismo territorial en el Estado Autonómico Español', *Revista de Estudios Políticos.* 46–7 (1985).

The historical roots of Spanish decentralization are outlined is S. Martin Retortillo, *Descentralización administrativa y Organización Política* (Madrid, 1973). See also L. Vandelli, *L'ordinamento regionale Spagnolo* (Milano, 1980).

For a treatment of the problems currently facing the Spanish Autonomous State, see *Informes Pi- i Sunyer sobre Comunidades Autónomas,* 1989 and 1990, ed. E. Aja (Madrid, 1990, 1991), and L. Martin Rebollo (ed.), *El Futuro de las Autonomías Territoriales* (Santander, 1991).

On the effect of Spanish entry into the European Community from the point of view of the structure of the territorial autonomy see A. Lopez Castillo, 'Creación y aplicación del derecho

Comunitario europeo y Comunidades Autónomas', *Revista Española de Derecho Constitucional*, 35 (1992).

On the mechanisms of the articulation in the working of the Autonomous State, see A. Perez Calvo, 'Actuaciones de cooperación y coordinación entre el estado y las Comunidades Autónomas", *Revista de Estudios de la Administración Local y Autonómica, 235 ff.* (1987), also J. Cano Bueso (ed.) *Comunidades Autónomas e instrumentos de cooperación interterritorial'* (Madrid, 1990). R. Punset, *El Senado y las Comunidades Autónomas* (Madrid, 1987) is also interesting.

12

The Reform of the Belgian State

ROBERT SENELLE

PART I: THE ROAD TOWARDS PACIFICATION[1]

It would not be worthwhile setting out the evolution of the Belgian State without bearing in mind that Belgium, just like Switzerland, constitutes the border between the Germanic and Roman cultures. Of course, there are remarkable differences between Belgium—the former southern or Catholic Low Countries—and Switzerland, although both countries are multi-lingual. Linguistic diversity was a characteristic of the Belgian principalities from their earliest history. The most important aspect of this diversity is a clearly demarcated linguistic boundary dividing the present state of Belgium into two parts from east to west, from the north of Lille to Aachen in Germany. To the north of this line Dutch is spoken, to the south French.

Abroad the question often arises whether Belgium is an artificial body which owes its existence to the struggle on the part of the European Great Powers to achieve a political and military balance. On the whole, this opinion is seriously mistaken. Belgium is no more artificial than Switzerland, that other multi-lingual nation in Europe. The northern and southern Low Countries (the present Kingdom of the Netherlands and the present Kingdom of Belgium) formed a single political entity, created during the fifteenth and sixteenth centuries, which consisted of various principalities. Due to the genius of the Dukes of Burgundy, they had been made into an exceptionally prosperous economic and political unit. We are not dealing here with the accidental joining together of miscellaneous principalities. The constituent parts of the Burgundian state spoke French and Dutch, but shared the same socio-economic culture and sovereign, who held all the constituent parts together within one personal union. That is why the modern Belgian State is based upon ancient historical foundations. The Burgundian period, from 1382 to 1477, entailed a step-by-step political expansion, until finally all the provinces of modern Belgium and the Netherlands, except the prince-bishopric of Liège, were united under one sovereign within a very centralized state.

Under the *ancien régime* there was no question of linguistic conflict in the southern Netherlands. Multi-linguality was to become a problem only at the end of the eighteenth century, when the country became the victim of the unrestrained imperialism of the French Republic. This should not be surprising. In the end, language constitutes the key to every change, whether it be cultural, commercial, or social. Linguistic alienation is the basis of all forms of cultural alienation.

The policy of Frenchification, so disastrous to Belgium, was launched when the law of 9 Vendémiaire in the Year IV (1 October 1795) took effect. This law ratified the annexation of the Belgian provinces to France by the French National Convention in March 1793. The French occupying forces imposed the absolute dominance of the French language so as to ensure that the annexation to France was irreversibly accepted. In order to achieve broad political merging, through linguistic unification, the French government aimed at systematically extirpating Dutch. French became the language used for administrative matters, in the army, education, justice, culture, and for public life, and steps were taken to ban the Dutch language. Thus the origin of the present regional problems of Belgium can be retraced to the manner in which language was associated with social class.

In 1830 Belgium obtained its independence. At that period, just as today, 60 per cent of the population spoke Dutch. That Dutch-speaking population consisted essentially of farmers, labourers, and merchants, constituting the major part of the Flemish population, that is to say the four northern provinces of Belgium: East Flanders, West Flanders, Antwerp, and Limburg, and also the northern half of the province of Brabant. The upper classes in Flanders, estimated at about 3 per cent of the population, spoke French. Obviously, the upper classes in Brussels were the same as the inhabitants of Wallonia; in practice the French-speaking élite had the monopoly of political power in the new Belgium and, as a consequence, state matters were almost exclusively a French-speaking issue.

However, in the middle of the nineteenth century a halt was called to the decline of Dutch, as an ever-growing number of intellectuals rediscovered their native language and became aware of its right to an identity of its own. Although this was not a reversal, it was nevertheless the first sign of a Flemish revival. Gradually the so-called Flemish movement gathered momentum, became more adequately organized, and tried to gain a hold on political life with a view to restoring the Dutch language in government circles and state affairs. In other words, initially and up to the First World War the struggle for the emancipation of the Flemish people was a cultural one. However, the topics under discussion between the Dutch-speaking population and the French-speaking population gradually acquired a financial and a socio-economic dimension. Hence the unavoidable trend towards a federal form of government.

It is obvious that the language conflict has played, in its successive phases, an essential part in the recent evolution of Belgian society. The language legislation that has resulted from this conflict has developed as follows:

1831. Constitutional freedom in respect of the use of language; laws and decrees are promulgated in French; there are Flemish translations, but only the French text has legal validity.

1873. A law imposes the use of Dutch on the courts (in criminal cases) in the Flemish part of the country, unless otherwise requested by the accused.

1878. A law imposes the use of Dutch on the government authorities in the Flemish part of the country, unless otherwise requested by the party concerned.

1883. In the Flemish part of the country part of the teaching in secondary education is henceforth to be in Dutch.

1890. Magistrates must prove that they have a command of Dutch in order to be eligible for appointment in the Flemish part of the country; at Ghent National University lecturing in some of the subjects (including criminal law and criminal procedure for future Flemish magistrates) is henceforth to be in Dutch.

1898. Laws and decrees are sanctioned, ratified, and promulgated in Dutch as well as in French; both texts have legal validity.

1912. At the Catholic University of Louvain, too, lecturing in some of the subjects is henceforth to be in Dutch.

1913. Military officers must henceforth also have a command of Dutch.

1921. Law concerning the use of languages in administrative matters:

- the central national administration becomes bilingual, as do its officials;
- local administrations become monolingual (the language of the region becomes the medium of communication);
- the Brussels communal administrations have the choice between the country's two languages;
- protection of the French-speaking minorities in the Flemish part of the country;
- language censuses every ten years whereby a commune can change its language status.

1928. Training of soldiers must be in their mother tongue, while military officers must be bilingual.

1930. Official use of the Dutch language at Ghent National University. The University of Brussels is gradually transformed into two separate linguistic entities, as is the University of Louvain.

1932. Abolition of individual bilingualism of officials of the central national administration; matters must be dealt with in the language of the case-file without resorting to translators. Officials are distributed between two language rolls (Dutch and French), with a fair balance in respect of appointments; in primary and secondary education in the Flemish part of the country bilingualism is abolished and Dutch becomes the medium of communication. In Brussels the theoretical principle of mother tongue as the medium of communication is applied.

At the end of the First World War, a second set of language laws introduced the principle of territoriality or regional monolingualism: the language of the region—Dutch in Flanders and French in Wallonia—became the language used for administration, education, and justice. The Brussels-Capital Region was, and still is, bilingual. A third set of language laws, enacted at the end of the Second World War, confirmed and strengthened those principles. The linguistic divide, finally settled in 1962, became a political-administrative frontier, dividing Belgium into four linguistic regions: the Dutch-speaking region (Flanders, with 5.847 million inhabitants); the French-speaking region (with just over 3.305 million inhabitants); the German-speaking region (in eastern Wallonia, with nine communes and a population of 69,000); and the bilingual Region of Brussels-Capital (with a population of 949,000), where Dutch and French are on an equal footing.

The language frontier only became a political line of demarcation in 1963, when the administrative boundaries of the local bodies were aligned along this frontier. Before then, this had never been the case, not even in the remote past. The language laws of 1962 and 1963—now co-ordinated by a Royal Decree of 18th July 1966—are based on the territoriality principle, which means that in mono-lingual regions the use of a given language which is that of the region is compulsory for all public acts issued by any official authority.

When the Belgian political classes realized in the early 1970s that the unitary state was a thing of the past, the political parties began the slow process that was to lead, a quarter-century later, to the federalization of the kingdom. That fundamental reform was carried out in four phases, each of which entailed a revision of the Constitution (1970—1980—1988—1993). Belgians gradually accepted the obvious truth that it was only under a federal system that Belgium would be able to survive. In their view, indeed, federalism is a principle that combines unity with diversity. The key feature of federalism is that it makes it possible for different component elements to live together, both at the federal (or national) level and at the regional level (cantons, *Länder*, provinces). Federalism is based on political, religious, and cultural pluralism, or on the dissimilar economic or social developments of certain regions within one state. It requires constant dialogue, conducted in a spirit of tolerance. Federalism is therefore a political principle, a guideline for state organization. It distributes public power at different levels: at the federal level (central power) and the level of federated bodies. Federalism is a tool for allocating powers so as to achieve a balance between the federal authority and the federated components.

Fundamentally, federalism may be seen to provide a solution to the problems that arise in the governance of humans in communities which are, for historical, social, geographical, linguistic, cultural, or economic reasons, refractory to the type of uniform political power implied by the unitary state. Federalism must reconcile the need for a common policy on certain issues that relate to the federal state, with the legitimate aspirations of the constituents of that state which wish to retain their own specific features. It is a recognized way of preventing, managing, and solving conflict in divided societies. It is a concept that is adaptable and flexible to suit regional needs and requirements.

Finally, the present constitutional system changing Belgium into a federal state was brought about as a result of the four revisions of the Constitution between 1970 and 1993. Article 1 of the new Constitution states that Belgium is a federal state.

According to Article 4 of the Constitution Belgium has four linguistic regions: the French-speaking Region, the Dutch-speaking Region, the bilingual Region of Brussels-Capital, and the German-speaking Region. Each commune of the Kingdom is part of one of these linguistic regions. The limits of the four linguistic regions can only be changed or modified by a law adopted by majority vote in each linguistic group in each House, on condition that the majority of the members of each group are gathered together and that the total of affirmative votes given by the two linguistic groups is equal to at least two-thirds of the votes cast.

According to Article 2 of the Constitution Belgium is made up of three Communities: the French Community, the Flemish Community, and the German-speaking Community. According to Article 3 of the Constitution Belgium is made up of three Regions: the Walloon Region, the Flemish Region, and the Brussels Region. According to Article 5 of the Constitution the Walloon Region is made up of the following provinces: Walloon Brabant, Hainaut, Liège, Luxemburg, and Namur. The Flemish Region is made up of the following provinces: Antwerp, Flemish Brabant, West Flanders, East Flanders, and Limburg. It is permissible by law to divide the territory into a greater number of provinces, if need be. The bilingual Brussels-Capital Region comprises nineteen Communes of the metropolitan area of greater Brussels.[2]

A law can shield certain territories defined by it from division into provinces; it can make them directly dependent on the federal executive power, and can make them subject to a statute of their own. This law must be adopted by majority vote as provided for in the last paragraph of Article 4 of the Constitution.

The above mentioned co-ordinated laws of 1962–3 on the use of language in administrative matters provide linguistic facilities for the inhabitants of twenty-seven Communes adjoining a different linguistic region.

PART II: THE PRESERVATION OF ECONOMIC AND MONETARY UNION

The strong budgetary constraints on economic and financial policies during the 1980s are of crucial importance for understanding the characteristics of the recent trends in the Belgian federalization process. The negotiations on the devolution of powers would probably have been less protracted and the compromises worked out would have been less complicated, if the government had not faced the constant need to assess all solutions on their compliance with the overriding priority of accomplishing a budgetary adjustment of unprecedented magnitude.

The nature of the difficulties involved becomes fully clear when one looks at some of the budgetary implications of the devolution of powers. The budgetary resources transferred to the Regions and Communities now represent some 10 per cent of gross national product or 35 per cent of the government's total budget receipts.

If one takes into account that 6.5 per cent of these receipts is earmarked to the financing of local authorities and the European Union budget, and that another 27 per cent is absorbed by interest payments on the government's public debt, one arrives at the conclusion that the resources on which the central government has real influence represent no more than 32 per cent of total budgetary resources; roughly the same amount as the resources transferred to the Regions and Communities.

It is apparent that in such a constellation the preservation and orderly functioning of economic and monetary union becomes a critical factor in the maintenance of sustainable relationships between national and subnational entities. EMU fulfills an essential role, not only as a binding element between centrifugal forces but also as a principal anchor on which the government should be able to rely to perform its essential functions.

Three of the characteristics of economic and monetary unions are of special relevance in the Belgian context. First, the maintenance of an integrated market in which goods and production factors are free to move without risk of creating misallocations or political tensions due to fundamental divergences in subsidy or taxation policies. Second, the establishment of an overall framework for budgetary discipline allowing the central government to continue its adjustment strategy without being obstructed by the financial powers which have been transferred to the subnational entities. And third, the preservation of monetary unity based on a strong and independent monetary policy aimed at the maintenance of stable price conditions and participation in the final stage of the European Monetary Union.

The new financing mechanism which has been devised to support the substantial devolution of powers decided in the 1980s has a critical role to play in connection with these three basic characteristics. Two general principles underlie the system established by the Special Financing Law of 23 January 1989: the financial responsibility of the Communities and Regions, and revertible solidarity. The balance between these two principles has been embodied in a complex mechanism, replacing the old system under which the funding of the federated entities took place according to a number of fixed-scale criteria decided on the basis of political compromises with a system linked to the revenue-generating capacity of each entity and corrected by appropriate solidarity provisions. After the transitional period, which will run until the end of this decade in order to allow for a progressive and harmonious transition from the old to the new system, the Regions and Communities will receive the greater part of their revenue in the form of a share of personal income tax receipts allocated on the basis of locational criteria or the so-called 'fair-return' principle.

It becomes immediately clear, however, that the financial autonomy which the Regions and Communities acquire under this new system in terms of independent revenue-raising powers remains tightly constrained: in essence their resources will continue to derive from the transfer of national taxation revenue, although allocated on the basis of other criteria, while their taxation powers will remain strictly limited. In point of fact, the regions have only received independent taxation powers with respect to a limited number of items including betting and gaming taxes, the value tax on property, and succession duties; from 1994 they have also had the competence to grant remissions and levy surcharges on national personal income tax, subject to prior consultation with the central government, which will in any event retain the power to impose ceilings on such remissions and surcharges.

Moreover, financial autonomy will also be restricted by the overriding priorities related to budgetary adjustment. Several safeguards have been built in which, at least during the transitional period, should extend budgetary discipline to the financial policies of the Regions and Communities. In addition, an overall surveillance of their borrowing policies should avoid the emergence of fundamental slippages which might endanger financial and monetary stability in the long term. The following sections will discuss these characteristics in more detail.

1. AN INTEGRATED MARKET

Economic and monetary unity implies first of all an integrated market, which, according to European Union standards, can be defined as a market characterized by the free movement of persons, goods, services, and capital, including the freedom of payments. However, the Belgian concept of EMU is clearly a more ambitious one: not only does it prohibit all internal barriers to the free movement of labour and capital, it also submits to very strict limitations all actions by subnational authorities which might distort the allocation of labour and capital without formally restricting their movement. In short, in the Belgian context the notion of market integration also incorporates the notion of market efficiency.

The most striking cases in point are the legal limitations on the Regions' powers to conduct an autonomous economic expansion policy. In conformity with their wide-ranging competences in economic matters, the Regions are free to employ the revenues from taxes over which they have full and unfettered powers to promote a policy of economic expansion, but this freedom is subject to a twofold restriction. First of all, any regulation enacted by a Region with regard to the tax advantages deriving from the national taxation system and granted pursuant to the laws on economic expansion is subject to the agreement of the competent national authority. Second, the national authority is competent to fix the general rules concerning ceilings on aid to undertakings within the context of economic expansion, which can be modified only with the agreement of the Regions. The general policy considerations underlying these restrictions are first, that regional economic initiatives should not erode the government's tax revenues and second, that they should not give rise to an uncontrolled bidding of financial incentives in order to attract business investment. The orderly and efficient functioning of an economic union implies that investment decisions are made on sound economic grounds; government aid in the framework of an economic expansion policy can play a useful role in this connection, but it should not distort the allocation of investments among the members of the union. By giving the national authority the final responsibility for fixing the general rules and ceilings on economic aid, the union should be adequately protected against the inefficiencies and waste of public funds which would arise from unrestricted competition between the Regions for investment.

Similar considerations also apply to the distribution of fiscal competences between national and subnational authorities. In view of the financial autonomy which the Regions and Communities have acquired in successive steps since the early 1970s, it was only logical to vest them with some form of fiscal autonomy. However, this autonomy has been subjected to strict limitations in order to avoid developments which might endanger the smooth functioning of the economic union. The complex mechanism worked out by the special financing law of 1989 establishes the following general principles in this connection: no taxes shall be levied in matters where a state tax is already levied, nor shall the Regions or Communities levy any surcharges on a state tax. No remission shall be granted of a state tax. Even with respect to their competence to grant remissions or levy surcharges on personal income taxes, the regions still have the obligation to consult the national government before taking any decision. Moreover, the government may impose a ceiling on such remissions and surcharges in order to preserve economic and monetary unity.

The rationale for these upper and lower limits on the Region's fiscal autonomy is very similar to the one which justifies the limitations on economic expansion aid. Their aim is to avoid the emergence of substantial discrepancies between the level of income resources and households which in turn would give rise to politically unsustainable situations and inefficiencies in the long term. Moreover, an excessive reliance on surcharges by the Regions would erode any room for manœuvre for the central government to conduct an independent tax policy, and would in any event place Belgium as an economic union in an unfavourable position to compete with neighbouring countries where lower levels of income taxation are applied. The alternative scenarios in which the Regions would embark on a process of 'competitive defiscalization' by means of an escalation of tax remissions would lead to equally unsustainable situations: first of all, it would lead to the same misallocations of productive resources as those which may arise from an excessive reliance on investment subsidies and second, it would erode the Regions' regular revenue base and therefore need to be reversed sooner or later.

To conclude this section, it is clear that the concept of a sound economic union implies more than just the absence of barriers on internal trade and on the free movement of persons and production factors. An overall framework avoiding the emergence of wide discrepancies between various forms of tax incentives and invest-ment subsidies is needed to preserve efficiency and sustainability in the long term. The present legislative framework provides sufficient safeguards in this connection. To protect it for the future will require a cautious approach to additional pressures for stronger regional autonomy and, above all, a harmonious development of the standards of living among the Regions.

2. BUDGETARY DISCIPLINE

Budgetary discipline avoiding the accumulation of excessive debt and undue pressures on interest rates is a basic characteristic of any monetary union. It is of special relevance in the Belgian context if one takes into account that the stepwise devolution of powers to the Regions and Communities took place during a period of strong budgetary adjustment. Despite the rising burden of the public debt, the Belgian budget deficit has, since 1982, been reduced by 8 per cent of GDP from more than 13 per cent to less than 6 per cent. The amplitude of this effort can be gauged even better by the primary budget balance (excluding interest payments) which has gone from a 6 per cent deficit of GDP to a 5 per cent surplus of GDP. A further adjustment is needed in order to bring about a lasting reduction of the public debt-to-GNP ratio, which at more than 130 per cent of GDP is still the highest in the European Union.

In view of these considerations it was essential for the drafters of the new financing mechanism of the Regions and Communities first, to avoid at the outset any relaxation in the overall expenditure policies; second, to extend the principles of budgetary restraint to the subnational entities at least during the coming years; and third, to avoid the build-up of excessive budget deficits by the Regions and Communities in the long run. Any other approach would have confronted the central government with the need to offset, through additional spending reductions, the relaxation of discipline allowed for at the subnational level, a task which is bound to become increasingly difficult because, precisely as a result of the devolution process, the spending categories on which the central government can act independently become smaller and smaller. In sum, such an outcome could never have resulted in a smooth functioning of the economic and monetary union. To create a stable budgetary framework a number of provisions have been included in the financing mechanism, as outlined below.

1. The resources allocated to the Regions and Communities at the start of the system are determined on the basis of what the central government would have spent on the expenditure items transferred to them in the absence of regionalization. Apart from education, for which a special regime applies, the amounts resulting from this calculation and adjusted to the evolution of the consumer price index will serve as a basis for the transfers to the Regions and Communities during the transitional period. This means that their current resources will at least initially be submitted to a zero real rate of growth, which is also the expenditure norm set for the central government by the present budget legislation.

2. The amounts established in this way will not be paid in full in cash; 14.3 per cent of the entitlement is transformed into a loan which will be paid in the form of ten-year annuities. This decision, which imposes on the subnational entities reliance on some borrowing to meet their needs, reflects the desire of the framers of the new financing law to have the Regions and Communities share to some extent in the fiscal adjustment effort of the central

government. The proportion of 85.7 per cent which they receive on a cash basis corresponds to the share of the government's current expenditure which is covered by current revenues.

3. The possibility for the Regions and Communities to borrow should not, however, become an inducement to imprudent budgetary policies. Although no direct control exists over budgetary developments in the Regions and Communities, the law has established an overall framework enabling the central government to keep their borrowing policies under close surveillance. Private bond loans issued on the Belgian capital market and short-term bills issued in Belgium are subject to prior notice to the Minister of Finance and all other forms of borrowing including public bond loans issues on the Belgian market and foreign bond issues denominated either in Belgian francs or foreign currency are subject to the Minister of Finance's prior approval. While these formalities are in essence aimed at ensuring an orderly functioning of the financial market, the control exerted by the High Board of Finance is basically of a budgetary nature. A new section—'Public Authorities' Borrowing Requirements'—has been created in this board, which, besides the delivery of an annual opinion on the borrowing requirements of the public authorities, has been empowered to deliver, either on its own initiative or on request by the Minister of Finance, an opinion on the advisability of restricting the borrowing capacity of any public authority. Eventually, this procedure may result in a Royal Decree limiting the borrowing capacity of a Community or Region for a maximum period of two years.

In sum, the safeguards to protect UMU against serious slippages in the subnational entities' public finances do exist. The experience so far shows that the consensus on the desirable direction of financial policies is strong enough to induce all government entities to co-operate closely with the aim of respecting the overall budget criteria established by the Treaty on European Monetary Union.

3. THE INDEPENDENCE OF MONETARY POLICY

The full acceptance of a single currency supported by a single monetary policy is the cornerstone of all economic and monetary unions. Monetary unity has never been seriously contested in

Belgium. In contrast to almost all other areas of public policy, monetary policy has so far stayed completely outside the scope of debate on the devolution of powers; nor have any fundamental divergences of opinion surfaced among the Regions about the conduct of monetary policy in Belgium. In point of fact, a similar absence of divergences on basic monetary orientations also characterizes the debate between Belgium's political parties.

By far the most important reason for this national consensus is the high degree of autonomy which the National Bank of Belgium enjoys in the conduct of its monetary policy and in the expression of its opinion on general economic policy orientations. In sum, the Belgian case illustrates that the implications of a single currency will be the more easily accepted, the greater the autonomy of the institution which is responsible for the monetary management of that single currency. This deserves some further elaboration, since in addition to purely legal provisions, the Belgian central bank also derives its autonomy from a combination of other factors.

First of all, a substantial reinforcement of the National Bank's autonomy has recently taken place, with the phasing out of the government's monetary refinancing facilities and with the formal dissociation of the government's short-term borrowing requirements from the day-to-day management of monetary policy. This dissociation will enable the central bank to pursue with even greater continuity its basic policy commitment to a strong exchange-rate position within the European Monetary System. This attachment to a strong currency zone in the European Union is an important second aspect of the Bank's autonomy, since it automatically submits all policy decisions to a priority on which there is a general consensus. The importance of a stable exchange-rate system for a small open economy such as Belgium and the benefits which participation in the European Monetary System has produced in terms of imposing financial discipline on its members are widely acknowledged both in the northern and in the southern parts of the country and the Bank's autonomy in defending their interests on this issue is not questioned.

All this does not, of course, mean that there is no political debate at all on monetary policy but in Belgium this debate is almost fully internalized within the national bank's own decision-making process. The responsibility for endorsing all important decisions on monetary policy is given to the Council of Regents, which is composed of personalities representing all important social and political interest-groups in the country. It is a longstanding tradition to respect the confidentiality of the deliberations taking place in this Council and to accept its decisions without further questioning their validity at other political levels. The political accountability of monetary policy is thus preserved without being submitted to the same risks of controversy and political stalemate to which other policy areas are exposed.

PART III: THE FEDERAL LEVEL

1. THE KING AND THE FEDERAL GOVERNMENT

General Considerations

Before describing the exercise of federal powers, it may be useful by way of introduction to avoid any confusion by drawing the reader's attention to an important development in the exercise of political power in Belgium during the second half of the twentieth century. Regarding the monarchy the following articles of the Constitution are important:

Article 88: The King's person is inviolable; his ministers are responsible.

Article 105: The King has no powers other than those formally attributed to him by the Constitution and by specific laws established by virtue of the Constitution itself.

Article 106: No actions of the King may take effect without the countersignature of a minister, who, in doing so, takes responsibility upon himself.

As things now stand, when the Constitution cites the King as being head of the government, it is really referring to the government as a whole—in other words, the King, who is not responsible before the two chambers, and the government, which is. Clearly, in this type of political system, namely a monarchy under a modern parliamentary system, political initiative and the daily administration of state affairs are the concern of the government.

According to the current view of the monarchy, 'the King', to use a well-known expression, alludes to the King in Council: that means, the King together with the members of the government. It is quite out of the question for the King to take any political initiative without the approval of his ministers.

Under a Cabinet system, in which the team of ministers is the expression of a parliamentary majority, the government will always be the driving force. This is a system that necessarily sanctions the fundamental role of the government as the body responsible for managing and co-ordinating state affairs.

This modern form of parliamentarism cannot be presented as merely a reduction in the role played by a hereditary head of state in a living democracy. On the contrary, the King plays an extremely important psychological role, as national conciliator. The absence of political responsibility on the part of the King within a parliamentary democracy places him above suspicion of taking sides. It is a striking fact that the only monarchies that have survived into the twentieth century are all parliamentary monarchies. In this perspective, there can be no doubt that the monarchy and the parliamentary system have (and have had) what might be termed a mutually protective effect on each other.

Partly because the reform of the Belgian state is moving towards federalization, the monarchy is now of supreme importance. To transform a unitary state that has been highly centralized for more than two centuries (ever since the Belgian provinces were annexed by France in 1795), into a federal state is a difficult and hazardous political venture. All federal structures presuppose what is referred to as 'federal loyalty', or to use the time-honoured German expression, *Bundestreue*. The Belgians are now in the position of having to accustom themselves to observe federal loyalty, a notion quite unknown to them as recently as a quarter of a century ago. Were it not for the monarchy as symbol of the cohesion of the kingdom and therefore the visible incarnation of federal loyalty, the Belgian experiment would be doomed to failure.

Even prior to the 1993 Reform, the Constitution had ruled that the Council of Ministers should be composed of an equal number of French- and Dutch-speaking ministers, with the possible exception of the Prime Minister. However, this linguistic parity does not hold for Secretaries of State.

The 1993 Reform has introduced a number of changes to the

federal government, as regards the number of ministers making up its members, its independence, and above all its stability.

A reduced federal government.   It is now written into the Constitution that there cannot be more than fifteen federal ministers, including the Prime Minister. There is no limit to the number of Secretaries of State.

A more independent federal government.   The Constitution provides that from now on the offices of Minister and Member of Parliament may not be combined. Once a member of the Chamber or of the Senate has been appointed minister and has accepted that office, he or she will be replaced in Parliament. The parliamentary mandate will only be resumed after the King has terminated the appointment as minister. The same principles apply to the function of Secretary of State.

A more stable government.   The Constitution has introduced (subject to certain provisos) a device referred to as a constructive vote of no-confidence (Article 46). This means that the Chamber of Representatives cannot force the government to resign by passing a vote of no-confidence, nor by withholding its vote of confidence, without simultaneously designating a successor as head of the government: in other words, the Chamber of Representatives must submit to the King the name of a new Prime Minister for appointment. Though appointed by the King, the new Prime Minister will only take up office once the new government has been sworn in. In the interim, the outgoing government will continue to deal with day-to-day business.

The King may dissolve the Chamber of Representatives if a government finds itself in a minority and there is no new majority available. The monarch may also dissolve the Chamber of Representatives in the event of the resignation of the government, after obtaining its assent expressed by a simple majority of its members. From now on, the Chamber of Representatives will hold exclusive powers to operate a political review of the government. Hence the Chamber of Representatives and not the Senate has the power to force the government or one of its ministers to resign. The dissolution of the Chamber of Represenatives automatically brings about the dissolution of the Senate.

2. REFORM OF THE BICAMERAL SYSTEM

The Composition and Powers of the Chamber of Representatives and the Senate[3]

The reform of Belgian's bicameral (i.e. two-chamber) system is based on three principles:

1. The political control of the government and of state finances must be the exclusive preserve of one legislative chamber: the Chamber of Representatives.
2. The other legislative chamber—the Senate—is a 'chamber of deliberation', guaranteeing the quality of legislation and enabling the Communities to express their feelings, by virtue of the presence of members elected by the Councils of the Communities.
3. The institutional foundations of the Belgian state and the relations between the federal authority, the Communities, and the Regions fall within the shared competence of the two legislative chambers.

Since the Chamber of Representatives, and not the Senate, is the political chamber, the Chamber of Representatives holds exclusive powers to pass votes of confidence and no-confidence. In addition, legislative power is exercised by the Chamber of Representatives as regards:

1. the granting of naturalization;
2. the laws on the civil and criminal liability of the King's ministers;
3. state budgets and accounts, except the funding of the Senate;[4]
4. establishing the level of military conscription.

The Chamber of Representatives and the Senate have equal powers as regards:

1. The declaration of a constitutional revision and the subsequent implementation of such revision.
2. Texts that need to be drafted by the two legislative chambers in accordance with the Constitution, notably powers related to the monarchy (such as regency, guardianship, and succession).
3. Laws giving effect to the Articles of the Constitution on state structures.

4. Laws to be adopted by a majority vote in each language group (French-speaking and Dutch-speaking) of each of the chambers, on condition that the majority of the members of each language group are assembled, and providing that the total number of favourable votes given by the two language groups constitute two-thirds of the votes cast (special majority); and the laws enacted in pursuance of them.
5. Laws vesting specific powers in institutions of international public law.
6. Laws assenting to treaties; however, draft laws assenting to treaties laid before the chambers at the instance of the King are always lodged with the Senate and then transmitted to the Chamber of Representatives.
7. Laws adopted on behalf of a Community or Region in order to ensure compliance with international and supranational obligations.
8. Laws concerning the Council of State.[5]
9. The organization of the courts of law.
10. Laws approving co-operation agreements between the State, the Communities, and the Regions.

Laws adopted by the majority referred to under point 4 may designate other laws over which the Chamber of Representatives and the Senate shall have equal powers. Draft laws and/or proposed legislation over which the two chambers have equal powers travel back and forth between the Chamber of Representatives and the Senate until agreement has been reached on an identical text.

The Senate acts as a chamber of deliberation, but the last word always goes to the Chamber of Representatives as regards legislation over which the Chamber does not have exclusive powers, or to which the classic bicameral model does not apply. As a chamber of deliberation, the task of the Senate is to guarantee the quality of the legislation. It is also the duty of the Senate to take important legislative initiatives, for which the Chamber of Representatives and the government often have no time.

This new distribution of powers has necessitated the creation of a completely new legislative procedure. The Chamber, the Senate, and the King are all separately entitled to initiate legislation, with the proviso that the King must always exercise his right in this regard in the Chamber of Representatives and not in the Senate.

Whenever the Chamber adopts a draft law on its own initiative or on that of the King, it submits it to the Senate. The Senate may take up the draft law and examine it within a period of sixty days. On the expiry of this deadline at the latest, the Senate must send the draft law back to the Chamber, amended or unamended. If the Senate has amended the draft law, the Chamber will re-examine it. If the Chamber adopts an amendment other than the one proposed by the Senate, the draft law will be sent back to the Senate for the last time. The Senate has fifteen days in which to examine it. If the Senate amends the draft law, the Chamber will have to express an opinion one last time, and enjoys complete freedom in doing so. It may amend the draft law in ways contrary to those proposed by the Senate. Whatever the decision of the Chamber, the legislative procedure is then over.

When the Senate adopts a draft law in the exercise of its right to initiate legislation, it will transmit the draft to the Chamber, which will have sixty days in which to consider it. If the Chamber adopts or rejects the draft, the legislative procedure will be over. However, if the Chamber amends the draft, it will be sent back to the Senate one last time. If the Senate amends the draft within the deadline of fifteen days, the Chamber must give its last opinion on it—rejecting it, adopting it as it stands, or amending it.

The above deadlines may all be extended by a Parliamentary Liaison Committee (Commission de concertation parlementaire) which is also empowered to deal with any conflicts of powers between the two legislative chambers. Indeed, such conflicts may arise in the future: the Senate may claim that a proposed law or draft law is a bicameral issue, whereas the Chamber may perhaps consider itself to have sole competence. The Committee's membership is drawn in equal numbers from the Chamber and from the Senate. It gives rulings by a simple majority in both its constituent parts, or by a two-thirds majority of its members.

Although this new legislative procedure may seem complex, it is an attempt to maintain the advantages of classic bicameralism whilst attenuating its disadvantages. Specifically, an endless procedure is thereby avoided. Moreover, binding deadlines will be imposed on the Senate so that a draft law already approved by the Chamber cannot be delayed indefinitely. At the same time, the fact that the two chambers are both involved in legislative work guarantees the quality of that legislation. Furthermore, the need to have all legislation approved by both chambers is avoided.

The Senate is a forum for contact between the federal authority and the federated bodies: its composition testifies to this. Thus the Senate is the perfect venue for settling conflicts of interest between the legislative assemblies. It will issue a reasoned opinion on any conflict of interest between the assemblies (federal, Community, and Regional) which generate legislation.

The principle of loyalty to the federal principles is also inserted in the Constitution. It should be noted that this principle does not serve as a criterion for the distribution of powers, observance of which is monitored by the Court of Arbitration and other courts. The only purpose of the principle of federal loyalty is to state that the sound functioning of a federal state presupposes good faith. Adherence to that principle limits conflicts of interest to the bare minimum.

The Appointment of Members

The Chamber of Representatives has 150 members who are elected directly. There are twenty-one electoral constituencies. For each constituency the number of seats available is determined by dividing the population figure by the federal divisor, calculated by dividing by 150 the population figure for Belgium as a whole. Belgium has officially 9,978,681 inhabitants. The federal divisor is calculated in the following manner: $9,978,681/150 = 66.525$.

The Senate is composed of seventy-one senators of whom forty are directly elected by the Flemish and Walloon electoral colleges: twenty-five by the former and fifteen by the latter. The electoral colleges are the same as those for European elections. Twenty-one senators are appointed by the Community Councils. Of these:

- ten senators are appointed by the Flemish Council;
- ten senators are appointed by the Council of the French-speaking Community;
- One senator is appointed by the Council of the German-speaking Community;

Ten co-opted senators are chosen by the two previous groups, in the ratio of six senators nominated by the Dutch-speaking senators, to four senators by the French-speaking senators. They are appointed for a four-year term following each comprehensive renewal of the Senate.

The Senate also includes 'entitled' senators. The relevant paragraph of the Constitution reads as follows:

Article 72. The children of the monarch, or failing them the Belgian descendants of the ruling branch of the royal family, become senators as of right at the age of 18. They have voting rights at the age of 21. They are disregarded for the purpose of establishing a quorum.

Overall, the principle of proportional representation prevails in the composition of the Senate.

3. FEDERAL POWERS

Until the 1993 Reform the Communities and Regions had only the powers vested in them, the residual powers being held by the national authority, by virtue of a combination of constitutional provisions. Article 35 of the Constitution reads as follows:

The federal Authority has powers only in matters expressly assigned to it by the Constitution and the laws enacted thereunder.

The Communities or Regions, in their respective domains, have powers in other matters, subject to the conditions and rules established by law. That law must be adopted by a majority as defined in the last paragraph of Article 4.

'Majority' here means a majority of the votes in each language group of each chamber, on condition that the majority of the members of each group is assembled, and further provided that the total votes given in favour by both language groups represent two-thirds of the votes cast.

In stressing the dynamics of federalism, the revised Constitution provides that from now on residual powers will be vested in the Regions and the Communities, in their respective domains. However, this new system will not come into effect until a list of federal powers has been drawn up. This list must be drafted by a legislator acting under a special majority.

It should be emphasized that the Belgian constitutional system includes exclusive powers held by the federal authority and by the Communities and Regions. Thus, in Belgium there can hardly be said to be concurrent powers such as exist in most federal constitutional systems—for example, Switzerland or the Federal

Republic of Germany. Though regrettable, this state of affairs is the consequence of the process through which Belgian federalism has been fashioned: it has always had to contend with a profound mistrust of the central authority on the part of the advocates of federalism. In am convinced that in a few years' time the Belgian constituent power will have the sense to list, under a new article of the Constitution, the subjects falling within the concurrent powers of the federal authority and the federated entities.

PART IV: THE COMMUNITY AND REGIONAL LEVELS

1. GENERAL CONSIDERATIONS

The subdivision of the federated states of Belgium into Communities and Regions is one of the oddest aspects of Belgium's federal system. Community issues fall within the competence of the Flemish Council for the Flemish Community, that of the Council of the French-speaking Community for the French Community. Regional issues are handled by the Flemish Council for the Flemish Region, and by the Regional Walloon Council for the Walloon Region. Since 1980 the Constitution has allowed the exercise of the Flemish Region's powers to be devolved to the Flemish Community. and those of the Walloon Region to the French Community. This prerogative was immediately taken up by the Dutch-speaking Community but has never been used by the French-speaking Community. As far as the Dutch-speaking side is concerned, the Community is a privileged collective entity, whereas on the French-speaking side there is a strong tendency to give the Region more prominence.

With a view to meeting the aspirations apparent among the French speakers, the 1993 reform has introduced machinery whereby some of the powers of the French-speaking Community may be exercised by the Council and government of the Walloon Region in the French-language region, and by the French-language group of the Council of the Region of Brussels-Capital and its college in the bilingual Region of Brussels-Capital. The transfer of the exercise of those powers must, however, be approved by agreement with the three institutions involved—by a two-thirds majority within the Council of the French-speaking Community and by a simple majority of votes cast in the Council of the Walloon Region and the French-language group contained in the Council of the Region of Brussels-Capital, always provided that a majority of members are present.

As far as the German-speaking region within Wallonia is concerned, the Walloon Regional Council has powers over all regional matters in that region. None the less, the Constituent Assembly has created an option whereby certain regional powers may be conferred upon the Council of the German-speaking Community in the future. This transfer of powers must be regulated by a decree of both the Council of the German-speaking Community and the Walloon Regional Council, acting on a proposal from their executive bodies.

2. THE COUNCILS

The Election of Councils

The Councils are elected on a regional basis. Thus the members of the Regional Councils are elected directly. The Flemish and French-speaking Community Councils are made up of (a) members elected directly in the Flemish and Walloon regions (respectively), and (b) members of the Dutch or French-speaking group within the Council of the Region of Brussels-Capital. The Councils are elected for a period of five years, unless there is an early dissolution. The Council elections were held the same day as the next general election to the Chamber of Representatives, 21 May 1995; thereafter, they will be brought into line with the European Parliament elections in 1999 (see Art. 117 of the Constitution).

The Flemish Council (Region and Community) is composed of:

- 118 members directly elected in the Flemish Region; and
- the first six elected members of the Dutch-speaking group of the Council of the Region of Brussels-Capital.

The Walloon Regional Council is composed of the seventy-five directly elected members. The Council of the French-speaking Community is composed of:

- the seventy-five members of the Walloon Regional Council; and nineteen members appointed by and from the members of the French-speaking group of the Council of the Region of Brussels-Capital, divided among the political groups in proportion to the election results.

The office of councillor is not compatible with that of member of the Chamber of Representatives. It is also incompatible with the office of senator, with the exception of the twenty-one senators appointed by and from the Community Councils, who continue to act as Councillors.

Members of the Councils have full parliamentary status. Article 59 of the Constitution is rendered applicable to these members. According to that Article:

No member of either Chamber may, for the duration of the session, be prosecuted or arrested for criminal activity without the authorization of the Chamber to which he belongs, unless he is discovered *in flagrante delicto.*

No member of either Chamber may be imprisoned for the duration of the session, without the authorization of the Chamber to which he belongs.

The imprisonment or the prosecution of a member of either Chamber will be suspended for the duration of the session, if the Chamber so wishes.

The conditions for eligibility to vote in elections to the Flemish Council, the Walloon Regional Council, the Council of the Region of Brussels-Capital, or the Council of the German-speaking Community are identical. Members of the Council are directly elected by Belgians who have turned 18 years of age, are registered in the population register of a municipality in the territory of the Region, and do not come under any of the exclusion or suspension clauses referred to in the Electoral Code; each voter is entitled to only one vote.

To be directly elected to a Council it is necessary:

1. to be Belgian;
2. to enjoy civil and political rights;
3. to have turned 21 years of age;
4. to be resident in a municipality situated in the territory of the Region, and therefore to be registered in the population register of that municipality;[6]

5. not to come under any of the exclusion or suspension clauses set out in the Electoral Code.

Conditions of eligibility must be fulfilled as on the day of election, with the exception of the conditions as to residence and registration, which must be fulfilled six months prior to the election.

Three Councils—the Flemish Council, the French Community Council, and the Walloon Regional Council—have a certain degree of constitutive autonomy. This means that a decree of the Community or of the Region, adopted by a special majority, can settle certain issues to do with the elections, the composition, and the operation of Councils and Governments. Although the principle to this effect is contained in the Constitution (Arts. 118 and 123), it is the Special Law that defines the issues which can be regulated by the Councils themselves.

Those three Councils may, in their respective domains, deal with the following matters by a decree adopted by a two-thirds majority:

1. the number of Council members;
2. the constituencies for Council elections;[7]
3. changes to the number of members in their government and the rules governing their operation;
4. basic rules on the functioning of the Council, including (see the Special Law of 8 August 1980): the election of officers (president, vice-presidents, and secretaries) and their responsibilities, and the tasks of a registrar; whether sessions are public or secret; petitions; and assembly days;
5. the status and financial allowances of members;
6. functions deemed incompatible with those of a member.

The Councils can also decide by decree (adopted by a two-thirds majority) to involve directly elected senators in their work, albeit without voting rights. Senators who accept this invitation are statutorily debarred, on grounds of incompatibility, from holding office at any other political level.

The Governments of the Communities and Regions

The members of the governments of the Communities and Regions are elected by their respective Councils, but not necessarily from within the Council. They must be resident in the administrative constituency of the Council in question.

As part of their 'constitutive autonomy' the Councils may, by a decree adopted by a two-thirds majority and within their respective domains, change the number of members in the governments of the Flemish Community, the French Community, or the Walloon Region, and may regulate the way in which they operate. The Flemish government has eleven members; the Regional Walloon government has seven members; the government of the French-speaking Community has four members. It should be borne in mind that it is not possible to be a member of the government of a Community or Region and at the same time a member of the federal government.

3. POWERS OF COMMUNITIES AND REGIONS

Powers of the Communities

Cultural Issues.   Cultural issues can be divided into four groups:
- cultural issues in the strict sense, including the protection and diffusion of language, the fine arts, the cultural heritage, museums and other cultural or scientific institutions, libraries, record-libraries, and similar services;
- media-related issues, including the power to regulate radio and television advertising, and support for the press;
- leisure and tourism, excluding conditions of establishment;
- issues related to education and training, for example pre-school activities, further education, and extra-mural activities, art courses, and so on.

Education.   The provision in question is Article 24 of the Constitution:

§ 1. Education is free; any preventative measure is forbidden; the repression of offences is only governed by law or decree.

The Community offers free choice to parents.

The Community organizes neutral education. Neutrality implies notably the respect of the philosophical, ideological or religious conceptions of parents and pupils.

The schools organized by the public authorities offer, until the end of obligatory scholarity, the choice between the teaching of one of the recognized religions and non-denominational moral teaching.

§ 2. If a Community, in its capacity as an organizing authority, wishes to delegate competency to one or several autonomous bodies, it can only do so by decree adopted by a two-third majority vote.

§ 3. Everyone has the right to education with the respect of fundamental rights and freedoms. Access to education is free until the end of obligatory scholarity.

All pupils of school age have the right to moral or religious education at the Community's expense.

§ 4. All pupils or students, parents, teaching staff, or institutions are equal before the law or decree. The law and decree take into account objective differences, notably the characteristics of each organizing authority, that justify appropriate treatment.

§ 5. The organization, the recognition and the subsidizing of education by the Community are regulated by law or decree.

The only functions now withheld from the Communities are 'determining the commencement and end of compulsory school attendance; the minimum requisites for the award of diplomas; and the pension scheme'. Those three specific heads continue to lie with the federal state.

Personalizable issues. The Special Law of 8 August 1980 (Art. 5) divides personalizable issues into two blocks: health-care policy, including nursing, health education, and preventive medicine; and welfare, including family policy, social assistance, the reception and integration of immigrants, and policies regarding the disabled, the aged, youth protection, and social assistance for prisoners. In the sphere of personalizable issues, the Communities' powers are tempered by important reserves in favour of the federal state: thus, powers over health and disability insurance, powers in the area of health-care policy, and powers over some aspects of civil and criminal law and the administration of justice for the protection of minors lie outside the Communities' competence.

Languages. This power concerns the French-speaking and Flemish Communities, but not the German-speaking Community. Regarding the competence of the communities Art. 127 of the Constitution provides as follows :

Art. 127

§ 1. The French and Dutch Community Councils, respectively, establish
    by decree;
    1° cultural issues;
    2° education, with the exception of:
    a) the determination of the beginning and of the end of mandatory
       scholarity;
    b) minimum standards for the granting of diplomas;
    c) attribution of pensions;
    3° inter-Community co-operation, in addition to international co-
       operation, including the drafting of treaties for those matters de-
       scribed in 1° and 2°.
    A law adopted by majority vote as described in Article 4, last para-
    graph, establishes those cultural matters described in 1°, types of co-
    operation described in 3°, in addition to terms governing the
    conclusion of treaties described in 3°.
§ 2. These decrees have force of law in French-language and in Dutch-
    language Regions respectively, as well as in those institutions estab-
    lished in the bilingual Region of Brussels-Capital which, on account of
    their activities, must be considered as belonging exclusively to one
    Community or the other.

The cultural matters referred to in Art. 127 of the Constitution are
as follows:

    1. The defence and promotion of the language;
    2. The promotion of training for research workers;
    3. The fine arts;
    4. The cultural heritage, museums and other cultural and scientific
       institutions;
    5. Libraries, record libraries and kindred services;
    6. Radio and television broadcasting, with the exception of broadcasts
       by the National Government and of commercial advertising;
    7. Youth policy;
    8. Permanent education and cultural animation;
    9. Physical education, sport, and open-air activities;
    10. Leisure and tourism;
    11. Preschooling in nursery and day care units;
    12. Further education and parascholastic training;
    13. Artistic training;
    14. Intellectual, moral and social formation;
    15. Social advancement;
    16. Professional reconversion and retraining, with the exception of rules

governing intervention in the expenses incurred by the selection, professional training and rehabilitation of personnel recruited by an employer with a view to founding a business enterprise or to the enlarging or retooling of an existing enterprise;

17. Applied scientific research with respect to the matters listed above.

Scientific research.   Powers are vested in the Communities, within the limits of their responsibilities, to deal with scientific research, including research conducted under international or supranational agreements. However, the federal authority, having responsibility for scientific research as one of its inherent powers, may also intervene in the Communities' powers when international agreements are involved or if the matter extends beyond the interests of a Community, once it has heard the opinion of the Federal Council on Scientific Policy. A Community may nevertheless refuse to co-operate where it, as a Community, or establishments falling within its authority, are concerned.

Administrative supervision of subordinate bodies in Community matters.   The organization and conduct of administrative supervision are assigned to the Regions, but without prejudice to the power of the Communities to organize specific supervision within their own spheres of responsibility.

Powers of the Regions

Town and country planning.   Town and country planning has been entirely regionalized. The Regions are therefore sovereign in the planning of their own territory and in the protection of regional monuments and sites.

Environmental and water-management policy.   Most of the powers relating to the environment and water-management policy lie with the Regions. This covers:

- protection of the environment, especially the soil, subsoil, water, and atmosphere against pollution and interference, and noise control;
- waste policy;
- policing of dangerous, unhealthy, and undesirable premises,

without prejudice to internal inspection measures on labour protection;
- the production and distribution of water, including technical regulations on the quality of drinking water, the treatment of liquid waste, and drainage.

Rural re-development and nature conservation. The Regions, with certain exceptions, have responsibility in ten areas: the reallocation of rural property and rural re-development; nature protection and conservation; green-belt areas, parklands, and rural areas; forestry; hunting and trapping; river fishing; fish breeding; agricultural hydraulics and non-navigable waterways; land reclamation; and polders and coastal drainage.

Housing. Regions are responsible for housing and the inspection of premises hazardous to public health and hygiene.

Agricultural Policy

The economy. This covers four spheres:
- economic policy;
- the regional aspects of loans policies;
- marketing and export policy. The federal authority none the less remains responsible for co-ordination and co-operation in this area and for promotion in collaboration with the Regions—if possible under co-operation agreements. Hence, whilst concertation is a substantial formality, breach of which may be condemned by the Court of Arbitration, a co-operation agreement is no more than an aspiration, and its absence does not involve sanctions. Guarantees against risks arising from exportation, importation, and investment remain a federal affair. This, however, does not debar Regions from providing further safeguards from their own resources;
- natural resources.

Energy policy. The Regions are responsible for the regional aspects of energy (distribution and local transmission of electricity and gas, etc.), but the federal authority retains powers over those areas which, being technically and economically indivisible, call for standardization.

Subordinate powers. The Regions enjoy important prerogatives with respect to local communities (provinces and communes).

Employment policy.   Regions are responsible for employment, programmes to absorb unemployment, and the enforcement of rules on the use of foreign workers. With respect to this last field, however, the 1993 reform provides that the federal authority is also responsible for monitoring compliance.

Public works and transport.   This covers roads, waterways, ports, dikes, public transport in towns and neighbourhoods, including taxis and chauffeuring services, the equipment and use of public airports (excluding the Brussels national airport) and, since 1993, the legal system governing roads and waterways, excluding the railways run by the Belgian national railway company (SNCB).

Scientific research.   Within the limits of their powers, the Regions, like the Communities, are responsible for research, including research carried out under international or supranational agreements or instruments. Nevertheless, these regional powers do not mean that the federal authority is not entitled to embark on certain projects when the subject-matter falls under international agreements or extends beyond the interests of a Region.

Additional Powers

At the moment, Communities and Regions only wield the powers vested in them. However, it was necessary to prevent the efficacy of those powers from being nullified through being unduly constrained, and various measures protect them:

1. The Communities and Regions are empowered to enact provisions and other measures with respect to the infrastructure required for the exercise of their powers.
2. They are empowered to set up decentralized facilities, establishments, and undertakings, or to hold share capital.
3. Decrees may make it an offence to fail to comply with their provisions; they may introduce—within certain limits—penalties for such non-compliance. The Communities and Regions may in certain special cases derogate by decree from the provisions of the first book of the Penal Code. This means that the Communities and Regions can introduce penalties not envisaged by the Penal Code. However, any draft Decree drawn up by the Government of a Region or Community on

this subject must receive the assent of the Council of Ministers. The Communities and Regions can appoint sworn officials as police officers, can rule on the evidential value of official reports, and can determine the circumstances warranting a search of premises. The purpose of this provision is to enable the Communities and Regions to enforce their rules and regulations, since some claim that the traditional judicial bodies have been rather too passive.

4. Communities and Regions may now intervene in reserved areas by virtue of inherent powers. This means that Communities and Regions will be able to organize administrative courts and tribunals in their spheres of responsibility on the basis of their inherent powers of the Special Law of 8 August 1980.

5. Governments of Communities and Regions are permitted to expropriate property in the public interest.

6. Communities and Regions may instruct provincial or municipal authorities to give effect to their decrees and regulations.

PART V: BRABANT

The principal change brought about by the 1993 reform in the decentralized institutions was the splitting-up of the Province of Brabant. Situated in the heart of the federal kingdom of Belgium, Brabant is composed of a Dutch-speaking part, a French-speaking part, and a bilingual part, namely the linguistic region of Brussels-Capital. As the linguistic divide runs right across the Province, as from 1 January 1995 it has been split—the experience of keeping it in its present form having proved administratively disastrous.

1. INSTITUTIONS AND THEIR POWERS

The Province of Flemish Brabant

The Province of Flemish Brabant is established over the Dutch-speaking part of the present territory of the Province of Brabant. A separate provincial council was elected for Flemish Brabant at the provincial elections which coincided with the elections of October 1994.

The Province of Walloon Brabant

The Province of Walloon Brabant is established over the French-speaking part of the present territory of the Province of Brabant. A separate provincial council was elected for Walloon Brabant at the provincial elections, held simultaneously with the elections of October 1994.

The Bilingual Region of Brussels-Capital

The area covering the nineteen Brussels communes will not be included in the division into provinces. The reason is that it was absurd to establish a third Brabant province solely for Brussels, since its territorial jurisdiction would have been mixed up with that of the Region of Brussels-Capital, generating an undesirable duplication of powers. As regards that part of the territory of the present Province of Brabant which lies within the bilingual Region of Brussels-Capital, the powers of the Province will be transferred to existing Community and Regional institutions, in keeping with the division of powers between the federal authority and the federated entities.

PART VI: THE INSTITUTIONS OF THE REGION OF BRUSSELS-CAPITAL

1. LIMITS

The Region of Brussels-Capital covers the nineteen communes of the bilingual district of Brussels-Capital: the city of Brussels, plus the Communes of Schaerbeek, Anderlecht, Uccle, Ixelles, Molenbeek-Saint-Jean, Forest, Woluwe-Saint-Lambert, Saint-Gilles, Etterbeek, Woluwe-Saint-Pierre, Jette, Evere, Auderghem,

Watermael-Boisfort, Ganshoren, Saint-Josse-ten-Noode, Berchem-Saint-Agathe, and Koekelberg.

In order to avoid any confusion, it should be pointed out that the territory of Brussels-Capital is just the same as that of the bilingual region of Brussels-Capital, and indeed of the Brussels Urban Area. We may note that the Region of Brussels-Capital is the only bilingual part (both Dutch- and French-speaking) of the Kingdom of Belgium. The Region of Brussels-Capital has a legal persona.

2. THE COUNCIL

The Council of the Region of Brussels-Capital—the parliament of the Brussels region—consists of seventy-five members elected directly every five years. The first elections were held in 1989. The date of the elections is the same as the date appointed for the other Regional Councils. As a transitional measure, the next elections of all the councils were held at the same time as the next elections to the Chamber and the Senate, namely on 21 May 1995.

The voting rules are identical to those for the Flemish and Walloon Councils. Voters must be entered in the population register of one of the nineteen communes of the Region of Brussels-Capital. The candidates of the French-language group and the candidates of the Dutch-language group are set out on separate lists. On being elected, members of the Council are divided into two language groups: the French-language group and the Dutch-language group. Elections follow single-language rolls. The number of members belonging to each language group depends on the results of the elections.[8] A pooling system has been introduced to limit the disadvantages to the smaller parties due to proportional representation: the seventy-five seats are first split up between all the French rolls on the one hand, and all the Dutch rolls on the other.

The Council exercises its regional powers in the form of orders (*ordonnances*), which have the force of law. Unlike a law or a decree, an order may be subjected to judicial review, to ascertain its compliance with the Constitution and with the Special Law of 12 January 1989 itself. The Council exercises its powers over the urban area in the form of regulations (*règlements*).

3. THE GOVERNMENT

Executive power is vested in the Government of the Region of Brussels-Capital, which is composed of five members elected by the Council from amongst its own members: the President, plus two members of the French-language group and two members of the Dutch-language group.

There are also three regional Secretaries of State (of whom at least one belongs to the Dutch-speaking language group), elected by the Council from amongst its members, on a proposal from the Government of the Region. They are not members of the Government but are entitled to attend its meetings. However, they are responsible to the Council.

The decisions of the Government are collegial, and based on consensus. 'Collegial' means that the decision comes from the Government acting as a single body, as opposed to being attributable to one or more members, whilst 'consensus' means that all the members have to signify their assent.

4. POWERS

Regional Powers

The Region of Brussels-Capital has the same regional powers as the Walloon and Flemish Regions, namely:

1. town planning;
2. environment;
3. nature conservation;
4. housing;
5. water husbandry;
6. economy;
7. energy policy;
8. employment policy;
9. public works and transport;
10. subordinate powers (Article 4 of the Special Law of 12 January 1988).

Powers of the Urban Area

The powers of the Brussels Urban Area, which has a legal persona, are exercised by the Council and the Government of the Region of Brussels-Capital. The Brussels Urban Area is responsible for some matters of public interest which cannot be managed by any one commune, such as the fire service and the collection of refuse.

5. THE COMMUNITY COMMISSIONS OF BRUSSELS (COMMISSIONS COMMUNAUTAIRES BRUXELLOISES)

The decrees of the Flemish and French-speaking communities on cultural matters—education and 'personalizable' subjects—are legally binding in the territory of Brussels-Capital on those institutions which, by virtue of their activities (cultural events and education) or their organization ('personalizable' subjects), are to be regarded as belonging solely to either the French or the Flemish Community. This means that the decrees of either community may apply throughout the territory of Brussels-Capital. It was therefore necessary to set up institutions to be responsible for the implementation of such decrees in the territory of Brussels-Capital. Those institutions are the French-language Community Commission and the Flemish Community Commission. Where the subject-matter is common to both communities there is a Joint Community Commission.

The French-language and Flemish Community Commissions act, in their respective communities, as organizing authorities in education, and exercise cultural and personalizable powers together with those delegated to them by the Council of their Community. In practice they are responsible for the setting up, management and funding, within their particular community sited in the territory of the Region of Brussels-Capital establishments such as schools, theatres, cultural places, rest homes for the elderly, and monolingual home-care services. Each community Commission has its own parliamentary and executive body. The parliamentary body of each Commission is made up of the members of the relevant language group in the Council of the Region of Brussels-Capital.

Since the 1993 reform the college has consisted of the members of the government of the Region and the regional Secretaries of State belonging to the relevant language group. The Brussels member of Government of the French-speaking Community and the Brussels member of the Government of the Flemish Community attend the sessions of the relevant college in an advisory capacity.

The Joint Community Commission is responsible for 'personalizable' matters common to both Communities, such as bilingual hospitals. The bodies of this Commission are the Assembly composed of the members of both language groups referred to above, and the joint college, composed of the members of the two colleges referred to above. The President of the Brussels Executive chairs the sessions of the joint college and has advisory status. Some institutions continue to fall within the responsibility of the federal authority. Examples include the Théâtre Royal de la Monnaie, the Palais des Beaux-Arts, and the Royal Museums.

6. CO-OPERATION COMMITTEE

In order to decide on initiatives to be taken jointly by the State and the Region of Brussels-Capital with a view to fostering and promoting the international rôle and function of the capital, a separate body, the Cooperation Committee, has been set up. This Committee is composed of an equal number of ministers of the federal Government and members of the Government of Brussels-Capital. Each delegation contains the same number of French- and Dutch-speaking members.

PART VII: THE GERMAN-SPEAKING COMMUNITY

1. TERRITORIAL AND LANGUAGE ARRANGEMENTS

Pursuant to Article 3 of the Ordinary Law of 31 December 1983, the German-language Region includes the communes of Amel, Büllingen, Burg-Reuland, Bütgenbach, Eupen, Kelmis, Lontzen, Raeren, and Sankt-Vith. The Communes of Malmedy and Waimes fall within the French-language Region, but special facilities are provided for German speakers.

According to the Law of 2 August 1963 on the use of language for administrative purposes, German is the official administrative language in the communes of the German-language Region. There are special provisions for the protection of the cultural identity of the French-speaking minority. The German-language Region was formally created by Article 4 of the Constitution.

The German-Speaking Community Council

The Council of the German-speaking Community consists of twenty-five members, directly elected by the citizens of the communes making up the German-language Region who are entitled to vote at legislative elections. As is customary in Belgium, the German-speaking Community Council is elected by proportional representation. The ballot is confidential and compulsory.

The ordinary meeting of the electoral college held to replace outgoing Council members takes place every five years, on the same date as that appointed for elections to the European Parliament. However, if the complete renewal of the Flemish Council and the Regional Walloon Council takes place on some other date, the ordinary meeting will fall on that date.

The following—if they are not members of the Council—are entitled to attend the sessions in an advisory capacity:

1. Members of the Chamber of Representatives and members of the Walloon Regional Council elected in the constituency of Verviers who are resident in the German-language Region and who have taken the constitutional oath either exclusively or primarily in German;
2. Senators elected by the French electoral college and also senators elected by the Senate, as long as they meet the two conditions referred to in point 1 above;
3. Provincial councillors elected in the district of Eupen, as long as they meet the two conditions referred to in point 1 above.

Members of the Council must: be Belgian; have reached twenty-one years of age; have been registered in the population registers of a commune of the German-language Region for at least six months prior to the day of the election; and not be in any of the circumstances entailing the removal or suspension of voting rights, nor be deprived by a judicial conviction of the right to stand for election (Article 5 of the Law of 6 July 1990). Since the Council is not composed of members of Parliament, Article 120 of the Constitution grants the members of the Council parliamentary immunity under Articles 55 and 59 of the Constitution.

The Government of the German-speaking Community

The government includes three members elected by the Council on the majority principle. They need not be elected from within the Council. The candidates' applications must be signed by at least three members of the Council. They cannot simultaneously be members of the national government or of any other government. They are not entitled to vote in the Council unless they are members of the Council (Law of 31 December 1983).

Powers

On Community matters, the institutions of the German-language Region have the same powers as the Flemings and the Walloons, except that the federal State alone has jurisdiction over the use of languages. On Regional matters, the German speakers are part of the Walloon Regional Council.

PART VIII: FINANCIAL RESOURCES OF THE COMMUNITIES AND REGIONS

To illustrate the general scale of the funds received by the Communities and Regions, one need only mention that, on the basis of the preliminary 1995 budget, the total revenue paid to the Communities and Regions amounted to BF 837.3 bn., representing 34.9 per cent of total state income from fiscal and non-fiscal sources, amounting to BF 2,397.7 bn. Compared with the total finances managed by the state, that is to say including the income from loans, the percentage accruing to the Communities and Regions is 24.3 per cent.

1. FINANCIAL RESOURCES OF THE COMMUNITIES

The financial resources of the Communities are derived from the following sources:

- autonomous non-fiscal receipts, derived from the exercise by the Communities of the powers vested in them;
- fiscal receipts (from Community taxes);
- taxes shared between the federal authority and the Communities: the remission of part of the VAT revenue and of the tax on natural persons;
- borrowing: the Communities are allowed to engage in private or public borrowing, in Belgian francs or in other currencies (subject to certain conditions as to notification or authorization);
- conditional endowments: these are yearly budgetary credits for the financing of foreign students in university education (except students who come under a development co-operation agreement).

2. FINANCIAL RESOURCES OF THE REGIONS

The financial resources of the Regions come from the following sources:

- autonomous non-fiscal receipts, deriving from the exercise by the Regions of the powers vested in them;
- regional taxes (autonomous taxation): tax on the opening of premises serving alcoholic drinks; tax on automatic amusement machines; tax on gaming and betting; withholding tax on real estate (*précompte immobilier*); registration fees on real estate transferred against payment; inheritance tax and tax on change of ownership occurring on death; vehicle licence tax;
- joint tax, imposed on natural persons;
- borrowing: Regions may issue private or public loan stock in Belgian francs or other currency (subject to certain conditions as to notification of or authorization by the federal authorities);

- national solidarity payment, whose purpose is to mitigate the disparities in regional prosperity;
- credit entitlements for employment programmes: this is a financial grant from the state for each full-time job taken over by a Region.

PART IX: INTERNATIONAL TREATIES

Several new provisions on treaty-making have just been introduced by the constituent chambers at both the constitutional level and at that of special and ordinary legislation. As the Kingdom of Belgium is now a federal state, these provisions seek—often in novel ways—to enable the different components of the federal state to participate in international life. To explain in simple terms, we shall first enumerate the entities having treaty-making power, then turn to the various phases of the *jus tractati*, and finally discuss certain specific problems.

1. WHO HAS *JUS TRACTATI*?

Pursuant to Article 167 of the Constitution treaties may be concluded, in matters over which they have exclusive powers, by the following:

- at the federal level, by the King, as head of the federal government;
- at the Community level, by the respective governments of the Flemish Community, the French-speaking Community, and the German-speaking Community;
- at the Regional level, by the respective governments of the Flemish Region, the Walloon Region, and the Region of Brussels-Capital.

It should be noted that the schedule of the powers vested in the federal state has not yet been defined in the course of reforming the state. *Jus tractati* is conferred on the Flemish and French-speaking Communities by Articles 127 and 128 of the Constitution, and on the German-speaking Community by Article 130 of the

Constitution. As far as the Regions are concerned, no powers are conferred by the Special Law of 8 August 1980 implementing the former Article 107 *quater* of the Constitution. Reference to the *jus tractati* of the Regions is made in Article 167(3) of the Constitution, which does not grant powers as such, but regulates the exercise of certain powers.

For treaties that are not confined to matters falling within the domain of the Communities or Regions—the 'mixed treaties'—the new Article 167 of the Constitution refers to a Special Law establishing detailed rules for treaty-making. This Special Law on the international relations of Communities and Regions, adopted on 5 May 1993, amends (in Article 3(2)) Article 92 *bis* of the Special Law of 8 August 1980 and adds the obligation on the part of the state, the Communities, and the Regions to conclude a co-operation agreement in order to define those detailed rules. That agreement was negotiated between the various entities of the Kingdom and was published in the *Moniteur Belge*.

2. OPENING OF NEGOTIATIONS

The King and each of the governments of Communities or Regions may take the initiative in commencing negotiations with third states when the subject-matter of such negotiations falls within their exclusive powers. However, Article 167(1) of the Constitution specifies that the King shall direct international relations. The governments of the Communities and Regions are under an obligation—inserted into Article 81 of the Special Law of 8 August 1980 by Article 2 of the Special Law of 5 May 1993—to give the King prior notice of their intention to start negotiations with a view to concluding a treaty, and of any subsequent legal step they may wish to take in this regard.

The special legislator has chosen not to use the expedient of submitting the *jus tractati* of the federated bodies for the approval of the federal authority. However, the new Article 81 of the Special Law of 8 August 1980 introduces a procedure whereby the King may declare that there are objections to the treaty envisaged. Under this procedure, which sets deadlines, the parties may reach an agreement by consensus. If there is no consensus, the King can confirm that the initiative of the government is suspended, if:

(1) the contracting party is not recognized by Belgium;
(2) Belgium does not have diplomatic relations with the contracting party;
(3) it is apparent from a decision or act of the State that the relations between Belgium and the contracting party have been broken off, suspended or seriously compromised;
(4) the proposed treaty is contrary to any international or supranational obligations on the part of Belgium.

Article 2 of the Special Law of 5 May 1993 (new Article 81(5) of the Special Law of 8 August 1980) also provides that the King may suspend the performance of a treaty concluded by the Communities and the Regions acting in pursuance of their exclusive powers, on the same grounds as those permitting him to suspend a government's initiative to start negotiations.

Reference should also be made to a new rule that places the King and the governments under an obligation to inform the relevant parliamentary body of any commencement of negotiations designed to amend in any way the treaties establishing the European Communities, or the treaties and acts that amend or supplement them (Article 168 of the Constitution; new Article 16(2) of the Special Law of 8 August 1980).

3. NEGOTIATION, INITIALLING, AND SIGNATURE

For treaties that fall within the respective exclusive powers of the entities of the Kingdom, responsibility for negotiating, initialling, and signing treaties lies with the King for the federal authority, and with the various governments for the Communities and Regions. It is worth noting that the signature of the diplomatic instrument does not have to be authorized by the King, as is often the case in federal systems. Rules have not yet been laid down for 'mixed treaties'.

4. ASSENT

No treaty, regardless of its diplomatic form (whether a treaty, agreement, convention, exchange of letters, or other) comes into effect until it has received parliamentary assent: treaties governed by exclusive powers are approved by the relevant chambers or Councils; 'mixed treaties' require the assent of each parliamentary assembly whenever the provisions of the diplomatic instrument affect the powers of both the federal authority and the Communities and/or Regions. The joint Community Assembly of the Region of Brussels-Capital must give its assent to any treaty containing provisions which are the subject of the current bi-community powers in the territory of the bilingual Region of Brussels-Capital.

5. RATIFICATION, ACCESSION, AND TERMINATION

The government that has negotiated and signed the diplomatic instrument is responsible for ratification, accession, and termination, since these are all part of treaty-making procedures. Rules have not yet been laid down for the 'mixed' treaties. Article 167(5) of the Constitution contains a special measure whereby the King may repudiate any treaties made before that Article came into force, on subjects falling under the exclusive powers of the Communities and Regions, but does so by agreement with the Governments of the Communities and Regions.

6. PARTICULAR PROBLEMS

Article 2 of the Special Law of 5 May 1993 on the international relations of the Communities and Regions amends Article 81 of the Special Law of 8 August 1980. Pursuant to Article 81 §7, the King is responsible for defending the interests of the Communities and Regions before international and supra-national courts. Consultation must be arranged between the different authorities for that purpose—the detailed rules being set out in a co-operation agreement between the federal authority, the Communities, and the Regions (Art. 92 *bis*, new paragraph 4 *qua ter*, of the Law of 8 August 1980).

Article 169 of the new Constitution specifies that, in order to guarantee compliance with the international or supra-national obligations of the Kingdom, the federal state may temporarily act in lieu of the bodies of the Communities and Regions. The conditions for this substitution are listed in Article 1 of the Special Law of 5 May 1993, which inserts a new Article 16(3) into the Law of 8 August 1980. Any expenses due to non-compliance on the part of a Community or Region with an international or supra-national obligation may be recovered by the federal state from the defaulter.

The Special Law of 5 May 1993 places the national authority, the Communities, and the Regions under an obligation to conclude a co-operation agreement among themselves with a view to establishing rules as to how the components of the Kingdom are to participate in the activities of international organizations (new Art. 92 *bis* §4 *bis*, of the Special Law of 8 August 1980).

An inter-ministerial conference has been set up. It is composed of the members of the various governments in charge of international relations. The purpose of this inter-ministerial conference is to ensure that Belgium acts consistently at the international level (Ordinary Law of 5 May 1993 on the international relations of the Communities and Regions).

PART X: THE COURT OF ARBITRATION

1. POWERS

Actions for Annulment

Actions for annulment seek to quash all or part of a law, decree, or order violating: a) the distribution of powers; b) Articles 10 and 11 of the Constitution about equality and non-discrimination and Article 24 about free education. It is abstract, in that proceedings are instituted against a provision of law without reference to any specific situation generated by the provision. Actions for infringement of the rules on the division of powers may be made brought with a view either to obtaining the Court's settlement of an actual conflict—if two provisions issued by different deliberative assemblies purport to solve the same issue—or to resolving a potential conflict, if a deliberative assembly has overstepped its powers.

Ambit. Article 142 of the Constitution defines the jurisdiction of the Court of Arbitration, and Article 1 of the Special Law of 6

January 1989 gives effect to that rule in infringement proceedings seeking annulments. There are provisions established by, or under, the Constitution to determine the respective powers of the state, the Communities and the Regions. Since its creation in 1983, the Court of Arbitration has had jurisdiction over questions as to whether the constitutional and legislative rules defining the powers of the various political communities have been complied with. In order to give a ruling, it must make a careful examination of the basis for the powers held by the various legislatures involved in the conflict.

The powers of the Communities and Regions are those vested in them. Accordingly, Community and Regional matters are always expressly defined in the Constitution. Sometimes the federal legislature will implement the constitutional provisions in a body of provisions specifying their content. The Court of Arbitration will ensure that the autonomy of the Communities and Regions is respected in all these matters.

The powers of the federal legislature are not always expressly defined. The Court of Arbitration obliges the federal authorities, the Communities, and the Regions not to go beyond the constitutional and legislative framework of their powers. There is no exhaustive list or precise definition of the rules for the division of powers on the basis of which the Court of Arbitration is to exercise its review powers. In this area, therefore, it is endowed with a definite discretionary power, which allows it to define the concept exactly and hence to establish the ambit of its own powers.

Article 107 *ter* was amended and became Article 142 of the new Constitution, so that the Court of Arbitration could address conflicts other than those concerning the distribution of powers. Thereafter, the court was authorized to review the conformity of laws, decrees, and orders with Articles 10, 11, and 24 of the Constitution. The extension of the court's power is fully consistent with the Communities' responsibility for education, which accompanied the 1988 institutional reforms. The court must guarantee freedom of education. Articles 10 and 11 of the Constitution, enjoining observance of the principles of equality and non-discrimination, are linked to Article 24 (discussed above), because they constitute the basis underlying it and are clearly the prerequisites for such transfer of powers to the Communities.

In the preparatory phase of the drafting of the Special Law of 6 January 1989, it was often stressed that the three Articles of the

Constitution could be invoked separately. Indeed, from its very first judgments, the Court of Arbitration construed Articles 10 and 11 independently. Since the two Articles are simply the formulation of the principles of equality and of non-discrimination, that interpretation of its additional powers means that the court is able to monitor compliance with many Articles of the Constitution.

Bringing an action.   According to Article 142 of the Constitution, an action for annulment may be commenced before the Court of Arbitration by any authority designated by the law and any person showing a legitimate interest. Article 2 of the Special Law of 6 January 1989 provides that such actions may be commenced:

1. By the Council of Ministers, and by the government of a Community or of a Region;
2. By any individuals or legal entities showing a legitimate interest;
3. By the presidents of the legislative assemblies, at the request of two-thirds of the members.

Requests for Suspension

The purpose of a request for suspension is to obtain the suspension of the contested law, decree, or order so that its implementation shall not have irreversible effects. This request is an ancillary measure since it presupposes the institution of proceedings. Actions for annulment are not, however, necessarily accompanied by applications for suspension. Suspension is a completely separate procedure and the outcome of the application has no impact on the outcome of the main proceedings.

Preliminary Questions

Preliminary questions are raised by a court of law in relation to a particular dispute: the Court of Arbitration is requested to rule as to the validity or invalidity of a law, decree, or order. It is a strictly case-specific application, presented in the context of a dispute pending before a court, and designed to enable the latter to give a decision. The Court of Arbitration does not have the power to quash an unconstitutional provision, but simply sets out the law and declares that certain powers have been exceeded.

As to preliminary questions, the sole duty of the Court of Arbitration—without going into the details of the dispute pending before the court making the referral—is to inform the latter whether or not the law or the decree referred to in the question, and capable of being applied to the dispute in question, entails a breach of its powers on the part of one or other legislature.

The judicial handling of preliminary questions is specific in so far as it consists of a dialogue between judges. The parties to the dispute giving rise to the question may intervene before the Court of Arbitration but without ever entering into a debate with it.

The parties before the Court of Arbitration—whether they be the parties before the referring court or others—have not been granted the right of altering or seeking the alteration of, the content of the questions raised before the Court of Arbitration. (Judgments No. 12, 13, and 15.)

A preliminary question addressed to the Court of Arbitration is never accompanied by a request for suspension. The only consequence of the referral of the matter to the Court of Arbitration is the automatic suspension of the proceedings until the court notifies its decision, and the procedural time-limits and time-bars attaching to the main proceedings.

2. ORGANIZATION

Composition

The Court of Arbitration is a forum of law. It is composed of judges and legal secretaries (*référendaires*). Clerical and administrative staff also help it to function properly.

According to Article 31 of the Special Law of 6 January 1989, the Court of Arbitration is composed of twelve judges. The judges are selected according to a double rule of parity. There is a rule of linguistic parity: six French-speaking judges form the French-language group of the court and six Dutch-speaking judges form the Dutch-language group. And there is a rule of parity as to qualifications: six judges hold legal qualifications and six judges hold political qualifications. The two rules of parity also intersect: in each language group, three of the judges are lawyers and three are politicians.

PART XI: CO-OPERATION AND SETTLEMENT OF CONFLICTS BETWEEN THE FEDERAL AUTHORITY, THE COMMUNITIES, AND THE REGIONS

1. CO-OPERATION

As already indicated, powers are allocated exclusively between the federal authority, the Communities, and the Regions. The federated bodies also enjoy extensive autonomy, since their legal provisions (decrees and orders) are not in principle subordinated to those of the federal authority. The Belgian Constitution does not contain the famous principle set out in Article 31 of the Constitution of the Federal Republic of Germany, under which federal law takes precedence over the law of the *Länder*—hence the importance attached by the Constituent body and the legislature to co-ordination and co-operation between the various authorities. By virtue of the concertation and co-operation procedures the authorities are able to harmonize their policies on similar issues and thus achieve optimum efficiency: it often happens that several authorities may have responsibility for a given issue, each being in charge of one particular aspect of it.

Formal Co-operation Agreements

The co-operation agreement is the classic device used by the federal authority and the federated bodies to harmonize their policies in accordance with the content of the agreement, each respecting the autonomy of the other. Some agreements must be approved by law, decree, or order. Co-operation agreements are compulsory on certain issues, such as transport between adjacent areas, and roads and waterways that extend beyond a single region.

Any disputes that may arise in relation to a co-operation

agreement cannot be brought before an ordinary court but must come before special co-operation tribunals having sole juridiction over disputes of this type: they are not permanent but are set up whenever a conflict arises. They are composed of a presiding judge and two or more members appointed by the parties to the dispute. If the parties fail to reach agreement on this point, the President of the Court of Arbitration will act as chairman of the tribunal. Its reasoned decision is binding on the parties and cannot be appealed against.

Methods of Concertation

In addition to the co-operation agreements, a vast array of concertation methods have also been provided by statute to ensure optimum harmonization of the policies pursued by the various authorities. The following are just some of the main features of concertation: exchange and communication of information; consultation; the involvement of other authorities in drawing up rules; the settlement of certain matters by consent; the delivery of a simple official opinion; notification of a formal assent; and the representation of other authorities in decision-making and administrative bodies. Several Community Councils and Regional Councils also have a special committee for fostering co-operation between the different authorities.

2. SETTLEMENT OF CONFLICTS

Other conflict-solving mechanisms besides the co-operation and concertation procedures have been provided to solve conflicts between the federation, the Communities, and the Regions. A conflict may fall into one of two types: conflict of powers and conflict of interest. Conflicts of powers are those that arise whenever the federation, a Community, or a Region, in pursuing its policies, oversteps its powers and encroaches upon those of another authority. Conflicts of interest are those that arise whenever a given authority, in pursuing its policies within the limits of its powers, risks seriously damaging the interests of another authority.

The conflict may concern an act emanating either from the Legislature (such as a law, decree, or order) or from the Executive (a decree).

Conflicts of powers always take precedence over conflicts of interest. Thus, any procedure commenced on the ground of conflict of interest will always be suspended if proceedings on the same issue are already pending before the Court of Arbitration for excess of powers. A political solution is often found for such conflicts. A number of bodies, procedures, and time-limits have been set up to promote the smooth running of that political concertation process. The main body is the Concertation Committee, composed of members of the federal government and the Community and Regional governments; it seeks by way of consensus to reach agreement between the authorities involved. It consists of the Prime Minister and five other federal ministers, the President and one member apiece from the respective governments of the French-speaking and Flemish Communities; the President of the Walloon government; the President and one member of the government of the Region of Brussels-Capital, the latter belonging to a language group other than that of the President.

Conflicts of Powers

Conflicts of powers arise when the federal authority, a Community, or a Region impinges upon the powers of another authority. Certain mechanisms have been introduced to forestall such conflicts, and to resolve them should they arise.

The Legislation Division of the Council of State plays an important role in preventing conflicts of powers. It gives its opinion on preliminary draft laws, decrees, and orders, and on certain proposed laws, decrees, and orders. If the application for an opinion raises problems of jurisdiction the Council of State will deliver its opinion in a joint session. Should it consider a text to exceed the powers of the authority concerned, the issue will generally be referred to the Concertation Committee within forty days.

Conflicts of powers can also arise once a law, decree, or order has been adopted, if such law, decree, or order is at odds with the rules on the division of powers. Article 142 of the Constitution empowers the Court of Arbitration to settle such conflicts.

Conflicts of Interest

Conflicts of interest arise whenever an authority, in implementing its policy within the limits of its powers, threatens to encroach seriously on the interests of another authority. Article 143(1) of the Constitution provides that the authorities must respect federal loyalty in the exercise of their respective powers. The Concertation Committee is the central body for the prevention and settlement of conflicts of interest. This decision must be adopted by a three-quarters majority. It can also be adopted by the joint assembly of the Community Commission of the Region of Brussels-Capital, in which case a simple majority in each of the two language groups is required.

Such a decision will entail suspension of examination of the contested proposal or draft for sixty days. This period could be termed a 'cooling-off period', during which political concertation may take place in an effort to reach a compromise. If this procedure fails, the Senate must communicate its reasoned opinion to the Concertation Committee within thirty days. The latter then has a further thirty days in which to reach a final decision. Given that this decision has to be adopted by consensus and that almost all authorities are represented in the Concertation Committee, the authority engaged in considering the proposal or draft law still holds a power of veto. This means that in principle no authority can be forced to amend or abandon the contested proposal or draft against its will.

The same procedure can also be commenced by the Chamber or the Senate, if either assembly believes that a proposed decree or order may encroach upon its interests. In that eventuality, however, the Senate does not deliver a reasoned opinion to the Concertation Committee once the cooling-off period is over, since it would then be both judge and interested party. If the cooling-off period expires without a solution having been found, the issue will be immediately submitted to the Concertation Committee, which has sixty days in which to take a decision.

Relations between Communities

Here, conflicts of interest arise not between two or more authorities but within an assembly composed of two language groups, where a qualified majority of one of the groups believes that a draft law or a proposal may seriously damage relations between the linguistic communities. The procedure entails bringing the conflict before the government, composed of an equal number of members of each language group. The Council of Ministers has thirty days in which to give a reasoned opinion. The issue will then be referred back to the chamber concerned. The purpose is to promote political concertation within the Council of Ministers so as to allow the appropriate changes to be made to the contested proposal or draft law.

Notes

1. This study is not the same as the report presented at the forum organized by the Centre for European Studies at the University of Oxford, but sets out an account of the current constitutional arrangements in Belgium following the latest revision of the Constitution in 1993.
2. The city of Brussels, plus the Communes of Schaerbeek, Anderlecht, Uccle, Ixelles, Molenbeek-Saint-Jean, Forest, Woluwe-Saint-Lambert, Saint-Gilles, Etterbeek, Woluwe-Saint-Pierre, Jette, Evere, Auderghem, Watermael-Boisfort, Ganshoren, Saint-Josse-ten-Node, Berchem-Saint-Agathe, and Koekelberg.
3. Document of the Chamber of Representatives: *Report on Behalf of the Commission of Constitutional Reform*, No. 894/3, 17 Mar. 1973, 2–7.
4. Every year the Chamber of Representatives and Senate each establish their financial entitlement.
5. The Conseil d'Etat (Council of State) is the highest administrative body in Belgium. It consists of an administrative section and a legislative section. The administrative section, acting as an administrative court, delivers rulings on appeal in the last instance. The legislative section gives legal opinions on any draft law presented to the federal chambers by the federal government, and also on any draft decree or order laid by a Regional government before a Community Council or Regional Council.
6. It follows that Dutch-speaking inhabitants of Brussels may not be directly elected to the Flemish Council.
7. The electoral constituencies may not, of course, extend beyond the Regional boundaries; and seats must be allocated strictly in proportion to the number of inhabitants.
8. Following the 1995 elections, there are 65 members of the French-language group and 10 members of the Dutch-language group in the Council of the Region of Brussels-Capital.

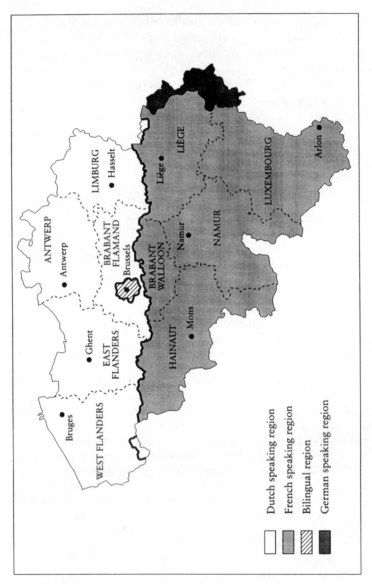

FIG. 12.1. The Communities of Belgium

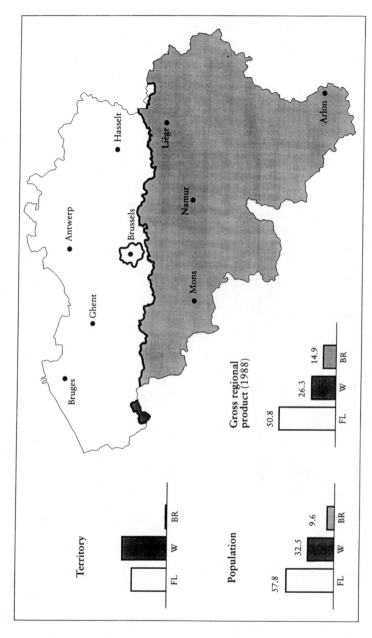

FIG. 12.2. The Regions of Belgium: their populations and gross national product

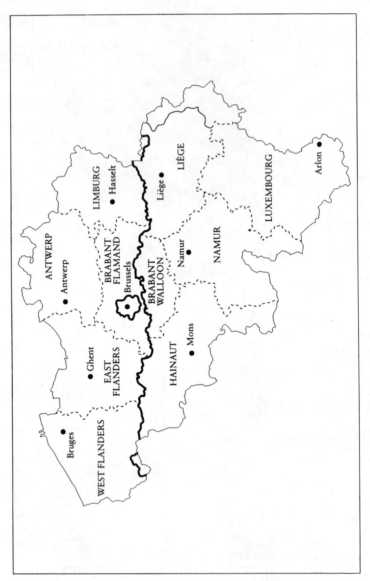

Fig. 12.3. The Provinces of Belgium

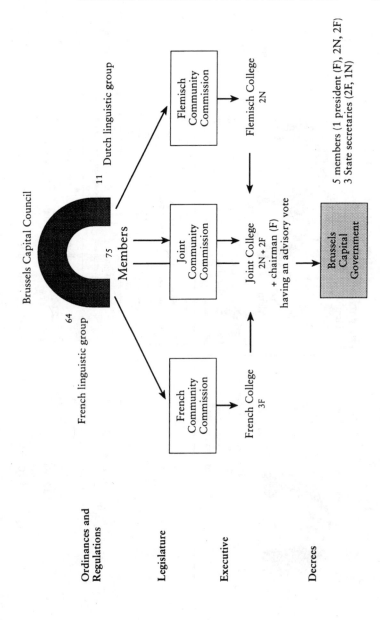

FIG. 12.4. The political structure of the Brussels-Capital Region

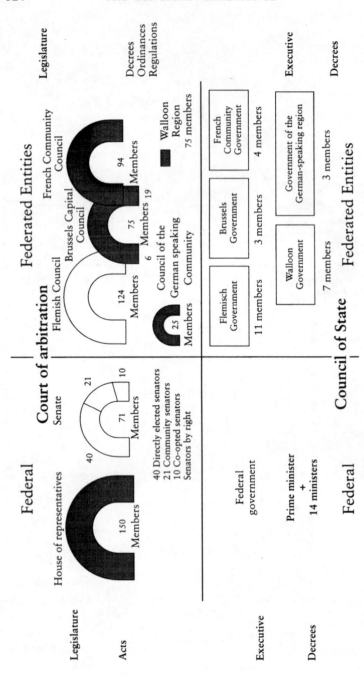

FIG. 12.5. The political structure of Belgian government

13

From the USSR to the Commonwealth of Independent States: Confederation or Civilized Divorce?

STEPHAN KUX

1. INTRODUCTION

The dissolution of the Union of Soviet Socialist Republics and the creation of the Commonwealth of Independent States (CIS) mark a crucial turning-point in the political landscape of Europe and indeed in world history. The revolutionary process of systemic change and national liberation is, however, not yet terminated, and the CIS also seems to be on the brink of collapse. The republics are shaken by domestic instabilities, powerful centrifugal forces are pulling the post-Soviet states further apart, and interrepublican ties are beset with serious political, military, and economic conflicts. The ambitious plans to create a common market, a political union, and a military alliance at the same time could not be realized. Most observers have written off the CIS as a viable institution. Despite the serious challenges facing this heterogeneous confederation of states *in statu nascendi*, some progress towards institutionalization and integration can nevertheless be observed. Moreover, despite the often confusing, chaotic nature of alliance politics in the new Commonwealth, the republican leaders, have a fairly good track-record in managing conflicts, finding compromises, and co-ordinating policy.

While the new institutional arrangements in the CIS are still weak, uncertain, and of an *ad hoc* nature, relations among the republics do not start from zero. Elements of this new political framework became visible as early as 1988, when the USSR's constituent parts started to challenge the imperial centre and to claim sovereign rights. In the course of the tug-of-war between the Union and the republics, new federalism-like elements emerged over the years. The republics started to forge direct, horizontal ties with one another. Union and republican agencies began to co-ordinate their activities. Opposing political forces at the centre and on the periphery agreed to share power, and to form coalition governments. Some sort of federalist political culture emerged in the USSR. These proto-federalist elements are characteristic of the initial stage of confederation-building. The process of transition was thus shaped by the destruction of the empire on the one hand, and the simultaneous evolution of alternative patterns of political organization on the other. The emergence of proto-federalist ties can be called the achievement of *perestroika*. The Soviet Union did not collapse, but was rather transformed into a radically different form of association. Whether the new power structure will last in the present form or is merely playing a transitional role as the post-Soviet republics consolidate their independence, and develop new economic relations, remains an open question. The survival of the CIS as a cohesive, well-structured, confederal institution as envisaged in the Minsk treaties is, indeed, rather doubtful. In any case, the new patterns of proto-federalist co-operation and organization will provide inter-republican ties with some degree of stability. Even after the demise of the Soviet Union, and the difficulties encountered by the CIS, confederalism thus remains an issue in the territories of the former USSR. The emerging ties among the Soviet successor states provide an interesting case of federation-building which will last far beyond the year 2000. In order to understand current developments, it is essential to analyse the preceding processes of systemic change and devolution in the USSR.

2. THE GRADUAL DISINTEGRATION OF THE SOVIET UNION

The dissolution of the Soviet Union and the creation of the Commonwealth of Independent States are the product of a truly revolutionary process which resulted in a fundamental reorganization of society and power structures in the former USSR.[1] This process is remarkable in three respects. First, despite the enormous potential for conflict, the demise of the USSR proceeded fairly smoothly and did not result in large-scale violence, chaos, or inter-state war, as was the case in the dissolution of the Austro-Hungarian, Manchu, Ottoman, or Roman empires. Second, while the outcome of the process can be described as revolutionary, the transformation itself was much more gradual. The relatively peace-ful nature of the revolution can be explained only by the gradual, evolutionary changes in the political system in the preceeding three to four years. The centre withered away piece by piece, the will to exert power faded, the coercive instruments of the old system slowly disintegrated, and the balance of power gradually shifted in favour of the republics. Third, the revolution did not result in a political vacuum as was the case in other processes of decolonization and national liberation. The republics emerged as relatively stable, independent entities, took over power from the centre, and formed with the CIS a new horizontal, confederal, inter-state alliance.

The heterogeneous structure of the USSR itself facilitated the emancipation of the republics. First, ethnic diversity provided the republics with a distinct identity. Ethnicity formed an important aspect of what can be described as the national liberation struggle. Political, economic, or environmental issues inevitably took on an ethnic dimension. Second, centre–periphery relations in the Soviet Union resembled those of an empire.[2] While the imperial centre exercised absolute control over the peripheral lands, the republics nevertheless retained their character as distinct societies with dis-tinct élites. The existence of a national *nomenklatura* and local political structures formed an important precondition for decen-tralization and federalization. The fact that there was, for instance, a Ukrainian parliament passing laws on the basis of a republican constitution played a decisive role in the emancipation process. A unique feature is that an organizational, not a territorial-state struc-ture formed the imperial centre. It was not Russia, but the central apparatus, which ruled over the empire based on an imperial philosophy—socialism, democratic centralism, and a planned economy—on a political class, the *nomenklatura*—and on an im-perial-administrative structure—the party and state bureaucracies. Thus the USSR resembled an overblown, twentieth-century version of the British East India Company. Third, at least in theory, the Soviet Union was constituted as a federation. Even in practice, the republican governments performed wide-ranging administrative functions. Following changes in Union leadership or policy, the degree of republican autonomy varied over time. In their tug-of-war with the centre, the republics were thus able to justify their demands for sovereignty by referring to the token rights and freedoms assigned to them in the USSR Constitution.[3]

The first three years of Gorbachev's reforms had little impact on the status of the republics and the structure of the quasi-federation. In a first phase of the Andropov-type system acceleration, the new Soviet leader attempted to widen the macroeconomic parameters, and to mobilize society within the existing systemic framework. The renewed efforts at centralizing and streamlining the administrative command system actually meant less autonomy for the republics. In a second phase of system reform, which was essentially identical with the programme of *perestroika* initiated at the January 1987 Central Committee Plenum, Gorbachev resorted to more radical measures in order to create the political preconditions for economic reforms. In July 1988 the 19th Party Conference decided to transfer power from the party to the state, and to create new executive and legislative structures. A Federation Council was established, which included the highest executive officers from the constituent states. The republics' access to decision-making at the Union level was thus improved. *Perestroika* also resulted in the transfer of more administrative and macroeconomic management functions from the centre to the periphery. However, Gorbachev's insistence on 'democratic socialism', the monopoly of the party, and the primacy of the centre set clear limits to the political freedom of the republics.

Perestroika did not, however, reinforce the system, but released pent-up centrifugal forces. The Soviet population, especially the nations on the periphery, did not respond as expected to the new opportunities Gorbachev offered. During 1988 and 1989, informal local opposition groups became more vocal and started to organize themselves into popular fronts, first in the Baltic states, later in the European parts of the USSR. They began to present demands for the official recognition of their languages, the teaching of their national culture and history, the protection of their environment, and the self-administration of the economy.[4] These popular movements tested the limits of *glasnost* and *perestroika*, exploited the newly created parliamentary institutions, redefined the political agenda on their own terms, and thus induced much more extensive change than was originally contemplated. *Perestroika* began to develop its own momentum. Limited reform guided from above turned into transformation from below; the centre started to lose the initiative. The turning-point came with the elections to the republican parliaments in March 1990: in most republics, new political forces were elected, the extra-parliamentary opposition moved into positions of local power.

In Armenia, Moldova, Russia, and Ukraine, the apparatchiks were forced to bargain or share power with the popular fronts. In the Baltic states and Georgia, non-communist forces took over power. The political monopoly of the local Communist party was broken, and the existing power structures undermined. Local leaders were infected by ideas of democracy and national self-determination, and shifted their allegiance to the national opposition movements. The existing republican structures were turned into platforms for the articulation of dissent and the struggle for national liberation and democracy. The republican governments abandoned their role as governors of the empire, and started to mediate between the centre and the local population and to pursue their own political agenda. In their declarations of sovereignty issued in summer 1990, the republics mapped out their alternative programmes. At this point, demands were still limited to claims for more sovereignty and self-determination. The declarations were mainly adopted to improve the republics' bargaining power and to help preserve the position of the national Communist leadership, yet they began to take on a momentum of their own. The assumption that real power derived only from Moscow was thus called into question, the political monopoly of the central party and state authorities was broken, alternative centres of authority emerged, and the republics started to act on their own. This process of emancipation of subordinated political entities, and the resulting vertical differentiation of interests, fundamentally transformed the balance of forces in the USSR, a redistribution of powers and the creation of new co-ordination mechanisms between centre and periphery became necessary.

Gorbachev was very slow in responding to these developments. Only in late 1989 did he put the renewal of the federation on his agenda.[5] During the course of 1990 he presented a series of measures to strengthen the Union, including the conclusion of a new Union treaty, the revision of the constitution, the redistribution of powers between Union and republics, and the reorganization of federal institutions and economic reforms. The Law on the Definition of Powers between the Union and the Republics passed in April 1990, for instance, envisaged a transfer of substantial competences to the republics, and thus formed a first step towards creating a federation based on the principle of subsidiarity. The responsibilities delegated to the republics included construction, health services, education, and other deficitary tasks, while the centre retained control over natural resources, taxation, and other sources of revenue. Republican incomes did not match exploding expenditures. The costs of federalization were higher than the benefits. Since 1990 the republics have been burdened with enormous budget deficits which threaten their economic stability. The struggle for control of economic assets subsequently became a key issue in the centre–periphery conflict, and contributed to the collapse of the Soviet economic complex. Gorbachev's approach bore a striking resemblance to Ronald Reagan's 'new federalism'. In 1983 the US President transferred costly tasks such as public health, transportation, or social security to the state governments in order to reduce the federal budget deficit.

In brief, Gorbachev's federal reforms offered too little, too late. His philosophy of new federalism was neither particularly federalist nor democratic, and failed to address the key issue, namely the systemic crisis. In its implementation, it merely aggravated the situation it was intended to alleviate. The centre's ill-fated attempts to preserve the old structures accelerated the disintegration of the Union. As subsequent developments illustrated, a co-ordinated transition towards a new democratic, post-colonial, federal or confederal system managed from above was not conceivable. Given the deterioriation of the economic situation, the repeated postponement of reforms, and the declining leadership of the centre, the republics were increasingly left on their own—whether they were seeking it or not. Once the republican leaders understood that under Gorbachev a coherent, comprehensive reform of the political and economic system was unlikely to happen, they started to take over powers from the centre, and to initiate programmes of *perestroika* on their own. They began to co-ordinate their activities and to forge direct, horizontal ties with one another. Thus, the failure of reform from above did not necessarily mean the complete end of *perestroika*. Rather, economic and political reforms started to take place on a republic-by-republic basis, and to be more successful at that. The balance of power between centre and periphery shifted decisively.[6] The result was a growing polarization and a protracted tug-of-war between the Union and the republics. The republican governments pursued a policy of gradual political, economic, and military disengagement, a strategy which was best reflected in the declaration in the summer of 1990 by both Belorussia and Ukraine to become independent, neutral, and non-nuclear states.[7] Their tactics resembled those of the feudal struggles between the vassals and their superiors in the Middle Ages, including the withholding of customs and taxes, the boycott of the military draft, and other measures of insubordination and revolt. The unregulated power struggle escalated in late 1990, after Gorbachev's shift towards authoritarian rule. Boris Yeltsin and other republican leaders declared outright war on the centre, with the stated goal of ousting the Union government and of creating more democratic, confederal power structures. The republics threatened to form a union on their own should Gorbachev refuse to go along with their demands.

The escalating centre–periphery struggle led to a political pact and a paralysis of power. Then, on 23 April 1991, the Soviet President and the leaders of nine Union republics achieved a *compromesso storico*. In a surprising move, they decided to overcome the political and economic crises and signed an agreement calling for the speedy conclusion of a new Union treaty, new parliamentary elections in 1992, and the implementation of a joint emergency economic programme. The so-called 'nine-plus-one agreement' envisaged a radical redistribution of power in favour of the republics, a fundamental reorganization of the centre, and a far-reaching reallocation of resources. It set the stage for the creation of a loose confederation or commonwealth of states. Key attributes of federation, such as common citizenship, a central tax authority, or Union property, were abandoned. After six years of 'preperestroika', economic and political reforms thus entered the decisive phase. A polarization of positions and interests, an intensification of the political struggle, and a showdown between centralists and federalists were almost inevitable. In fact, on 19 August 1991, party hawks, generals, and industrial managers launched a last-ditch struggle in order to defend their powers and privileges, to save the Union as they knew it, and to prevent chaos, economic break-down, and widespread unrest. The timing of the coup was no coincidence. On 20 August five republics—Belorussia, Kazakhstan, Kyrgyzstan, Russia, and Uzbekistan—intended to sign the Union treaty. The putsch was thus anti-federalist in essence, and marked the climax of the power struggle between centre and periphery. It formed a catalyst for change, fatally weakened the centre, discredited Gorbachev, and hastened the demise of the dying empire.

In the first days after the coup, under the leadership of the Russian parliament, the main pillars of central power were dismantled, suspended or put under new leadership. Most of the central organs continued to function in some way, although considerably weaker, and in a state of permanent reorganization. Some *ad hoc* bodies were created in order to fill the vacuum and ensure a minimum of central government during the period of transition. The republican governments seized the opportunity, declared their full independence, nationalized state and party property, took control of the industries, the infrastructure, and other assets on their territory, and created parallel power structures, including republican central banks and defence ministries. The republics also started to control revenues. They paid into the Union budget only what they considered appropriate. The centre became increasingly irrelevant; real power was essentially transferred to the republics. Gorbachev's attempts to revive the idea of a Union treaty, to preserve the central structures, and to keep the country together were condemned to fail. The centre fell terminally ill in December 1990, died after the August coup, and was finally buried in December 1991.

The demise of the Union was thus the product of a slow-motion revolution. While central power eroded and the Union disintegrated, new centres of power emerged and more solid structures formed at lower levels of government. The process of transition was characterized by the destruction of the empire on the one hand, and the simultaneous construction of alternative patterns of political organization on the other. The transition in the USSR can be compared with the formation of tectonic structures during the glacial period, when powerful forces moved new tectonic layers above, below, or between existing ones, resulting in multi-layered tectonic formations. In the USSR, elements of a new, confederal political and economic order emerged above, below, or in-between the structures of the old system. The Soviet Union did not collapse, but was rather transformed into a radically different form of association.

3. THE COMMONWEALTH OF INDEPENDENT STATES

In a referendum on 1 December 1991, the Ukrainian population overwhelmingly voted in favour of complete independence. This decision destroyed all lingering hopes of patching up the ailing Union, and precipitated the final dissolution of the USSR. Boris Yeltsin made it clear that Russia would not enter a Union treaty should Ukraine not participate. Moscow was afraid of finding itself locked into an alliance with the largely conservative, impoverished Central Asian republics. Without Ukraine, the economic burden would be on Russia alone, the country's centre of gravity would shift towards Asia and the Islamic world, and Moscow would be isolated from Eastern and Western Europe. Hence, the Russian government acted quickly to preserve its ties with Ukraine. On 8 December 1991 the leaders of the three Slavic republics of Belorus, Russia, and Ukraine met near Brest. They stated unambiguously that negotiations on the Union treaty had reached a dead end, declared that the USSR had actually ceased to exist 'as a subject of international law and a geopolitical reality', proclaimed the Commonwealth of Independent States, and thus confronted Gorbachev with a *fait accompli*. On 21 December, the newly independent states of Armenia, Azerbaijan, Kazakhstan, Kyrgyzstan, Moldova, Tajikistan, Turkmenistan, and Uzbekistan joined the Commonwealth as co-founders on equal terms. Of the twelve former Soviet republics, only Georgia remained outside the CIS. In the meantime, the Azerbaijani parliament unanimously denied ratification of the CIS treaty and thus ended the country's membership. In the words of Abulfaz Elchibey, the new president of Azerbaijan, the CIS was but a soap bubble—pretty on the surface, but empty. The parliament of Moldova has not yet discussed ratification and may never do so.

The Commonwealth agreement, and other accords, outline the purpose, activities, and institutions of the Commonwealth in very general terms.[8] The signatory states pledged 'to build democratic states ruled by law'; they recognize the full independence and the territorial integrity of one another within existing borders; and they express their intention of creating 'a common political, economic, and strategic space'. Initial goals included the co-ordination of foreign and security policy; the creation of a single market including open borders and freedom of movement for citizens of CIS states; and joint development of transport, communication, and energy systems. The Council of Heads of State and the Council of Heads of Government form the co-ordinating bodies, meeting on a regular basis to set basic policy guidelines. Ministerial committees co-ordinate policy at the operational level. The CIS is, therefore, designed as a loose confederation, i.e. a league or political union between formally independent states which retain exclusive jurisdiction, but co-ordinate foreign, defence, and macro-economic policies, and delegate limited powers to joint authorities.[9]

At first, the CIS had a difficult, slow start. The centrifugal forces that had led to the break-up of the Soviet Union prevailed. The Russian–Ukrainian conflicts over the status of the Crimea, the division of the Black Sea fleet, or the control of nuclear weapons dominated the agenda. Initial plans to create an EC-type single market, a political union, and a NATO-type military alliance in one stroke proved to be far too ambitious. In the meantime, the initial euphoria of independence has worn off. Most CIS states are beginning to face the reality of their continuing interdependence and are realizing the need to co-operate, at least for the time being. The CIS meetings are better prepared, more business-like, and more productive. In 1992, the CIS states signed over 200 agreements, half of which deal with military matters. In order to maintain goods and energy supplies, the republican administrations jointly operate CIS-wide power grids, communication networks, railways, and shipping lines. Interstate committees have been set up in the spheres of transport, ecology, space, statistics, standardization, and the fight against crime. With the creation of these co-ordinating bodies at the operational level, the Commonwealth states hope to institutionalize intergovernmentalism.

At least from an international perspective, the most important aspect of the CIS is joint control over the huge nuclear arsenal of the disintegrating world power. Under strong outside pressure, the republics agreed to subordinate strategic forces to a joint command under Russian control during a transitional period. A decision to use nuclear weapons may be made by the Russian president in 'agreement' with the heads of the other republics where strategic nuclear weapons are based—Belorus, Kazakhstan, and Ukraine—and in 'consultation' with the leaders of the other republics. However, joint command over nuclear forces is likely to fade away as soon as all long-range nuclear forces outside Russia are eliminated or withdrawn to Russia by the end of 1994. [10] The reorganization of general purpose forces is a more contentious issue. Most republics would prefer to create a CIS armed forces based on professional and territorial formations under the joint command of a general staff or joint chiefs-of-staff. The military organization of NATO serves as a model. In May 1992, seven of the ten member states—Armenia, Belorus, Kazakhstan, Kyrgyzstan, Russia, Tajikistan, and Uzbekistan—signed a collective security pact pledging mutual assistance in case of outside attack. Moldova and Ukraine, in turn, insist on the creation of fully independent republican forces and the definition of national security doctrines. CIS peacekeeping efforts contributed to the de-escalation of conflicts in Abkhasia, Moldova, and Tajikistan.

There is also an agreement to create some sort of economic organization in order to preserve the existing trade links and the unified economic space. The Soviet economy was based on such intense regional specialization that it cannot easily be taken apart. The republican economies depend to a large degree on barter trade with the other republics. Almost every branch of industry relies on suppliers and customers in another republic. Even before the demise of the Union, the republics started to restrict trade, to establish various quotas and licences, and to raise customs and taxes. The relapse into protectionism and separatism proved to be very costly for the republics. Another reason for preserving the economic space relates to the balance of payments of inter-republican trade. Under the old, centrally administered trade system, Russia sold energy and other raw materials cheap, and bought consumer goods at inflated prices. None of the republics could afford to pay world-market prices and hard currency for essential imports of fuel, energy, food, and industrial goods. Thus the post-Soviet republics are stepping up efforts to form a free-trade zone and a payments union in order to avoid customs barriers and trade wars.

The plan for an International Economic Commonwealth is roughly modelled on the original 1957 plan for the European

Economic Community.[11] It draws upon an earlier agreement on the formation of an economic union signed in October 1991. The common market which is envisaged is supposed to ensure the free flow of goods, services, and capital, and the co-ordination of monetary policy. There is more disagreement on forming a joint banking and credit system and retaining monetary union. While most republics have agreed to form a banking union based on the republican central banks, and modelled after Western reserve systems, they refuse Russia's claim to play a dominating role in the rouble zone. In economic and financial matters, Moscow is not willing to grant the other CIS states an equal say. The republics are also supposed to co-ordinate their macro-economic management including marketization and privatization. Other areas of joint activity include the co-ordination of customs and migration, environmental protection, and law enforcement. A series of special Commonwealth funds has been established to finance specific union expenditures, such as transportation, communication, defence, or space research.

At least in theory, economic union does not necessarily require political union. A relatively centralized system of economic integration and a relatively decentralized political confederation are not mutually exclusive, since they have different focuses and operate at different levels. While political union assumes the permanent delegation of some competences to a joint, supranational institution, economic integration starts with the joint performance of certain tasks which will eventually lead to political institutionalization.[12] Since economic union is much less restrictive, it is more palatable to the Soviet successor states than political union or military alliance. In the Commonwealth agreement, the republics try to separate economic integration, political union, and military alliance. It grants each republic the right to leave the political and military structures, while participating in the planned common market. The parliaments of Moldova and Ukraine have already expressed their preference for selective membership. They joined the Commonwealth charter only under the condition that it will not prejudice political union or military association. The preservation of economic ties, while pursuing political and military disengagement, is considered as a smooth process of secession.[13]

In practice, the separation of the economic and political dimensions of association will prove difficult. Economic union actually requires the formation of some joint political structures. In order to co-ordinate and integrate economic activities in a common, organic market to the extent most Commonwealth members envisage, an autonomous centre comparable with the Commission of the European Union is necessary. The process of European integration has illustrated that economic integration without political union is not possible. Or, as the example of former Yugoslavia demonstrates, a joint monetary policy is doomed to fail in a situation of rapid economic decline, and in a system in which monetary policy is centralized, and political power and fiscal control are decentralized. In December 1990 the central government lost control over macro-economic management. The republican governments started to plunder the Central Bank, to print Dinar notes on their own, and to spend money at their own discretion. The monetary system collapsed; inflation sky-rocketed. The coexistence of two principles of organization, political versus economic union, also creates serious problems of co-ordination, equalization, and integration. In many respects, integration in the CIS is proceeding in reverse, since it started as a highly integrated economic complex and centralized political system comparable to what the EU hopes to achieve by the end of this century. The final outcome is likely to be a loose association of relatively independent states comparable with the EEC of the 1950s or 1960s. The years of Soviet power have so inoculated each republic against any form of centralization that further co-ordination will be a struggle. The difficult task for the reformers is to create co-ordinating bodies which are powerful enough to be viable, while weak enough not to infringe upon the republics' newly gained freedoms. While there are strong economic incentives for the republics to unify, the forces that keep states apart are basically political, not economic. Political will could well triumph over economic common sense.

Basic disagreements over the objectives of the CIS, weak institutions, and non-implementation undermine its viability. First, the provisions of the CIS are sufficiently imprecise and ambiguous to accommodate the diverging interests and aspirations of all its member states. The republics continue to hold fundamentally different views on the *finalité* the new association should pursue. Moldova, Ukraine, and—to some extent—Turkmenistan apparently feel able to take a more independent stand. They reject the notion of Commonwealth citizenship, joint armed forces, or a common foreign and security policy. And they oppose the creation of strong co-ordinating bodies, which they see as the re-creation of the old imperial centre. Ukraine especially wants to exert full independence and places its sovereignty before the unity of the Commonwealth members. At best, Kiev hopes to maintain existing trade links with other republics, and to ensure energy deliveries from Siberia. Moldova seeks closer ties with Romania. Most Central Asian republics in turn are interested in the preservation of central institutions strong enough to guarantee their equality among equals, to administer the redistribution of funds, and to provide protection against outside threats. At the same time, they are starting to look to their natural partners, the other Muslim states to the south and east. The only republic still wedded to the idea of the CIS as a fully fledged confederation is Russia. Since it lost most of its ports and other 'windows' on Europe when the Baltic states, Belorus, and Ukraine became independent, Moscow has a strategic interest in maintaining close ties with the other republics in order to avoid isolation. A Commonwealth of the Soviet successor states would give a reassuring sense that borders are what they were, and that Russia is still a great power. The Russian government also fears what will happen to the Russian soldiers and the huge Russian minorities living outside the republic should the CIS collapse.

The CIS is thus an uneasy compromise between opposite points of views and contradictory national agendas. As with the EU or NATO, the Commonwealth has its 'footnote nations'. To most CIS agreements, one or more participants have added dissenting opinions or comments. The republics have considerable leeway to co-operate or not. Parallels with the British or Danish position within the European Union exist. Some politicians have suggested the creation of different categories of CIS membership, so that those in favour of greater integration can go ahead without waiting for the non-signers. Yet Moscow is rather reluctant to form a closer union consisting of Russia and the Central Asian states but excluding Ukraine. It prefers to pursue closer integration through bilateral arrangements.

Second, there are no clear decision-making procedures. The new power-house, the Council of Heads of States, is—as its predecessor, the Federation Council was—an informal body without clear procedural rules. The agreement on its creation is provisional, as are the statutes of the working group responsible for its organization.

Decisions are taken by consensus, which gives individual republics a veto. The republics also have the right to declare their lack of interest in a given question. The Council can be compared with a *ting*, the assembly of the chieftains of the ancient Germanic tribes, with equally assertive, uncompromising republican leaders such as Ukraine's Leonid Kravchuk, Armenia's Levon Ter Petrosian, or Russia's Boris Yeltsin sitting around the bargaining table. It remains unclear how the republican leaders intend to co-ordinate their activities, to achieve and sustain compromises, and to enforce agreements in the absence of a mediating authority. There is no clearing-house or arbitration procedure in case of conflict, and there is no statute providing guidance.

Moreover, the Council has yet to demonstrate its viability as a collective decision-making body. Government by consensus does not make for strong government. The republican leaders continue to hold greatly diverging views on key questions such as marketization, privatization, military reform, or international relations. For instance, as in previous blueprints for economic reform, the Commonwealth agreement is based on the assumption that marketization and privatization can be co-ordinated, and can proceed at the same pace in all republics. The economic structures and political preferences of the republics differ so widely as to make co-ordination of macro-economic reforms between the conservative Central Asian republics and the progressive European republics an almost impossible task. Especially since the last pillar of power of some republican leaders is control over the economy, they are unlikely to agree voluntarily to destatification and privatization.

Third, most documents signed so far are merely declarations of intent. Few of the agreements have been observed, since there are no mechanisms for sanctions in case of non-compliance. Fourth, the Commonwealth is based on an executive agreement and lacks democratic legitimation. The new bodies co-ordinating CIS affairs do not consist of elected deputies, but of representatives appointed by the republican government. They are dominated by former Union bureaucrats and Russian officials. Thus power-sharing is limited to the executive level. The role of republican parliaments has been reduced to the rubber-stamping of inter-state agreements. In April 1992 a CIS Interparliamentary Assembly was created to broaden the political basis of the Commonwealth, to make the new coalition more representative, and to provide it with more legitimacy. Yet the capacity of the new Commonwealth bodies for interest articulation, interest aggregation, and conflict resolution still remains limited.

4. CENTRIFUGAL FORCES

Domestic Uncertainties

Attempts to establish a stable and peaceful new order on the territory of the former Soviet Union are indeed confronted with enormous problems. One set of difficulties refers to developments within the republics. Most of them still lack the economic and political bases for sovereignty and independence. First, after the creation of the CIS, the economic situation has further declined, undermining the economic viability and social stability of the republics. Second, while some progress has been made, political change is proceeding very slowly. National liberation has been achieved, yet democratization, federalization, and institution-building have only just started in the republics. Non-communist governments are in power in only three of the ten Commonwealth states—Armenia, Kyrgyzstan, and Moldova. Three republics—Belorus, Russia, and Ukraine—are headed by coalition governments. In most parts of Central Asia, the post-communist leaders managed to defeat the opposition and to stay in power. Institutions are simply changing their colours like chameleons, the Communist Party organization continues under a new name, and the old apparatchiks turn into champions of nationalism and democracy. As in Albania or Romania, a twilight situation of transsocialism persists; strong pockets of the old system survive. The August coup probably did not last long enough to uproot the old structures thoroughly. It will take years to achieve political conversion and to remove the deep structures of the system. Most republics have not yet adopted new, legitimate, and democratic constitutions. Political institutions remain largely unchanged and lack legitimacy. The republican parliaments, for instance, were elected in 1990 in semi-free elections, before political parties had been formed. The next parliamentary elections are only scheduled for 1995. Important political forces are not represented, the rural farmers, and urban workers especially remain sleeping giants. The weak institutions seem increasingly unable to respond to the growing discontent and escalating radicalism among the population. An increasingly vocal extra-parliamentary opposition is left out on the streets. As long as there are no new, fully free multi-party parliamentary elections, polarization and unregulated power struggles within the republics will continue.

Third, as a by-product of the difficult process of emancipation and national liberation, nationalist feelings are on the rise. During the tug-of-war between centre and republics, nationalism and national identity served as an instrument of political mobilization, and provided an alternative ideology to communism. *Ethnos* was as much a driving-force of change as *demos*. A particular concern is the tendency towards strong executive or nationalist-authoritarian government. In order to consolidate government and to promote tough economic reforms, the republican leaders have increased their ordinary and extraordinary powers at the cost of the parliaments. Especially in Central Asia, the South Korean, Taiwanese, or Turkish models of authoritarian transition to a market economy are popular. Republican leaders can also justify strong government with the requirements of bargaining and effective interest representation at the negotiating table of the CIS. Nationalism thus serves to preserve power.

Fourth, most republics are also beset by serious national problems: the quest for self-determination has trickled down to lower levels of government. Most republics have turned into ethnocratic states in that the titular nationality enjoys a privileged position. The growing self-assertiveness of the new élites, the ill-considered reorganization of government structures, or discriminatory language or citizenship laws have led to polarization within the republics, and contributed to the escalation of ethnic conflicts. In Moldova, for instance, the declaration of independence by the Romanian majority has provoked violent conflicts with Russian and Gagauz minorities seeking to protect their identity and existence. With the support of the motherland and the 14th Army stationed in the area, the Russians on the left bank of the Dniester have refused to obey the Moldovan government and proclaimed their autonomy. The conflicts resemble those between Croatia and its Serbian minorities in the Kraijna. The heterogeneous Russian Federation especially is faced with disintegration into ethnic homelands.

Some constituent republics are seeking complete independence from Moscow. One approach is federalization, i.e. the granting of more self-determination to national-territorial entities at lower administrative levels and the creation of federal institutions within the republics.[14] The Russian government, for instance, has been fairly successful in negotiating a new federal treaty delimiting powers between the Federation and its constituent parts. Another approach is democratization and the strengthening of human and minority rights. The draft constitutions of Russia, Ukraine, and other republics stipulate far-reaching human and minority rights which are modelled on the United Nations Human Rights Charter and recent accords on the human dimension of the Conference of Security and Cooperation in Europe (CSCE). Moreover, republican governments have demonstrated their willingness to respond to the demands of the nationalities and to grant more autonomy to ethnic territories. Thus, most minorities seem to accept that their aspirations can be met within renewed, more democratic, sovereign republics. Yet the growing chauvinism and the brutal suppression of Abkhazian and South Ossetian minorities in Georgia demonstrate that even democratically elected governments are no guarantee of non-discrimination against minorities. Political reforms and economic improvements may reduce some manifestations of nationalism, but exacerbate others. The post-Soviet republics, linked together in a new and more open political environment within a less rigid system of inter-state relations will probably face an increase, rather than a decrease, of nationalism, particularism, and localism, less manageable and prone to more ethnic conflict and competition.

The Commonwealth members are thus going through a difficult, uncertain period of transition. Even after the disintegration of the Soviet empire, their territorial integrity, independent statehood, and economic stability are still in jeopardy. Narrow national interests are taking priority over common objectives within the CIS. The republics are becoming more and more introverted. Under these circumstances, co-operation and compromise among the republics are becoming extremely difficult. As the developments in Tajikistan illustrate, instability in one of the member states also has adverse repercussions on the stability and cohesion of the entire CIS. Republican leaders might be tempted to export internal difficulties to the inter-state level.

Inter-Republican Tensions

The potential for interrepublican conflict also seems to be considerable. Divisions have already opened up among the ten Commonwealth members over economic, political, and military questions. In the fight against the centre, the republics were natural allies, they sided with one another out of necessity, not sympathy or congruence of interests. After the demise of the centre, the republics no longer face a common opponent to rally against, and long-buried conflicts are re-emerging. First, while the CIS is based on the principle of equality, power is not distributed equally among the republics. The non-Russian republics are afraid that Russia will simply supplant Soviet power and pursue a hegemonic policy. Zyanon Paznyak, leader of the Belorussian Popular Front, speaks of a 'Russian metropolis with non-Russian colonies'; Leonid Kravchuk, President of Ukraine, refers to an emerging Russian 'tsarist empire' and an 'imperial disease'. On the international stage, Russia has indeed emerged as the successor state to the Soviet Union. It acts as the guarantor of foreign credits and negotiates new arms control agreements. And it occupies the Soviet seat in the UN Security Council. Within the CIS, the Russian President Boris Yeltsin has emerged as the dominant figure. There are accusations that Moscow takes more than its fair share of former Soviet assets. Russia, for instance, has nationalized virtually all Union banks including hard currency and gold reserves. Boris Yeltsin is, however, unlikely to reintroduce semi-imperial methods of government. He has demonstrated his commitment to democratic principles, supported the sovereignty and independence of the other republics, and forged equitable horizontal relations with them. The Russian leader will rather play a constructive role as *primus inter pares* in the Commonwealth within a democratic framework comparable to the position of the USA within NATO or unified Germany within the European Union. Given the instability of the governing coalition, the strength of more conservative and nationalist forces in the Russian parliament, and the rapid deterioration of the political and economic situation, the emergence of a more hegemonic Russia cannot, however, be fully excluded.

Second, the dismantling of the USSR will inevitably bring up territorial claims and unresolved border problems. Under Soviet rule, internal borders had only administrative significance and were largely irrelevant. Repeatedly, the territories of the republics were altered at the discretion of the central government. With the dissolution of the Soviet Union as a state, these administrative delineations were turned into international borders of military, political, and economic importance. They have become defence lines of nation-states and sources of tariff income. Consequently, border conflicts are on the rise. The creation of a customs union, or a collective security organization, among the Commonwealth states would also help to reduce the significance of borders, accommodate conflicting claims, and prevent economic and political nationalism.

Third, the distribution of Union assets, debts, and liabilities continues to constitute a potential source of tension. After the republican leaders could not agree to form a CIS army under joint control or to share defence expenditure, the division of the army and its arsenal has become the main bone of contention. In spite of all the agreements Commonwealth leaders have signed, it is not clear whether any operational joint commands actually exist. Most republics, including Russia, have now decided to form their own army and general staff. The redistribution of the multinational forces causes many problems. Russian officers serving in units on Ukrainian territory, for instance, refuse to swear an oath to Ukraine. For strategic reasons, Russia wants to retain certain early-warning facilities and to preserve a naval presence in the surrounding seas. Ukraine views a viable republican army as the best guarantee against Russian hegemony. Thus Kiev claims, for instance, the entire Black Sea fleet except for strategic units. Russia and other republics insist that the fleet must remain an integrated entity protecting the interests of all CIS members in the Mediterranean Sea region. Armenia and Azerbaijan, in turn, are involved in a fully fledged inter-state war over Nagorno Karabakh and have mobilized their military resources. There is thus a danger of inter-republican arms races which might violate existing arms control agreements and undermine regional stability in eastern Central Europe and the Black Sea region. Other potentially conflictual issues include the redistribution of Union assets such as gold reserves, property abroad, civilian aircrafts, or the merchant fleet. The post-Soviet problems are thus complex and potentially conflictual. For a long time, relations between the successor states will be bedevilled by territorial disputes, minority issues, and economic competition.

5. PROTO-FEDERALISM

What began in December 1991 as a device by the presidents of Russia and Ukraine to eliminate the USSR and to remove Mikhail Gorbachev has thus already turned into a mechanism for the civilized divorce of the republics. Galina Starovoitova, the Russian parliamentarian describes it as 'a gentlemen's agreement between prisoners who have escaped from jail but are still linked by one chain'. And Irina Demchenko, an *Izvestiya* commentator, referred to the CIS as 'a forced alliance, generated more by the impossibility of parting than a desire to continue to live together'.[15] Most observers have actually written off the CIS as an institution. There are, however, good reasons for a more cautious assessment. The danger of inter-republican conflicts, for instance, should not be exaggerated. The CIS states are confronted with the difficulties of unregulated inter-state relations. In many respects, the disagreements between the republics are not unlike those between Western countries. Under current circumstances, conflict situations are possible. There is no reason to dramatize them as long as the political will and the appropriate mechanisms exist to solve them by peaceful, equitable means. The track-record of the republican leaders in managing conflicts, finding compromises, and co-ordinating policy has been fairly good so far. They display an impressive problem-solving capacity, try hard to play down inter-republican confrontations, and seek negotiated solutions. Most of the new élites have demonstrated political far-sightedness, realism, and responsibility.

The reason for the relatively peaceful nature of inter-republican ties is that the CIS members do not start from zero. Co-operation among the republics has a history and has grown organically, based on free will and genuine interests. After 1989, during the difficult years of transition, the republics started to forge new, federalistic ties with one another: they concluded direct, mutual horizontal ties. Union and republican agencies co-ordinated their activities. Opposing political forces at the centre and on the periphery agreed to share power and to form coalition governments, and signs of a federalist political culture facilitating the negotiation of compromises and the peaceful resolution of conflicts appeared.

The first aspect of proto-federalism is the institutionalization and intensification of inter-republican relations. Under Soviet rule, co-operation among the republics took place only within the framework of the Union and under central control. With the acquisition of more autonomy, however, the republics began to exploit their treaty-making powers and to negotiate directly with one another. In the course of 1990 and 1991, the republican governments concluded numerous bilateral agreements ranging from cultural exchange programmes to comprehensive economic and political state treaties. The contracting parties recognized one another as fully sovereign states. The accords were signed on the basis of international law and not, as was previously the case, of Soviet constitutional law. Thus they formed the prelude to genuine, bilateral state-to-state relations. The Treaty on the Fundamentals of Relations Between Russia and Ukraine concluded in December 1990 set new standards for inter-republican ties. It covered most aspects of interstate relations, including the recognition of independence, the guarantee of existing borders, and the protection of minorities.[16] The accord laid the foundation for a Russian–Ukrainian special relationship and led to the conclusion of the Friendship Treaty in September 1991.

A remarkable achievement of these horizontal agreements is the inclusion of provisions for the protection of minorities and the granting of equal rights to citizens living on one another's territory. In the Estonian–Russian accord of 12 January 1991, for instance, the Russian minority living in Estonia has achieved more rights than in any of the acts passed by the Union government or most inter-state treaties covering minorities. Some of the horizontal agreements contained mutual security guarantees, and took the form of Treaties of Friendship, Cooperation, and Mutual Assistance. A new form of inter-republican solidarity emerged and new mechanisms of mediation and crisis management were tested in the USSR. During the attempted military crack-down in the Baltic in January 1991, for instance, the presidents of Kazakhstan, Russia, and Ukraine intervened on behalf of the democratically elected governments in Estonia, Latvia, and Lithuania, and contributed to the de-escalation of the conflict. As another example, Boris Yeltsin repeatedly consulted with President Sviad Gamsakhurdia of Georgia in order to resolve the dispute in South Ossetia, and several republican leaders attempted to mediate in the Armenian–Azerbaijani conflict over Nagorno-Kharabakh. Thus the horizontal ties were remarkably innovative and progressive in their content.

The republican governments aimed at promoting peaceful, demo-cratic change rather than continued violence among Soviet nations. They set new standards for inter-republican relations.

Most inter-republican agreements focused on direct trade and economic co-operation. The devolution of decision-making and the collapse of the centrally administred supply system also reinforced tendencies towards genuine horizontal integration of the republican economies. A series of embryonic regional markets built on existing networks of local purchasing, the shadow economy, and other direct ties among enterprises and regions emerged. Leningrad started to negotiate directly with Baltic producers on meat deliver-ies in exchange for appliances, whilst managers from the Tyumen oilfields deal directly with enterprises in Ukraine to guarantee en-ergy supplies and to make sure that spare parts arrive on time. The promotion of direct, horizontal ties thus contributed to a process of integration from below. As a result, a patchwork of multi-levelled, cross-cutting, and interlocking horizontal relations emerged which reinforced the perception of mutual interests and interdependence, strengthened the spirit of commonwealth (*sodruzhestvo*), changed the traditional approach to political and economic management, and provided an alternative to the collapsing structures of internal empire. The promotion of direct inter-republican ties also contrib-uted to the replacement of the old administrative command methods with the practices and procedures of international rela-tions. Yet the emerging new relationships were still too weak to provide a viable alternative to the existing unitary state structure. More especially, the intensification of direct economic relations did not materialize. In the absence of an internal market, with the depreciation of the rouble and with the central government's stub-born refusal to transfer pricing authority to the republics or to free prices, the negotiation of fair prices for direct republic-to-republic trade was not possible. In 1991 the volume of inter-republican trade continued to decline. Attempts at economic co-operation, co-ordination, and integration were thus limited to the *ad hoc* manage-ment of the economic crisis. The patchwork of horizontal ties remained inherently unstable, incomplete, and inadequate. The republics continued to depend on the Union authorities and on the fate of the 'national economic complex'.

After the demise of the Union, the heterogeneous patchwork of horizontal ties provided a solid framework for sustaining inter-republican relations. The republics stepped up their efforts to improve bilateral co-operation. By the end of 1991, of the 105 possible pairs of republics (including the Baltic states), one or several agreements had been concluded between 102 of them, mostly on economic co-operation. The republics have an interest in continuing the old trade relationships with one another.[17] In January 1992 Kazakhstan and Russia, for instance, concluded a comprehensive agreement On Removing Restrictions in Economic Activities in which the parties agree to abandon quotas and licensing in commodity exchange, and import and export taxes on goods in transit through their territories.[18] Most republics have also created bilateral co-ordinating bodies and exchanged quasi-diplomatic missions enjoying status similar to foreign embassies. The growing frequency of bilateral meetings of republican leaders also indicates that efforts at policy co-ordination are increasing.

A second aspect of proto-federalism is the emergence of power-sharing arrangements between the centre and the republics, and among the republics respectively. Coalitions were first formed at the local and republican level, where elections forced the communists to share or to transfer power. Formal and informal round-table arrangements and coalition governments became new features of local politics. The most prominent case is Russia, where Boris Yeltsin depended on the support of reformist communists and nationalists to win the chairmanship of the Supreme Soviet in the summer of 1990. The Russian leader had to include these groups in his government, and to make political concessions in order to build and sustain a workable coalition. Even today, after his overwhelming victory in the presidential elections, Yeltsin is faced with constantly shifting and often hostile majorities in parliament. The unstable political situation in Russia has similarities to the politics of Israel or Italy. The twists and turns of the Russian government thus can only be understood as an outcome of coalition politics.

Attempts at forming a coalition at the Union level have been less successful. While Gorbachev demonstrated his extraordinary skill in forming coalitions within the *nomenklatura*, he was rather reluctant to share power with the republican leaders or the new political forces in the Union parliament. At the same time, the republics started to form horizontal alliances and coalitions directed against the centre. Republican leaders and opposition figures called for the formation of government structures parallel to those of the Union. In their eyes, the evolving horizontal ties could lay the foundations for a genuine confederal arrangement, a commonwealth of nations, or an economic community based on the free choice of the constituent parts and built from below. Thus it was hoped to provide an alternative to the existing hierarchical system, which would lead to the conclusion of a new Union treaty dictated from above. In December 1990, dissatisfied with the slow progress of reforms, the 'Big Four', i.e. Belorus, Kazakhstan, Russia, and Ukraine, started negotiations on a quadrilateral agreement. Such an *entente cordiale* posed a serious threat to the power of the Union, but the negotiations proved to be more complicated than originally assumed. In February 1991 the four republics and Uzbekistan succeeded in establishing a multilateral standing group co-ordinating and supervising direct barter trade among the republics. In April 1991 Armenia, Estonia, Georgia, Latvia, Lithuania, and Moldova also decided to co-ordinate their activities and to intensify multilateral co-operation. And in July 1991 the five Central Asian republics formed an inter-republican consultative council reminiscent of the historical ties of former Turkestan. This networking among the republics provided an important leverage against the centre. It laid the foundation for the subsequent creation of the Commonwealth, which is in essence a horizontal coalition among the independent republics. Government through coalition provided an *ad hoc* alternative to federal institution-building. It can thus be considered as some form of ersatz federalism. Yet none of these coalition agreements lasted very long. Therefore, the question is how to render these power-sharing arrangements more stable and durable.

A third, rather neglected aspect of proto-federalism is the co-ordination of activities of Union and republican agencies. With the gradually shifting balance of forces between centre and periphery, the relationship between Union and republican bureaucracies changed significantly. In some cases, agencies were decentralized and transferred to republican jurisdiction. In others, the republics unilaterally took control of Union agencies on their territory or formed parallel administrative structures. As a result, the central authorities were forced to recognize the growing authority of local and republican governments in order to sustain their functions at the grassroots level. A series of formal and informal agreements on inter-agency co-ordination were concluded. With the decentralization of the police, the federal law enforcement agencies, for instance, were forced to deal with their semi-independent branches in the republics. Republican bureaucracies also started to co-ordinate activities between one another in fields in which they assumed responsibilities. New forms of intergovernmentalism emerged. After the demise of the Union agencies, increased efforts at inter-republican co-ordination became necessary in order to secure Union-wide operations such as railways, aviation, power grids, or communication networks. A number of standing committees, working groups, and councils have been created. They include a council for railway transportation, a council of procurators-general, a sports council, a council for the protection of the environment, and a bank for the repayment of foreign debts. Co-operation in these technical fields reinforces existing interlocking ties and could lead to spill-overs into more substantial areas.

A fourth aspect of proto-federalism refers to changes in Soviet political culture. Traditionally, political life in the USSR did not necessarily reflect a conception of the federal idea, a strong persuasion or ideology endorsing federal solutions. Exceptional communication barriers caused by social, ethnic, political, or ideological polarization existed. Notions of tolerance, mutual respect, power-sharing, compromise, and consociationalism were not the characteristic traits of the Soviet polity. The Soviet Union first had to learn to bargain with itself. With the democratization and decentralization of Soviet society, elements of a federalist political culture became visible. In the Federation Council, at round tables, and in a variety of coalition arrangements, the republican leaders gained some experience in bargaining, co-ordination, compromise, and conflict resolution. Arend Lijphart refers to two essential conditions for consociationalism to work. In the first place, all the groups concerned must be willing to work towards accommodation and be ready to bargain, i.e. to make creative use of both substantive and procedural solutions avoiding zero-sum game situations. Second, the leaders of the parties involved must be able to secure the support of their followers, otherwise the consociational bargains will fail.[19] To some extent, both conditions have been fulfilled in the case of the reconstructed, post-Soviet republics.

While the institutionalization of inter-republican ties will probably take an extended period of time, some proto-federalist elements have emerged in the former Soviet Union which may create the conditions for the emergence of a new confederal polity.

The emergence of these proto-federalist ties can be considered the achievement of *perestroika*. The demise of the centre and the emergence of alternative, proto-federalist forms of inter-republican association proceeded simultaneously, and were linked dialectically. In many respects, the Commonwealth draws upon previous blueprints for reorganizing inter-republican relations, and is built on the pillars of proto-federalism. The republican leaders could base their co-operation on concepts which were defined and tested months or years ago. The idea of a Commonwealth of Independent States, for instance, was first presented by Andrei Sakharov in June 1989 and was promoted thereafter by opposition groups such as Democratic Russia. The idea of an Economic Union was debated by economists such as Mikhail Bronshteyn, Stanislav Shatalin or Grigorii Yavlinskiy as early as 1990,[20] whilst the concepts of confederation have been widely discussed by Kazakh President Nazarbayev, Kyrgyz President Akayev, or Russian President Yeltsin since late 1990. In addition, the blueprints for the current decentralized, confederal reorganization of the armed forces were worked out by opposition defence experts such as Major Vladimir Lopatin in late 1989. Thus the slow-motion transition was remarkably well prepared and conceptualized. The republican leaders had a trial-and-error-phase and sufficient lead-time to prepare for the new situation. None of these elements can be considered as attributes of federalism *per se*, since they do not yet reflect some specific conception of the federal idea, some persuasion or ideology which endorses federal solutions, some particular application of the federal principle, or some particular federal framework. Proto-federalism merely forms a precondition for the emergence of federal or confederal ties.

6. CONFEDERATION AND STABILITY

In the former USSR, a very loose, dynamic confederationalism is emerging. The CIS is a loose association of states built on a series of bi- or multilateral agreements and a multitude of *ad hoc* committees and joint institutions with changing membership. In a renewed form of functionalism, the republics are co-operating in a very pragmatic way on a bi- or multilateral basis in those fields where there is common interest and comparative advantage. The result is not a fixed state structure, with each republic having a clear status in the concentric circles of union, and assuming well-defined rights and duties. Rather, the CIS resembles a system of overlapping circles with changing networks of co-operation at various levels, and in different issue areas. Within the framework of the CIS, sub-alliances are emerging. Clusters of republics unite along historical lines. Belorus, Moldova, and Ukraine have intensified co-operation in a trade-zone stretching from the Baltic to the Black Sea, while the Central Asian republics are considering the creation of a Turkic commonwealth. After the break-up of the monetary union, the CIS is also likely to be divided into several currency zones. Russia will dominate the rouble zone, the Central Asian republics may form a separate monetary union, and Ukraine may create its own currency system.[21] Thus various forms of bi- and multilateral organization and integration will coexist for some time.

In such a variable geometry of co-operation and organization, the importance of the newly emerging nation-states could be modified, growing nationalism and regionalism could be accommodated, and centrifugal and centripetal forces could be balanced. The problem of such an *à la carte* association is, however, that co-ordination will hardly be possible. There will be conflicting or overlapping commitments, and equality of rights and duties will be difficult to achieve. There is also little co-ordination, harmonization, or standardization of bilateral agreements at a multilateral level. Kazakhstan or Kyrgyzstan, for instance, do not receive the same terms as Russia from Ukraine. While most-favoured-nation provisions have been agreed upon in some cases, equal treatment and non-discrimination are becoming sensitive political issues. The likely result is a multi-tiered structure of the Commonwealth. In such an asymmetrical arrangement combining various forms of association conflicts are pre-programmed, and centrifugal forces are reinforced. Without agreement on a statute establishing a legal, normative basis, and on proper mechanisms of co-ordination and self-regulation, the post-Soviet states will hardly stay together. Comparative federalism does indeed suggest that confederations and other loose associations are inherently unstable. They either disintegrate or reintegrate. Switzerland or the United States existed as confederations for some years and then unified into a federation. The Malaysian confederation in contrast disintegrated into sovereign nation-states. With the exception of the confederation between Tanzania and Zanzibar, no other confederative organization exists today. Confederations are, therefore, either completely out-dated, or very modern structures. Recently, the idea of confederation has gained new prominence. It is viewed as a promising new form of organization of inter-state ties. Some statesmen have proposed, for instance, to base the new European architecture on the principle of confederation of nation-states. The European Union agreed upon at the Maastricht summit of the EC is also described as a confederative structure.

Another caveat refers to the international status of the CIS. The republics have been recognized as independent states and are busy establishing ties with foreign countries and international organizations. The newly independent states are redirecting their international orientation and are joining regional groups outside the CIS. Ukraine, for instance, is seeking to join the EU or at least the eastern Central European states as a political partner and economic ally. Kiev has signed an agreement with the Czech Republic, Slovakia, Poland, and Hungary aimed at easing trade among the border regions, setting up a free-trade zone, establishing an inter-regional bank, and improving co-operation between state and private enterprises. The five countries have also set up a permanent body, the Subcarpatian Council on Interregional Cooperation. Hence Ukraine sees no comparative advantage in a highly integrated Commonwealth. Kyrgyzstan, Tajikistan, Turkmenistan, and Uzbekistan, in turn, joined the Economic Co-operation Organization, which originally consisted of Iran, Pakistan, and Turkey. The group plans to work towards the creation of a common market of Muslim states based on free-market economies and modelled on the European Community. Thus international integration is pulling the CIS further apart.

The balance-sheet of costs and benefits of association in the Commonwealth is, therefore, mixed. It unites ten very dissimilar states with different agendas, all subject to varying kinds of internal pressures and differing centrifugal forces. Whether the CIS as a cohesive, well-structured confederal institution (as envisaged in the Minsk treaties) can be realized or merely serves as a framework for civilized divorce as the post-Soviet republics consolidate their independence, and develop new economic and political ties, remains open. At best, it is facilitating the transition, and is minimizing the danger of chaos and violence inevitably linked with the dissolution of an empire. The exchange of permanent missions, the formation of joint committees, and the definition of standard operational procedures do not necessarily provide for the integration of ties as long as the purpose and terms of the Commonwealth remain unclear. Despite the current difficulties and uncertainties, the development of proto-federalist ties over the years and the rather impressive track-record of the new leaders suggest that there will be evolutionary stability, a process of institution-building from below will take place, once the republics have sorted out their interests and common purposes. As long as the railways between Minsk and Kiev keep operating, there is power in the grid, the communication lines function, and the republics manage to share a common currency, there will be a margin of intergovernmental co-ordination. Even if the CIS does not survive as an institution, the patterns of proto-federalist co-operation and organization which have emerged over the last few years provide a framework for inter-republican relations.

The loose, contradictory forms of association emerging on the territory of the former Soviet Union in many respects reflect the dialectics of the transitional period. The CIS members are faced almost simultaneously with several processes of transformation including the dismantling of the old centralized structures, the decolonization of the republics, the transfer and redistribution of power, the building of new institutions and economic emergency measures, reform, and reintegration. The dynamics and inter dependences of these processes are complex, and sometimes conflicting. In the words of Ukrainian President Leonid Kravchuk, the post-Soviet states are moving through two parallel processes: the division of everything that had been jointly accumulated, and the consolidation of strong ties within the CIS on new, civilized foundations.[22] As in the cases of Switzerland and the United States, confederation-building was preceded by decolonization, democratization, and nation-building.[23] The Republican leaders are faced with the difficult task of how to dismantle the old system without sacrificing the stability and integrity of the Commonwealth and the republics. The question is whether the federalization and institutionalization of the CIS can be managed and stabilized at a certain level or whether the simultaneous processes of democratization and decentralization are simply reinforcing the centrifugal tendencies. Given the acceleration of change, the rapid disintegration of the old structures, and the deterioriating economic situation, institution-building is taking place under enormous time-pressure. Lenin spoke of 'war communism' to describe the emergent Soviet system. Today, the term 'war democracy' would be appropriate to describe the current situation in the post-Soviet republics. In the August revolution and the subsequent months, freedom was won: now it has to be ordered and maintained. How long this confusing, chaotic stage of transition will take remains unknown. The Western desire for stability and order will be unfulfilled for a lengthy period of time.

The quintessential question relates not so much to the purpose of the new arrangements or to the nature of the future alliance structures, but to how genuine ties emerge, co-operation proceeds, and integration occurs. It is not the structures but the processes which matter. Moreover, much depends on the expectations of the observer. Some recent commentaries on the political situation in the CIS or on the individual republics are reminiscent of the cognitive bias and bad faith images of the Cold War. The basic political assumptions have changed: one-dimensional scenarios and worst-case thinking are not in favour any more. Progress in the post-Soviet republics cannot be measured against the scale of presumably ideal-type democracies and free-market economies such as Germany or the UK. More modest comparisons with imperfect cases such as India, Portugal, or Turkey are more appropriate. Nor can the CIS be compared with the Swiss confederation or the European Union. Like other regional associations, the EU was formed by fully independent, politically stable and relatively prosperous states. It took them more than 30 years to achieve the degree of integration the EU enjoys today. The CIS currently lacks these conditions. The old system is in a progressive stage of collapse, the economy is in a protracted structural crisis and the republics have just entered the process of nation-building. As the long cycle of the Soviet transformation demonstrates, system change in a complex, heterogeneous, multi-ethnic empire hardly proceeds in simple, linear patterns.

Notes

1. E. Zimmermann, *Political Violence, Crises and Revolutions: Theories and Research* (Cambridge, 1983) provides a detailed discussion of revolutions.

2. A. J. Motyl, 'Empire or Stability? The Case for Soviet Dissolution', *World Policy Journal*, 8 (summer 1991), 499–524.

3. S. Kux, *Soviet Federalism—A Comparative Perspective* (Institute for East–West Security Studies Occasional Paper, no. 18; Boulder, Colo., 1990).

4. G. Hosking, 'The Roots of Dissolution', *The New York Review of Books*, 16 (Jan. 1992), 34–8.

5. See the 'Draft Nationalities Policy of the Party Under Present Conditions, adopted by the CPSU Central Committee Plenum', *Pravda*, 24 Sept. 1989, 1–2.

6. The actual strength of the republics is best reflected in the redistribution of expenditures between the Union and the republican budgets. In 1981 the percentage of republican expenditures amounted to only 38%. In 1991 the Union budget envisages expenditures of approximately 540 bn. roubles, while republican expenditures amount to 322 bn. roubles, or roughly 60% of Union expenditures (*TASS*, 8 Jan. 1991; *TASS*, 25 Oct. 1991). In Switzerland, in contrast, the cantons' expenditures amounted to approximately 115% of the federal budget in 1988 (*Finance publiques en Suisse 1988* (Berne, 1990), 2–3).

7. Article IX of the Declaration of Sovereignty, *Pravda Ukrainy*, 17 July 1990, 1; Art. X of the Belorussian Declaration on Sovereignty, repr. in *Argumenti i fakti*, 31 (1990), 2.

8. For the text of the proclamation by the heads of states, the statement of the principles of the commonwealth agreement and the declaration on the co-ordination of economic policy, see *TASS*, 9 Dec. 1991.

9. Cf. the discussion of various models of federal associations in the fields of politics, economy, and the churches in I. Duchacek, *Comparative Federalism: The Territorial Dimension of Politics* (Lanham, Md., 1987), 18 ff.

10. 'Agreement on Strategic Forces', *TASS*, 31 Dec. 1991.

11. *Izvestiya*, 13 Jan. 1992.

12. P. Robson, *The Economics of International Integration* (London, 1987).

13. The argument can be compared with the proposal for 'independence within Europe' put forward by Scottish and Slovak separatists. The assumption is that secession could be achieved more easily if combined with membership of the European Union. Economic union would provide for open borders and close co-operation, thus making independence politically and economically more palatable to the former mother country.

14. It has to be noted, however, that Western models of federalism are based on the notion of sovereign political entities, i.e. states, provinces, or cantons and not on ethnic groups. Federalism is a model of organizing a state structure which generally can accommodate a broad

range of social, political, cultural, and ethnic aspirations and not a specific form of managing inter-ethnic relations.

15. *International Herald Tribune*, 21 Feb. 1992. 2; *Izvestiya*, 2 Jan. 1992, 4.
16. Treaty between Ukrainian SSR and the Russian SFSR, *Radianskaya Ukraina*, 21 Dec. 1990, 1–2.
17. B. Slay, 'On the Economics of Interrepublican Trade', *RFE/RL Report on the USSR*, 29 Nov. 1991, 1–7.
18. *Izvestiya*, 18 Jan. 1992, 3.
19. A. Lijphart, *Democracy in Plural Societies: A Comparative Explanation* (New Haven, Conn., 1977).
20. M. Bronshteyn, 'The Baltic Knot', *Literaturnaya Gazeta*, 17, 25 Apr. 1990; cf. *id.*, 'Our Common Market is an Alternative,' *Izvestia*, 21 Feb. 1990, 3; S. Shatalin, Interview in *La Stampa*, 19 Sept. 1990, 5.; G. Yavlinskiy, interview in *Sovetskaya Rossiya*, 20 Sept. 1990, 1–2.
21. In February 1992 Belorus, Kazakhstan, and Russia, for instance, agreed to create a rouble zone, in which there is to be free movement of goods, services, capital, and labour.
22. Reported in *RFE/RL Daily Report*, 21 Feb. 1992, 2.
23. See the discussion in W. H. Riker, Federalism: Origin, *Operation, Significance* (Boston, 1964), 5 f.

BIBLIOGRAPHY

Bahry, D., *Outside Moscow: Power, Politics, and Budgetary Policy in the Soviet Republics* (New York, 1987).

—— 'Perestroika and the Debate over Territorial Economic Decentralization', *Harriman Institute Forum*, 5 (1989), 1–8.

von Beyme, K. 'Federalism', in C. D. Kernig (ed.), *Marxism, Communism and Western Society—A Comparative Encyclopedia*, iii (New York, 1972), 314–28.

Bialer, S. (ed.), *Politics, Society, and Nationality Inside Gorbachev's Russia* (Boulder, Colo., 1989).

Brunner, G. and Meissner, B. (eds.), *Nationalitätenprobleme in der Sowjetunion und Osteuropa* (Cologne, 1982).

Carrère d'Encausse, H., *Decline of an Empire: The Soviet Socialist Republics in Revolt* (New York, 1979).

Dienes, L., 'Dilemmas of Resource Development in the USSR', *Nationalities Papers*, 1 (1989), 25–9.

Gleason, G., *Federalism and Nationalism in the USSR* (Boulder, Colo., 1990).

Hazard, J. N., 'Political Reform and the Soviet State', *Nationalities Papers*, 1 (1989), 6–12.

Hough, J. F. and Fainsod, M., *How the Soviet Union is Governed* (Cambridge, 1979).

Katz, Z. (ed.), *Handbook of Major Soviet Nationalities* (New York, 1975).

Kux, S., *Soviet Federalism—A Comparative Perspective* (Institute for East-West Security Studies Occasional Paper, no. 18, Boulder, Colo., 1990).

——*Decline and Reemergence of Soviet Federalism* (Zurich, 1992).

Motyl, A. J., *Will the Non-Russians Rebel? State, Ethnicity, and Stability in the USSR* (Ithaca, NY, 1987).

——*Sovietology, Rationality, Nationality—Coming to grips with Nationalism in the USSR* (New York, 1990).

——'Empire or Stability? The Case for Soviet Dissolution', *World Policy Journal*, 8 (summer 1991), 499–524.

Nahaylo, B. and Swoboda, V., *A History of the Nationality Problem in the USSR* (London, 1990).

Tucker, R. C., *Political Culture and Leadership in the Soviet Union: From Lenin to Gorbachev* (New York, 1987).

PART IV
Conclusion: Federalizing Europe

14

Can there be a Stable Federal Balance in Europe?

FRITZ W. SCHARPF

In its present shape, the European Union is more than a mere alliance of nation-states. But it is also far from being a fully developed political system with a democratically legitimized government of its own. The Union has remained at this halfway house between confederacy and federation much longer than both the optimistic and the pessimistic theorists of European integration would have thought possible in the 1950s and early 1960s. However, at the beginning of the 1990s the European constellation is changing, and new factors seem to increase the pressure towards political integration. As a result, Europe will have to deal with increasing tensions between the urgency of effective central regulation and the equally compelling need to respect the cultural diversity and institutional autonomy of its nations and regions.

With the completion of the internal market and the commitment to move towards monetary union, the capacity of Member States to deal directly with a wide range of economic and economy-related problems will be greatly reduced. If we distinguish between 'negative integration' and 'positive integration', the former has severely constrained the ability of Member States to respond to increasingly pressing problems with measures that might have the effect of restraining the free movement of goods, services, capital, and persons—and that free movement, in turn, is curtailing their *de facto* power to impose burdens or restrictions on firms or investors within their own boundaries that would reduce the economic attractiveness of the country in comparison with other European locations. The result is a competition among regulatory systems that can only reduce the ability of all Member States to regulate economic activity in accordance with their own political preferences. Moreover, if monetary union should come about, national policy-makers would not only lose their control over interest rates and the money supply—and hence over the national rate of inflation—but they would also lose the option of adjusting exchange rates in response to changes in the international competitiveness of their country.

In view of the high political costs associated with this loss of national self-determination, the completion of economic and monetary union is by no means assured. If it should be realized, however, pressure for the development of complementary problem-solving capacities at the European level will come precisely from those countries that find themselves most painfully constrained in their own efforts. Thus, the country that has had its own attempt to regulate road transport struck down by the European Court will have no choice but to become the promoter of a European form of regulation—and it will also be compelled to champion institutional reforms that will increase the legitimacy and the capacity for decisive political action at the European level.

At the same time, German Unification has added political urgency to the constitutional development of a European state. One obvious reason is the desire on the part of Germany's neighbours to restrict her freedom for unilateral action. But even if Germany were expected to concentrate loyally and exclusively on playing her role within the Union, European union would still gain in importance. The need arises from the basic structural conditions of EU policy-making, which still resemble more the pattern of classical alliance politics among European states in the nineteenth century than the domestic politics of a modern federal state. Leadership in the Union is not primarily exercised, in spite of the personal authority of its presidents, by the European Commission, and it certainly is not exercised by majorities in the European Parliament or by European political parties. Formally, the leadership role is assigned to the semi-annual presidency in the European Council, and substantively major policy initiatives in the European Union are promoted by changing coalitions of Member States. In order to be successful, however, they have generally depended on joint promotion by France and Germany.

However, the system of flexible alliances has been unbalanced by German Unification. By the size of her population and of her economic potential, the Federal Republic is now clearly the largest member of the Union, and it is most likely that this will also change the character of Franco-German relations, which hitherto depended on the fundamental equality of status and influence between both countries. Even if the Germans should in no way aspire to a position of dominance in Europe, they will be suspected of doing so, and other countries will want to protect themselves against that eventuality—which surely will alarm not only hard-line Conservatives in Britain. The long drawn-out dispute over the number of seats which the larger Germany should have in the European Parliament is sufficient warning on this point.

In the context of alliance politics, of course, the most likely response would be the formation of defensive coalitions against the presumptive German hegemony. But while there is every reason to expect that such strategies would be completely successful in frustrating the underdeveloped German willingness and ability to assume leadership responsibility, it is also most likely that such coalitions against the strongest member of the Union would be too weak and too heterogeneous successfully to shape the future of Europe. What is to be feared, therefore, is a throw-back to the pattern of European politics of the 1970s and early 1980s—if not to the style of international relations that was characteristic of Europe in the inter-war period.

That may be an excessively pessimistic scenario. But since it is unlikely that Germany will be divided again or that her attractiveness as a potential leader will greatly increase, the hope that it might be avoided must depend mainly on developments which will reduce the salience of the relative weight of Germany in European politics. That hope presupposes that the Union will outgrow its inappropriate pattern of international alliance politics, and that it will be transformed into a system resembling the domestic politics of a federal state.

From a functional perspective (i.e. disregarding issues of political feasibility) the necessary changes are easy to identify. The most important step would be the transformation of the European Commission into a politically responsible European Government which is elected, and may be deposed, by the European Parliament. This would focus political attention, political controversies, and political aspirations on processes at the European level, and it would create an action centre at that level that would be capable of dealing with national governments from an autonomous basis of political legitimacy. A complementary condition would be the concurrent competence of the European Parliament in all legislative and budgetary matters. As a consequence, the role of the Council of Ministers would then be reduced to that of a—very important—second chamber. Under such conditions, surely, the relative weight of Germany among the Member States of the European Union would lose its political importance—just as the even greater preponderance of North Rhine-Westphalia within the Federal Republic never produced major political irritation.

The Maastricht conference has shown, however, that European governments are not yet willing to accelerate the pace of political integration, and to consider constitutional solutions which would not only transfer decision-making powers from the national to the European level but would, as a consequence, also reduce their influence on the process of European policy-making. Nevertheless, decision-making powers are being transferred, and if Maastricht is any indication, will continue to be transferred to the European level as a consequence of economic integration. If political integration should lag behind, that merely means that these powers will continue to be exercised through negotiations among national governments which, even in the absence of anti-German alliances, will be greatly affected by the enormous diversity of interests among European countries. Their most likely outcomes are compromise solutions at the lowest common denominator.

But even if these should be unsatisfactory solutions from every point of view, that does not mean that Europe would escape the problems of over-centralization associated with any upward transfer of regulatory powers. They are already manifest in complaints about the ridiculous degree of bureaucratic detail that is characteristic of regulations and directives drafted by the Commission and adopted by the Council of Ministers. And they are likely to increase as the areas that must be regulated at the European level expand. These problems are inherent in any multi-level political system in which central authorities must specify general rules that have to be implemented by lower-level governments. They must be particularly acute in Europe, however, where the extreme diversity of national administrative organizations, administrative procedures, and administrative styles must increase the perceived need for precise specifications, while the resentment produced by uniform and detailed specifications must also be much greater than it would be in a unitary or even a federal nation-state.

It is clear by now that a European Union that must be constituted of many nations cannot grow into a large nation-state resembling the United States of America. The successful integration of Switzerland into a multi-national state represents a special case whose conditions are hard to reproduce. If proof were needed, it is provided by the continuing or renewed virulence of linguistic and ethnic conflicts in long-established states such as Canada, Belgium, or Spain—and much more so in Yugoslavia, Romania, and in the successor states of the Soviet Union. These examples should serve as a warning of the potentially explosive power inherent in the multiplicity of nationalities and languages within the European Union. If it is to succeed, its constituent states and regions must be granted a high degree of autonomy. They must be able to maintain not only their cultural identities, but also the vitality and problem-solving capacities of their own political institutions, and they must remain as far as possible masters of their own fates.

The institutional evolution of the European Union thus leads to a constitutional dilemma: the effects of economic integration and of German Unification appear to generate problems whose solution would require a much higher level of political integration and centralization than would be compatible with the national and cultural diversity and the need for autonomy of the Member States of the Union. There is reason to believe, moreover, that this dilemma cannot be overcome through the mechanisms of joint decision-making, that have worked reasonably well in German federalism or through the institutionalization of the principle of subsidiarity in the Maastricht Treaty.

In German federalism, the *Länder* have been able to compensate for their loss of legislative authority by maximizing their participation rights in decision-making processes at the national level—a pattern which is also characteristic of the relationship between Member States and EU decision-making. In Germany, however, joint decision-making has in no way helped to protect the autonomy of the *Länder*. Rather, West Germany has long been described as a 'unitary federal state' in which the goal of uniform living conditions has taken precedence over other concerns. In constitutional theory, German federalism is justified as an additional (and most effective) set of checks and balances restraining the exercise of central government power, rather than as an effective protection of regional identities, diversity, and autonomy. In political terms, it is fair to say that *Länder* governments have traded their autonomy for political influence at the federal level.

As a result, policy-making is constrained by high consensus requirements among governments representing diverse constituencies. If West Germany was, by and large, served well by these arrangements, that does not mean that similar structures would work equally well in the European Union (or that they will continue to work in the larger Germany, for that matter). In West Germany, inter-regional economic disparities were comparatively low; cultural diversity was mitigated by post-war mass migration; and a political orientation towards national issues was reinforced by the pervasive influence of national parties on *Land* elections. At the same time, the political salience of the constitutional standard of uniform living conditions, and its approximation in actual practice, made uniform nation-wide regulations both politically acceptable and administratively practicable. In the European Union, by contrast, economic disparities and cultural differences are extremely important, and conflicts among national interest positions are not mitigated at all by common European party political orientations and loyalties. As a consequence, uniform living conditions are not only far from being a European reality—they are not even an acceptable goal, if the term is meant to suggest (as it does in Germany) not only economic convergence, but also institutional and cultural amalgamation. In short, the evolution of a European Union cannot follow the German model of the unitary federal state. It cannot count on the factors which facilitate both the adoption of uniform central rules and their uniform application by formally separate, but substantively homogeneous, *Land* administrations. If it should proceed at all, it must develop much looser forms of coupling between central and Member State policy-making than is characteristic of German federalism.

If German-style government by consensus seems beyond reach, one should also not place too much hope on the subsidiarity principle which is now formally enshrined in Article 3*b* of the Maastricht Treaty. According to this clause, the Union will exercise its concurrent powers only if its goals cannot be attained through measures taken by Member States. As an appeal to the self-restraint of European decision-makers this may have some political effect.

But the legal effectiveness of such a clause should be regarded with considerable scepticism. One reason lies in the expansive dynamism of the Union's economy-related competences.

European integration has so far meant economic integration. But with the completion of the internal market, not only the Union's power to regulate economic transactions, but also the derivative powers to secure the preconditions of the internal market and to deal with its secondary problems, will gain a new urgency. By their own logic, these regulatory powers must also extend to matters which, when considered in isolation, might seem to be non-economic in character. Modern capitalist societies are so thoroughly 'economized' that it is difficult to think of areas for which it cannot plausibly be argued that they either have effects upon the economy or are themselves affected by economic developments.

There can be no question, to cite just two current controversies between the European Union and the German *Länder*, that television is not only a medium of political communication and cultural identity, but that it is also a branch of economic services for which it seems perfectly legitimate to regulate market access at the European level. By the same token, the right to vote in local elections is not only a matter close to the core of local and regional self-government, but it is also a matter that directly affects the free movement of persons within the internal labour-market. Similarly, the recognition of education and training certificates, company law, access to trades, or regulations of packaging to promote waste avoidance and recycling—all are of such obvious importance for the openness of the internal market that one could hardly think of plausible legal arguments to oppose their European regulation. By the same logic, the Union has extended its concern to the support of arts and sciences and the fight against white-collar crime, and in response to the removal of border controls, the creation of common European police forces is already on the agenda. In short, the powers derived from responsibility for the internal market do not contain any implicit limitations on their own scope; potentially they extend to all matters of relevance for, or affected by, the free movement of goods, services, capital, and labour. To put it in the words of the US Supreme Court: 'If it is interstate commerce that feels the pinch, it does not matter how local the operation which applies the squeeze' (*United States* v. *Women's Sportswear Mfrs. Ass'n*, 336 US 460, 464 (1949).

In the European Union, this expansionary logic can assert itself even more sweepingly than it would in a nation-state, where economic concerns must compete at the same level with a multitude of other politically salient problems and purposes—from social welfare and health policy to education, environmental protection, or defence. In the Commission, by contrast, any consideration relating to the free movement of goods and services seems to prevail unconditionally—as it were 'lexicographically'—over all other concerns. There is reason to hope, however, that the monomania of the internal-market perspective will give way to a more balanced political outlook once non-economic policy areas other than agriculture gain in importance on the European agenda.

From the viewpoint of the effectiveness of the subsidiarity principle, however, little would be gained from such a diversification of European responsibilities. Rather, one might expect a reciprocal escalation of centralizing tendencies if European regulations in one area entail European responsibilities for coping with the effects of that regulation in another policy field (which is exactly the spillover effect predicted long ago by neo-functionalist theorists of European integration). It seems, therefore, that, even apart from the specific imperialism of economic policy competences, there is an inherent centralizing dynamic in all constitutional allocations of power which specify only the central government pole of an inherently bi-polar relationship.

With few exceptions (for example, in Canada), federal constitutions allocate powers asymmetrically. While the federal level is empowered to exercise only specifically enumerated competences, the constituent units—states, provinces, cantons, or *Länder*—are left with the unspecified residuum of powers. In theory, this arrangement is meant to protect lower-level units by creating a constitutional presumption in their favour. In practice, however, almost everywhere it has failed to prevent the increasing centralization of legislative authority. The reason is succinctly contained in the old poker rule that 'you cannot beat something with nothing'. In the present context this means that even the weakest argument creating a link to one of the enumerated powers of the central government will prevail—in court as well as in political debate—against unspecific appeals to the residual competence of Member States.

In order to change that pattern, the European constitution would itself have to create political and legal counterweights against the imperialism of central powers which could be enforced through judicial review (and by the anticipation of judicial review in political debate). One such solution was provided by the doctrine of 'dual federalism' which had dominated American constitutional law until the New Deal of 1937. At bottom, the doctrine rested on the simultaneous recognition not only of enumerated federal powers, but also of a substantively specific 'police power' of the states. Where one of these applied, the other one had to yield, and vice versa.

In the US Supreme Court, the doctrine ultimately failed because of the difficulties of defining an intellectually defensible line of demarcation between the equally legitimate claims of the national government and of the states. Regulating the national economy in a unitary market, and regulating local conditions affecting the health, safety, and working conditions of their citizens, both levels of government were ever more frequently dealing with the same subject-matter. Searching for either–or solutions, before 1937 the Supreme Court had almost always favoured the 'states rights' position; and when this position became politically untenable in a direct confrontation with Roosevelt's New Deal legislation, dual federalism was abandoned altogether. At any rate, no single federal statute has been struck down as an unconstitutional interference with the reserved powers of the states since then.

But the demise of dual federalism was perhaps not inevitable. The West German Constitutional Court has also read into the Constitution a core competence of the *Länder* in the cultural field, including education and mass communications. Unlike the US Supreme Court, however, it has never tried to define a precise dividing-line between, say, the federal foreign relations power and the cultural competences of the *Länder*. Recognizing the inevitable interdependence among policy areas, the German Court has opted for a balancing approach that is sensitive to the relative weights of the respective governance interests involved in the specific case. Even more importantly, the Court has developed a principle of 'federal comity' (*bundesfreundliches Verhalten*), according to which each side, even in the exercise of its undisputed powers, is obliged to avoid undue interference with the constitutional prerogatives of the other level of government. If there is to be any solution to the European dilemma described above, it is likely to be found through the systematic extrapolation of the underlying logic of these principles.

An important precondition, given the centralizing drift of past decisions of the European Court of Justice, would be the explicit commitment of the European Union to a bi-polar constitutional order. Treaties should avoid the asymmetrical allocation of powers, which is characteristic of most federal constitutions, by explicitly enumerating the goals and competences not only of the central (European) level of government, but also those of the Member States. In addition to their—however comprehensively defined—residual powers, Member States should also insist on the positive specification of at least the core areas of their own responsibility for the maintenance of their institutional and cultural identity and autonomy. It should be made clear, in other words, that European claims to jurisdiction—while strongest in the regulation of transnational transactions—will not automatically override national or regional competences in these core areas.

In order to succeed, a bi-polar constitutional order would have to avoid the pitfalls of American-style dual federalism. In the light of a growing interdependence among all policy areas and subject-matters, even explicitly enumerated powers could no longer be treated as if they were watertight compartments. There is no question that central measures relating to external economic relations or to the internal market will have effects on subject areas within a competence of Member States; and measures of national or regional education policy or cultural policy may, of course, affect the free movement of workers or the market axis of cultural or information services. Unable to rely on the simple rule that any plausible reference to a central government power will always win out over any Member State interest, a bi-polar constitutional order would necessarily have to cope with strong internal tensions. It would not only require Member States to respect the core of central–state competences in the exercise of their own powers, but would also require that the central state exercising its explicitly specified powers would still have to consider their potential impact on the reserved rights of Member States.

Thus, the rules of federal comity developed by the German Constitutional Tribunal would have to become the guiding principle of all levels of government within a European Union. By the same token, the judiciary in a bi-polar constitutional order could no longer afford to treat the potential reach of an explicitly enumerated power as a question of political discretion: it would be compelled in cases of conflict to balance the relative weights of—in principle equally legitimate—functions and interests of both levels of government. This would rule out the abstract resolution of conflicts over competence in favour of a dominant central government, and it would require a practical balancing of interests under the circumstances of the specific case—at least in cases where two preliminary questions have been answered in the affirmative: first, whether the measure in question is plausibly employed for purposes entrusted to that level of government and, second, whether the means employed will have real (and not merely hypothetical) and significant negative effects on policy areas whose regulation is reserved to another level of government. If the answer to either question were negative, there would obviously be no need for balancing. But, if balancing is necessary, cases would then have to be decided by the relative weights of the constitutionally legitimate and practically affected governance interests involved.

Such balancing operations may be difficult, but they are by no means unusual in constitutional adjudication. The less constitutional courts succumb to the temptation of excessive abstraction, and the more they insist on the practical comparison of the specific consequences and interests associated with the exercise, or denial, of governance powers on either side, the more one may hope that governments themselves will develop practices that will systematically minimize co-ordination conflicts. Such hopes are rooted in the insight that almost all regulatory purposes can be achieved by a wide variety of means which are likely to differ significantly in the nature and intensity of the negative externalities that will be imposed on other jurisdictions.

Under the rule of federal comity, all levels of government would thus be obliged to take care, in the exercise of their own powers, to minimize interference with the functions assigned to another level of government. In this spirit, central government would have to choose forms of intervention that will maximally respect the autonomy of Member States, while Member States in turn would be required to pursue their own goals through means which are maximally Union compatible. Even if we do not yet have a general theory of interference-minimizing policy choices, it is nevertheless possible to mention some plausible examples.

At the central or European level, one might think of the grossly under-utilized opportunities to rely on framework regulations instead of fully specified regulations, and one might also think of central rules specifying minimal or maximal requirements which may be superseded by more demanding national or subnational regulations. Of potentially even greater importance, in view of the economic inequality among Member States, might be proposals to achieve harmonization in, say, environmental protection, not through the enunciation of uniform pollution standards but through levies whose volume is determined by a wealth-related criterion—perhaps as a percentage of GNP. Similar solutions taking account of national differences in the ability to pay might also be helpful in other policy areas—for social welfare, health, or education policy, for instance. Moreover, national and subnational governments should remain free to deal with matters transcending national boundaries without requiring Union-wide action through multilateral agreements and inter-state compacts.

Conversely, at lower (national or subnational) levels of government, the imposition of emission or energy-consumption related levies for automobiles or furnaces would be much more Union compatible than the prescription of technical solutions or the imposition of fixed standards of emission. By the same logic, in the areas of secondary, tertiary, and vocational education, admissions tests (which any applicant could take after individual preparation) would create lower impediments to mobility than the requirement of certificates of completion of particular courses of education. In this area, European countries could profit greatly from the experience of American states. Similar solutions might be found in the field of social security, where combinations of collectively financed basic income support with private insurance (arranged individually or through collective bargaining) would create significantly lesser impediments to mobility throughout the community than is presently true under systems of public social security that provide complete coverage. The list could easily be extended.

To conclude, the completion of the internal market will increase the importance of governance functions that can only be performed at the European level, and it will increase pressures for institutional changes that could improve the democratic legitimacy of European decisions. Nevertheless, a European Union cannot develop along the lines of a (federal) nation-state. If it is to survive, it must respect and protect the vitality and autonomy of its institutionally and culturally diverse constituent members to a much greater degree than is usual in federal states. This can only be achieved in a bipolar constitutional order which explicitly balances the legitimate concerns of the Union and the core responsibilities of Member States and regions under rules which will amount to the institutionalization of constitutional conflict.

In order to succeed in practice, such arrangements depend on the presumption, shared by all parties involved, that every political level should be able to define and pursue its own purposes within its own sphere of competence and with its own means—provided that these purposes will be pursued with the utmost consideration for the responsibilities and purposes of all other levels of government. It is only under constitutional rules and practices inspired by the principles of dual federalism and federal comity that a European Union would be capable of gaining legitimacy without destroying the political and cultural autonomy of its multiple national Member States. And unless it is clear that it will not be able to overwhelm national and regional governance systems, it is unlikely that a European Union will be given the chance to develop even those essential governing capacities on which the internal market depends.

15

Federalizing Europe: The Path to Adjustment

JOACHIM JENS HESSE AND VINCENT WRIGHT

This book has hopefully contributed to a more balanced assessment of the political, economic, and socio-cultural potential of federal arrangements through an exploration of the costs, benefits, and preconditions of federalization. The basic questions addressed were the following: To what extent do we discern federalization processes at work in Europe, and why such processes? What, on the basis of theoretical understanding and empirical studies (not confined to Europe), can reasonably be expected from federal systems, at what price, and under what conditions?

Given the combination of theoretical and empirical questions involved, it proved useful to complement the analytical and conceptual discussion of the costs, benefits, and preconditions of federalization with empirical studies of individual federations. After all, it was reasonable to assume that the costs and benefits would vary widely between countries, and that the preconditions might shape costs and benefits. It was none the less plausible to posit that some benefits might be realized in specific institutional settings, just as particular institutional arrangements could give rise to certain costs.

For this reason, the first part of the book was devoted to a reconsideration of the classical approaches to federalism, whilst the second concentrated on the political, economic, and socio-cultural costs and benefits of federalization. These were followed by a look at the performance of traditional Western constitutions (such as Austria, Switzerland and Germany, and Belgium and Spain), whose constitutional make-up contains distinctive federal elements. The Western experience was then contrasted with a chapter on the former Soviet Union, leading to a concluding general discussion on the opportunities and limits of federalization.

1. THE CASE FOR FEDERALISM—CLASSICAL APPROACHES RECONSIDERED

Whether there are any useful lessons to be learned from the historical development of federal systems for the analysis of contemporary federalization processes and their preconditions is open to dispute. According to William H. Riker,[1] a comparison of the different historical circumstances that have given rise to federations underlines the importance of one central factor: the objective most frequently sought in federalization is military. In fact 'the rulers of all successful federations, that is, federations that have lasted for more than a few years, have initially displayed some kind of military purpose'. Such a military purpose can take many forms: federation as preparation for rebellion or civil war; defence against the imperial ambitions of neighbouring countries; the wish to absorb neighbours in order to prepare for aggressive expansion; the intention of absorbing neighbours, with less cost than conquest, or of mollifying them with the appearance of continuing sovereignty.

In so far as federalization is understood as closer integration (rather than as a way to decentralize authority in a unitary state), military considerations are of outstanding significance: 'initially, there must be a compelling reason to aggregate resources, and this compulsion is invariably military, though sometimes framers prefer imperial to federal institutions to solve military problems at, perhaps, less cost'. Where federations have failed in the past, the absence of any military purpose needs to be counted amongst the principal reasons. On the basis of this analysis, the present prospects for a European Federal Union appear gloomy. As the Soviet military threat recedes, it is not clear what can be gained by federation. Consequently, for Riker it would appear that 'the future of a united Europe is as chimerical as a united world'.

Riker's thesis may be disputed, especially by pointing to cases of successful federations where military motives were said to have been of secondary importance from the outset, if such considerations had played a role at all. Perhaps more importantly, it is questionable to what extent historical analysis could have any predictive force. In particular, in quite a number of cases it appears that economic competition and conflict might have superseded military ambition as the prime stimulus to federalization. In this perspective, the decisive motivation for pooling national resources in Europe would be the desire to safeguard economic positions in a global environment. Even where military concerns had historically been of supreme significance, they in themselves had, in turn, often been shaped by other factors, especially rival economic interests. Furthermore, it has been noted that whilst military considerations might have played a powerful role in the creation of federations out of previously independent polities, they seem to have been far less important in those cases where federalization meant the fragmentation of hitherto strongly centralized, unitary political systems. Moreover, federation-building could be conceived of as a special case of state-building. Although it might be correct in identifying military concerns as a dominant force in the emergence of states, this did not distinguish federations from other forms of government. The military factor can, therefore, hardly explain the type of government which emerged.

Whilst Riker's analysis concentrated on the historical preconditions for the emergence of federal polities, trying to assess their contemporary relevance, Murray Forsyth's chapter re-examined classical theories of federalism; the historical experience of federations was thus confronted with the history of political thinking about the federal organization of the body politic. The leading question here again is: What lessons might be drawn from such a re-reading of classical authors for an analysis of present federalization processes?[2]

Concentrating on the question of European integration, four main groups of propositions which underline the continued relevance of classical political theories of federalism are identified. First, older theories are valuable because they provide an overall framework which enables us to identify what is of fundamental constitutional importance in the changing, diverse, and increasingly opaque processes of European integration. Older approaches tended to place particular emphasis on constitutional questions, and they could thus offer guidance and insight in trying to extract constitutional issues from 'the tangled mass of policies and objectives and processes that make up the Community system'. Secondly, a study of older theories of federalism might help to correct those images of federal systems (which still tend to dominate discussions in Britain), which see them as always involving a concentration of power at the centre and a reduction of the constituent units to near insignificance. Thirdly, classical theory emphasized the point that federalism is always and by definition a two-way process of the delegation and the reservation of powers. It is worth keeping this point in mind at a time when EU Member States, worried about the progressive draining away of their powers, seek to draw a line, and 'often represent this process of line-drawing as a rejection or brake on federalism'. Finally, older theories might be able to avoid the myopic focus on the economic dimension in the European integration process. True, federal union has nearly always tended to involve some measure of economic union, but this end has invariably been balanced and complemented by other goals, whether of a power-political or cultural nature.

The importance of these goals in explaining the foundations of federal government is stressed by several authors. What makes the writings of some of the older political theorists, such as Hamilton, of especial significance, though, is not merely that they drew attention to the wide range of ends to be pursued through a federal construction, but that they highlighted the importance of thinking about both ends and means. The topicality of this point is obvious in relation to the European Union, where the discussion centred almost exclusively on specific legal-institutional arrangements, whereas the fundamental constitutional aims and objectives of creating an ever-closer union were for a some time rarely debated.

The historical experience of federalization and the body of political ideas within which it needs to be embedded were then complemented by a comparative analysis of modern federal constitutional arrangements.[3] The aim here was to cast light on the potential and limitations of specific constitutional arrangements, and the preconditions of their successful operation. Drawing on empirical examples, not merely from Europe, but also from the United States, Canada, and, in particular, Australia, Cheryl Saunders demonstrates the wide variations which exist between federal constitutions and between federal systems of government. It is because of this variety that extensive debate over whether a system of government is a federation, in form or function, is unproductive: 'federalism is not created by federal institutions and rules alone, but depends also on attitudes towards the process of government. Thus, some of the advantages of federalism may be obtained without traditional federal structures. Equally, they may be lost in a country which otherwise is federal in form.'

None the less, the constitutional and institutional framework of federal governance has a decisive impact on the political process; the latter, in turn, largely defines the spectrum of feasible legal-institutional arrangements. Processes of federal constitution-alization typically involve decisions on: amendment and enforce-ment procedures; the division of powers (which types of govern-mental powers are allocated by what method); economic union (e.g. what are the features of an internal market; what is the appropriate balance of power and responsibility between a feder-ation and its constituent parts; what is the relationship between these considerations and the federal financial framework); and the acceptable degree of disparity between the constituent units of the federation. These issues, which directly concern federal arrange-ments, must be viewed in the context of the rest of the governmen-tal system with which they are closely interwoven. The empirical variety of institutional arrangements underlines here the flexibility of federal governance, thus partly explaining its attraction.

It has to be noted, however, that the individual elements of a federal system cannot be considered in isolation from one another, but are often mutually conditional. Consequently, there is little scope for 'constitutional shopping', or *federalisme à la carte*, in which the federal arrangements are mixed with little regard to their interdependence. This issue is acutely relevant to Central and East-ern European attempts at building new federal structures.

2. THE COSTS AND BENEFITS OF FEDERALIZATION— POLITICAL, ECONOMIC, AND SOCIO-CULTURAL ASPECTS

To assess the costs and benefits of federalization it is arguably necessary to examine in more detail the specific advantages and drawbacks of federal governance in political, economic, and socio-cultural terms. The rational utility category obviously has to play an important role in such a broadly conceived cost–benefit analysis;

however, analytical discussion cannot be restricted to the essentially apolitical weighing-up of legal-institutional options. The successful organization of governance requires the balancing of a wide range of political, economic, and socio-cultural requirements and preferences, which, because of their frequently conflicting nature and inevitable externalities, call for political choices. Thus, in discussing costs and benefits in a comparative manner, it is impossible to determine the relative weight of different categories objectively; value-judgements are, therefore, inevitable when it comes to assessing the relative advantages and disadvantages of federally structured polities. A comparative analysis is also made difficult by the need to define costs and benefits in relation to particular national needs and settings. What may appear a benefit in one national context may be regarded as a cost in another, and vice versa.

The German case seems to be of particular interest here: hence the chapter by Uwe Leonardy. In examining the political potential and limitations of the respective federal arrangements, the flexibility and adaptability of the intergovernmental system, which has been stressed by a number of German observers in recent years, is subject to a double challenge posed by German Unification and the evolution of a European federal system in the shape of the European Union.[4] Three central questions need to be raised: first, what was the impact of Unification on German federal structures? Second, in what ways do the legal-institutional framework and policy-making processes characteristic of German federalism need to be adjusted to the emerging European Union, in order to preserve the advantages of the federalized nation-state? Finally, does the German experience of federalism hold any lessons for the construction of a federal Europe, if only by pointing to key problems which need to be addressed in the European constitutionalization process?

The first of these questions is dealt with in Lehmbruch's contribution to this book. With respect to the impact of European federalization on German national arrangements, it is above all the role of the *Länder* (states) in national decision-making on EU-related issues, and their position in Union-level policy-making, for which satisfactory solutions need to be found if progressive European integration is not to be accompanied by an erosion of *Länder* powers. The aim of the *Länder* is to preserve what they see as the undeniable benefits of a decentralized polity, in which subnational units of government exercise substantive responsibilities on their own, whilst fully participating in closely integrated federal working structures that are characterized by intensive horizontal and vertical co-ordination, co-operation, and joint policy-making. To achieve this end, the *Länder* have formulated a catalogue of demands, designed, on the one hand, to safeguard their traditional (national) role in a new Union treaty and, on the other, to give them wider powers in national decision-making on Union matters. Not surprisingly, however, the views of the *Länder* on the distribution of powers in a European Union, and their proposals for the participation of subnational governments in Union-level decision-making, reflect very closely the German experience of federalism.

This raises the obvious question of whether the German federation provides a 'model' for the European federalization process, even though the export of legal-institutional arrangements is, for quite a number of observers, neither a viable nor desirable option. However, there are a number of significant similarities between German and European problems which suggest that it might be useful to study the implications of the German case. In particular, these similarities concern: the federal allocation of powers (discussed under the heading of 'subsidiarity'); the conduct of intergovernmental relations (viewed under the perspective of 'federal loyalty' or 'federal comity'); the question of the institutional and economic comparability and homogeneity of constituent units; and the danger of a 'democratic deficit' in decision-making systems dominated by members of the executive ('executive federalism'). These issues and the problems linked to them coincide with most of the core areas of constitutional choice in federal constitutional processes which have been discussed above, in the chapter by Saunders.

The element of choice and discretion in federalization processes is also emphasized in discussing economic approaches to the analysis of the costs and benefits of federal structures. As Biehl pointed out, 'dealing with the costs and benefits of federalization requires . . . an extended framework in order to avoid too narrow a perspective'. With its emphasis on efficiency criteria, the theory of fiscal federalism might help to decide on the allocation of powers in, and the fiscal constitution of, a (federal) polity; however, resource costs need to be considered together with preference or frustration costs, which accrue when efficient allocation conflicts with other political, economic, or social values. Consequently, there cannot be an optimal degree of centralization or decentralization as such; rather, the application of an extended economic reference framework could produce different systems of government, depending on the relative weight attached to resource versus preference costs. These general observations are then made concrete with reference to the fiscal constitution of the European Union. Here, as Biehl makes clear in his chapter, it is obvious that the Union structure displays considerable inefficiencies, falling short of preference criteria as set out in the Union treaties. In other words, an extended economic analysis reveals that the costs of the federal construction of Europe are much higher than necessary. The compromise at the Edinburgh Summit, to increase the Union budget only moderately from 1.0 per cent of EU GNP in 1993 to 1.72 per cent in 1999 will certainly not serve as an appropriate answer, because it basically retains the old financing system.

The federal elements in the Union's constitution, i.e. 'federalization as a building-up or integrative process', also provided the focus for Leslie's chapter on the socio-cultural costs and benefits of federal-type arrangements. The basic question here is whether the diversity of national cultures, especially as associated with linguistic differences, forms an obstacle to the federalization of previously independent states, or to the conversion of a confederal political association, such as the European Community, into a federal union?[5] At first sight, the more recent troubled history of Canadian federalism holds some sombre lessons for a future European federation:

In Canada, the 'national unity' issue has frequently been presented in the same terms as appear in European debates about political and economic integration. The supposed benefits are mainly or exclusively economic, while many (although not necessarily all!) of the anticipated costs are cultural, in the broad sense that national values and habits and preferences . . . may be undermined by political centralization and what a Canadian economic historian once called 'the penetrative powers of the price system'.

However, as Leslie points out, there are a number of vital differences between the Canadian case and the European situation.

First, the co-existence of cultural communities of unequal size in Canada is accompanied by the threat of assimilation, whereas cultural absorption is not (yet) an issue in the EU. Secondly, the terms of the trade-off between economic benefits and political-cultural costs of integration seem increasingly unfavourable to many Quebec nationalists, who see little economic advantage in staying in the federation. By contrast, in the EU most political and economic leaders in the Member States appear convinced that further economic integration offers significant economic benefit—or at least, that failure to participate in further steps towards integration would entail significant economic costs. Thirdly, relations between Quebec and the rest of Canada are intertwined with the relations with the United States as the dominant economic and cultural force to which Canadians 'are simultaneously attracted and repelled'; this situation does not exist in Europe. Fourthly, the Canadian federation has become much more involved than the EU in the funding of social policy programmes, where values and preferences vary by region; as a result, the federal government's gradual withdrawal from these programmes—spurred by an acute federal financial crisis—exacerbates federal–state conflict, regional strains, and inter-regional disparities.

All this is not to say that the analysis of the causes of the Canadian conflict does not open up some stimulating perspectives on the future of the Union. For instance, the formation of a dominant bloc in the EU and 'an acquiescent group of states tagging along' could result in dualism (although it would not be based on language differences), in which economic costs and benefits might ultimately become indistinguishable from cultural ones. Also, the extension of Union competences in areas with direct and economic issues would be closely entangled. As the Union pursues more explicitly redistributive policies, it is delving ever deeper into the realm of government activities that obviously have cultural or value-laden implications. According to Leslie, it is unlikely that ethnic or linguistic differences would be at the core of the resulting political controversies; none the less, 'language and ethnicity could well become important tools of political mobilization, and consequent disruption', especially when considering the further enlargement of the Union.

3. COSTS, BENEFITS, AND PRECONDITIONS—THE WESTERN EUROPEAN EXPERIENCE

The discussion of Western European political systems with more or less pronounced federal constitutional features centres on the political implications of the dual nature of federalization as a centralizing or decentralizing principle. In particular, the debate revolves around the question of how (prospective) EU Member States with federal-type constitutions can maintain their decentralized political structure within a Community that is itself slowly developing into a federal union. The Austrian and German *Länder*, the Swiss Cantons, the Belgian regions, and the Spanish autonomous communities are intent on preserving and, if possible, extending their powers, not only in the national, but also in the Union context. The gradual transformation of the Union from an intergovernmental organization into a political institution with unmistakably federal features is inevitably accompanied by a certain upward transfer of powers to the Union; what seems less clear is whether this process will primarily affect national parliaments and governments or subcentral tiers. The European Parliament and the Commission have, in recent years, shown greater willingness to recognize regional demands for a closer co-operation between Community institutions and subnational governments;[6] national governments, by contrast, have, on the whole, shown much more reluctance to respond to such pressures. Attempts by the Commission to 'by-pass the national state' (and thus reinforce its own position) by strengthening direct contacts with regional and local administrations have, accordingly, been viewed with suspicion by central governments.[7]

It is interesting to note that the impact of a federalization of the Community on national federal structures is already being broadly debated in both Austria and Switzerland. In fact, the prospect of joining the EU within the foreseeable future has probably proved the single most important stimulus for a renewed debate on a revision of the federal constitution in both countries. As Rack points out in his chapter on the Austrian federation, the decision taken in July 1989 to apply for EC membership immediately raised the problem of the status of the *Länder* within the Community. Thus far, the Union is *länderblind*, i.e. the legal bases of the EU do not take into account the internally federalized structure of Member States. Membership in the Union will inevitably mean that the Austrian *Länder* will be weakened in their regulatory power, and thus in their capacity for self-government. In order to minimize the political-constitutional costs this imposes on the *Länder*, they are already seeking adequate compensation. The strategy of the Austrian *Länder* to ensure that they continue to be centres of substantial political decision-making closely resembles that adopted by the German states. Thus, the *Länder* are insisting that the federation give up some regulatory powers in their favour; demand extensive participatory rights in national Union-related decision-making; and seek the closer direct involvement of regional governments in EU policy-making.[8] It is by no means certain that this three-pronged strategy will produce the results hoped for; however, it underlines the importance of considering the inevitably profound effects of the constitutional development of the European Union on the legal-institutional structures of federal (future) Member States.

The development of Austrian federalism will, in the coming years, certainly be decisively shaped by EU membership. It seems more likely that a decision in favour of joining the Union would have an even greater impact on the Swiss federation. Daniel Thürer even predicts, in his chapter, a 'revolution' in Swiss federalism should his country eventually become an EU member. The fact that Swiss EU membership is regarded as a serious possibility has given a new impetus and urgency to the long-standing controversy over a comprehensive revision of the Swiss federal constitution.

According to Thürer, such a revision would need to preserve what he identifies as the two central strengths of the Swiss federal model: first, the Cantons' constitution-making capacity, which has resulted in a salutary diversity of constitutional law and practice at the cantonal level; and second, the openness of the federal system for inter-regional transborder arrangements, which stems from the Cantons' right to enter into international agreements. These undeniable advantages could not, however, compensate for two key weaknesses in Swiss federalism: the failure to restructure central–cantonal relations in a meaningful way, and the formidable difficulties which Switzerland will inevitably experience if and when it needs to adjust its legal-institutional arrangements to the requirements of political and economic

European integration. As in Austria, the debate on the implications of EU membership on Switzerland's federal structure is fully underway,[9] but it would appear that the challenge to the adaptability of Swiss federalism is greater than that faced by either Austria or Germany. The negative result of the Swiss referendum revealed the unease of the Swiss population when confronted with the daunting prospects.

This does not mean that Germany has few adjustment problems. Indeed, in Germany, the difficulty of adjusting the federal constitution in response to further European integration is compounded by the immense challenge of Unification.[10] After the collapse of the Communist regime in the German Democratic Republic, the decision to restore the five East German *Länder*, which had been abolished in 1952, was but a question of time. As Lehmbruch points out in his chapter, it was motivated by a widely shared popular desire for decentralization and for emotional identification with regional and local traditions, as a reaction to the centralized rule of the Communists. After Unification, it soon became apparent that the fiscal provisions made for the new *Länder* in the Unification treaty were inadequate, and that their resource needs were far greater than was originally assumed. Therefore, 'the important and complex problems of fiscal federalism . . . are at the centre of present controversies over how federalism might cope with the problems of unification'.

In contrast to many other observers, who tend to focus on the dysfunctional effects of the federal structure on the process of political integration of the two Germanies, Lehmbruch emphasizes the positive impact of federalism on the political and societal cleavage structure. True, the debate over the financial provisions for the new *Länder* suggests that the efficacy and adaptability of German federalism might have been impaired. The new *Länder* still lack effective and efficient administrative structures, and they possess insufficient resources to carry out their responsibilities. Financially, the eastern *Länder* are heavily dependent on the federation. The consequences of this reliance on federal grants can be far-reaching: 'the—not unlikely—perpetuation of this situation would mean that the German federal system is cut into a western half where, in principle, the status quo is maintained, and an eastern half with a much more centralist federal-state relationship.' The adoption of the 'solidarity pact' (*Solidarpakt*) has certainly not yet created a new intergovernmental arrangement in this respect.[11]

Despite these serious difficulties, the positive contribution of federalization to the gradual unification of the country in social and political terms should not be overlooked. The dysfunctional effects of federalism have been at least partly counterbalanced by the emergence of a system of party government in the new states: the net result is an increase in diversity within the parties that promises to contribute to innovation and will probably facilitate the adaptation of the German political system to the challenges of Unification. Secondly, and perhaps more importantly, 'the federal structure of the united Germany is the organizational basis for potential "horizontal" alliances that cut across (the "vertical") east–west cleavage'. In this way, federalization can promote political integration.[12]

Whereas, in the German case, federalization promises to function as an integrative force, the progressive federalization of the Belgian state has been accompanied by increasing disintegration, fragmentation, and intractable intercommunal and intergovernmental conflicts. In Belgium, it has not been the effects of Europeanization on the intergovernmental system that have dominated the constitutional debate; rather, constitutional reforms have largely been sought in an attempt to preserve the unity of the Belgian state whilst accommodating highly vocal demands for increased regional autonomy.[13] As Robert Senelle emphasizes in his chapter, the adopted 'gradualistic' approach to federalization has not served institutional stability well. The practice of superimposing new reforms on existing arrangements has contributed to confusion and conflict about competences and has created a climate in which the balance of power between federal and federated entities is constantly exposed to the risk of revision under political pressure.

As a result of this perception, the federalization process has been fundamentally influenced by the exigencies of reducing Belgium's vast public-sector deficits:

The negotiations on the devolution of powers would probably have been less protracted and the compromises worked out would have been less complicated, if the government had not faced the constant need to assess all solutions on their compliance with the overriding priority of accomplishing a budgetary adjustment of unprecedented magnitude.

The result has been an extremely complex web of economic and monetary provisions regulating the relations between Belgium's regions, communities, and the central state.

It should come as no surprise, therefore, that a number of critical observers are raising doubts about the longer-term future of the Belgian state.[14] It is argued that one of the central pre-conditions of a working federal structure, namely the basic willingness of the political, economic, and social élites representing the constituent parts to work together, seems critically eroded. Whilst the legal-institutional hardware of a federal structure has been put into place, affirmative federal practices do not seem to be taking root. The prospect of creating a federal European Union or a 'Europe of the regions' has further helped to weaken integrative forces in Belgium: the more likely a federalized Europe, in which regions will play a major role, the less convincing the case for maintaining a unified Belgium.

The importance of good federal practice as an essential prerequisite for the survival of a highly decentralized or federalized state, is also stressed in the contribution on the Spanish state of Autonomous Communities. An adequate constitutional arrangement needs to guarantee at least a margin of political manœuvre to the constituent states of a federation; this applies both to their capacity for effective self-government, and to their opportunities for participating in central-level decision making. However, mutual faith or loyalty (what in German constitutional doctrine is called 'federal comity' or *Bundestreue*) are required to keep both centralizing forces and centrifugal tensions in check. A willingness to co-operate could compensate for deficiencies in the constitutional framework. None the less, it was important that the basic tenets of the legal-institutional structure of the decentralized or federalized state were universally accepted. It was this acceptance of the constitutional framework by all democratic forces which laid the ground for the success of Spain's transformation from a unitary state into a state of Autonomous Communities with wide-ranging powers, including a genuine legislative capacity.[15] This is not to argue that the transformation has been an easy one, or that relations between central government and the Autonomous Communities are necessarily harmonious. Conflicts over the intergovernmental distribution of powers are, in fact, frequent, although judicial review through the Constitutional Court has gradually led to a clarification of competences.

Summarizing these experiences, what lessons might be drawn from the Western European examples of federalization? One of the central issues touched upon only briefly in the various reports is the role of political parties in federal systems. It has to be noted that political parties could be expected to act as integrative forces in relatively homogeneous federations. By contrast, in heterogeneous federal polities, the party system is likely to reflect the central divisions or tensions in the federation. Belgium is normally cited as an example where the party system has gradually fragmented along the linguistic divide, thus heightening the political salience of the dominant cleavage. But in discussing integrative linkages, the perspective needs to be widened from a narrow focus on political parties to encompass a wide range of other social organizations. It has been argued, for instance, that in Germany the degree of centralization in interest groups and functional organizations is high, and that, therefore, the danger of social fragmentation is reduced. The integrative effects of centralized social intermediaries have recently been shown through what has been described as a 'pact' between peak organizations concerning the restructuring of the East German economy. In Belgium, on the other hand, the universe of social institutions is, like the party system, split along the linguistic dividing-line. As a consequence, functional organizations reflect rather than contain societal divisions. Leading on from this, the more general question to be raised is whether federal structures are not often exacerbating and artificially perpetuating the societal conflicts they are supposed to resolve. Are decentralized unitary states not perhaps—in the longer term—more capable of accommodation than fragmented federations? The United Kingdom, in spite of recent centralizing trends, is often mentioned as an example of a politically unitary state with a high degree of decentralization; here, it is said, a constitutional settlement has evolved which, since it respects different legal, administrative, and cultural traditions, possesses a significant capacity for social accommodation, whilst at the same time offering a stable institutional framework in which centrifugal forces can be effectively contained.[16]

So the importance of considering potential functional equivalents to federalization becomes fairly obvious. Where the potential costs of federalization seem too high a price to pay for limited tangible benefits, other forms of decentralized and territorialized governance might offer realistic alternatives. The cases of France, which has been pursuing a successful strategy of political decentralization and of administrative deconcentration, and of Italy, which has steadily regionalized its intergovernmental arrangements, provide ample evidence of viable alternative options. Perhaps more importantly, the institutional and procedural complexity of mature federations, and their dependence on quite specific preconditions, make it advisable to look for other viable options which might stand a greater chance of success. An examination of the political situation in Central and Eastern Europe underlines the need for innovative legal-institutional arrangements, in which—at least for a transition period—elements of unitary and federal systems might be combined in an unorthodox mixture. This is particularly evident in the case of the former Soviet Union. Similarly, the imagination of constitutional legislators has been put to the test in the Czech and Slovak Federal Republic, where political conflict between the two major ethnic-linguistic groups jeopardized the intertwined processes of democratization and economic reform, and led, at the end of 1992, to the eventual break-up of the federation.

4. THE CENTRAL AND EASTERN EUROPEAN CHALLENGE

With the exception of the Belgian case, the post-war experience of federalization in Western Europe has, on the whole, been a positive one. Despite problems of adaptation to changing political, economic, and social requirements, an overall assessment of the performance of the Austrian, Swiss, and German federations is likely to arrive at favourable conclusions. Spain, whilst not (yet?) a federal state, displays many of the essential attributes of a federalized polity, and her achievements in accommodating strong regionalist and nationalist feelings in a largely acceptable legal-institutional framework have been impressive. In these countries, then, central preconditions for a successful federal structure seem to have been fulfilled, and, at least in the eyes of the functional élites, the benefits of federal government have, on balance, outweighed the costs it imposes. By contrast, Central and Eastern Europe have recently provided examples of the actual or potential dissolution of federal structures. In the case of the former Soviet Union, Yugoslavia, and the Czech and Slovak Federal Republic (CSFR) the old federations have broken down completely, and it is by no means certain that any longer-lasting form of federal settlement, which would have to be radically different from previous arrangements, will eventually be put into their place. In the context of a comparative analysis of the costs, benefits, and preconditions of federations, these examples of failed federal structures, or exceptionally precarious federation-building processes, can be particularly instructive. They serve to highlight the complex and interrelated political, economic, and social requirements which need to be fulfilled if federalist systems are to work effectively.

Turning, therefore, to the link between federalization and democratic reconstruction, the problems of achieving a viable federal formula are readily apparent. The process by which consensus on a federal solution is reached must adhere to the principles which are to be established by federalization itself. Put differently: a commonly accepted federal practice of decision-taking must already be in place to reach a dependable settlement on the constitutionalization and institutionalization of a federal polity. Successful federalization cannot normally be decreed or imposed; paradoxically, federalization may be viewed as the precondition of the success of federalization.

Since the Czech and Slovak politicians were not able to stabilize or to revive their federation, there seems, at first sight, even less reason to assume that new federal structures might emerge after the rapid dissolution of the Soviet Union. As Stephan Kux notes in his chapter, which analyses the future of federalism in the territory of the former Soviet Union, there is currently much speculation about the breakdown of what was called the Union of Sovereign States (USS), an event seen by many as 'comparable to the collapse of the Habsburg, Ottoman, or Roman empires'. Unlike some other observers, however, Kux identifies a number of important 'proto-federalist' elements, which could furnish the foundations of a renewed federal polity. They include: the consolidation of relatively sovereign republics as independent actors and relatively stable political entities; the building of direct, horizontal ties among the republics; inter-agency co-ordination between the centre and the periphery; attempts at coalition politics at the Union level; and the emergence of a federalist political culture.

To be sure, these developments are not the outcome of a widespread belief in the desirability of federal co-operative structures: 'they do not (yet) fully reflect some specific conception of the federal idea, some persuasion or ideology which endorses federal solutions, some particular application of the federal principle, or some particular federal framework'. Current arrangements still lack institutionalization, their precise terms remain unclear, and they constitute an inconsistent, contradictory mixture of federal and confederal elements; also, the chances of the eventual re-emergence of a coherent, tightly structured federation are slim. Yet there are signs that it might still be possible to accommodate various nationalisms and regionalisms in a loose asymmetrical and flexible confederal framework. The USS may come to resemble a set of overlapping circles, with changing networks of co-operation at various levels and in various issue areas. It will be a confederation built on a series of bi- or multilateral agreements and a multitude of *ad hoc* committees and joint institutions with changing membership. The emergence of the loosely structured Commonwealth of Independent States would appear to provide some evidence in support of this thesis.

As regards the other countries of Central and Eastern Europe, it is worth noting that aspects of federalizing the domestic political arrangements are intimately linked to the future of the intermediate levels of government. Here, one detects a significant uncertainty and confusion about intergovernmental arrangements at large. Whilst the previous district offices were abolished almost everywhere, since they served as organs of state government, the future of the regional level is wide open. Taking Poland, the former Czechoslovakia, and Hungary as examples, it has not been possible to provide a satisfactory solution so far. Whereas the old intermediate authorities have been discredited and, accordingly, decisively weakened, the new policies have led to a proliferation of specialized deconcentrated units of state administration. What is emerging is an attempt to disentangle governmental levels, although there is a growing awareness that the problems of co-ordination and control may be at the forefront of reform processes for several years to come. Since there is a multitude of institutions with partly overlapping competences, it should come as no surprise that a clear performance deficit tends to worry reformers. Unusual models, such as the Commissioner of the Republic in Hungary, are, therefore, under close scrutiny. However, there seems to be significant evidence that they are not really appropriate for the given political and administrative structure. Taking all the factors together, intergovernmental arrangements and especially the intermediate level seem to have developed into a serious bottle-neck of the ongoing reform process. Since they serve as the main level of implementing administrative policies, intermediate institutions undoubtedly deserve special consideration over the coming months and years.

5. THE FEDERALIZATION OF THE EUROPEAN UNION

Turning to the European Union, it has rightly been observed that, in its present shape, it is more than a mere alliance of nation-states without yet being a fully developed political system with a democratically legitimate government of its own. As Scharpf notes in his chapter, the Union has remained a kind of halfway-house between confederacy and federation for much longer than both the optimistic and pessimistic theorists of European integration would have thought possible in the 1950s and early 1960s. The question today, however, is whether this situation is likely to change under the impact of the Maastricht Treaty and its attempt to complement economic and monetary union with political union.[17]

Although feared by some and denied by others, political union will, due to its underlying logic, almost certainly lead to a European federal state. In fact, the text of the Maastricht Treaty, though trying to avoid the term 'federal', because of the sensitivities of the UK representatives in particular, argues clearly enough:

The Community will act within the limits of the powers conferred upon it by the Treaty and of the objectives assigned to it. In areas which do not fall within its exclusive competence, the Community shall take action, in accordance with the principle of subsidiarity, only if and insofar as the objectives of the proposed action cannot be sufficiently achieved by the member states and can therefore, by reason of the scale or effects of the proposed action, be better achieved by the Community.

Subsidiarity, the compromise label,[18] is obviously linked here to the broader issues of greater democratic control and more transparency in Union legislation and other actions. And the Commission is indeed prepared, as drafts of papers for the Edinburgh Summit clearly indicated, to acknowledge that all three elements need to be carried through and ought to be part of the practices of the Union. However, whether the adoption of the subsidiarity principle will make the Union more accountable to the public is still open for discussion. There are good reasons to believe that subsidiarity is (and has always been) a quasi-philosophical concept, derived from Catholic social doctrine and enshrined in the 1931 Encyclical 'Quadragesimo Anno' by Pope Pius XI. It served its purpose in defining state–church relationships in fascist Italy, for instance, and it significantly influenced the state-theoretical debates of Christian Democratic parties after the Second World War. But the principle was certainly never used to resolve specific questions of allocating powers and competences between various levels of government or specific policy areas. That might explain why subsidiarity has become so extraordinarily popular among politicians (an admittedly somewhat cynical conclusion), since it seems to offer safeguards against centralization processes that are to be detected not only at the Union level but within national environments, too—without committing the partners to binding agreements. Subsidiarity ought, therefore, to be perceived as a rather nebulous political consensus-category. It is certainly in need of specification. It should not be confused with the real underlying agenda, the federalization of the Union.

Given this background, it might make more sense to analyse the existing attempts to pay increased attention to the needs of sub-central governments in European policy-making and implementation. Here, the pronouncements by the President of the European Commission on the role of regional governments in the Union and the pertinent resolutions and reports of the European Parliament[19] have shown that there is a growing awareness that sub-national governments might gain in importance. Article 198 of the Maastricht Treaty introduces a Committee of the Regions which is to serve as a consultative body to the Commission and which could develop into a significant player on the Brussels scene. All this reflects institutional reactions towards ongoing processes of decentralization and regionalization, which were initially linked to movements of ethnic minorities, and have since been fostered by reactions towards the alienation engendered by centralized welfare-state policies, and ultimately led to constitutional reforms in a number of West European countries.

The case of the Federal Republic might be of relevance in this context again, since many of the arguments used by the Commission and the European Parliament refer primarily to distinctive structural components of German federalism. This becomes most obvious when one leaves aside the enumeration of the most basic elements of implementing the subsidiarity principle or relevant policies of regionalization, and turns instead to the proposals regarding the structural characteristics of the decentralized authorities. What emerges is more or less (though expressed in a different terminology, of course) the model of German federalism and the specific role played by the *Länder*.[20] It stresses the need for government accountability to an elected assembly, for a separate constitution, separate administrative systems and resources, fiscal equalization schemes to avoid regional and social disparities, to name but some of the key characteristics. Thus, one observes a strong attachment to the idea of decentralized, regionalized, 'meso-level' forms of government, although it should be borne in mind that the European initiatives are certainly not without tactical undertones and are at least partly motivated by self-interest: weak nation-states and strong regional units will strengthen the European case, and a certain regionalization of European policies is expected to off-set the loss of competences which sub-central governments face in the course of a progressive Europeanization of decision-making. Since EU institutions need meso-level governments for the purposes of implementation, they might be well advised to court them.

Turning again to the empirical evidence of the German case, one must conclude that it is not primarily self-interest that leads to the proposed regionalization of politics and policies, but a functional reaction towards a significantly changed societal environment as well. The obvious limits to the central state's capacity to steer and control complex processes of problem-solving and service delivery; the need to adjust to economic structural change by taking advantage of the more flexible and adaptive structures provided by regional and even local bodies; the growing awareness of a socio-cultural transformation that renders regulatory public behaviour (irrespective of the needs of target groups) much more difficult—all these issues call for a certain regionalization of political and administrative processes, at least in those policy areas which are based on a certain societal consensus and co-operative response patterns of the parties involved.

But does the relative success of the German way of responding to these developments justify references to a model for overcoming the problems of multi-level problem-solving, and to a recommendation of the *Länder* as a structural component worth testing under different institutional circumstances? In answering these questions, one should first bear in mind the unusual origins of the *Länder*. In their present form they represent neither historical territories nor distinct economic, geographical, and cultural phenomena; this applies both to the old *Länder* and to the five new states on the territory of the former GDR.[21] As far as the Western *Länder* are concerned, they are primarily the product of the post-war division of Germany into occupational zones, and only Hamburg, Bremen, and Bavaria have more or less retained their traditional boundaries. It is quite surprising that despite these artificially imposed boundaries, there exists quite a high degree of regional identity. Secondly, it should be noted that the Federal Republic—not being faced with ethnic minorities—was one of the few European countries that did not experience a regional protest movement during recent decades, a fact which facilitated the evolution of 'co-operative federalism'. Finally, the first forty years of the Federal Republic's existence were characterized by a tendency to arrive at consensual positions and the development of many common behaviour patterns and informal rules shared among the actors. The parties involved tended to approach discussions with the assumption that they would probably have to modify their original positions in order to minimize conflict and to reach compromise. The willingness of individual *Länder* to accept a compromise and to defend it is part of the tradition of fair-play which evolved between the federal government and the *Länder*, a tradition now being severely tested under the double impact of Unification and Europeanization.

If German-style government by consensus seems, given these unusual prerequisites, beyond reach, and if it is equally misplaced to put too much hope on the subsidiarity principle now formally enshrined in Article 3*b* of the Maastricht Treaty, it might make sense to develop further the rule of 'federal comity' instead, in which all levels of government would be obliged to take care, in the exercise of their own powers, to minimize interference with the functions assigned to another level of government. 'In this spirit, central governments would have to choose forms of intervention that will maximally respect the autonomy of Member States, while Member States in turn would be required to pursue their own goals through means which are maximally "Union compatible".' Framework regulations, rather than fully specified regulations and the adoption of rules specifying minimal or maximal requirements, which may be superseded by more demanding national or subnational regulations, might play a significant role here. Of potentially even greater importance, not least in view of the economic inequality amongst EU Member States, might be proposals to achieve harmonization in certain policy areas not through the enunciation of uniform standards but through levies whose volume is determined by wealth-related indicators such as, for example, a percentage of GNP.

This leads to the conclusion that the completion of the internal market will certainly increase the importance of governance functions that can be performed only at the European level, but that political union will not develop along the lines of a federal nation-state. If it is to survive, it will almost certainly have to respect and protect the vitality and autonomy of its institutionally and culturally diverse constituent members to a much greater degree than is usual in federal states. This might be achieved only in a bipolar constitutional order which explicitly balances the legitimate concerns of the Union and the core responsibilities of Member States and regions under rules which will amount to the institutionalization of constitutional conflict.

6. THE COSTS, BENEFITS, AND PRECONDITIONS OF FEDERALIZATION: SOME TENTATIVE CONCLUSIONS

With respect to the feasibility of further federalization processes in Europe, four points emerge as a tentative conclusion. In the first place, a performance analysis of existing federations must take into account both the distinct advantages and disadvantages of federalized governance. It is a more costly form of government than many convinced federalists are prepared to concede, and the benefits of federalization do not necessarily outweigh the political, economic, and socio-cultural costs. In terms of economic prosperity, as well as social and political stability, Western Europe's federations compare well with other countries. But it is not easy to determine the role which their federal structures of government played in their relative success. The problem-solving capacity of the Western federations seems high. Yet, it is by no means certain and is, in fact, somewhat unlikely, that similar legal-institutional arrangements could produce comparable results in very different societal circumstances. This suggests that there are very severe limitations on a West–East transfer of federal models.

Second, the outcome of federalization processes is decisively influenced by the political, economic, and socio-cultural contexts in which they take place. Although there is, of course, room for political choice, decisions on federal governance seem to be unusually preconditioned. The requirements of successful federalization appear more stringent than the prerequisites of unitary democratic government. This is not to argue that it is possible to specify universally applicable minimum requirements, be they of an economic, social, or cultural character, which need to be fulfilled if a federal polity is to work in the longer term. Such an attempt would quickly founder on the actual variety of federal institutions and practices, and the impossibility of defining an ideal-type federation. However, the findings of this volume underline the importance of taking a very close, and critical, look at contextual conditions in trying to assess the viability of federation-building.

Third, on the basis of these considerations, the chances for the progressive federalization of the European Community must be viewed with some scepticism. A historical analysis of federal systems raises doubts as to whether basic requirements for the successful creation of a federal union are already fulfilled. In this connection, it is not very helpful to argue that the European Union would be a federation *sui generis*. Obviously, all federations are to some extent unique, but they would appear to share certain preconditions, which can neither be ignored nor created at will.

Finally, there is some evidence to suggest that—at least in Western Europe—the differences between federal and unitary political systems are beginning to lose some of their salience. Thus, it has been noted that the structures and procedures of governance in Western Europe are showing signs of increasing convergence, perhaps not least due to the European Union's harmonizing influence on national governmental and administrative traditions. The gradual permeation of previously unitary systems of government with distinct federal elements constitutes one of the main forces behind such a process of convergence. At the same time, in the established federations (and perhaps most obviously in Germany) the limits of subcentral policy-making and the need for central governmental capacities are (once again) beginning to be more clearly recognized. It is too early, however, to predict whether the 1990s will be a decade of recentralization for the traditional federations. Clearly, however, a critical reassessment of the potential for regional and local policy-making and problem solving is now under way.

Notes

1. See as his seminal text W. H. Riker, *Federalism: Origins, Operation and Significance* (Boston, 1964).
2. Apart from Forsyth's analysis, attention should be drawn to Daniel Elazar's continuous attempts to reinterpret classical authors.
3. For early attempts see, among others, C. J. Friedrich, *Trends of Federalism in Theory and Practice* (New York, 1968); W. S. Livingston, *Federalism and Constitutional Change* (Oxford, 1956); A. W. Macmahon (ed.), *Federalism, Mature and Emergent* (New York, 1955); R. L. Watts, *New Federations: Experiments in the Commonwealth* (Oxford, 1966); K. C. Wheare, *Federal Government* (London, 1946).
4. Whereas the impact of Unification is not very well analysed yet, a reasonable summary of the challenges posed by German reunification is to be found in *German Politics*, 3 (1992).
5. The special issue of *Regional Politics and Policy* on 'The Territorial Management of Ethnic Conflict', Spring 1993, provides interesting material on this issue.
6. This refers not only to the resolution of the European Parliament on the future of regional policies and the reform of the structural funds, but also to the establishment of the Committee of the Regions as stipulated by Art. 198 of the Maastricht Treaty. This Committee is supposed to act as a consultative body but might turn into a serious player within Brussels decision-making, not least under the influence of the constitutionally and economically powerful subnational governments in Europe.

Belgium, Communities (cont.):
 powers 292–8
 relations with federal authority and Regions 315–19
Belgium, Constitution:
 1993 changes 281–4
 on Communities and Regions 310
 on federation: components and territory 323–4
 on Regions and Communities 310
Belgium, federal authority 280–8
 1993 changes 281
 relations with Communities and Regions 315–19
Belgium, King of 280–2, 283–5
 and international treaties 307–10
Belgium, Regions 288–98, 321
 additional powers 297–8
 budgeting 276–8
 and Constitution 311
 financial resources and responsibilities 272–4, 305–7
 governments 291–2
 and market 274–6
 powers 295–8
 relations with Communities and federal authority 315–19
Belorussia/Belorus 331, 332, 335, 338, 340, 343, 349, 352
benefits of federalization, see costs and benefits
Behl, Dieter 380–1
Bismarck, Prince Otto von 170, 171, 172, 174
Bourbons 241
Brabant 298–9
Britain, see UK
Brussels-Capital Region 271, 299–303, 323
Buchanan, J. M., and Tullock G., The Calculus of Consent 101–2, 104
Bundesfreundliches Verhalten, see federal comity
Bundestreue, see federal loyalty

Calhoun, John C. 33, 36, 38
Canada:
 break-up in prospect? 16
 central and provincial governments 150
 Confederation 140, 143
 Constitution: Act and amendments 50, 51, 137
continentalism, values and 155–8
decentralization 151
difference from Europe 381–2
dualism, linguistic and cultural 139–43, 144, 156
economic and cultural affairs merged 149–50
economic development 58–9
federation: origin 139–40
francophones 140–1
government roles and responsibilities 143–51
linguistic polarization 141
minorities 146, 152–3, 154
social security 146–8
trade restrictions 22–3
and United States 156–7
 see also Quebec
Canary Islands 250
CAP (Common Agricultural Policy) 112, 113, 114, 115
Castile 242
Catalonia 241, 253
Central and Eastern Europe 389–92
centralization 17–18
 degrees of 11, *11*
 increasing 368–9
Charlottetown Accord 50, 137
Churchill, Winston (1874–1965) 230
CIS (Commonwealth of Independent States) 325–55, 391
 beginnings and foundation 325–6, 333–40
 Big Four 349
 borders within 343–4
 centrifugal forces 340–5
 as confederation 334, 351–5
 contradictions and tensions within 338, 343–4
 Council of Heads of States 338–9
 currency zones 352
 economic organization 335–6, 351
 federal institutions 342
 human and minority rights 342, 346
 international status 353
 military forces 334–5, 344, 351
 nationalist feelings 341
 and nuclear arsenal 334–5
 parallels drawn with 355
 political change, speed of 340–1
 political union within? 336–7
 power-sharing 348
 proto-federalism 345–51

7. The attempts to 'bypass the national state' should, on the other hand, not be overestimated. Even if the Commission might be tempted to develop respective policies, the prevailing distrust between some Member States and the EU will almost certainly induce the Commission to adopt a rather careful attitude.

8. This has led, in the meantime, to the creation of a 'Europa Article' (Art. 23) within the Basic Law. It is questionable, though, whether the enhanced powers of the *Länder* will really improve their standing at the Union level, not least due to limited administrative capacities.

9. The Swiss case is furthermore complicated by the need to overcome the longstanding and more explicit political neutrality of this country as compared to some of its neighbours. It would even make sense to distinguish between different cultures shaping the accession process.

10. For a comprehensive analysis See J. J. Hesse and T. Ellwein, *Das Regierungssystem der Bundesrepublik Deutschland*, 7th edn. (Opladen, 1992).

11. It is most interesting to observe how the routines of joint decision-making and co-operative federalism have changed due to the pressures brought about by Unification. The negative-sum games observed might even induce a reconsideration of the problem-solving capacities of the German federal system.

12. It should be kept in mind, though, that the German case clearly indicates the need to distinguish between formal and material integration.

13. On the most recent reform of the Belgian state (May 1993) see R. Maes and S. De Rynck (1993), 'Belgium: The Regions and Communities in the European Integration Process' (MS. Leuven, forthcoming).

14. Given the current developments in Central and Eastern European countries, it would make sense to distinguish clearly between a break-up of a federation and gradual changes towards confederative arrangements.

15. See, among many, A. Elvira Perales, 'Implementing the Spanish Constitution', in J. J. Hesse and N. Johnson (eds.) *Constitutional Policy and Change in Europe* (Oxford, forthcoming).

16. See, for example, R. A. W. Rhodes, *Beyond Westminster and Whitehall* (London, 1988).

17. A good summary is to be found in European Research Associates (ed.), *Europe in the 90s: From Maastricht to European Union* (Brussels, 1992).

18. For a critical discussion of the subsidiarity principle see A. Adonis and S. Jones, 'Subsidiarity and the European Community's Constitutional Future', in *Staatswissenschaften und Staatspraxis*, (1991), 179–96.

19. ABl. Nr. C 326 of 19 Dec. 1988, 289 ff.
20. See J. J. Hesse, *West German Federalism: Effects, Outputs and Implications for European Integration*, Centre for European Studies, Nuffield College, Oxford, Discussion Paper Series, No. 3 (Oxford, 1991).
21. A broad discussion is to be found in the special issue of *German Politics*, 3 (1992) on 'Federalism, Unification and European Integration'.

Index

accountability, blurred, versus
    proximity to citizen 76–7
alliances 10–11
Andalusia 250
Armenia 329, 333, 335, 340, 344,
    346, 349
Australia:
    constitutional amendments 49–50
    court system 53
    fiscal federalism 59–60
    individual states 61
    trade 57–8
Austria:
    balance of power within 204, 211
    constitution 55, 205–6, 209, 210
    and EU membership 207, 209–10
    federal council 204–5
    federal law adaptation 210
    federalism: future? 208, 213
    indirect administration 205
    land sales 212
    Landeshauptmann 206
    legislative power 204
    states (*Länder*), competences 209–
        12, 379–80
Azerbaijan 333, 344, 346

Baltic states 328, 346, 347, 349
Basque country 241, 250, 253, 255,
    260
Belgium:
    agricultural policy 296
    bicameral system reform 283–7
    break-up in prospect? 386
    budgetary discipline 276–8
    Chamber of Representatives 282,
        283–6
    Communities *see separate entry*
    Constitution *see separate entry*
    Councils 280, 281, 286–90
    Court of Arbitration 311–14
    cultural issues 292, 294
    devolution of powers: financing
        mechanism 272
    economic and monetary union 272–
        80
    economy 296

education 292–3
employment 297
energy policy 296
as entity 266
environmental and
    management poli
federal authority *se*
as federal state 27(
fiscal competences
Flemish movement
Frenchification of
German-speaking
government, politi
history 266–72
housing 296
international treati
King of *see separa*
languages and lan
    70, 293–4
market, integrated
Ministers, Counci
monetary policy i
    80
National Bank 2
Parliamentary Lia
    285
party system 388
personalizable iss
Provinces 322
public works and
reform, state 26
Regents, Counci
Regions *see sepa*
rural re-developi
    conservation
scientific researc
Senate 283–7
social institution
town and count
Belgium, Commu
    98, 320
additional pow
budgeting 276–
Constitution ar
financial resou
    responsibiliti
governments 2

purposes, activities and institutions 333–4
and republican agencies 349–50
republics: developments within 340–2
trade within 347–8
viability? 325–6
weaknesses 337–40
civil law tradition 51
civil war 12
classical theory, *see* federalization, classical theory
collective identity, government and 125
common law tradition 51, 53
competences:
  freedoms within different levels of 370
  optimal differentiation/assignment 107–9, 111–12, 114
competition between regional units, versus blurred accountability 76–7
confederations 32, 351–5
  instability 352–3
consociationalism 350
constituent instruments 48–52
  amendments 49–50
  enforcement 50
constitution function 105, 106
constitutional arrangements 46–69
  see also Belgium, Constitution
constitutional courts, government levels and 51
constitutionalism versus functionalism 232–3
constitutionalization, federal 379
correspondence principle 109
CSFR (Czech and Slovak Federal Republic) 390, 391
culture:
  accretion process 126
  and federalization 121–63;
    conclusion 158–63
  homogeneous populations 129–30
Czechoslovakia, former 390–1

decentralization 388–9
democracy:
  and federalism 34–5, 62
  versus solidarity 234–5
'democratic deficit' 92–3
diversity, ethnic and linguistic 33

'dual federalism' 370
dual monarchies 13

Economic Co-operation Organization 353
economic development 58–9
economic method, and federal costs and benefits 101–19
economic union 56–60
Edinburgh Summit 118, 381, 393
EEA (European Economic Area):
  Agreement 224, 225, 226, 227, 228, 235 n.
EEC (European Economic Community/Common Market) 26, 38, 39
EFTA (European Free Trade Association) 225, 232
empires, collapse of 17
employers and employees 128
Estonia 346
'ethnies' 125–6
'ethnonationalism' 126–7
EU (European Union)/EC (European Community):
  autonomy of states and regions 365
  bi-polar constitutional order 373
  budgetary decisions 116
  Committee of the Regions 393
  comparability and homogeneity 87–8
  competences 367
  confused view of 95
  and democratization 124
  dominant bloc emerging in? 157
  'ever closer union' 86
  expenditure competition, proposal to end 117
  federal elements 38–40
  federalization of 392–6
  federalization: prospects 397
  financial constitution: current deficiences 111–16
  and German federal model 366
  Germany as potential leader 362–4
  homogeneity and comparability 87–8
  institutions, member states *vis-à-vis* 150–1
  as *länderblind* 383
  laws 39
  leadership 362
  linguistic and cultural assimilation 143
  major institutions 28–9

EU (European Union)/EC (European
  Community) (*cont.*):
  nature of? 41
  overall spending 112–13
  own resources distribution *118*
  potential regulations 372
  as pragmatic 'going concern' 27
  present shape 361
  present structures as inadequate 123
  proposed tax authority 116
  revenue sources 112
  sovereign powers 39
  transnational organizations 207–8
  Treaties as constitutions 52
  Treaty 27
  as union 40
  see also EU/EC; EEC
Europe:
  Common Market (EEC) 26, 38, 39
  federal 20
  over-centralization 364
Europe, federalization:
  as ambiguous term 122–4
  classification of 134
  path to adjustment 374–98
European Commission 28–9, 393
European Court of Justice 39, 87,
  228, 370
European federalism, lessons of
  past 9–24
European federation, projected 158
  and decentralization 154–5
  institutional framework 169
  nation-states and 142
European Government 363–4
European integration process 367
  core of 25
  federal-constitutional spirit 40–4
  philosophy underlying 28
  purposes 124–5
  speed of 364
  technical-functional spirit 26, 42–3
  two souls of 40–1
European Parliament 363–4
European Regional Committee 90
executive, power of 33–4
extended distribution function 106
extended-cost approach 101–6, *103*,
  115

federal comity (*bundesfreundliches
  Verhalten*) 369–72, 395–6
federal constitutionalization 378

federal constitutions, powers allocated
  asymmetrically 368
federal government, typical powers 54
federal loyalty (*Bundestreue*):
  Belgium 281
  Germany 86–7, 387
  Switzerland 223
federal principle, reflected in organs of
  government 61
federal theory, streams of 34–6
Federalism: Mature and Emergent (ed.
  A. W. Macmahon) 26
federalism:
  co-operative 257
  commitment to 64
  costs and benefits, Canada and
    Europe 136–58
  history of 9–24
  nature 9–10
  non-institutional feeling for 47
  as tier-structure 10
Federalist, The 36, 37
federalization:
  characteristics 122–4
  classical theory 35–7, 375–8
  costs and benefits 47–8, 124–58, *130*
  downward (decentralization) 127,
    129, 160
  typical objective 375
  upward (centralization) 127, 129,
    132
federalization, costs and benefits 74–
  96, 378–82
  conclusions 94–6, 396
  Western Europe 383–9
federalizing Europe, path to
  adjustment 374–98
federations:
  and central power 55
  engendering nationalistic loyalty 16–
    17
  history in Europe 17
  non-surviving 13–16
  of states 133–4
fiscal equalization 110–11, 114–15
fiscal federalism 59–60
  principles 106–11
Flemish Region 271
Forsyth, Murray 476
France 389
free trade 20, 21
freedom-generation 19
frustration costs 102, 106

'functionalism' 29–31
functionalism versus constitutionalism
    232–3

Galicia (Spain) 250
Georgia 333, 342, 346, 349
German Democratic Republic (GDR),
    former, see Germany, East
Germany
    Basic Law 55, 82–3
    Bundesrat 80–1, 90, 93, 172, 181,
        230
    Bundestag 80, 182
    capital cities 179
    centralization 173–5, 388
    comparability and homogeneity 87
    costs, compared with United
        Kingdom's 79
    decentralization 185
    distinctive political system 173, 174
    East, see separate entry
    'federal comity' 369, 370
    federal system accepted 75
    federal unitarization 173–6
    fiscal federalism: quandaries 188–91
    'golden lead' 83
    industrial relations 177–8
    intergovernmental bargaining
        system 171–3
    'interlocking polities'
        (Politikverflechtung) 173, 177,
        182
    'modern' bureaucratic state 171
    party government 181, 194–6
    political costs and benefits 84
    as polycentric or centralized
        society? 177–9
    as potential EU leader 362–4
    public finance integrated in fiscal
        federalism 176–7
    regionalization of policy
        networks 179–81
    Reichstag 171–2
    social and political cleavages,
        organization 177–81
    Solidarity Pact 190
    sovereignty 94
    states (Länder), see separate entry
    television, public 178
    'third level' (Dritte Ebene) 80
    unification, see separate entry
    unitary federalism 191–2
    vertical separation of powers 75
    war defeats 174
    West 365–6
    whole state (Gesamtstaat) 80
    working structures, levels of 79–80
    writers on federalism 36
Germany, East:
    education 191
    identity 186
    income equalization 192
    Länder restored 184–7, 193–5, 385
    public sector 186
    reconstruction of economy 193–4
    trust establishment
        (Treuhandanstalt) 194
    West German view 187
Germany, federal state (Bundesstaat)
    80–4, 170–2
Germany, federalism:
    as European model? 380, 394–5
    institutional logic of 170–6
    intergovernmental relations 170
    as model for Europe? 380
Germany, states (Länder):
    Basic Law and 80–1
    and Bund 80
    controversies with EU 367
    core competence 369
    in doubly federalized structure 81–2
    eastern, restored 183–5, 193–6, 385
    economic policies 180
    and EU 113–14
    and European federalism 89–92
    functions and powers 80–1, 369,
        379–80
    largest 188
    origin 395
    political influence 366
    rich and poor: revenue-sharing
        188–91
    sponsorships 185–7
Germany, unification 133, 169–70,
    182–96
    and EU 363–4
    and German federal structures 379–
        80
glasnost 328
Gorbachev, Mikhail 328–32, 345, 348
government
    powers at different levels 52–3
    structures, and federalism 62

Habsburgs 242
Hallstein, Dr 32

heterogeneity versus practicability in regionalism 89–92
Hungary 391–2

identity, diversity through, versus lack of uniformity 74–5
imperialism 11–12, 14
individual states, federation and 61
Indonesia 14
integration process, federal component 31–40
intergovernmental processes 93
internal market 57–8, 373
  versus regionalism 233–4
Italy 130, 132, 389

judicial power 53
judicial review 50–2
Jura, Switzerland 222

Kant, Immanuel 34
Kazakhstan 332, 333, 335, 346, 348, 349, 351, 352
Kilpatrick, James Jackson 35
Kohl, Chancellor 183
Kravchuk, Leonid 339, 343, 354
Kux, Stephan 390
Kyrgyzstan 332, 333, 335, 340, 351, 352, 353

legislative, power of the 34
Lehmbruch, Gerhard 379, 385
Lenin, V. I. 15
Lijphart, Arend 350
List, Friedrich 36

Maastricht Summit 27
Maastricht Treaty 84, 232–3, 392, 393
  and European integration ambiguities 40–1
MacDougall Report 111
Madison, James 18, 36
market, internal 57–8
markets:
  efficiency 104
  see also internal market
Meech Lake Accord 50, 137
military objectives 12–19, 376–7
Minsk treaties 353
mistake-avoidance, versus time-consuming procedures 77–8
Mitrany, David 29–31

Moldova 329, 333, 335, 336, 337–8, 340, 341, 349, 352
monarchies, see Belgium, King of; dual monarchies
multiple cultural communities, states with 131
Musgrave, R. A. 103

nation states, and federalism 9–10
'national', defined 127–8
national culture, civic expression of 128
Navarre 250
neighbouring·states, absorption of 12–13
Nigeria 13–14

Pakistan 13–14
Pareto optimality 135
perestroika 326, 328–9, 330–1
  achievements of 351
plebiscites 222
Poland 391
political and administrative structures: costs 78–9
political costs and benefits, see federalization, costs and benefits
political dimension in federalism 73–98
political parties in federal systems 388
political theory of federalism 25–45
population, cultural attributes 129
powers, vertical separation of, versus complexity 75–6
powers, distribution and division of 52–6, 233
preference costs 102, 106
provision function 105
'public sector' functions 105

Quebec 16
  as 'Canadian' 154
  constitutional demands 155
  and constitutional powers 136–7
  entrepreneurialism 144–5
  and federal government 143–8, 382
  identity 140–2
  'Inc.' 149
  liberal and restrictive measures 152
  nationalism 153
  power-seeking by 145
  secession threat 136–8

Rack, Reinhard 383
Reagan, Ronald 330
rebellion 12
regional disparity 60–1
regionalism:
  heterogeneity versus practicability
    89–94
  versus internal market 233–4
Riker, William H. 375–6
'Roman Fountain' 234
Rome, Treaty of 28
Russia 327, 329, 332, 333, 335, 336,
  338, 340, 342, 343, 344, 345,
  346, 348, 349
  and Ukraine 334, 346, 352

Sakharov, Andrei 351
Saunders, Cheryl 377
Scharpf, Fritz W. 392
Schäuble, Wolfgang 192
Schmitt, Carl 36, 37
Schuman, Robert 28
Senelle, Robert 386
Smith, Anthony 125–7
social security 128
solidarity:
  pact 385–6
  versus democracy 234–5
sovereignty 94
Soviet Union, see USSR
Spaak Report 28
Spain:
  autonomous communities see under
    separate entry
  autonomous sentiment in regions
    244
  Autonomy, Statute of 247
  central state 240–3, 248–50, 257
  Constitutional Court 250–3, 255,
    262, 263
  constitutional position 254–5
  in crisis 240–3
  decentralization 245–50
  entry into EC 260–3
  federal model as unavailable 243–4
  as federation in the making? 240–63
  Franco regime 240
  history 241–3
  legal order 251–2
  nationalism 242–3, 253–5
  pluralism, reducing 254
  regional planning 241

second chamber (Senate) 246–8,
  255, 257–8
secular pluralism 241–2
special communities: powers 256
Spain, autonomous communtities 255,
  387
  and central state 256
  Constitutional Court and 250–3
  and EU 260
  parliament workings 259–60
  power variations between 248–50
Spain, autonomous state 253
  foundation 240–4
  organizational and legal features
    245–50
  perspectives and problems 255–63
Stalin, Joseph 12
structures, high costs of political and
  administrative 78–9
Styria 210
subsidiarity 84–94, 366–8, 392–3
  and competences 107–8
  origin 393
  presumptions about 84
  principle 113, 233
Swiss cantons 223, 226–7
  and constitution-making 222
  international character of 223
Swiss federation:
  constitution 220–1, 234–5
  Council of States 230
  drawbacks 223–5
  and EEA Agreement 235 n.
  and European integration 224–32
  European law implementation 228–
    9
  features of system 219–25
  federal loyalty (Bundestreue) 223
  future revision? 384–5
  as model for Europe? 230–2
  as model needing adaptation 219–
    35
  origins and political foundation 220
  political careers 229
  psychological conception of 221
  regional openness 222
  representative federalism 229–30
  strengths and benefits 222–3

Tajikistan 333, 335, 342, 353
tax burden-sharing 110, 110–11, 114–
  15
territory, communities defined by 132

Thürer, Daniel 384
time-consuming procedures, versus
    mistake-avoidance 77–8
Tito, President 12, 15
Tocqueville, Alexis de 36, 235
trade:
    country's size as factor in 22
    restriction of 19–24
Trudeau, Pierre 121, 151–2, 153
trust 10, 87
Turkestan 349
Turkmenistan 333, 337–8, 353

UK (United Kingdom) 393
    contributions to EU 115
    costs compared with Germany's 79
    as decentralized 388
    as proponent of federation 13
Ukraine 329, 331, 333, 335, 336,
    337, 338, 340, 342, 344, 345,
    347, 349, 352, 353
    and Russia 334, 345, 352
uniformity, lack of, versus diversity
    through identity 74–5
unitary political systems, compared
    with federations 398
upper houses of federal legislature 61
USA (United States):
    Civil War 33
    Constitution 32–3
    dual federalism 370
    federation: beginnings 18

government theory disregarded 30–1
    slavery 19–20
    Supreme Court 51
    trade restrictions 22–3
USS (Union of Sovereign States) 390–1
USSR (Soviet Union):
    communism defeated 326
    disintegration process 326–33
    end of 332
    as federation 15
    heterogeneous structure 327
    'nine-plus-one' agreement 331
    nomenklatura 327, 348
    political culture 350
    popular movements 328–9
    special features 325–6
    subsidiarity 330
Uzbekistan 332, 333, 335, 349, 353

Valencia 250
VAT (Value Added Tax) 112, 113,
    114

Walloon region 271, 320–2
West Germany 365–6
Wheare, Q. C., Federal Government
    226
world, projected as federal 20

Yeltsin, Boris 331, 333, 339, 343,
    346, 348, 351
Yugoslavia 12–13, 15–16, 337, 390

7. The attempts to 'bypass the national state' should, on the other hand, not be overestimated. Even if the Commission might be tempted to develop respective policies, the prevailing distrust between some Member States and the EU will almost certainly induce the Commission to adopt a rather careful attitude.

8. This has led, in the meantime, to the creation of a 'Europa Article' (Art. 23) within the Basic Law. It is questionable, though, whether the enhanced powers of the *Länder* will really improve their standing at the Union level, not least due to limited administrative capacities.

9. The Swiss case is furthermore complicated by the need to overcome the longstanding and more explicit political neutrality of this country as compared to some of its neighbours. It would even make sense to distinguish between different cultures shaping the accession process.

10. For a comprehensive analysis See J. J. Hesse and T. Ellwein, *Das Regierungssystem der Bundesrepublik Deutschland*, 7th edn. (Opladen, 1992).

11. It is most interesting to observe how the routines of joint decision-making and co-operative federalism have changed due to the pressures brought about by Unification. The negative-sum games observed might even induce a reconsideration of the problem-solving capacities of the German federal system.

12. It should be kept in mind, though, that the German case clearly indicates the need to distinguish between formal and material integration.

13. On the most recent reform of the Belgian state (May 1993) see R. Maes and S. De Rynck (1993), 'Belgium: The Regions and Communities in the European Integration Process' (MS. Leuven, forthcoming).

14. Given the current developments in Central and Eastern European countries, it would make sense to distinguish clearly between a break-up of a federation and gradual changes towards confederative arrangements.

15. See, among many, A. Elvira Perales, 'Implementing the Spanish Constitution', in J. J. Hesse and N. Johnson (eds.) *Constitutional Policy and Change in Europe* (Oxford, forthcoming).

16. See, for example, R. A. W. Rhodes, *Beyond Westminster and Whitehall* (London, 1988).

17. A good summary is to be found in European Research Associates (ed.), *Europe in the 90s: From Maastricht to European Union* (Brussels, 1992).

18. For a critical discussion of the subsidiarity principle see A. Adonis and S. Jones, 'Subsidiarity and the European Community's Constitutional Future', in *Staatswissenschaften und Staatspraxis*, (1991), 179–96.

19. ABl. Nr. C 326 of 19 Dec. 1988, 289 ff.
20. See J. J. Hesse, *West German Federalism: Effects, Outputs and Implications for European Integration*, Centre for European Studies, Nuffield College, Oxford, Discussion Paper Series, No. 3 (Oxford, 1991).
21. A broad discussion is to be found in the special issue of *German Politics*, 3 (1992) on 'Federalism, Unification and European Integration'.

Index

accountability, blurred, versus
    proximity to citizen 76–7
alliances 10–11
Andalusia 250
Armenia 329, 333, 335, 340, 344,
    346, 349
Australia:
    constitutional amendments 49–50
    court system 53
    fiscal federalism 59–60
    individual states 61
    trade 57–8
Austria:
    balance of power within 204, 211
    constitution 55, 205–6, 209, 210
    and EU membership 207, 209–10
    federal council 204–5
    federal law adaptation 210
    federalism: future? 208, 213
    indirect administration 205
    land sales 212
    Landeshauptmann 206
    legislative power 204
    states (*Länder*), competences 209–
        12, 379–80
Azerbaijan 333, 344, 346

Baltic states 328, 346, 347, 349
Basque country 241, 250, 253, 255,
    260
Belgium:
    agricultural policy 296
    bicameral system reform 283–7
    break-up in prospect? 386
    budgetary discipline 276–8
    Chamber of Representatives 282,
        283–6
    Communities *see separate entry*
    Constitution *see separate entry*
    Councils 280, 281, 286–90
    Court of Arbitration 311–14
    cultural issues 292, 294
    devolution of powers: financing
        mechanism 272
    economic and monetary union 272–
        80
    economy 296

education 292–3
employment 297
energy policy 296
as entity 266
environmental and water-
    management policy 295
federal authority *see separate entry*
as federal state 270–1, 280, 386–7
fiscal competences 275–6
Flemish movement 268–70
Frenchification of 267–8
German-speaking region 289, 303–5
government, political structure *323*
history 266–72
housing 296
international treaties 307–11
King of *see separate entry*
languages and language laws 266–
    70, 293–4
market, integrated 274–6
Ministers, Council of 281
monetary policy independence 278–
    80
National Bank 279
Parliamentary Liaison Committee
    285
party system 388
personalizable issues 293
Provinces *322*
public works and transport 297
reform, state 264–319
Regents, Council of 280
Regions *see separate entry*
rural re-development and nature
    conservation 296
scientific research 295, 297
Senate 283–7
social institutions: divide 388
town and country planning 295
Belgium, Communities 131, 271, 288–
    98, *320*
    additional powers 297–8
    budgeting 276–8
    Constitution and 310
    financial resources and
        responsibilities 272–4, 305–7
    governments 291–2

Belgium, Communities (*cont.*):
  powers 292–8
  relations with federal authority and
    Regions 315–19
Belgium, Constitution:
  1993 changes 281–4
  on Communities and Regions 310
  on federation: components and
    territory 323–4
  on Regions and Communities 310
Belgium, federal authority 280–8
  1993 changes 281
  relations with Communities and
    Regions 315–19
Belgium, King of 280–2, 283–5
  and international treaties 307–10
Belgium, Regions 288–98, 321
  additional powers 297–8
  budgeting 276–8
  and Constitution 311
  financial resources and
    responsibilities 272–4, 305–7
  governments 291–2
  and market 274–6
  powers 295–8
  relations with Communities and
    federal authority 315–19
Belorussia/Belorus 331, 332, 335, 338,
  340, 343, 349, 352
benefits of federalization, *see* costs and
  benefits
Biehl, Dieter 380–1
Bismarck, Prince Otto von 170, 171,
  172, 174
Bourbons 241
Brabant 298–9
Britain, *see* UK
Brussels-Capital Region 271, 299–303,
  323
Buchanan, J. M., and Tullock G., *The
  Calculus of Consent* 101–2, 104
bundesfreundliches Verhalten, see
  federal comity
Bundestreue, see federal loyalty

Calhoun, John C. 33, 36, 38
Canada:
  break-up in prospect? 16
  central and provincial governments
    150
  Confederation 140, 143
  Constitution: Act and
    amendments 50, 51, 137

continentalism, values and 155–8
decentralization 151
difference from Europe 381–2
dualism, linguistic and cultural
  139–43, 144, 156
economic and cultural affairs
  merged 149–50
economic development 58–9
federation: origin 139–40
francophones 140–1
government roles and responsibilities
  143–51
linguistic polarization 141
minorities 146, 152–3, 154
social security 146–8
trade restrictions 22–3
and United States 156–7
see also Quebec
Canary Islands 250
CAP (Common Agricultural
  Policy) 112, 113, 114, 115
Castile 242
Catalonia 241, 253
Central and Eastern Europe 389–92
centralization 17–18
  degrees of 11, *11*
  increasing 368–9
Charlottetown Accord 50, 137
Churchill, Winston (1874–1965) 230
CIS (Commonwealth of Independent
  States) 325–55, 391
  beginnings and foundation 325–6,
    333–40
  Big Four 349
  borders within 343–4
  centrifugal forces 340–5
  as confederation 334, 351–5
  contradictions and tensions
    within 338, 343–4
  Council of Heads of States 338–9
  currency zones 352
  economic organization 335–6, 351
  federal institutions 342
  human and minority rights 342, 346
  international status 353
  military forces 334–5, 344, 351
  nationalist feelings 341
  and nuclear arsenal 334–5
  parallels drawn with 355
  political change, speed of 340–1
  political union within? 336–7
  power-sharing 348
  proto-federalism 345–51

purposes, activities and institutions
  333–4
and republican agencies 349–50
republics: developments within 340–
  2
trade within 347–8
viability? 325–6
weaknesses 337–40
civil law tradition 51
civil war 12
classical theory, *see* federalization,
  classical theory
collective identity, government
  and 125
common law tradition 51, 53
competences:
  freedoms within different levels
    of 370
  optimal differentiation/assignment
    107–9, 111–12, 114
competition between regional units,
  versus blurred accountability
  76–7
confederations 32, 351–5
  instability 352–3
consociationalism 350
constituent instruments 48–52
  amendments 49–50
  enforcement 50
constitution function 105, 106
constitutional arrangements 46–69
  see also Belgium, Constitution
constitutional courts, government
  levels and 51
constitutionalism versus functionalism
  232–3
constitutionalization, federal 379
correspondence principle 109
CSFR (Czech and Slovak Federal
  Republic) 390, 391
culture:
  accretion process 126
  and federalization 121–63;
    conclusion 158–63
  homogeneous populations 129–30
Czechoslovakia, former 390–1

decentralization 388–9
democracy:
  and federalism 34–5, 62
  versus solidarity 234–5
'democratic deficit' 92–3
diversity, ethnic and linguistic 33

'dual federalism' 370
dual monarchies 13

Economic Co-operation Organization
  353
economic development 58–9
economic method, and federal costs
  and benefits 101–19
economic union 56–60
Edinburgh Summit 118, 381, 393
EEA (European Economic Area):
  Agreement 224, 225, 226, 227, 228,
    235 n.
EEC (European Economic Community/
  Common Market) 26, 38, 39
EFTA (European Free Trade
  Association) 225, 232
empires, collapse of 17
employers and employees 128
Estonia 346
'ethnies' 125–6
'ethnonationalism' 126–7
EU (European Union)/EC (European
  Community):
  autonomy of states and regions 365
  bi-polar constitutional order 373
  budgetary decisions 116
  Committee of the Regions 393
  comparability and homogeneity 87–8
  competences 367
  confused view of 95
  and democratization 124
  dominant bloc emerging in? 157
  'ever closer union' 86
  expenditure competition, proposal to
    end 117
  federal elements 38–40
  federalization of 392–6
  federalization: prospects 397
  financial constitution: current
    deficiences 111–16
  and German federal model 366
  Germany as potential leader 362–4
  homogeneity and comparability
    87–8
  institutions, member states *vis-à-vis*
    150–1
  as *länderblind* 383
  laws 39
  leadership 362
  linguistic and cultural assimilation
    143
  major institutions 28–9

EU (European Union)/EC (European
  Community) (*cont.*):
  nature of? 41
  overall spending 112–13
  own resources distribution *118*
  potential regulations 372
  as pragmatic 'going concern' 27
  present shape 361
  present structures as inadequate 123
  proposed tax authority 116
  revenue sources 112
  sovereign powers 39
  transnational organizations 207–8
  Treaties as constitutions 52
  Treaty 27
  as union 40
  see also EU/EC; EEC
Europe:
  Common Market (EEC) 26, 38, 39
  federal 20
  over-centralization 364
Europe, federalization:
  as ambiguous term 122–4
  classification of 134
  path to adjustment 374–98
European Commission 28–9, 393
European Court of Justice 39, 87,
  228, 370
European federalism, lessons of
  past 9–24
European federation, projected 158
  and decentralization 154–5
  institutional framework 169
  nation-states and 142
European Government 363–4
European integration process 367
  core of 25
  federal-constitutional spirit 40–4
  philosophy underlying 28
  purposes 124–5
  speed of 364
  technical-functional spirit 26, 42–3
  two souls of 40–1
European Parliament 363–4
European Regional Committee 90
executive, power of 33–4
extended distribution function 106
extended-cost approach 101–6, *103*,
  115

federal comity (*bundesfreundliches
  Verhalten*) 369–72, 395–6
federal constitutionalization 378

federal constitutions, powers allocated
  asymmetrically 368
federal government, typical powers 54
federal loyalty (*Bundestreue*):
  Belgium 281
  Germany 86–7, 387
  Switzerland 223
federal principle, reflected in organs of
  government 61
federal theory, streams of 34–6
Federalism: Mature and Emergent (ed.
  A. W. Macmahon) 26
federalism:
  co-operative 257
  commitment to 64
  costs and benefits, Canada and
    Europe 136–58
  history of 9–24
  nature 9–10
  non-institutional feeling for 47
  as tier-structure 10
Federalist, The 36, 37
federalization:
  characteristics 122–4
  classical theory 35–7, 375–8
  costs and benefits 47–8, 124–58, *130*
  downward (decentralization) 127,
    129, 160
  typical objective 375
  upward (centralization) 127, 129,
    132
federalization, costs and benefits 74–
    96, 378–82
  conclusions 94–6, 396
  Western Europe 383–9
federalizing Europe, path to
    adjustment 374–98
federations:
  and central power 55
  engendering nationalistic loyalty 16–
    17
  history in Europe 17
  non-surviving 13–16
  of states 133–4
fiscal equalization 110–11, 114–15
fiscal federalism 59–60
  principles 106–11
Flemish Region 271
Forsyth, Murray 476
France 389
free trade 20, 21
freedom-generation 19
frustration costs 102, 106

'functionalism' 29–31
functionalism versus constitutionalism 232–3

Galicia (Spain) 250
Georgia 333, 342, 346, 349
German Democratic Republic (GDR), former, see Germany, East
Germany
  Basic Law 55, 82–3
  Bundesrat 80–1, 90, 93, 172, 181, 230
  Bundestag 80, 182
  capital cities 179
  centralization 173–5, 388
  comparability and homogeneity 87
  costs, compared with United Kingdom's 79
  decentralization 185
  distinctive political system 173, 174
  East, see separate entry
  'federal comity' 369, 370
  federal system accepted 75
  federal unitarization 173–6
  fiscal federalism: quandaries 188–91
  'golden lead' 83
  industrial relations 177–8
  intergovernmental bargaining system 171–3
  'interlocking polities' (*Politikverflechtung*) 173, 177, 182
  'modern' bureaucratic state 171
  party government 181, 194–6
  political costs and benefits 84
  as polycentric or centralized society? 177–9
  as potential EU leader 362–4
  public finance integrated in fiscal federalism 176–7
  regionalization of policy networks 179–81
  Reichstag 171–2
  social and political cleavages, organization 177–81
  Solidarity Pact 190
  sovereignty 94
  states (*Länder*), see separate entry
  television, public 178
  'third level' (*Dritte Ebene*) 80
  unification, see separate entry
  unitary federalism 191–2
  vertical separation of powers 75
  war defeats 174
  West 365–6
  whole state (*Gesamtstaat*) 80
  working structures, levels of 79–80
  writers on federalism 36
Germany, East:
  education 191
  identity 186
  income equalization 192
  Länder restored 184–7, 193–5, 385
  public sector 186
  reconstruction of economy 193–4
  trust establishment (*Treuhandanstalt*) 194
  West German view 187
Germany, federal state (*Bundesstaat*) 80–4, 170–2
Germany, federalism:
  as European model? 380, 394–5
  institutional logic of 170–6
  intergovernmental relations 170
  as model for Europe? 380
Germany, states (*Länder*):
  Basic Law and 80–1
  and *Bund* 80
  controversies with EU 367
  core competence 369
  in doubly federalized structure 81–2
  eastern, restored 183–5, 193–6, 385
  economic policies 180
  and EU 113–14
  and European federalism 89–92
  functions and powers 80–1, 369, 379–80
  largest 188
  origin 395
  political influence 366
  rich and poor: revenue-sharing 188–91
  sponsorships 185–7
Germany, unification 133, 169–70, 182–96
  and EU 363–4
  and German federal structures 379–80
glasnost 328
Gorbachev, Mikhail 328–32, 345, 348
government
  powers at different levels 52–3
  structures, and federalism 62

Habsburgs 242
Hallstein, Dr 32

heterogeneity versus practicability in regionalism 89–92
Hungary 391–2

identity, diversity through, versus lack of uniformity 74–5
imperialism 11–12, 14
individual states, federation and 61
Indonesia 14
integration process, federal component 31–40
intergovernmental processes 93
internal market 57–8, 373
  versus regionalism 233–4
Italy 130, 132, 389

judicial power 53
judicial review 50–2
Jura, Switzerland 222

Kant, Immanuel 34
Kazakhstan 332, 333, 335, 346, 348, 349, 351, 352
Kilpatrick, James Jackson 35
Kohl, Chancellor 183
Kravchuk, Leonid 339, 343, 354
Kux, Stephan 390
Kyrgyzstan 332, 333, 335, 340, 351, 352, 353

legislative, power of the 34
Lehmbruch, Gerhard 379, 385
Lenin, V. I. 15
Lijphart, Arend 350
List, Friedrich 36

Maastricht Summit 27
Maastricht Treaty 84, 232–3, 392, 393
  and European integration ambiguities 40–1
MacDougall Report 111
Madison, James 18, 36
market, internal 57–8
markets:
  efficiency 104
  see also internal market
Meech Lake Accord 50, 137
military objectives 12–19, 376–7
Minsk treaties 353
mistake-avoidance, versus time-consuming procedures 77–8
Mitrany, David 29–31

Moldova 329, 333, 335, 336, 337–8, 340, 341, 349, 352
monarchies, see Belgium, King of; dual monarchies
multiple cultural communities, states with 131
Musgrave, R. A. 103

nation states, and federalism 9–10
'national', defined 127–8
national culture, civic expression of 128
Navarre 250
neighbouring·states, absorption of 12–13
Nigeria 13–14

Pakistan 13–14
Pareto optimality 135
perestroika 326, 328–9, 330–1
  achievements of 351
plebiscites 222
Poland 391
political and administrative structures: costs 78–9
political costs and benefits, see federalization, costs and benefits
political dimension in federalism 73–98
political parties in federal systems 388
political theory of federalism 25–45
population, cultural attributes 129
powers, vertical separation of, versus complexity 75–6
powers, distribution and division of 52–6, 233
preference costs 102, 106
provision function 105
'public sector' functions 105

Quebec 16
  as 'Canadian' 154
  constitutional demands 155
  and constitutional powers 136–7
  entrepreneurialism 144–5
  and federal government 143–8, 382
  identity 140–2
  'Inc.' 149
  liberal and restrictive measures 152
  nationalism 153
  power-seeking by 145
  secession threat 136–8

Rack, Reinhard 383
Reagan, Ronald 330
rebellion 12
regional disparity 60–1
regionalism:
    heterogeneity versus practicability 89–94
    versus internal market 233–4
Riker, William H. 375–6
'Roman Fountain' 234
Rome, Treaty of 28
Russia 327, 329, 332, 333, 335, 336, 338, 340, 342, 343, 344, 345, 346, 348, 349
    and Ukraine 334, 346, 352

Sakharov, Andrei 351
Saunders, Cheryl 377
Scharpf, Fritz W. 392
Schäuble, Wolfgang 192
Schmitt, Carl 36, 37
Schuman, Robert 28
Senelle, Robert 386
Smith, Anthony 125–7
social security 128
solidarity:
    pact 385–6
    versus democracy 234–5
sovereignty 94
Soviet Union, see USSR
Spaak Report 28
Spain:
    autonomous communities see under separate entry
    autonomous sentiment in regions 244
    Autonomy, Statute of 247
    central state 240–3, 248–50, 257
    Constitutional Court 250–3, 255, 262, 263
    constitutional position 254–5
    in crisis 240–3
    decentralization 245–50
    entry into EC 260–3
    federal model as unavailable 243–4
    as federation in the making? 240–63
    Franco regime 240
    history 241–3
    legal order 251–2
    nationalism 242–3, 253–5
    pluralism, reducing 254
    regional planning 241

second chamber (Senate) 246–8, 255, 257–8
secular pluralism 241–2
special communities: powers 256
Spain, autonomous communties 255, 387
    and central state 256
    Constitutional Court and 250–3
    and EU 260
    parliament workings 259–60
    power variations between 248–50
Spain, autonomous state 253
    foundation 240–4
    organizational and legal features 245–50
    perspectives and problems 255–63
Stalin, Joseph 12
structures, high costs of political and administrative 78–9
Styria 210
subsidiarity 84–94, 366–8, 392–3
    and competences 107–8
    origin 393
    presumptions about 84
    principle 113, 233
Swiss cantons 223, 226–7
    and constitution-making 222
    international character of 223
Swiss federation:
    constitution 220–1, 234–5
    Council of States 230
    drawbacks 223–5
    and EEA Agreement 235 n.
    and European integration 224–32
    European law implementation 228–9
    features of system 219–25
    federal loyalty (Bundestreue) 223
    future revision? 384–5
    as model for Europe? 230–2
    as model needing adaptation 219–35
    origins and political foundation 220
    political careers 229
    psychological conception of 221
    regional openness 222
    representative federalism 229–30
    strengths and benefits 222–3

Tajikistan 333, 335, 342, 353
tax burden-sharing 110, 110–11, 114–15
territory, communities defined by 132

Thürer, Daniel 384
time-consuming procedures, versus
    mistake-avoidance 77–8
Tito, President 12, 15
Tocqueville, Alexis de 36, 235
trade:
    country's size as factor in 22
    restriction of 19–24
Trudeau, Pierre 121, 151–2, 153
trust 10, 87
Turkestan 349
Turkmenistan 333, 337–8, 353

UK (United Kingdom) 393
    contributions to EU 115
    costs compared with Germany's 79
    as decentralized 388
    as proponent of federation 13
Ukraine 329, 331, 333, 335, 336,
    337, 338, 340, 342, 344, 345,
    347, 349, 352, 353
    and Russia 334, 345, 352
uniformity, lack of, versus diversity
    through identity 74–5
unitary political systems, compared
    with federations 398
upper houses of federal legislature 61
USA (United States):
    Civil War 33
    Constitution 32–3
    dual federalism 370
    federation: beginnings 18

government theory disregarded 30–1
slavery 19–20
Supreme Court 51
trade restrictions 22–3
USS (Union of Sovereign States) 390–1
USSR (Soviet Union):
    communism defeated 326
    disintegration process 326–33
    end of 332
    as federation 15
    heterogeneous structure 327
    'nine-plus-one' agreement 331
    nomenklatura 327, 348
    political culture 350
    popular movements 328–9
    special features 325–6
    subsidiarity 330
Uzbekistan 332, 333, 335, 349, 353

Valencia 250
VAT (Value Added Tax) 112, 113,
    114

Walloon region 271, 320–2
West Germany 365–6
Wheare, Q. C., Federal Government
    226
world, projected as federal 20

Yeltsin, Boris 331, 333, 339, 343,
    346, 348, 351
Yugoslavia 12–13, 15–16, 337, 390